Lecture Notes in Computer Scie

T0230180

Commenced Publication in 1973
Founding and Former Series Editors:
Gerhard Goos, Juris Hartmanis, and Jan van Leeuwen

Springer
Berlin
Heidelberg
New York
Hong Kong
London
Milan
Paris
Tokyo

Maurice Bruynooghe (Ed.)

Logic Based Program Synthesis and Transformation

13th International Symposium, LOPSTR 2003
Uppsala, Sweden, August 25-27, 2003
Revised Selected Papers

 Springer

Volume Editor

Maurice Bruynooghe
Katholieke Universiteit Leuven, Department of Computer Science
Celestijnenlaan 200A, 3001 Heverlee, Belgium
E-mail: Maurice.Bruynooghe@cs.kuleuven.ac.be

Library of Congress Control Number: 2004107503

CR Subject Classification (1998): F.3.1, D.1.1, D.1.6, I.2.2, F.4.1

ISSN 0302-9743
ISBN 3-540-22174-3 Springer-Verlag Berlin Heidelberg New York

Springer-Verlag is a part of Springer Science+Business Media

springeronline.com

© Springer-Verlag Berlin Heidelberg 2004
Printed in Germany

Typesetting: Camera-ready by author, data conversion by Olgun Computergrafik
Printed on acid-free paper   SPIN: 11010531   06/3142   5 4 3 2 1 0

Preface

This volume contains selected papers from LOPSTR 2003, the 13th International Symposium on Logic-Based Program Synthesis and Transformation. The LOPSTR series is devoted to research in logic-based program development. Particular topics of interest are specification, synthesis, verification, transformation, specialization, analysis, optimization, composition, reuse, component-based software development, agent-based software development, software architectures, design patterns and frameworks, program refinement and logics for refinement, proofs as programs, and applications and tools.

LOPSTR 2003 took place at the University of Uppsala from August 25 to August 27 as part of PLI 2003 (Principles, Logics, and Implementations of High-Level Programming Languages). PLI was an ACM-organized confederation of conferences and workshops with ICFP 2003 (ACM-SIGPLAN International Conference on Functional Programming) and PPDP 2003 (ACM-SIGPLAN International Conference on Principles and Practice of Declarative Programming) as the main events. The LOPSTR community profited from the shared lectures of the invited speakers, and the active scientific discussions enabled by the co-location.

LOPSTR 2003 was the thirteenth in a series of events. Past events were held in Manchester, UK (1991, 1992, 1998), Louvain-la-Neuve, Belgium (1993), Pisa, Italy (1994), Arnhem, The Netherlands (1995), Stockholm, Sweden (1996), Leuven, Belgium (1997), Venice, Italy (1999), London, UK (2000), Paphos, Cyprus (2001), and Madrid, Spain (2002).

I wish to thank the PLI Organizing Committee and especially Kostis Sagonas for welcoming LOPSTR as part of PLI 2003 and taking care of the many organizational matters. Special thanks go towards Roland Bol for taking care of LOPSTR specific matters in Uppsala, towards Wim Vanhoof for assistance with the Program Chair work, and towards Qiang Fu for the help in preparing this volume. The sponsorship of the Association for Logic Programming (ALP) is gratefully acknowledged, and the LNCS team of Springer-Verlag is thanked for publishing this volume with the selected and revised papers. Last but not least, authors, PC members and additional reviewers are thanked for all the work that went into preparing this selection of revised papers.

Out of 32 submissions, the program committee selected 18 works for presentation; 16 were revised and submitted for this volume. The program committee selected 12 of them for inclusion in this volume. In addition, a paper based on the invited talk of Michael Leuschel is included as well as some abstracts based on the other papers presented at LOPSTR.

The preproceedings were printed in Uppsala and are also available at http://www.cs.kuleuven.ac.be/ dtai/lopstr03/, a page with all information about LOPSTR 2003.

March 2004   Maurice Bruynooghe

Program Chair

Maurice Bruynooghe   Katholieke Universiteit Leuven, Belgium

Local Chair

Roland Bol   Uppsala University, Sweden

Program Committee

Elvira Albert	Complutense University of Madrid, Spain
Roland Bol	Uppsala University, Sweden
Maurice Bruynooghe	Katholieke Universiteit Leuven, Belgium
Michael Butler	University of Southampton, UK
Jim Caldwell	University of Wyoming, USA
Włodek Drabent	Polish Academy of Sciences, Poland
	Linköping University, Sweden
Tom Ellman	Vassar College, USA
Norbert E. Fuchs	University of Zurich, Switzerland
Robert Glück	Waseda University, Japan
Gopal Gupta	University of Texas at Dallas, USA
Ian Hayes	University of Queensland, Australia
Catholijn Jonker	Vrije Universiteit Amsterdam, The Netherlands
Andy King	University of Kent, UK
Mario Ornaghi	Universitá degli Studi di Milano, Italy
Maurizio Proietti	IASI-CNR, Rome, Italy
Germán Puebla	Technical University of Madrid, Spain
Julian Richardson	RIACS/NASA Ames Research Center, USA
Olivier Ridoux	University of Rennes 1/IRISA, France
Sabina Rossi	Università Ca' Foscari di Venezia, Italy
Wim Vanhoof	University of Namur, Belgium

Local Organizers

Roland Bol
Kostis Sagonas

Additional Referees

José Alferes
Olaf Chitil
Nicoletta Cocco
Dario Colazzo
John Cowles
Agostino Dovier
Thomas Eiter
Samir Genaim
Silvio Ghilardi
Roberta Gori
Stefan Gruner
Hai-Feng Guo
Ángel Herranz
Juliana Küster-Filipe
Kung-Kiu Lau

Lunjin Lu
Alberto Momigliano
Alberto Pettorossi
Isabel Pita
Enrico Pontelli
Alessandra Raffaetá
Konstantinos Sagonas
Alexander Serebrenik
Jan-Georg Smaus
Colin Snook
Vera Stebletsova
Bert Van Nuffelen
Pedro Vasconcelos
Germán Vidal

Table of Contents

Invited Talk

Specification and Synthesis

Verification

Analysis

Transformation and Specialisation

Constraints

Author Index

Inductive Theorem Proving
by Program Specialisation:
Generating Proofs for Isabelle Using Ecce

Helko Lehmann and Michael Leuschel

Department of Electronics and Computer Science
University of Southampton
Highfield, Southampton, SO17 1BJ, UK
{hel99r,mal}@ecs.soton.ac.uk

Abstract. In this paper we discuss the similarities between program specialisation and inductive theorem proving, and then show how program specialisation can be used to perform inductive theorem proving. We then study this relationship in more detail for a particular class of problems (verifying infinite state Petri nets) in order to establish a clear link between program specialisation and inductive theorem proving. In particular, we use the program specialiser ECCE to generate specifications, hypotheses and proof scripts in the theory format of the proof assistant ISABELLE. Then, in many cases, ISABELLE can automatically execute these proof scripts and thereby verify the soundness of ECCE's verification process and of the correspondence between program specialisation and inductive theorem proving.

1 Introduction

Program specialisation aims at improving the overall performance of programs by performing source to source transformations. A common approach, known as partial evaluation [8], is to exploit partial knowledge about the input by precomputing parts of the program. In the context of logic programming, partial evaluation is sometimes called partial deduction and is achieved through a well-automated application of parts of the Burstall-Darlington unfold/fold transformation framework.

The relation between program specialisation and theorem proving has already been raised several times in the literature [23, 7, 24, 21]. In this paper we will examine in closer detail the relationship between partial deduction and inductive theorem proving.

Partial Deduction. At the heart of any technique for *partial deduction* is a program analysis phase: Given a program P and an (atomic) goal $\leftarrow A$, one aims to analyse the computation-flow of P for all instances $\leftarrow A\theta$ of $\leftarrow A$. Based on the results of this analysis, new program clauses are synthesised.

M. Bruynooghe (Ed.): LOPSTR 2004, LNCS 3018, pp. 1–19, 2004.

In partial deduction, such an analysis is based on the construction of finite and usually incomplete[1], SLD(NF)-trees. More specifically, following the foundations for partial deduction developed in [17] (see also [12] for an up-to-date overview), one constructs

- a finite set of atoms $S = \{A_1, \ldots, A_n\}$, and
- a finite (possibly incomplete) SLD(NF)-tree τ_i for each $(P \cup \{\leftarrow A_i\})$,

such that:

1) the atom A in the initial goal $\leftarrow A$ is an instance of some A_i in S, and
2) for each goal $\leftarrow B_1, \ldots, B_k$ labelling a leaf of some SLD(NF)-tree τ_l, each B_i is an instance of some A_j in S.

The construction of the set S is referred to as the *global control*, while the construction of the trees τ_i are called the *local control*. The conditions 1) and 2) are referred to as *closedness* and ensure that *together* the SLD(NF)-trees $\tau_1, \ldots, \tau_n$ form a complete description of all possible computations that can occur for all concrete instances $\leftarrow A\theta$ of the goal of interest. Finally, a code generation phase produces a *resultant clause* for each non-failing branch of each tree, which synthesises the computation in that branch. This phase also typically generates a fresh predicate name for every element of the set S and rename the clauses in an appropriate manner.

The approach has been generalised to specialising a set of *conjunctions* rather than just atoms in [4]. The basic principle remains roughly as outlined above; the only difference being that we have a set S of conjunctions rather than atoms and that the closedness condition becomes slightly more involved to allow the leaf goals $\leftarrow B_1, \ldots, B_k$ to be split up into sub-conjunctions. This technique has been implemented within the program specialiser ECCE [15, 4] . An overview of control techniques that are used in partial deduction and conjunctive partial deduction in general and by ECCE in particular, such as determinacy, homeomorphic embedding, or characteristic trees, can be found in [12].

A Small Example. Let us illustrate conjunctive partial deduction on the following simple program.

```
even(0).
even(s(X)) :- odd(X).
odd(s(X)) :- even(X).
```

Suppose we only wish to use this program for queries of the form $\leftarrow C$ with $C = even(X) \wedge odd(X)$ Conjunctive partial deduction can then specialise this program by constructing the incomplete SLD-tree for $\leftarrow C$ depicted in

---

[1] As usual in partial deduction, we assume that the notion of an SLD-tree is generalised [17] to allow it to be incomplete: at any point we may decide not to select any atom and terminate a derivation.

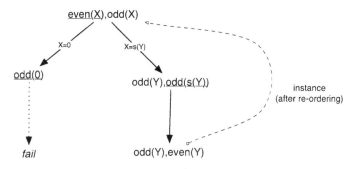

Fig. 1. Specialisation of even-odd

Fig. 1. The set S mentioned above would simply be $S = \{C\}$. Supposing that we produce the new predicate name **even_odd** for C, the specialised program we obtain, is:

```
even_odd(s(X)) :- even_odd(X).
```

It is immediately obvious that $even\_odd(X)$ will never succeed, and hence that no number is even and odd at the same time. The ECCE system [15, 4] basically produces the above result[2] and can also automatically infer the failure of $even\_odd(X)$ by applying its bottom up more specific program construction phase [18] in the post-processing.

Inductive Theorem Proving. Now, the above result corresponds to an inductive proof showing that no number can be both even and odd. The left branch of Fig. 1 corresponds to examining the base case $X = 0$, while the right branch corresponds to the induction step whereby $even(s(Y)), odd(s(Y))$ is rewritten into the equivalent $odd(Y), even(Y)$ so that the induction hypothesis can be applied.

In a sense the conjunctive partial deduction has identified a working induction schema and the bottom-up propagation [18] has performed the induction proper. This highlights a similarity between partial deduction and *inductive theorem proving*. Indeed, in the induction step of an inductive proof one tries to transform the induction assumption(s) for $n + 1$ using basic inference rules so as to be able to apply the induction hypothese(s) and complete the proof. In partial deduction, one tries to transform the atoms in A (or conjunctions for conjunctive partial deduction) by unfolding so as to be able to "fold" back all leaves. The set of atoms A thus plays the role of the induction hypotheses and resolution the role of classical theorem proving steps. In summary,

- there is a striking similarity between the control problems of partial deduction and inductive theorem proving. The problem of ensuring A-closedness is basically the same as finding induction hypotheses where the induction "goes through." Many control techniques have been developed in either camp (e.g., [1] for inductive theorem proving) and cross-fertilisation might be possible.

---

[2] Using the default settings, ECCE produces a slightly bigger specialised program because it does not re-order atoms by default. But the overall result is the same.

– if basic resolution steps correspond to logical inference rules one may be able to perform inductive theorem proving directly by partial deduction.

The only difference is that unfolding steps are not guaranteed to decrease the induction parameter, so program specialisation is only guaranteed to perform valid inductive theorem proving if the predicates to be specialised are inductively defined.

A More Complicated Example. Let us now have a look at a slightly more involved example. The following is a simple theory expressed in the proof assistant ISABELLE [19]. (We will provide more details about ISABELLE later in the paper.) The theory defines a datatype for binary trees and then defines the function mirror which simply produces the mirror image of tree (i.e., reversing left and right children for all nodes). We then define a lemma stating that applying mirror twice produces the same result and then instruct Isabelle to use induction on the tree in order to show this lemma.

```
theory ToyTree = PreList:
  datatype 'a tree = Tip              ("[]")
                   | Node "'a tree" 'a "'a tree"
  consts mirror :: "'a tree => 'a tree"
  primrec
    "mirror([]) = []"
    "mirror((Node ls x rs)) = Node (mirror(rs)) x (mirror(ls))"
lemma mirror_mirror [simp]: "mirror(mirror(xs)) = xs"
apply (induct_tac xs)
```

Loading this theory int ISABELLE results in the following output:

```
proof (prove): step 1
fixed variables: xs

goal (lemma (mirror_mirror), 2 subgoals):
 1. mirror (mirror []) = []
 2. !!tree1 a tree2.
      [| mirror (mirror tree1) = tree1; mirror (mirror tree2) = tree2 |]
      ==> mirror (mirror (Node tree1 a tree2)) = Node tree1 a tree2
```

It is now possible to use ISABELLE to prove this lemma, by interactively performing the required rewriting steps and twice applying the induction hypothesis[3].

Let us now try to achieve the same result using program specialisation. First, we have to encode the mirror function and the lemma as a logic program:

```
mirror(tip,tip).
mirror(tree(L,N,R),tree(RR,N,RL)) :- mirror(L,RL), mirror(R,RR).
lemma(X,R) :- mirror(X,Z),mirror(Z,R).
```

---

[3] E.g., first calling the simplifier `apply(simp)` and then the automatic prover `apply(auto)` will perform the required proof steps.

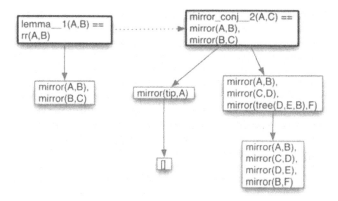

Fig. 2. ECCE specialisation tree for mirror

Now, one would like to be able to infer that for all valid trees the the second argument of `lemma` must be identical to the first argument. Surprisingly this is exactly what we obtain when we specialise the above program for the call `lemma(X,R)` using the ECCE program specialiser (with the most specific version [18] postprocessing enabled):

```
/* Transformation time: 130 ms */
/* Specialised Predicates:
lemma__1(A,B) :- lemma(A,B).
mirror_conj__2(A,B) :- mirror(A,C1), mirror(C1,B). */

lemma(A,A) :- mirror_conj__2(A,A).
lemma__1(A,A) :- mirror_conj__2(A,A).
mirror_conj__2(tip,tip).
mirror_conj__2(tree(A,B,C),tree(A,B,C)) :-
    mirror_conj__2(A,A),  mirror_conj__2(C,C).
```

Again, ECCE has managed to rewrite the lemma in such a way that the induction hypothesis could be applied (in this case it was applied twice as can be seen from the two instances of `mirror_conj__2` in the last clause of the specialised program). The specialisation tree produced by ECCE can be seen in Fig. 2. The dashed arrows indicate a descendance at the global control level (see, e.g., [12]), whereas the solid arrows indicate unfolding steps. By carefully inspecting the proof trace of ISABELLE and the specialisation tree of ECCE it turns out that there is a one-to-one correspondence between the steps performed by Isabelle and by ECCE.

An obvious question is now whether there is a systematic way to exploit this correspondence? In the next sections we show how ECCE can be used to perform inductive theorem proving as applied to verification tasks and how the specialisation trees produced by ECCE can be automatically translated into induction schemas for the proof assistant Isabelle [19].

2   Infinite Model Checking by Program Specialisation

In recent work it has been shown that logic programming based methods in general, and partial deduction in particular, can be applied to model checking [2] of infinite state systems. As this problem can also be tackled by inductive theorem proving [19] we choose this as the basis of a more formal comparison. Indeed, one of the key issues of model checking of infinite systems is *abstraction* [3]. Abstraction allows to approximate an infinite system by a finite one, and if proper care is taken the results obtained for the finite abstraction will be valid for the infinite system. This is related to finding proper induction schemas for inductive theorem proving, which in turn is related to the control problem of partial deduction.

In earlier work we have tried to solve the abstraction problem by applying existing techniques for the *automatic* control of *(logic) program specialisation*, [12] and modelling the system to be verified as a logic program by means of an interpreter [16]. Thereby, the interpreter describes how the states of the system change by executing transitions. By applying partial deduction to the interpreter we expect a finite abstraction of the possibly infinite state space of the system to be generated. This abstraction may then be used to verify system properties of interest. This approach proved to be quite powerful as it was possible to obtain decision procedures for the coverability problem, if "typical" specialisation algorithms, as for example implemented in the ECCE system [15, 10], are applied to logic programs that encode Petri nets [14].

Technically, the dynamic system specified in the input for the partial deduction algorithm can also be viewed an inductive system describing the set of finite behaviours, i.e. the set of finite *paths*. Thereby, the set of initial states form the inductive base and each transition represents an inductive step. For the output of the partial deduction algorithm to be a sound abstraction each of the states reachable by a path must be contained in a state representation of the output. It is desirable to verify this property if we cannot ensure that the partial deduction algorithm is correctly implemented. The goal of this work is to show that such proofs can be generated and executed automatically. To this end we employ the partial deduction system ECCE for the automatic generation of the theory and the proof scripts. The proof assistant ISABELLE [20] is used to execute the proof scripts.

If we can use ISABELLE to verify the soundness of the output of the partial deduction method we may also ask whether it is possible to generate the hypotheses automatically and thereby use ISABELLE directly as a model checker of infinite systems. To this end, similar to the partial deduction system, ISABELLE needs to perform some kind of abstraction while searching for a proof of some dynamic property such as safety.

In this paper we focus on the specification and verification of Petri nets. This is due to their simple representation as a logic program as well as in a ISABELLE theory. The following section describes how we can specify Petri nets in ISABELLE. Then we discuss how such specifications are generated using ECCE and how ECCE output can be translated into ISABELLE. In Section 5 we demonstrate how proof scripts can be used in ISABELLE for automatic theorem proving. In Section 6 we demonstrate the complete verification process using an example specification. The last section gives a conclusion and proposes some further work. All relevant source code of the ECCE system can be found in the technical report [9].

3 Specification of Petri Nets in ISABELLE

The proof assistant ISABELLE [19] has been developed as a generic system for implementing logical formalisms. Instead of developing an all new logic for our purposes we will use the specification and verification methods realised by the implementation of Higher Order Logic (HOL) in ISABELLE. HOL allows to express most mathematical concepts and, in contrast to, for example, First Order Logic, it allows the specification of and the reasoning about inductively defined sets. This latter feature is crucial for our purposes. Hence, strictly speaking, we will develop specifications in ISABELLE/HOL. Furthermore, the current ISABELLE system provides the language ISAR for the specification of theories and the development of proof scripts. In this work we will use ISAR instead of ISABELLE's implementation language ML since ISAR is much easier to use as it hides most implementation details of ISABELLE. However, the possibilities to develop proof tactics using ISAR only are very limited. Consequently we conjecture that for efficient automatic theorem proving the use of ISAR allone is insufficient (see also Section 7).

ISABELLE allows specifications as part of *theories*. A theory can be thought of as a collection of *declarations*, *definitions*, and *proofs*. ISABELLE/HOL is a typed logical language where the *base types* resemble those of functional programming languages such as ML. To specify new types ISABELLE provides *type constructors*, *function types*, and *type variables*. We will introdce the particular concepts as we will use them and refer for additional information to [19].

Terms are formed by applying functions to arguments, e.g. if f is a function of type $\tau_1 \Rightarrow \tau_2$ and t a term of type τ_1 then ft is a term of type τ_2.

Formulas are terms of base type `bool`. Accordingly, the usual logical operators are defined as functions whose arguments and domain are of type `bool`.

We specify the Petri net theory `PN` as a successor of the theory `Main` which is provided by ISABELLE/HOL. `Main` contains a number of basic declarations, definitions, and lemmas concerning often required basic concepts such as lists and sets. Thereby, every part of the theory `Main` becomes automatically visible in `PN`:

```
theory PN = Main:
```

To simplify the specification and to increase readability of the theory we define the type `state` which corresponds to a notion in Petri net theory: A *state* or *marking* is a vector of natural numbers representing the number of *tokens* on the *places* of a Petri net. The number of dimensions of the vector corresponds to the number of places of the particular net. In ISABELLE we use the type constructor $\times$ to define the type `state` as a product over the base type `nat`:

```
types
  state = "nat × nat ×...× nat"
```

Based on the type **state** we declare the functions **paths**, **trans**, and **start**. The function **start** represents the *initial state* of the Petri net. Note that since we allow parameters in the definition of **state** it actually may represent a set of initial states. The function **trans** describes how the firing of a *transition* can change the state of a Petri net. The additional parameter of type **nat** is used to refer to a particular transition of the net. The set of finite possible sequences of transitons starting in the initial state is represented by **paths**. Note that the declaration of **trans** and *paths* is independent of the particular considered Petri net.

```
consts
  start :: "nat ⇒ ...⇒ nat ⇒ state"
  trans :: "(state × state × nat) set"
  paths :: "(state list) set"
```

By assigning a unique number the transition names are defined as a of enumeration type. Consequently, for each transition t we include a declaration of the following form:

```
consts
  t :: "nat"
```

The initial state **start** is defined by a term *term* of type state:

```
defs
  start_def [simp]: "start list of variables ≡ term"
```

The optional [simp] controls the strategy of ISABELLE's built-in simplifier to apply this definition whenever possible. For our purposes *term* will be always a tuple of terms built using the unary successor function Suc, 0, and variables appearing in the *list of variables* (the number of variables in this list must correspond to the number of parameters in the declaration of **start**.

The transition function is defined as a set of transitions of the Petri net. Thereby each transition is represented as a tuple (x,y,n), where x and y are tuples of terms built by Suc and variables of the corresponding *list of variables*. The term n is the name of the transition.

```
defs
  trans_def: "trans ≡ {(x,y,n).
                    (∃ list₁ of variables. (x,y,n)= transition₁
                    ∨ (∃ list₂ of variables. (x,y,n)= transition₂
                    ⋮
                    ∨ (∃ listₙ of variables. (x,y,n)= transitionₙ}"
```

One of the important features of ISABELLE/HOL is the possibility of inductive definitions. We define `paths` inductively using the following two rules:

```
inductive paths
intros
  zero: "[(start list of variables)] ∈ paths"
  step: "[(y,z,n) ∈ trans; y#l ∈ paths] ⟹ z#(y#l) ∈ paths"
```

The first rule defines all initial states to be paths. The second rule allows the construction of new paths by extending an arbitrary path by a new state if there exists a transition from the state at the head of the path to the new state.

Finally, each transition t is defined as follows, where n is a unique natural number:

```
defs
  t_def [simp]: "t ≡ n"
```

The following example shows the the specification of a Petri net according to this scheme.

Example 1. We encode the Petri net depicted below in ISABELLE/HOL. The initial state is defined by one token on each of the places $p2$ and $p3$, and the parameter A representing an arbitrary number of tokens on place $p1$ ($p1$, $p2$, $p3$ correspond to the first, second, and third dimension, respectively, of the state vector.

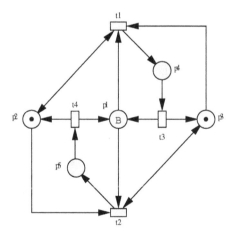

```
theory PN = Main:
types
  state = "nat × nat × nat × nat × nat"
consts
  start :: "nat ⟹ state"
  trans :: "(state × state × nat) set"
  paths :: "(state list) set"
  t1 :: "nat"
```

```
t2 :: "nat"
t3 :: "nat"
t4 :: "nat"
```
defs
```
start_def [simp]: "start ≡ (B,(Suc 0),(Suc 0),0,0)"
trans_def: "trans ≡ {(x,y,n).
              (∃ E D C B A. (x,y,n)=(((Suc A),(Suc B),(Suc C),D,E),
                                     (A,(Suc B),C,(Suc D),E),t1))
              ∨ (∃ E D C B A. (x,y,n)=(((Suc A),(Suc B),(Suc C),D,E),
                                       (A,B,(Suc C),D,(Suc E)),t2))
              ∨ (∃ E D C B A. (x,y,n)=((A,B,C,(Suc D),E),
                                       ((Suc A),B,(Suc C),D,E),t3))
              ∨ (∃ E D C B A. (x,y,n)=((A,B,C,D,(Suc E)),
                                       ((Suc A),(Suc B),C,D,E),t4))}"
t1_def [simp]: "t1 ≡ 0"
t2_def [simp]: "t2 ≡ 1"
t3_def [simp]: "t3 ≡ 2"
t4_def [simp]: "t4 ≡ 3"
```
inductive paths
intros
```
zero: "[(start B)] ∈ paths"
step: "⟦(y,z,n) ∈ trans; y#l ∈ paths⟧ ⟹ z#(y#l) ∈ paths"                    □
```

4 Generating ISABELLE Theories Using ECCE

Since we aim to verify the partial deduction results of ECCE, we have integrated the generation of the ISABELLE theory directly into ECCE. The generated IS-ABELLE theory consists of three parts:

1. the specification of the Petri net,
2. the specification of the coverability graph [5] as generated by ECCE,
3. the lemma to be verified together with a proof script.

In this section we deal with the first two parts while the third part is discussed in Section 5.

4.1 Generating Petri Net Specifications from Logic Programs

The ISABELLE theory generator integrated in ECCE assumes that the transitions of a Petri net are specified by a set of clauses of a ternary predicate. The first parameter represents a transition name, the second represents the set of states where the transition can be applied, and the third how the state changes if the transition is executed. Technically, the second and the third parameter of each clause are lists of the length corresponding to the number of places. Relying on unification, conditions and changes can be easily expressed. For example, the condition that at least two tokens are on place $p3$ in a Petri net with five places is expressed by the term [X0,X1,s(s(X2)),X3,X4] (thereby s can be interpreted as the successor function on natural numbers). Similarly, the state change can be expressed: the removal of one token on place $p3$ and generation of two tokens on $p1$ is represented as [s(s(X0)),X1,s(X2),X3,X4].

The initial state is simply represented as a single clause where the last parameter must be a list of the length corresponding to the number of places. Each element of the list can be constructed using 0, the unary function s, and variables.

Example 2. The following logic program encodes the Petri net of Example 1.

```
trans(t1,[s(X0),s(X1),s(X2),X3,X4],[X0,s(X1),X2,s(X3),X4]).
trans(t2,[s(X0),s(X1),s(X2),X3,X4],[X0,X1,s(X2),X3,s(X4)]).
trans(t3,[X0,X1,X2,s(X3),X4],[s(X0),X1,s(X2),X3,X4]).
trans(t4,[X0,X1,X2,X3,s(X4)],[s(X0),s(X1),X2,X3,X4]).

start([B,s(0),s(0),0,0]).                                              □
```

The implementation of the theory generator is part of the file "code_generator.pro" and can be found in [9]. The generation is initiated by a call to the clause print_specialised_program_isa. For example, the ISABELLE theory of Example 1 has been generated from the logic program of Example 2.

4.2   Generating Specifications of the Coverability Graph from Logic Programs

To use partial deduction techniques for model checking we need to specify also the verification task as a logic program. To this end we may implement the satisfiability relation of some temporal logic as a logic program, such as the CTL interpreter described in [16]. In this paper we restrict ourselves to *safety properties* and hence we only need definition of the *EU* operator of the temporal logic *CTL*, and we just need the following subset of the interpreter from [16]:

```
model_check_safety :- start(_,S), sat(S,eu(true,p(unsafe))).

sat(E,p(P)) :- prop(E,P).
sat(E,eu(F,G)) :-  sat_eu(E,F,G).
sat_eu(E,_F,G) :-  sat(E,G).
sat_eu(E,F,G) :-  sat(E,F), trans(_Act,E,E2), sat_eu(E2,F,G).
```

Depending on the safety property of interest, we have to define prop/2. E.g., the fact prop([X0,X1,X2,s(X3),s(X4)],unsafe) defines a state of a Petri net to be unsafe when there exist at least one token on each of the places $p4$ and $p5$.

Note that simply calling model_check_safety in Prolog would lead to an infinite derivation. Due to the potentially infinite state space of a Petri net also methods like tabling will be insufficient to deal with this problem.

To perform the verification we use the same approach as in [14]. Hence, before we apply the partial deduction system ECCE we will first perform a preliminary compilation of the particular Petri net and task. Thereby we will get rid of some of the interpretation overhead and achieve a more straightforward equivalence between markings of the Petri net and atoms encountered during the partial deduction phase. We will use the LOGEN offline partial deduction system [13] to that effect (but any other scheme which has a similar effect can be used).

After this precompilation we can apply ECCE to the resulting program, producing the code in Example 4:

Example 3.

```
model_check_safety :- sat__1__2(A).
    /* sat__1__2(A) --> [sat__1(A,s(0),s(0),0,0)] */
sat__1__2(A) :- sat_eu__2__3(A).
    /* sat_eu__2__3(A) --> [sat_eu__2(A,s(0),s(0),0,0)] */
sat_eu__2__3(s(A)) :- sat_eu__2__4(A).
sat_eu__2__3(s(A)) :-sat_eu__2__5(A).
    /* sat_eu__2__4(A) --> [sat_eu__2(A,s(0),0,s(0),0)] */
sat_eu__2__4(A) :- sat_eu__2__3(s(A)).
    /* sat_eu__2__5(A) --> [sat_eu__2(A,0,s(0),0,s(0))] */
sat_eu__2__5(A) :- sat_eu__2__3(s(A)).                                 □
```

While this program is hard to read at first, every specialised predicate represents a set of reachable markings and the whole specialised program corresponds to a coverability graph of the Petri net under consideration (see [14] for more details). From the output of ECCE we generate an ISABELLE theory representing the generated coverability relation. Independent of the particular domain this relation is declared as a set of pairs of states:

```
consts
    coverrel:: "(state × state) set"
```

For each predicate name of a clause in the specialised program, which represents a set of states we add a declaration of the form:

```
consts
    name :: nat ⇒ ...⇒ nat ⇒ state"
```

Thereby the number of parameters of type **nat** corresponds to the number of variables in the head of the clause. The definitions have the form:

```
defs
    name_def: "name list of variables ≡ term"
```

For our purposes *term* will be always a tuple of terms built using the unary successor function Suc, 0, and variables appearing in the *list of variables* (the number of variables in this list must correspond to the number of parameters in the declaration of *name*).

Finally, the coverability relation is defined as a set of pairs of states. In the specialised program every clause of the form $name_m(args_m)$:- $name_n(args_n)$ corresponds to such a pair. Formally, in the ISABELLE theory each pair is represented as a tuple (x,y), where x and y are tuples of terms built by Suc and variables of the corresponding *list of variables*:

```
defs
  coverrel_def: "coverrel ≡
```
$$\{(x,y).\ \exists\ list_1\ of\ variables.\ x=\ state_{11}\ \wedge\ y=\ state_{12}\}$$
$$\cup\ \{(x,y).\ \exists\ list_2\ of\ variables.\ x=\ state_{21}\ \wedge\ y=\ state_{22}\}$$
$$\vdots$$
$$\cup\ \{(x,y).\ \exists\ list_m\ of\ variables.\ x=\ state_{m1}\ \wedge\ y=\ state_{m2}\}"$$

The theory generator (cf. [9]) produces automatically the specification of the coverability relation from the specialised program.

Example 4. The following theory was generated by the theory generator [9] from the program of Example 4:

```
consts
  coverrel:: "(state × state) set"

  sat__1__2 :: "nat ⇒ state"
  sat_eu__2__3 :: "nat ⇒ state"
  sat_eu__2__4 :: "nat ⇒ state"
  sat_eu__2__5 :: "nat ⇒ state"
defs
  sat__1__2_def: "sat__1__2 A ≡ (A,(Suc 0),(Suc 0),0,0)"
  sat_eu__2__3_def: "sat_eu__2__3 A ≡ (A,(Suc 0),(Suc 0),0,0)"
  sat_eu__2__4_def: "sat_eu__2__4 A ≡ (A,(Suc 0),0,(Suc 0),0)"
  sat_eu__2__5_def: "sat_eu__2__5 A ≡ (A,0,(Suc 0),0,(Suc 0))"
  coverrel_def: "coverrel ≡ {(x,y). ∃ A. x=(sat__1__2 A)
                                     ∧ y=(sat_eu__2__3 A)}
                        ∪ {(x,y). ∃ A. x=(sat_eu__2__3 (Suc A))
                                     ∧ y=(sat_eu__2__4 A)}
                        ∪ {(x,y). ∃ A. x=(sat_eu__2__3 (Suc A))
                                     ∧ y=(sat_eu__2__5 A)}
                        ∪ {(x,y). ∃ A. x=(sat_eu__2__4 A)
                                     ∧ y=(sat_eu__2__3 (Suc A))}
                        ∪ {(x,y). ∃ A. x=(sat_eu__2__5 A)
                                     ∧ y=(sat_eu__2__3 (Suc A))}"
```
                                                                    □

5   Proof Scripts

In this section we demonstrate how we can prove theorems using ISABELLE/ISAR and how we can write proof scripts for automatic execution. Thereby we focus only on some of the "execution style" proof commands of ISABELLE/Isar. These commands can be considered to be the classical way of writing ISABELLE proofs although the actual ISABELLE proof methods are wrapped within the ISAR language. Note however that ISAR allows also a more "mathematical style" notation of proofs than the one we use here (see the *Isabelle/Isar Reference Manual* for details).

Furthermore we discuss only the proof methods we are going to apply in order to solve the verification task of ECCE. Keep in mind that ISABELLE/ISAR provides a much wider range of methods.

The proof mode of ISABELLE/ISAR is initiated by executing a `lemma`. When entering the proof mode ISABELLE/ISAR generates a single pending subgoal consisting of the lemma to be proven. The list of subgoals can be altered, mainly by executing *proof methods*. Proof methods are executed using the proof command `apply`. Thereby the list of subgoals defines the *proof state*. The proof mode can be left by executing `done` in the case that there are no pending subgoals (the proof state is the empty list of subgoals, in which case ISABELLE/ISAR prints `No subgoals!`).

Note that all proof methods described below only transform the first subgoal of the proof state. For finding a proof this may be inconvenient. Therefore, ISABELLE/ISAR provides commands to change the order of the subgoals. However, our aim in this paper is the automatic execution of proof scripts, not their interactive development.

Rewriting. To rewrite a subgoal using existing definitions and lemmas automatically we may execute ISABELLE's simplifier: `apply(simp)`. For the simplifier to automatically attempt to use new defintions and lemmas they have to be accompanied by the option `[simp]`. Such defined simplification rules are then applied from left to right. However, we have to take care if we define simplification rules in such a way as they may slow the simplifier down considerably or even cause it to loop. Instead of defining a general simplification rule we may also use the simplifier to only apply certain, explicitly stated definitions. E.g., the execution `apply(simp only: r_def)` causes to rewrite using the definition of r only.

Introduction and Elimination. Based on reasoning using *natural deduction* there are two types of rules for each logical symbol, such as $\vee$: *introduction rules* which allow us to infer formulas containing the symbol (e.g. $\vee$), and *elimination rules* which allow us to deduce consequences of a formula containing the symbol (e.g. $\vee$).

In ISABELLE an introduction rule is usually applied by `apply(rule r)`. Assume r being a rule of the form:

$$\frac{P_1, \ldots, P_n}{Q}$$

where Q is a formula containing the introduced logical symbol while the formulas $P_1, \ldots, P_n$ in the premise do not. Then, if r is applied as introduction rule the current first subgoal is unified with Q and replaced by the properly instantiated $P_1, \ldots, P_n$.

An elimination rule is usually applied using `apply(erule r)`. Assume r being a rule of the above form and the current first subgoal of the form $A_1, \ldots, A_m \Longrightarrow S$. Then, if r is applied as elimination rule S is unified with Q and some A_i is unified with P_1. The old subgoal is replace by $n-1$ new subgoals of the form $A_1, \ldots, A_{i-1}, A_{i+1}, \ldots, A_m \Longrightarrow P_k$ with $2 \le k \le n$.

In our verification proofs we will use explicitly only the elimination rules `disjE` for disjunction and `paths.induct` for induction over the length of paths.

Automatic Reasoners. Most classical reasoning of even simple lemmas can require the application of a vast amount of rules. To simplify this task ISABELLE provides a number of automatic reasoners. Here we will make use of `blast` which is the most powerful of ISABELLE's reasoners. Additionally, we will employ `clarify` which performs obvious transformations which do not require to split the subgoal or render it unprovable. The method `clarify` and the explicit application of the elimination rule `disjE` (see above) was necessary to tune the proof process. This tuning was necessary to complete the verification proofs of even very small Petri nets using the available computing resources.

Additionally to the two classical reasoners we also employ the simplifier `simp` as an automatic proof tool as it can also handle some arithmetics. Furthermore, for some cases in our verification task `simp` succeeded faster than `blast` if it was able to eliminate a subgoal at all.

Scripts. To improve the handling of large proofs and to allow a higher flexibility of a proof proof scripts can be extended by the following operators:

- $method_1, \ldots, method_n$: a list of methods represents their sequential execution;
- ($method$): mainly used to define the scope of another operator;
- $method$?: executes $method$ only if it does not fail,
- $method_1 | \ldots | method_n$: attempts to execute $method_k$ only if each $method_i$ with $i < k$ failed;
- $method+$: $method$ is repeatedly executed until it fails.

For our verification task the lemma and proof script are generated automatically by the theory generator [9]. The execution of the script in the example below is illustrated in the next section.

Example 5. The following lemma and script corresponds to the one automatically generated by ECCE for the Petri net specification of Example 1:

```
lemma "1 ∈ paths ⟹ ∃ y. ((hd 1),y) ∈ coverrel"

apply(erule paths.induct)
apply(simp only: start_def
                 coverrel_def)
apply(simp only: sat__1__2_def
                 sat_eu__2__3_def
                 sat_eu__2__4_def
                 sat_eu__2__5_def)
apply(simp)
```

```
apply(blast)
apply(simp only:trans_def)
apply(clarify)
apply(((erule disjE)?,
        simp only: coverrel_def, simp,
        ((erule disjE)?,
          simp only: sat__1__2_def
                     sat_eu__2__3_def
                     sat_eu__2__4_def
                     sat_eu__2__5_def,
          simp|blast)+)+)
```

□

6 Verifying ECCE

In this section we illustrate the automatic verification of the ECCE output by the
ISABELLE system. To this end the theory, lemma and proof script as generated by
ECCE for the Petri net of Example 1, are executed (the complete input consists
of the ISABELLE specifications of Example 1, Example 5, and lemma and proof
script of Example 6). Full details can be found in the technical report [9]. After
this, we can also apply the steps required to prove the lemma for transition
t1 in a similar fashion to the remaining transitions. The following proof script
attempts precisely this. Again, the elimination rule disjE is not applicable for
the last transition. Hence, we perform a test using ? before applying this method
in the first line.

```
apply(((erule disjE)?,
        simp only: coverrel_def, simp,
        ((erule disjE)?,
          simp only: sat__1__2_def
                     sat_eu__2__3_def
                     sat_eu__2__4_def
                     sat_eu__2__5_def,
          simp|blast)+)+)
```

For our example all cases could be verified, hence ISABELLE answers:

```
No subgoals!
```

□

Consequently, the coverability relation generated by ECCE for the Petri net
of Example 1 covers indeed all states reachable by any path (under the condition
that the theory generated by the automatic theory generator as implemented in
ECCE is correct).

Automatic Generation of Hypotheses. Instead of defining the coverability
as a relation as illustrated in Subsection 4.2 we may view the coverability graph
as an inductive definition of a set of states which covers the actual state space of

the Petri net. Similarly, instead of using the concept of paths, we may directly specify the set of reachable states inductively in ISABELLE/ISAR. Full details can be found in the technical report [9].

However, we did not yet succeed in implementing a complete proof script using this rule as the search for the appropriate alternative subgoal has to be controlled by the proof script. Within the execution oriented proof style we have focused on ISABELLE/ISAR does not seem to provide enough control without implementing new proof tactics on ISABELLE's ML-implementation level.

7 Conclusion and Further Work

We have shown the similarity between controlling partial deduction and inductive theorem proving. We have formally established a relationship between the program specialiser ECCE and the proof system ISABELLE when applied to verifying infinite state Petri nets. We have shown that verification of ECCE output using the proof system ISABELLE can be achieved for small nets. The execution of the proof script of Section 6 on a Pentium II/400 needed about 90s and the underlying PolyML required 80MB of memory. However, as further experiments with a net containing 14 places and 13 transitions reveiled, more specific proof methods have to be employed as the use of the method `blast` required more than the available 200MB of main memory and therefore had to be canceled. One way of tuning the proof process further is by restricting the number of rules potentially applied by `blast`. However, while rules can easily be removed from and added to the list of simplification rules in ISABELLE/ISAR, a similar simple manipulation of the "`blast` rules" without rewriting underlying ISABELLE proof tactics seems not possible. An indirect way of restricting the search space of `blast` could also be to derive the theory PN not from Main but from (sets of) more basic theories.

A way of improving the readability of the proof script could be to employ the mathematical proof style instead of the execution oriented style. In the mathematical proof style higher-order pattern matching can be used to control the proof. This may also increase the flexibility of the proof significantly, in particular if the results have to be generalised for other specifications than those of Petri nets.

Finally, for ISABELLE to automatically generate the coverability relation from the specification of the Petri net we believe that it is necessary to implement a new proof rule/proof method at ISABELLE's implementation level which allows to automatically backtrack over potential hypotheses which are more general than the subgoal to be shown. Another option worth exploring might be to attempt to define a proof scheme using the higher-order pattern matching of ISABELLE/ISAR, which performs the abstraction on proof level: E.g., if a state description matches a certain pattern we attempt to prove a lemma concerning a similar pattern where a constant is replaced by some variable.

Finally, to use program specialisers for proving more complicated inductive theorems one probably needs a tighter integration of (conjunctive) partial deduction with abstract interpretation, e.g., as detailed in [6, 22, 11]. We hope that future research will uncover more exciting parallels between inductive theorem proving and program specialisation.

Acknowledgements

We thank the participants of LOPSTR'03 for valuable feedback. We would also like to thank Maurice Bruynooghe and the LOPSTR'03 programme committee for their invitation to present this paper.

References

1. A. Bundy, A. Stevens, F. van Harmelen, A. Ireland, and A. Smaill. Rippling: a heuristic for guiding inductive proofs. *Artificial Intelligence*, 62:185–253, 1993.
2. E. M. Clarke, O. Grumberg, and D. Peled. *Model Checking*. MIT Press, 1999.
3. E. M. Clarke and J. M. Wing. Formal methods: State of the art and future directions. *ACM Computing Surveys*, 28(4):626–643, Dec. 1996.
4. D. De Schreye, R. Glück, J. Jørgensen, M. Leuschel, B. Martens, and M. H. Sørensen. Conjunctive partial deduction: Foundations, control, algorithms and experiments. *The Journal of Logic Programming*, 41(2 & 3):231–277, November 1999.
5. A. Finkel. The minimal coverability graph for Petri nets. In *Advances in Petri Nets 1993*, LNCS 674, pages 210–243. Springer-Verlag, 1993.
6. J. P. Gallagher and J. C. Peralta. Regular tree languages as an abstract domain in program specialisation. *Higher Order and Symbolic Computation*, 14(2–3):143–172, November 2001.
7. R. Glück and J. Jørgensen. Generating transformers for deforestation and supercompilation. In B. Le Charlier, editor, *Proceedings of SAS'94*, LNCS 864, pages 432–448, Namur, Belgium, September 1994. Springer-Verlag.
8. N. D. Jones, C. K. Gomard, and P. Sestoft. *Partial Evaluation and Automatic Program Generation*. Prentice Hall, 1993.
9. H. Lehmann and M. Leuschel. Generating inductive verification proofs for Isabelle using the partial evaluator Ecce. Technical Report DSSE-TR-2002-02, Department of Electronics and Computer Science, University of Southampton, UK, September 2002.
10. M. Leuschel. The ECCE partial deduction system and the DPPD library of benchmarks. Obtainable via http://www.ecs.soton.ac.uk/~mal, 1996-2002.
11. M. Leuschel. A framework for the integration of partial evaluation and abstract interpretation of logic programs. *ACM Transactions on Programming Languages and Systems*, May 2004. To appear.
12. M. Leuschel and M. Bruynooghe. Logic program specialisation through partial deduction: Control issues. *Theory and Practice of Logic Programming*, 2(4 & 5):461–515, July & September 2002.
13. M. Leuschel, J. Jørgensen, W. Vanhoof, and M. Bruynooghe. Offline specialisation in Prolog using a hand-written compiler generator. *Theory and Practice of Logic Programming*, 4(1):139–191, 2004.
14. M. Leuschel and H. Lehmann. Solving coverability problems of Petri nets by partial deduction. In M. Gabbrielli and F. Pfenning, editors, *Proceedings of PPDP'2000*, pages 268–279, Montreal, Canada, 2000. ACM Press.

15. M. Leuschel, B. Martens, and D. De Schreye. Controlling generalisation and poly-variance in partial deduction of normal logic programs. *ACM Transactions on Programming Languages and Systems*, 20(1):208–258, January 1998.
16. M. Leuschel and T. Massart. Infinite state model checking by abstract interpretation and program specialisation. In A. Bossi, editor, Logic-Based Program Synthesis and Transformation. *Proceedings of LOPSTR'99*, LNCS 1817, pages 63–82, Venice, Italy, 2000.
17. J. W. Lloyd and J. C. Shepherdson. Partial evaluation in logic programming. *The Journal of Logic Programming*, 11(3& 4):217–242, 1991.
18. K. Marriott, L. Naish, and J.-L. Lassez. Most specific logic programs. *Annals of Mathematics and Artificial Intelligence*, 1:303–338, 1990.
19. T. Nipkow, L. C. Paulson, and M. Wenzel. *Isabelle/HOL: A Proof Assistant for HIgher-Order Logic*. LNCS 2283. Springer-Verlag, 2002.
20. L. C. Paulson. *Isabelle: A Generic Theorem Prover*. LNCS 828. Springer, 1994.
21. A. Pettorossi and M. Proietti. Synthesis and transformation of logic programs using unfold/fold proofs. *The Journal of Logic Programming*, 41(2&3):197–230, November 1999.
22. G. Puebla and M. Hermenegildo. Abstract specialization and its applications. In *ACM SIGPLAN Workshop on Partial Evaluation and Semantics-Based Program Manipulation (PEPM'03)*, pages 29–43. ACM Press, June 2003.
23. V. F. Turchin. Program transformation with metasystem transitions. *Journal of Functional Programming*, 3(3):283–313, 1993.
24. V. F. Turchin. Metacomputation: Metasystem transitions plus supercompilation. In O. Danvy, R. Glück, and P. Thiemann, editors, *Partial Evaluation, International Seminar*, LNCS 1110, pages 482–509, Schloß Dagstuhl, 1996. Springer-Verlag.

Predicate Synthesis from Inductive Proof Attempt of Faulty Conjectures

Francis Alexandre[1], Khaled Bsaïes[2], and Moussa Demba[2]

[1] LORIA BP 239
54506 Vandoeuvre-lès-Nancy, France
alexandr@loria.fr
[2] Faculté des Sciences de Tunis, DSI
Campus Universitaire 2092 Tunis, Tunisie
{khaled.bsaies,moussa.demba}@fst.rnu.tn

Abstract. We present a method for patching faulty conjectures in automatic theorem proving. The method is based on well-known folding /unfolding deduction rules. The conjectures we are interested in here are implicative formulas that are of the following form: $\forall \overline{x} \; \phi(\overline{x}) = \forall \overline{x} \; \exists \overline{Y} \; \Gamma(\overline{x}, \overline{Y}) \leftarrow \Delta(\overline{x})$. A faulty conjecture is a statement $\forall \overline{x} \; \phi(\overline{x})$, which is not provable in some given program $\mathcal{T}$, defining all the predicates occurring in ϕ, i.e, $\mathcal{M}(\mathcal{T}) \not\models \forall \overline{x} \; \phi(\overline{x})$, where $\mathcal{M}(\mathcal{T})$ means the least Herbrand model of $\mathcal{T}$, but it would be if enough conditions, say P, were assumed to hold, i.e., $\mathcal{M}(\mathcal{T} \cup \mathcal{P}) \models \forall \overline{x} \; \phi(\overline{x}) \leftarrow P$, where $\mathcal{P}$ is the definition of P. The missing hypothesis P is called a corrective predicate for ϕ. To construct P, we use the abduction mechanism that is the process of hypothesis formation. In this paper, we use the logic based approach because it is suitable for the application of deductive rules.

Keywords: Corrective predicate, program synthesis, theorem proving, implicative formulas, folding/unfolding rules, abduction.

1 Introduction

Classical proof techniques can be seen as simplification methods, i.e. conjectures are transformed to trivial ones, *true*. Unfortunately, sometimes the proof ends up with an unprovable or a false conjecture. In general, a theorem prover will do nothing more but reject this conjecture. However, in many cases it is strongly interesting to know why the conjecture is false, and how it can be corrected.

In this paper, we are interested to correct faulty conjectures by synthesizing the missing hypotheses. To do that, we consider a theory $\mathcal{T}$ of definite logic programs (Horn clauses) and conjectures, called implicative formulas, of the form $\forall \overline{x} \; \exists \overline{Y} \; \Gamma(\overline{x}, \overline{Y}) \leftarrow \Delta(\overline{x})$, where Γ and Δ are conjunctions of atoms. Given a conjecture $\phi : \forall \overline{x} \; \exists \overline{Y} \; \Gamma(\overline{x}, \overline{Y}) \leftarrow \Delta(\overline{x})$ that is not valid in the least Herbrand model of $\mathcal{T}$, i.e.,

$$\mathcal{M}(\mathcal{T}) \not\models \forall \overline{x} \; \exists \overline{Y} \; \Gamma(\overline{x}, \overline{Y}) \leftarrow \Delta(\overline{x})$$

our aim is to turn ϕ into a theorem, by inserting assumptions into the right-hand side of ϕ. An assumption is represented by a (corrective) predicate say P defined by some program $\mathcal{P}$. P is said to be a corrective predicate of ϕ if we have:

M. Bruynooghe (Ed.): LOPSTR 2004, LNCS 3018, pp. 20–33, 2004.
© Springer-Verlag Berlin Heidelberg 2004

$$\mathcal{M}(\mathcal{T} \cup \mathcal{P}) \models \forall \overline{x} \; \exists \overline{Y} \; \Gamma(\overline{x}, \overline{Y}) \leftarrow \Delta(\overline{x}), P(\overline{x})$$

The definition of the corrective predicate P is obtained by proof-as-program paradigm [8]. To construct P, we exploit information derived from a failed proof attempt of ϕ. To do that, we use a theorem prover, a set of inference rules. This prover is particularly suitable to prove recursive definitions or to synthesize corrective predicates. This predicate synthesis may be viewed like a kind of abduction [14, 9].

The correction of conjectures has various applications. The patching faulty conjectures can be useful if the formula to be patched has been obtained by an overgeneralization technique otherwise the original (*true*) conjecture cannot be proved. It is then necessary to correct the generalized formula [2], [16] see section 4.1 for more examples. In [7], corrective predicates are also used to extend classes of formulas where inductive validity is decidable.

Here is a simple example illustrating our patching faulty conjectures method.

1.1   Example

Suppose that $\mathcal{PLUS}$ is the following program:

$$
\begin{array}{ll}
plus(0, x, x) & \leftarrow \\
plus(s(x), y, s(z)) & \leftarrow plus(x, y, z) \\
nat(0) & \leftarrow \\
nat(s(x)) & \leftarrow nat(x)
\end{array}
$$

where s and 0 are constructors. The atom $plus(x, y, z)$ is true if $z = x + y$ and $nat(x)$ is true if x is an integer. Let us consider the following specification for the subtraction function in natural numbers: given two natural numbers v and w, find U such that $v + U = w$. To this specification corresponds the implicative formula :

$$\forall v \; \forall w \; \exists U \; plus(v, U, w) \leftarrow nat(v), nat(w) \tag{1}$$

which is false, as we discover while attempting to prove it, for example there is no U verifying $2 + U = 1$. Nevertheless, there are particular values for the universally quantified variables for which the formula (1) is true. It is interesting to know these values of v and w. To do that, the formula (1) is associated with a corrective predicate $P(v, U, w)$. First at all, we try to prove (1) and to keep track of substitutions on P. After some unfolding steps on (1), we get the following formulas (without quantifiers):

$$plus(0, U, w) \leftarrow nat(w) \tag{2}$$

$$plus(s(v), U, 0) \leftarrow nat(v) \tag{3}$$

$$plus(v, U, w) \leftarrow nat(v), nat(w) \tag{4}$$

- formula (2) is true with the existential substitution $\{U/w\}$; and its corresponding predicate is the unit clause $P(0, w, w) \leftarrow$.
- while formula (3), it is fully false, then its corresponding corrective predicate is set to false.
- formula (4) is the same as formula (1), which plays the role of the induction hypothesis. An obvious folding step between (4) and (1) allows us to yield the formula true, and the following recursive clause for P : $P(s(v), U, s(w)) \leftarrow P(v, U, w)$.

We have then synthesized a definition, say $\mathcal{P}$, of P:

$$P(0, w, w) \leftarrow \tag{5}$$
$$P(s(v), U, s(w)) \leftarrow P(v, U, w) \tag{6}$$

Note that in the clause (6) occurs the existential variable U. We have to eliminate in some way this variable. For instance, a truncation of P w.r.t. its second argument yields the following program $\mathcal{P}'$:

$$P'(0, w) \leftarrow$$
$$P'(s(v), s(w)) \leftarrow P'(v, w)$$

We remark that P' is the predicate $\leq$ over natural numbers, and we have

$$\mathcal{M}(\mathcal{PLUS} \cup \mathcal{P}') \models \forall v \ \forall w \ \exists U \ plus(v, U, w) \leftarrow nat(v), nat(w), P'(v, w).$$

1.2 Proof Method

We present an extension of the systems defined in [18, 10] so as to make it capable of dealing with faulty conjectures using a synthesis mechanism. The system presented here uses deduction rules, that include unfolding and folding, that allow us to prove implicative formulas. Intuitively, unfolding is an extension of SLD-resolution whereas folding represents deductive reasoning. Indeed, whereas an unfold step replaces a term that "matches" the conclusion of a definition in the program by the corresponding hypothesis, a folding right (resp. left) step replaces a conjunction of atoms that match the hypothesis (resp. conclusion) of an induction hypothesis by the corresponding conclusion (resp. hypothesis).

In order to synthesize the definition of the corrective predicate, we propose an extension of the logic program extraction method of Fribourg [5]. Fribourg described a method for generating programs from (true) conjectures. The method of Fribourg makes use of an extended form of SLD-resolution and a form of structural induction. Our method does not use explicit induction and inductive rules of inference [4], but the folding rules are able to perform some induction proofs and to synthesize some recursive predicates.

So if our system is used to prove a given faulty conjecture, it will build a corrective predicate P, and if it is used to prove a true conjecture, the corrective predicate *true* will be generated.

The rest of the paper is structured as follows: section 2 presents some notations and definitions, in section 3 we describe our proof system. Section 4 presents an example illustrating the patching process and some results of experimentation. The last section is a comparison with the related works and a discussion.

2   Preliminaries

Throughout the paper, Γ, Δ and Λ denote conjunctions of atoms; ϕ, π and π' denote implicative formulas; A and B denote atoms and θ, σ denotes substitutions. In all formulas, existentially quantified variables are distinguished from universal variables by giving them upper-case letters. A program is a set of definite clauses, programs are denoted by calligraphic letters: $\mathcal{T}$, $\mathcal{P}$, ... An implicative formula is a first-order formula of the form $\Gamma(\overline{x}, \overline{Y}) \leftarrow \Delta(\overline{x})$, where $\overline{x}$ and $\overline{Y}$ are vectors of universally and existentially quantified variables respectively, and where no variable of $\overline{Y}$ occurs in Δ. The sub-formula Δ (resp. Γ) is the hypothesis (resp. conclusion). mgu means "most general unifier".

Definition 1 (Corrective predicate). *Let* ϕ : $\Gamma(\overline{x}, \overline{Y}) \leftarrow \Delta(\overline{x})$ *be a implicative formula,* $\mathcal{T}$ *the program defining the predicates occurring in* ϕ, P *a predicate and* $\mathcal{P}$ *a program defining* P.

  - *P is a corrective predicate of* ϕ *iff* $\mathcal{M}(\mathcal{T} \cup \mathcal{P}) \models \Gamma(\overline{x}, \overline{Y}) \leftarrow \Delta(\overline{x}), P(\overline{x})$
  - *P is a maximal corrective predicate of* ϕ *if for all corrective predicate* P' *of* ϕ, *we have:* $\mathcal{M}(\mathcal{P} \cup \mathcal{P}') \models \forall \overline{x}\ P(\overline{x}) \leftarrow P'(\overline{x})$ *where* $\mathcal{P}'$ *is a program defining* P'.

Definition 2 (Partial correctness [5]). *Let* ϕ : $\Gamma(\overline{x}, \overline{Y}) \leftarrow \Delta(\overline{x})$ *be an implicative formula whose predicates are defined by the program* $\mathcal{T}$. *Let* $\mathcal{P}$ *be a program defining a predicate* P. *The program* $\mathcal{P}$ *is partially correct for* $\mathcal{T}$ *with respect to* ϕ *iff* $\mathcal{M}(\mathcal{T} \cup \mathcal{P}) \models \forall \overline{x}\ \forall \overline{Y}\ \Gamma(\overline{x}, \overline{Y}) \leftarrow \Delta(\overline{x}), P(\overline{x}, \overline{Y})$.

Remark 1. Let us note that in the definition of "Partial correctness" the existential variables $\overline{Y}$ of the formula ϕ are universally quantified, the truncation of the predicate P with respect to the variables of $\overline{Y}$ will allows us generally to obtain a corrective predicate.

3   Proof System

Let $\mathcal{T}$ be a definite program, and π an implicative formula. To prove that $\mathcal{M}(\mathcal{T}) \models \pi$, we apply deduction rules in π step by step until we get trivial formulas. We describe the proof process and synthesis of corrective predicates as a proof tree. The nodes of the proof tree are labelled by $< \pi \mid P >$ where π is a formula and P is a predicate associated with π. The root of the proof tree is labelled by the initial formula and each branch of the proof tree is marked by a deduction rule. A deduction rules generates a set of pairs namely $\{< \pi_i \mid P_i >\}$ from a given pair $< \pi \mid P >$ and also some Horn clauses which establish the relationship between the predicates P and P_i. The synthesized program is the set of clauses generated during the proof.

3.1   Deduction Rules

Definition 3 (Folding right or CUTR). *Let* $\pi_1 : \Gamma \leftarrow \Delta_1, \Delta_2$ *and* $\pi_0 :$ $\Lambda \leftarrow \Pi$ *be two formulas satisfying the following conditions :*

- θ *is a substitution such that* $\Pi\theta = \Delta_1$
- *for any local variable* x *in* Π, $x\theta$ *is a variable and does not occur other than in* $\Pi\theta$
- θ *replaces different local variables in* Π *with different internal variables in* Δ_1.

CUTR yields the formula π_2 *defined as follows:*

$$< \pi_0 : (\Lambda \leftarrow \Pi) \mid P_0 >$$
$$\vdots$$
$$< \pi_1 : (\Gamma \leftarrow \Delta_1, \Delta_2) \mid P_1 >$$
$$\downarrow CUTR$$
$$< \pi_2 : (\Gamma \leftarrow \Lambda\theta, \Delta_2) \mid P_2 >$$

The clause $P_1 \leftarrow P_0\theta$, P_2 *is generated and added to the synthesized program.*

Remark 2. The formula π_0 has generally the role of the induction hypothesis and it is necessary to verify that π_0 is smaller than π_1 w.r.t. a well-founded ordering.

Proposition 1. *The rule CUTR preserves partial correctness.*

Proof. We suppose that the formulas $\Gamma \leftarrow \Lambda\theta, \Delta_2, P_2$ and $P_1 \leftarrow P_0\theta$, P_2 hold, we have to prove that the formula $\Gamma \leftarrow \Delta_1$, Δ_2, P_1 holds in the least Herbrand model of the program defining its predicates. Let $\Delta_1\sigma_0$, $\Delta_2\sigma_0$, $P_1\sigma_0$ be ground instances of Δ_1, Δ_2 and P_1 respectively, we must prove that $\Gamma\sigma_0$ holds.

- from $P_1\theta_0$ and the only-if part of $P_1 \leftarrow P_0\theta$, P_2 it follows that $P_0\theta\sigma_0$ and $P_2\sigma_0$ hold
- according the definition of $CUTR$, we have $\Pi\theta = \Delta_1$, then $\Pi\theta\sigma_0 = \Delta_1\sigma_0$.
- From the induction hypothesis $\Lambda \leftarrow \Pi, P_0$ and from the conjunctions $\Pi\theta\sigma_0$ and $P_0\theta\sigma_0$ that hold, we have $\Lambda\theta\sigma_0$.

Finally from the formula $\Gamma \leftarrow \Lambda\theta, \Delta_2, P_2$ and the three following conjunctions $\Lambda\theta\sigma_0$, $\Delta_2\sigma_0$ and $P_2\sigma_0$ that hold, we can conclude that $\Gamma\sigma_0$ holds too, Q.E.D.

Likewise, we define the rule of folding left.

Definition 4 (Folding left or CUTL). *Let* $\pi_1 : \Gamma_1, \Gamma_2 \leftarrow \Delta$ *and* $\pi_0 : \Lambda \leftarrow$ Π *be two formulas satisfying the following conditions:*

- θ is a substitution such that $\Lambda\theta = \Gamma_1$
- in Λ, $z\theta$ is a variable and does not occur other than in $\Lambda\theta$
- θ replaces different internal variables in Λ with different internal variables in Γ_1.

$CUTL$ yields the formula π_2 defined as follows:

$$< \pi_0 \ : \ (\Lambda \leftarrow \Pi) \mid P_0 >$$
$$\vdots$$
$$< \pi_1 \ : \ (\Gamma_1, \Gamma_2 \leftarrow \Delta) \mid P_1 >$$
$$\downarrow CUTL$$
$$< \pi_2 \ : \ (\Pi\theta, \Gamma_2 \leftarrow \Delta) \mid P_2 >$$

The clause $P_1 \leftarrow P_0\theta, P_2$ is generated and added to the synthesized program.

Proposition 2. The rule $CUTL$ preserves partial correctness.

Proof. the proof is similar to $CUTR$.

Definition 5 (Unfolding right or NFI). Let $\mathcal{T}$ be a program, $\pi_0 \ : \ \Gamma \leftarrow \Delta, A$ a formula and $C = \{c_1, \ldots, c_k\}$ the set of clauses of $\mathcal{T}$ such that $c_i \ : \ B_i \leftarrow \Delta_i$ and there exists a substitution $\theta_i = mgu(B_i, A)$. NFI yields the formulas π_i $(1 \leq i \leq k)$ defined as follows:

$$< \pi_0 \ : \ (\Gamma \leftarrow \Delta, A) \mid P_0 >$$
$$\downarrow NFI$$
$$< \pi_i \ : \ (\Gamma \leftarrow \Delta, \Delta_i)\theta_i \mid P_i >$$

The clauses $P_0\theta_i \leftarrow P_i$ $(1 \leq i \leq k)$ are generated and added to the synthesized program.

If $C = \emptyset$, i.e., $\mathcal{M}(\mathcal{T}) \not\models A$, then the formula π_0 is reduced to the (true) formula $\Gamma \leftarrow false$ and the unit clause $P_0 \leftarrow$ is generated.

Example 1. Let $\pi_0 : plus(u, \ v, \ w) \leftarrow plus(v, \ u, \ w) \mid P_0(u, v, w)$ be a formula to be corrected. NFI yields the two following formulas:

$$\pi_1 : plus(u, \ 0, \ u) \qquad \leftarrow \qquad \qquad \mid P_1(u)$$
$$\pi_2 : plus(u, \ s(v), \ s(w)) \leftarrow plus(u, \ v, \ w) \mid P_2(u, \ v, \ w)$$

The relationships between the predicates P_0, P_1 and P_2 are defined by the following clauses: $P_0(u, \ 0, \ u) \leftarrow P_1(u)$ and $P_0(u, \ s(v), \ s(w)) \leftarrow P_2(u, \ v, \ w)$.

Proposition 3. The rule NFI preserves partial correctness.

Proof. We have to prove that if for all $i \in [1, \ k]$ the formulas $\Gamma\theta_i \leftarrow \Delta\theta_i, \Delta_i\theta_i$, P_i and the clauses $P_0\theta_i \leftarrow P_i$ hold then the formula $\Gamma \leftarrow \Delta, A, P_0$ holds.

It is sufficient to note that the formulas $\Gamma\theta_i \leftarrow \Delta\theta_i, \Delta_i\theta_i, P_i$ may be obtain from the formula $\Gamma \leftarrow \Delta, A, P_0$ by the rule NFI by selecting successively the atoms A and P_0. We have the expected result because the rule NFI is equivalence-preserving [11].

We define a rule that simplifies an atom in the conclusion of an implicative formula.

Definition 6 (Simplification rule). *Let* $\pi : A, \Gamma \leftarrow B, \Delta$ *be a formula such that there exists* θ *satisfying* $A\theta = B$ *and* θ *substitutes only existential variables of* A. *The simplification rule applied on* π *yields the formula* π' *and is defined as follows:*

$$< \pi : (A, \Gamma \leftarrow B, \Delta) \mid P >$$
$$\downarrow SIMP$$
$$< \pi' : (\Gamma\theta \leftarrow B, \Delta) \mid P' >$$

The clause $P\theta \leftarrow P'$ *is generated and added to the synthesized program.*

Example 2.

$$< \pi : plus(u1, y, X), plus(X, z, u3) \leftarrow plus(u1, y, t),\ plus(t, z, u3) \mid P >$$
$$\downarrow SIMP$$
$$< \pi' : plus(t, z, u3) \leftarrow plus(u1, y, t),\ plus(t, z, u3) \mid P' >$$

The rule $SIMP$ can be applied on π with $\theta = \{X/t\}$ and yields π'. The clause $P(u1, y, t, z, u3, t) \leftarrow P'(u1, y, z, u3, t)$ is then generated.

Definition 7 (Unfolding left or DCI). *Let* $\mathcal{T}$ *be a program and* $\pi_0 : \Gamma, A \leftarrow \Delta$ *be a formula. Let* $C = \{c_1, \ldots, c_k\}$ *be the set of clauses of* $\mathcal{T}$ *such that* $c_i : B_i \leftarrow \Delta_i$ *and there exist existential substitutions* $\theta_i = mgu(B_i, A)$ (θ_i *does not modify universal variables). The rule DCI yields the formulas* π_i ($1 \leq i \leq k$) *defined as follows:*

$$< \pi_0 : (\Gamma, A \leftarrow \Delta) \mid P_0 >$$
$$\downarrow DCI$$
$$< \pi_i = ((\Gamma, \Delta_i)\theta_i \leftarrow \Delta) \mid P_i >$$

The clauses $P_0\theta_i \leftarrow P_i$ ($1 \leq i \leq k$) *are generated and added to the synthesized program.*

Definition 8 (POSTULATE). *Let* $< \pi : \Gamma \leftarrow \mid P >$ *be a pair (where* P *is a corrective predicate associated with the formula* $\Gamma \leftarrow$ *); the rule of* $POSTULATE$ *applied on* π *yields the formula true and generates the clause* $P \leftarrow \Gamma$ *which is added to the synthesized program.*

Remark 3. This rule allows us to stop the proof with π as a leaf of the proof tree and to establish a relationship between the new synthesized predicate, namely P, and the primitive predicates (i.e. these occurring in Γ).

The rules $SIMP$, DCI and $POSTULATE$ preserve partial correctness [5] and [1].

The $FAILURE$ rule allows us to detect the fully false conjectures.

Definition 9 (FAILURE). *Let $\mathcal{T}$ be a program and $< \pi : \Gamma \leftarrow \Delta \mid P > a$ pair where P is the corrective predicate associated with the formula $\Gamma \leftarrow \Delta$. If no atom of Γ is unifiable with no clause head of the program $\mathcal{T}$ and that $\mathcal{M}(\mathcal{T}) \models \Delta$ then the rule $FAILURE$ yields the couple $< false \mid false >$.*

$$< \Gamma \leftarrow \Delta \mid P >$$
$$\downarrow FAILURE$$
$$< false \mid false >$$

The predicate P is set to false.

Proof. The rule $FAILURE$ preserves partial correctness. It sufficient to note that the formula $\Gamma \leftarrow \Delta$, P holds, this is true because P is false.

Remark 4. This rule allows us to eliminate all the clauses of the synthesized program which contain the predicate P in accordance with the negation as failure principle.

Example 3. Going back to the formula (3) of our introductory example : $plus(s(v), U, 0) \leftarrow nat(v)$. The atom $plus(s(v), U, 0)$ is $false$, because, in one hand it cannot be reduced using the program $\mathcal{PLUS}$ and on the other hand we have $\mathcal{M}(\mathcal{PLUS}) \models \forall v \ nat(v)$. The formula $plus(s(v), U, 0) \leftarrow nat(v)$ is then (fully) false and its corresponding corrective predicate is set to $false$.

3.2 Corrective Predicate

The preservation of partial correctness for all the deduction rules guarantees the construction of a corrective predicate for the universally quantified implicative formulas. For the existentially quantified formulas, it is necessary to truncate the synthesized predicate with respect to the existentially variables. The following proposition gives a sufficient condition to get a corrective predicate.

Proposition 4. *Let $\pi : \Gamma(\overline{x}, \overline{Y}) \leftarrow \Delta(\overline{x})$ be a conjecture, $\mathcal{T}$ the program defining the predicates occurring in π and P the predicate associated with π. Let $\mathcal{P}$ be the synthesized program obtained by using the previous deduction rules, $\mathcal{P}$ defines P. Let P' be the predicate symbol obtained from P by truncating it with respect to its existential variables and $\mathcal{P}'$ the resulting program defining P'. If we have*

$$\mathcal{M}(\mathcal{T} \cup \mathcal{P} \cup \mathcal{P}') \models \exists \overline{Y} P(\overline{x}, \overline{Y}) \leftarrow \Delta(\overline{x}), \ P'(\overline{x}) \tag{7}$$

then P' is a corrective predicate of π.

Proof. From the partial correctness of P we have

$$\mathcal{M}(\mathcal{T} \cup \mathcal{P}) \models \forall \overline{x} \forall \overline{Y} \ \Gamma(\overline{x}, \overline{Y}) \leftarrow \Delta(\overline{x}), \ P(\overline{x}, \overline{Y})$$

and the condition (7) gives

$$\mathcal{M}(\mathcal{T} \cup \mathcal{P} \cup \mathcal{P}') \models \forall \overline{x} \exists \overline{Y} P(\overline{x}, \overline{Y}) \leftarrow \Delta(\overline{x}), \ P'(\overline{x})$$

it follows obviously that

$$\mathcal{M}(\mathcal{T} \cup \mathcal{P}') \models \forall \overline{x} \exists \overline{Y} \Gamma(\overline{x}, \overline{Y}) \leftarrow \Delta(\overline{x}), \ P'(\overline{x})$$

this expresses that P' is a corrective predicate of the formula π.

Remark 5. The condition (7) may generally be proved by using the rules $CUTR$, $CUTL$, NFI, DCI and $SIMP$, and the proof is often straightforward.

The termination of the method we propose, can be expressed by the following formula:

$$\mathcal{M}(\mathcal{T}) \models \forall \overline{x} \exists \overline{Y} P(\overline{x}, \overline{Y}) \leftarrow \Delta(\overline{x})$$

The termination is not guaranteed because of folding rules (CUTL and CUTR). This is due to the fact that the rules of folding do not preserve equivalence. If it is supposed that the predicates specify functions, the folding rules are equivalence-preserving and it is possible to show the termination of our method.

4 Experimentation

4.1 Example

The following program defines the multiplication of the natural numbers.

$$
\begin{array}{ll}
mul(0, m, 0) & \leftarrow \\
mul(s(n), m, r) & \leftarrow mul(n, m, u), \ plus(u, m, r) \\
plus(0, x, x) & \leftarrow \\
plus(s(x), y, s(z)) & \leftarrow plus(x, y, z) \\
nat(0) & \leftarrow \\
nat(s(x)) & \leftarrow nat(x)
\end{array}
$$

We consider the following false conjecture $mul(U, v, w) \leftarrow nat(v), \ nat(w)$ and $P1(w, v, U)$ the associated predicate. The figure 1 shows the proof tree of this conjecture.

The formulas occurring at the leaves of the proof tree are the following:

(11) $nat(v), nat(u2)$ $\qquad\qquad$ $\leftarrow nat(v), nat(u2)$
(15) $nat(V5), plus(V5, s(x), 0)$ $\quad$ $\leftarrow nat(x)$
(16) $nat(0)$ $\qquad\qquad\qquad\qquad$ $\leftarrow$
(17) $mul(U, 0, 0)$ $\qquad\qquad\qquad$ $\leftarrow$
(19) $\qquad\qquad\qquad\qquad\qquad$ $\leftarrow nat(x)$
(20) $mul(N, s(x), V8), plus(V8, s(x), 0) \leftarrow nat(x)$

The formulas (11), (16), (17) and (19) are *true*, and the formulas (15) and (20) are totally false. Finally, the program defining the predicates is made of the following clauses 1 to 19.

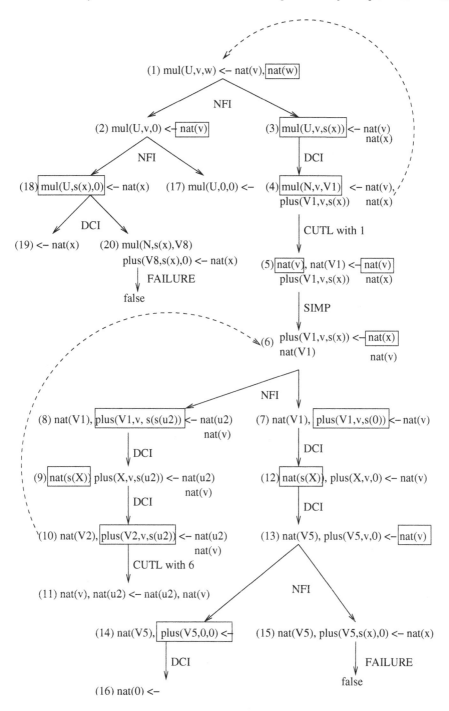

Fig. 1. Proof tree

(1) $P1(0, v, U)$ $\leftarrow P2(v, U)$
(2) $P1(s(x), v, U)$ $\leftarrow P3(x, v, U)$
(3) $P3(x, v, s(N))$ $\leftarrow P4(x, v, V1, N)$
(4) $P4(x, v, V1, N)$ $\leftarrow P1(V1, v, N), P5(x, v, V1)$
(5) $P5(x, v, V1)$ $\leftarrow P6(x, v, V1)$
(6) $P6(0, v, V1)$ $\leftarrow P7(v, V1)$
(7) $P6(s(u2), v, V1) \leftarrow P8(u2, v, V)$
(8) $P8(u2, v, s(X))$ $\leftarrow P9(u2, v, X)$
(9) $P9(u2, v, V2)$ $\leftarrow P10(u2, v, V2)$
(10) $P10(u2, v, V2) \leftarrow P6(u2, v, V2), P11(u2, v)$
(11) $P7(v, s(X))$ $\leftarrow P12(v, X)$
(12) $P12(v, V5)$ $\leftarrow P13(v, V5)$
(13) $P13(0, V5)$ $\leftarrow P14(V5)$
(14) $P13(s(x), V5)$ $\leftarrow P15(x, V5)$
(15) $P14(0)$ $\leftarrow P16()$
(16) $P2(0, U)$ $\leftarrow P17(U)$
(17) $P2(s(x), U)$ $\leftarrow P18(x, U)$
(18) $P18(x, 0)$ $\leftarrow P19(x)$
(19) $P18(x, s(N))$ $\leftarrow P20(x, V8, N)$

A straightforward program transformation by unfolding [19, 15] simplifies the synthesized program above as:

$P1(0, 0, V10)$ $\leftarrow$
$P1(0, s(u112), 0)$ $\leftarrow$
$P1(s(u54), u55, s(V23))$ $\leftarrow P1(V1, u55, V23), P6(u54, u55, V1)$
$P6(0, 0, s(0))$ $\leftarrow$
$P6(s(u100), u101, s(V51)) \leftarrow P6(u100, u101, V51)$

Once a program is extracted, the "uninteresting" variables in $P1$ can be eliminated. For instance, a truncation of $P1$ with respect to its third argument yields the following program.

$P'1(0, 0)$ $\leftarrow$
$P'1(0, s(u112))$ $\leftarrow$
$P'1(s(u54), u55)$ $\leftarrow P6(u54, u55, V1), P'1(V1, u55)$
$P6(0, 0, s(0))$ $\leftarrow$
$P6(s(u100), u101, s(V51)) \leftarrow P6(u100, u101, V51)$

The condition of the proposition 4 is expressed by the following formula $P1(x, y, U) \leftarrow nat(x), nat(y), P'1(x, y)$. It is easy to prove this formula by using the previous deduction rules. $P'1(x, y)$ means that y is a divisor of x and $P6(x, y, z) : x + y + 1 = z$.

4.2 Results

We have tested our method on various implicative formulas. One can see the results in the table 1. The missing hypotheses of the non-theorem below have been successfully synthesized using the method. Note that the conjecture 5 is only valid if x is even, we have then synthesized the predicate *even*. The table shows

Table 1. Examples

N°	Conjectures	Corrections	Definitions
1	$sup(x,n) \leftarrow half(x,n)$	$x \neq 0$	
2	$sup(y,x) \leftarrow double(x,y)$	$x \neq 0$	
3	$half(y,s(0)) \leftarrow$	$y = s^2(0)$ or $y = s^3(0)$	
4	$plus(x,Z,y) \leftarrow$	$P(x)$	$P(0,y) \leftarrow$ $P(s(x),s(y)) \leftarrow P(x,y)$
5	$eq(x,z) \leftarrow half(x,y), double(y,z)$	$P(x,y)$	$P(0) \leftarrow$ $P(s^2(x)) \leftarrow P(x)$
6	$sort(l,l) \leftarrow list(l)$	$P(l)$	$P([]) \leftarrow$ $P([a|l]) \leftarrow P(l), Q(a,l)$ $Q(a,[]) \leftarrow$ $Q(a,[b|l]) \leftarrow inf(a,b), Q(a,l)$
7	$even(z) \leftarrow plus(x,y,z)$	$P(x,y)$	$P(0,y) \leftarrow even(y)$ $P(s(0),y) \leftarrow even(s(y))$ $P(s^2(x),s^2(y)) \leftarrow P(x,y)$
8	$plus(v,U,w) \leftarrow nat(v), nat(w)$	$P'(v,w)$	$P'(0,w) \leftarrow$ $P'(s(v),s(w) \leftarrow P'(v,w)$
9	$mul(U,v,w) \leftarrow nat(v), nat(w)$	$P(w,v)$	$P(0,0) \leftarrow$ $P(0,s(u)) \leftarrow$ $P(s(w),v) \leftarrow Q(w,v,u), P(u,v)$ $Q(0,0,s(0)) \leftarrow$ $Q(s(x),y,s(z)) \leftarrow Q(x,y,z)$

that our method can also be useful if the formula to be patched has been obtained by an overgeneralization technique otherwise the original(*true*) conjecture cannot be proved. For instance, the generalization of the formula $sort(sort(x)) = sort(x)$ leads to an overgeneralization (formula 6) [2]: $sort(l,l) \leftarrow list(l)$. Clearly, the conjecture 6 is valid only if the list l is ordered. In this case our method finds a candidate corrective predicate P that is equivalent to the predicate *ordered*, and the corrective predicate Q is equivalent to the predicate *less_than_all* over lists, i.e., the atom $Q(a,l)$ stands for that the element a is less than all the elements in the list l. It is clear that the formula: $sort(l,l) \leftarrow list(l), P(l)$ is a theorem by construction. Hence, using the proposed method we may be able to prove formulas which are unprovable otherwise. Conjectures (8) and (9) contain existentially quantifiers.

5 Conclusion

5.1 Related Works

Franŏvà et al. [6] have investigated the problem of patching faulty conjectures and proposed a method called *PreS* (predicate synthesis from formal specification). Their approach is based on the paradigm of predicate synthesis by proofs-as-programs. They explained their method by examples. No formal system is clearly defined and no system is described.

Protzen [16] proposed a method which allows to synthesize a corrective predicate during the proof attempt of a faulty conjecture. His approach is similar to ours, but uses rewriting rules and induction rules, he gives some correctness results and dealt with universally quantified formulas.

Also Monroy et al. have introduced a method for correcting faulty conjectures[13]. However, they only partially deal with the problem of correcting faults. For example, they cannot build a corrective predicate, only identify it as long as it is present in the working theory. More recently, Monroy proposed in [12] another method that consists of a collection of construction commands and is able to synthesize corrective predicates. His approach is also based on the proofs-as-programs paradigm and guarantees the correction and the termination. There is a similarity between his predicates and ours, but his predicates are refined incrementally during the proof process. Monroy poses the problem of automation of the process and suggests to use a proof planning approach [3]. His technics deal with universally quantified formulas.

5.2 Final Remarks

We have presented a new method for patching faulty conjectures by synthesizing definite programs. The contribution of the paper is mainly the construction of corrective predicates by completing failed proof attempts. This method is original because it makes possible to correct formulas comprising of the existential quantifiers and it uses the powerful rules of folding. We proved the partial correctness of this method. We tested our method successfully on several examples borrowed from the literature, and we generally obtain some maximal predicates. The proposed method for patching faulty conjectures and extracting logic programs is implemented in the functional language OCaml (Objective Caml) [17]. So in our implementation, the user has to specify which rules to be applied. The full automation of the technique requires some proof strategies. We are investigating several ways. One is to implement some strategies in order to automate our system, a second track is to show that our method is useful in the domain of theorem proving, finally we intend to show that our method can be used to detect protocol attack.

References

1. A. Bouverot. *Comparaison entre la transformation et l'extraction de programmes logiques.* PhD thesis, Université Paris VII, 1991. en français.

2. R.S. Boyer and J.S. Moore. *A Computational Logic*. Academic Press, New York, 1979.
3. A. Bundy. The use of explicit plans to guide inductive proofs. In R. Lusk and R. Overbeek, editors, *9th Conference in Automated Deduction, CADE'88*, volume 310 of *Lecture Notes in Computer Science*, pages 111–120, 1988.
4. A. Bundy. *Handbook of Automated Reasoning*, chapter The Automation of Proof by Mathematical Induction. In A. Robinson and A. Voronkov, editors. Elseviers Science Publishers B. V. (North-Holland), 2000.
5. L. Fribourg. Extracting Logic Programs from Proofs that Use Extended Prolog Execution and Induction. In D.H.D. Warren and P. Szeredi, editors, *7th International Conference on Logic Programming*, pages 685–699, Jerusalem, 1990. MIT Press.
6. M. Frănová and Y. Kodratoff. Predicate synthesis from formal specifications. In B. Neumann, editor, *proceedings of the 10th European Conference on Artificial Intelligence ECAI'92*, pages 87–91, Chichester, England, 1992.
7. J. Giesl and D. Kapur. Decidable classes of inductive theorems. In *IJCAR 2001, First International Joint Conference on Automated Reasoning*, Siena, Italy, 2001.
8. W.A. Howard. The formulae-as-types notion of construction. In J.P. Sedlin and J.R. Hindley, editors, *To H.B. Curry; Essays on Combinatory Logic, Lambda Calculus and Formalism*, pages 479–490. Academic Press, 1980.
9. A. Kakas, R.A. Kowalski, and F. Toni. *Handbook of logic in Artificial Intelligence and Logic Programming*, volume 5, chapter The Role of Abduction in Logic Programming, pages 235–324. Oxford University Press, 1998.
10. T. Kanamori and H. Seki. Verification of Prolog Programs Using an Extension of Execution. In *3rd International Conference on Logic Programming*, volume 225 of *Lecture Notes in Computer Science*, pages 475–489. Springer-Verlag, 1986.
11. Tadashi Kanamori. Soundness and Completeness of Extended Execution for Proving Properties of Prolog Programs. Technical Report 175, ICOT, 1986.
12. R. Monroy. The use of Abduction and Recursion-Editor Techniques for the Correction of Faulty Conjectures. In *Automated Software Engineering*, pages 91–100, 2000.
13. R. Monroy, A. Bundy, and A. Ireland. Proof plan for the correction of false conjectures. In F. Pfenning, editor, *Proceedings of the 5th Int. Conf. on Logic Programming and Automated Reasoning, LPAR'94*, volume 822 of *LNAI*, pages 54–64, Kiev, Ukraine, 1994. Springer-Verlag.
14. C. S. Peirce. Collected Papers of Charles Sanders Peirce. C. Harston and P. Weiss. editors, Harvard University Press, 1959.
15. A. Pettorossi and M. Proietti. Synthesis and transformation of logic programs using unfold/fold proofs. *Journal of Logic Programming*, pages 197–230, (1999).
16. M. Protzen. Patching faulty conjectures. In M. McRobbie and Slaney, editors, *Proceedings of the 13th Int. Conf. on Automated Deduction , CADE13*, volume 1104 of LNAI, pages 77–91, New Brunswick, NJ,USA, 1996.
17. D. Rémy and J. Vouillon. Objective ML : An effective object oriented extension to ml. *Theory and Practice of Object Systems*, 4(1):27–50, 1998.
18. A. Sakurai and H. Motoda. Proving Definite Clauses without Explicit Use of Inductions. In K. Furukawa, H. Tanaka, and T Fujisaki, editors, *Proceedings of the 7th Conference, Logic Programming '88*, volume 383 of *Lecture Notes in Artificial Intelligence*. Springer-Verlag, 1988.
19. H. Tamaki and T. Sato. Unfold/Fold Transformation of Logic Programs. In *Proceedings of the 2nd International Logic Programming Conference*, Uppsala, 1984.

Correct OO Systems in Computational Logic

Kung-Kiu Lau[1] and Mario Ornaghi[2]

[1] Department of Computer Science, University of Manchester
Manchester M13 9PL, UK
kung-kiu@cs.man.ac.uk

[2] Dipartimento di Scienze dell'Informazione, Universita' degli studi di Milano
Via Comelico 39/41, 20135 Milano, Italy
ornaghi@dsi.unimi.it

Abstract. Object Oriented Design Frameworks (OOD frameworks) are groups of interacting objects. We have formalised them in computational logic as open systems of interacting objects. Our formalisation is based on steadfast logic programs in the context of open specification frameworks. However, we have considered only the static aspects, namely the specification of constraints and the correctness of queries (programs that do not update the current state). In this paper we extend this static model, by introducing actions that update the current state.

1 Introduction

In Object Oriented Analysis and Design (OOA&D), the traditional unit of design is of course the class. However, the observation that in the real world, design artefacts are rarely about single classes, but about groups of objects and the way they interact, has led to the introduction of *OOD frameworks*, which represent such groups of interacting objects. It is widely recognised that OOD frameworks are better design (and reuse) units than single classes.

Different characterisations of OOD frameworks as components have been proposed, using UML (Unified Modelling Language) [19]), e.g. *frameworks* in Catalysis [7] and *Komponents* in KobrA [2]. These approaches model OOD frameworks as UML subsystems. However, they do not define OOD frameworks (or components) precisely or formally.

A natural candidate for formalising OOD frameworks in UML would be the Object Constraint Language (OCL) [22]. OCL aims to become a standard for the formal specification of OO systems. It is being formalised in its various aspects [17] and there are Java tools (e.g., [6]), but its syntax and semantics are not yet fixed in a definitive and stable way.

Independently, we have been working on the formalisation of OOD frameworks in computational logic [12, 14]. In [14] we started with a more logically oriented formalisation of OO systems, because we believe that computational logic can offer a solid base for a formalisation of OO systems (and hence OOD frameworks). Moreover, we believe that OCL would benefit from a separate and more logically oriented approach. It would inherit a lot of knowledge, like Abstract Data Types, temporal logic, proof theoretical tools, and so on. We are

M. Bruynooghe (Ed.): LOPSTR 2004, LNCS 3018, pp. 34–53, 2004.

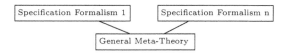

Fig. 1.

looking for a situation like the one depicted in Fig.1, where we can design specification formalisms for OO systems, on top of a meta-theory, i.e., a sound and general underlying logic formalisation.

To formalise OOD frameworks as open systems of interacting objects, we started from our previous work on steadfast programs in the context of open specification frameworks [15]. A specification framework is an open first-order theory that formalises a class of intended models. Specification frameworks can be instantiated (or reused) by theory morphisms, like in algebraic ADT's [23], and steadfast programs are open programs that correctly instantiate in every framework instance. Thus steadfast programs have the properties desired for the methods of correctly reusable units, and specification frameworks specifying and containing steadfast programs become good candidates for the formalisation of OOD frameworks.

In OO systems, instances are systems of interacting objects, that we call object-level instances. To give a precise definition of object-level instances, while preserving the features of open steadfast programs, we designed a three-tier approach, with an object, a specification and a meta level. The object level gives the semantics for our object-level instances. The specification level allows us to specify OO systems. The meta-level allows us to reason about OO systems, in particular, to reason about steadfast programs.

Although our aim was not the formalisation of UML, our three-level structure turns out to be very close to the multi-level approach of UML. The UML object and model levels correspond to our object and specification levels, while our meta-level has the role of the meta-model and meta-meta-model levels of UML. As a consequence, the approach developed in [14] allows us to formalise class and object UML diagrams in the context of computational logic. However, in that paper, we could only reason about the open correctness of queries, that is, open logic programs that do not update the current system state. In this paper we extend our approach by adding the ability to specify programs that update the current state. Moreover, we generalise our three-tier approach. We consider the meta level and the object level as general meta-theory of Fig.1, and we allow many different specification formalisms, to be built on top of it.

This paper is organised as follows. First we briefly review our past work in Section 2, and we discuss the general features of our approach. In Section 3, we introduce the object level, and we discuss the object-level semantics. In Section 4, we introduce the meta-level, we introduce projections (suitable semantic maps between object and meta levels). All this is used in Section 5, to show how intermediate specification formalisms, tailored to different aspects, can be defined, together with their object- and meta-level semantics. The paper is centred on the basic features of OO systems, which can provide a basis for important aspects like classes, polymorphism and modularity, as briefly discussed in the conclusion.

2   Static Aspects of OO Systems

In this section we give an overview of the static approach to OO systems given in [14], where OO systems are formalised on the basis of open steadfast programs and specification frameworks [15, 11].

A specification framework is an open first-order theory, where we distinguish *open* and *defined* symbols, and we have two kinds of axioms: *constraint* and *definition* axioms. The former constrain the possible interpretations of the open symbols, and the latter fix the intended meaning of the defined symbols in terms of the open ones. It may happen that the meaning of some defined symbols is completely fixed, independently from the open symbols. These symbols will be called *closed symbols*, and the axioms fixing their intended meaning will be called *closed axioms*.

A closed specification framework contains only closed symbols and closed axioms. In an open specification framework, the sub-signature of its closed symbols, together with their closed axioms, forms a closed sub-framework, that we will call the (closed) *kernel*.

The model-theoretic semantics of closed and open specification frameworks is based on isoinitial models [13], and we require the following *adequacy* [12] conditions.

A closed specification framework $\mathcal{F}$ is *adequate* if it has a *reachable isoinitial model* i. i is unique up to isomorphism and represents the intended meaning of the signature of $\mathcal{F}$. For an open specification framework $\mathcal{F}$, a *pre-interpretation* is an interpretation of the open and closed symbols, that interprets the closed ones according to the kernel and the open ones according to the constraints. $\mathcal{F}$ is *adequate* if for every pre-interpretation j, there is a *j-isoinitial model* of $\mathcal{F}$, indicated by $j^{\mathcal{F}}$. $j^{\mathcal{F}}$ is unique up to isomorphism and gives the interpretation of the defined symbols that corresponds to j. The *intended models* of $\mathcal{F}$ are the models $j^{\mathcal{F}}$ determined by the pre-interpretations j. Finally, specification frameworks can be built incrementally, by means of *adequate extensions* [11].

Example 1. First-order arithmetic $\mathcal{NAT}$ is a closed specification framework. The standard structure $\mathcal{N}$ of natural numbers is the (unique up to isomorphism) isoinitial model of $\mathcal{NAT}$. It is the kernel of the following open framework, which axiomatises lists with generic elements X and a generic total ordering $\lhd$ on X:

> **SpecFramework** $\mathcal{LIST}(X, \lhd)$ **with** KERNEL $\mathcal{NAT}$;
> ODECL: $X : sort$; $\lhd : [X, X]$;
> DDECL: $ListX : sort$;
> $nil : [\,] \to ListX$; $. : [X, ListX] \to ListX$;
> $\_@(\_,\_) : [X, Nat, ListX]$; $nocc : [X, ListX] \to Nat$;
> DAX1: $FreeAx(nil, . : ListX)$;

DAX2:   for $x, y : X, i : Nat, l, m : ListX$:
$x@(0, l) \leftrightarrow \exists y, m \,.\, l = y.m \land x = y$;
$x@(si, l) \leftrightarrow \exists y, m \,.\, l = y.m \land x@(i, m)$;
$nocc(x, nil) = 0$;
$x = y \rightarrow nocc(x, y.l) = nocc(x, l) + 1$;
$\neg x = y \rightarrow nocc(x, y.l) = nocc(x, l)$;

CONSTR: $\lhd : TO(\lhd)$.

X and $\lhd$ are declared as open in ODECL, and the defined symbols are declared in DDECL. The constraints CONSTR contain the total ordering axioms $TO(\lhd)$ for $\lhd$. The definition axioms DAX1 contain the *freeness axioms* [20] and induction for list constructors. DAX2 axiomatise $x@(i, l)$ (x occurs at position i in l) and $nocc(x, l)$ (number of occurrences of x in l).

A specification framework can be instantiated (or reused) by theory morphisms, and steadfast programs are open programs that correctly instantiate in every framework instance. Thus steadfast programs have the properties desired for the methods of correctly reusable units, and specification frameworks specifying and containing steadfast programs become good candidates for the formalisation of reusable units. A *reusable unit* is composed of an open *specification framework*, that formalises the problem context, a set of *specifications*, and a set of *steadfast* (i.e., correct) open programs. Each program predicate p has a declarative specification S_p, and each program P has a program specification $P : S_\pi \Rightarrow S_\delta$, which means that P correctly computes the predicates δ specified by S_δ, whenever it is composed with programs correctly computing π specified by S_π. Reusing a unit means instantiating it in the context of reuse. The inherited programs can be reused by composing them with other programs, according to their specifications.

Because of the properties of steadfast open programs, in [14] we considered reusable units as good candidates for a formalisation of OO systems. In OO systems, instances are systems of interacting objects, that we call object-level instances. The first problem here is to give a precise definition of object-level instances, while preserving the features of open steadfast programs. We studied different possibilities, that we briefly discuss here, together with their correspondence to UML static diagrams.

The simpler approach is the renaming approach, that is, the dot notation is considered as a renaming notation. This allows a simple and formal definition of the instance semantics by theory morphisms. For example, the left-hand side of Fig. 2 shows an UML diagram with a Car class and two Car objects; in our formalisation the Car class is an open unit, and the the two car objects are obtained by instantiating Car by the theory morphisms μ_{c1} and μ_{c2}, as shown in the right-hand side. At the class level, the attribute .km is open and the invariant states that it must be greater than 0 in every instance. μ_{c1} renames .km by c1.km and closes it by the axiom $c1.km = 3050$, while satisfying the invariant. Similarly for the morphism μ_{c2}.

The renaming approach has a clean semantics in terms of theory morphisms, but has problems when considering associations and groups of related objects.

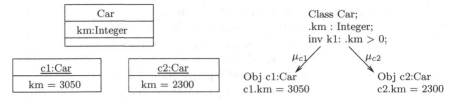

Fig. 2. Renaming.

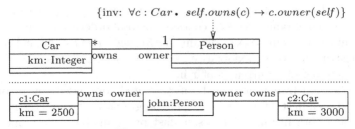

Fig. 3. Extra-argument.

For example, in the invariant inv of Fig.3 we have to quantify over c, but quantified renaming does not belong to the syntax and semantics of first order logic.

For this reason, usually dot is considered as a syntax for introducing c as an extra-argument, that is, $\forall c : Car \cdot self.owns(c) \leftrightarrow c.owner(self)$ represents a syntactical variant of $\forall c : Car \cdot owns(self, c) \leftrightarrow owner(c, self)$.

But extra-arguments also have problems. For example, by introducing an extra-argument, the $c1.km$ attribute becomes a function $km(c1)$ and it cannot be completely known unless we know all the Car objects. We believe that this is not natural in OO and in UML object diagrams, where an attribute like km should represent a *local* property of the single, isolated car object. Finally, in the extra-argument approach the semantics based on theory morphisms is lost.

Thus in [14] we came up with a many-level solution, with an object-level, a meta-level, and an intermediate specification level. At the *object level* dot works as renaming, each object has its own signature and a system can be considered as the union of its objects. This level corresponds to the object level of UML/OCL. At the *meta-level*, dot introduces an extra-argument of a special sort Obj, and an OO system $\mathcal{S}$ is formalised by a *meta-unit* $\mathcal{U}(\mathcal{S})$, which allows us to predicate over live objects and their classes, and to reason about steadfastness. Its framework has the role of the UML meta- and meta-meta-model. Since the syntax of the meta-level is redundant, we introduce the intermediate specification level, to allow simpler and more natural specifications. It is similar to the UML/OCL model level. The three levels are linked by syntactic maps and semantic maps. Syntactic maps work in a way similar to theory morphisms, and semantic maps have properties similar to the properties of reducts. This guarantees that the meta-level can be used to reason about the other levels.

In the next sections, we extend our previous static model, by introducing programs that update the current state and explicit time.

3   The Object Level

We model an *OO system* as a possibly distributed set of live *objects*, that dynamically evolve through a sequence of *states*, and collaborate to achieve a common goal. Each object has an *identity* and is created by a *template class*, which fixes the *signature* of its attributes and methods (programs) and the *implementation* of methods. We may have *query*, *action* and *activity* methods. Each object has one template (class)[1], and we write $o : T$ to indicate an object with identity o and template T.

We distinguish between *data* and *objects*. For simplicity, we assume that data are represented by the ground terms of a *predefined* data type $\mathcal{D}$. To represent *object identities*, $\mathcal{D}$ is always assumed to contain a closed framework $\mathcal{OBJ}$, axiomatising a special sort OBJ, generated by a denumerable set of constants. An object identity is a constant o of sort OBJ.

3.1   States

A state can be formalised as a first-order interpretation, or, under the hypothesis that each datum is represented by a unique *normal* ground term of $\mathcal{D}$, as a propositional interpretation. Here we consider the latter case, because it allows simpler definitions and is compatible with approaches based on propositional temporal logic. Moreover it is not too restrictive in the context of standard logic programs, where our propositional interpretations coincide with Herbrand models.

The attribute declarations of a template class T may be constant declarations $.c : [\,] \to s$, or relation declarations $.r : [s_1, \ldots, s_n]$, where $s, s_1, \ldots, s_n$ are sorts of $\mathcal{D}$. In the propositional approach *ground atoms* are considered as proposition symbols, and the attribute signature of an object $o : T$ is defined as follows.

Definition 1. (Object Attribute Signature). *Let $o : C$ be an object with class C. The* attribute signature *of $o : C$ is the propositional signature containing two kinds of symbols:* assignments, *of the form $o.c\,\mathrm{is}(t)$, and* attribute atoms, *of the form $o.p(t_1, \ldots, t_n)$, where $.c : [\,] \to s$ and $.r : [s_1, \ldots, s_n]$ are attribute declarations of C, and $t, t_1, \ldots, t_n$ are normal ground terms of $\mathcal{D}$.*

A population $\mathbf{P}$ is a set of objects, where each object has one template. The attribute signature of a population is the union of the signatures of its objects, and a state is characterised by a population $\mathbf{P}$ and by an interpretation of the signature of $\mathbf{P}$. We will indicate by $\mathbf{P}.Atb$ the signature of a population $\mathbf{P}$. The special syntax $o.c\,\mathrm{is}(t)$ is used only for the assignments. We will call $o.c$ a *constant* of $\mathbf{P}.Atb$.

Definition 2. (States). *A state of an OO system is a pair $S = (\mathbf{P}, \mathbf{I})$, where $\mathbf{P}$ is a population and $\mathbf{I} \subseteq \mathbf{P}.Atb$ is a $\mathbf{P}$-interpretation where each constant has one assignment.*

---

[1] Classes, interfaces, inheritance and polymorphism can be introduced, but we do not have space to consider them here.

The proposition symbols of an object o represent its local properties. Their current interpretation $\mathbf{I}$ represents the current state of o, as shown in Example 2, which also illustrates the correspondence of states with UML object diagrams.

Example 2. The classes of Fig. 3 introduce the following attribute declarations:

$$\textbf{Class } Car: \quad \text{NAVATB}: .owner: [\,] \rightarrow \text{OBJ};$$
$$\text{ATB}: \quad .km: [\,] \rightarrow Integer;$$
$$\textbf{Class } Person: \quad \text{NAVATB}: .owns: [\text{OBJ}];$$

where navigation attributes NAVATB are a special kind of attributes, representing links to other objects.

The attribute signature of a car object c contains the assignments $c.km\,\text{is}(n)$ and $c.owner\,\text{is}(o)$, with $o:\text{OBJ}$ and $n:Integer$. The attribute signature of a person object p contains the atoms $p.owns(o)$, with $o:\text{OBJ}$. The *navigation attributes* are declared according to the multiplicities of the class diagram of Fig.3, $.owner$ is declared as a constant (by multiplicity 1 each car has one owner), and $.owns$ as a predicate (by multiplicity $*$ a person may own many cars)[2].

The object diagram of Fig. 3 corresponds to the state with population $\mathbf{P} = \{c1:Car, c2:Car, john:Person\}$ and interpretation $i = \{c1.owner\text{ is } john, c1.km\text{ is } 2500, c2.owner\text{ is } john, c2.km\text{ is } 3000, john.owns(c1), john.owns(c2)\}$.

The navigation attributes $c1.owner$ is $john$ and $c2.owner$ is $john$ link $c1$ and $c2$ to $john$, and $john.owns(c1)$, $john.owns(c2)$ link $john$ to $c1, c2$.

The example introduces the *navigation attributes*, which link objects. Links are defined as follows.

Definition 3. (Links). *Let $o, o':\text{OBJ}$ be two object identities. A link from o to o' is an assignment $o.n\,\text{is}(o')$ or an atom $o.n(\underline{\tau})$, where n is a navigation attribute and o' occurs in $\underline{\tau}$.*

A link from o to o' allows o to send messages to o', i.e., call methods of o'.

3.2   Queries

Since we are in computational logic, we consider relational queries, that is, a template T may contain query declarations of the form $.q: [s_1, \ldots, s_n]$, where $s_1, \ldots, s_n$ are sorts of $\mathcal{D}$.

For every object $o:T$, the query atoms of o are the ground terms of the form $o.q(\underline{\tau})$, and (in the propositional approach) query methods are propositional programs.

Definition 4. (Query Methods). *Let $o:T$ be an object and $.q$ be a query declared in T. A query method of o for $.q$ is a set of ground clauses of the form $o.q(\tau) \leftarrow \mathcal{B}$, where the body $\mathcal{B}$ may contain assignments, attribute atoms and query atoms.*

---

[2] In OCL, the type of $.owns$ would be $Set(Person)$.

An object may call queries or attributes of other objects. In this case, the clauses of the query method must be navigable. A navigation from o_1 to o_n is a sequence of navigation atoms $o_1.N_1, \ldots, o_k.N_k$ such that, for $1 \leq i < k$, $o_i.N_i$ is a link from o_i to o_{i+1}. Navigability is defined as follows.

Definition 5. (Navigable Objects and Clauses). *Let $\mathcal{B}$ be the body of a clause. An object o' is $\mathcal{B}$-navigable from o iff $o = o'$, or $\mathcal{B}$ contains a navigation sequence from o to o'; a clause $o.Q \leftarrow \mathcal{B}$ is navigable iff, for every atom $o'.A$ in $\mathcal{B}$, o' is $\mathcal{B}$-navigable from o.*

For each object $o : C$ and each query $.q$ declared in C, there is a set of clauses defining $.q$ in the context of o. To model object collaboration, we consider a population as a whole:

Definition 6. (Distributed Programs). *Let $S = (O, I)$ be a state. Let Q_S be the set of all clauses defining the queries in the contexts of the objects of O; we will call Q_S the* distributed program *of S.*

The semantics of Q_S can be defined by minimum I-models:

Definition 7. (Minimum I-models). *Let Q_S be the distributed program of a state $S = (O, I)$; the* minimum I-model *of Q_S is the minimum model of $Q_S \cup I$.*

We say that a ground query $o.q(\tau)$ is *true* (succeeds) in S, iff it is true in the minimum I-model of P_S. To indicate that $o.q$ is true in S, we will write $S \models o.q$, The truth of a set F of compound formulas is defined in the usual way and will be indicated by $S \models F$.

Example 3. In the class Car of Example 2 we declare the query $.sameOwner$: [OBJ] and implement it by the program

$$self.sameOwner(C) \leftarrow self.owner(P) \wedge P.owns(C).$$

In the state of Example 2, $.sameOwner$ is represented at the object level (see Section 5) by the distributed program

$$c1.sameOwner(c1) \leftarrow c1.owner \text{ is } john \wedge john.owns(c1).$$
$$c1.sameOwner(c2) \leftarrow c1.owner \text{ is } john \wedge john.owns(c2).$$
$$c2.sameOwner(c1) \leftarrow c2.owner \text{ is } john \wedge john.owns(c1).$$
$$c2.sameOwner(c2) \leftarrow c2.owner \text{ is } john \wedge john.owns(c2).$$

where the first two clauses define $.sameOwner$ in the context of $c1$ and the other two clauses define $.sameOwner$ in the context of $c2$.

3.3 Actions and Events

In a template T, an action declaration is of the form $.a : [s_1, \ldots, s_n] \to$ ACTS, where $s_1, \ldots, s_n$ are sorts of $\mathcal{D}$ and ACTS is a special sort introduced for the actions. The *actions* of an object o are all the ground terms $o.a(\tau)$, for every action declaration $o.a : \alpha \to$ ACTS of o.

Definition 8. (Action Methods). *Let $o : T$ be an object and $.a$ be an action declared by T. An action method of o for $.a$ is a set of update-clauses of the form $U \leftarrow \mathcal{E}$, where $\mathcal{E}$ is the enabling condition and U is of one of the forms $new(o.a, o_n : T)$, $del(o.a, o_d)$, $toT(o.a, o'.c\, is(t))$, $toT(o.a, o'.p_t)$, $toF(o.a, o.p_f)$.*

The enabling condition $\mathcal{E}$ has the syntax of a body navigable from o, and states when $o.a$ may occur. It is the same in all the update-clauses of the same action. The update clauses define the updates caused by the action $o.a$.

When $o.a$ occurs, all the updates of $o.a$ occur simultaneously and give rise to a new state. We say that o_d is an object *deleted* by $o.a$, $o_n : T$ is an object *created* by $o.a$ with template T, $o'.c\, is(t)$ is an assignment *forced* to true by $o.a$, $o'.p_t$ is an attribute atom *forced* to true by $o.a$, and $o.p_f$ an attribute atom *forced* to false by $o.a$. If an assignment $o'.c\, is(t)$ is forced to true with a new value t, then the old assignment is *implicitly* forced to false.

A created object is added to the current population, while a deleted one is eliminated. To avoid inconsistency, an attribute atom cannot be forced to both true and false. If an atom or an assignment is not forced, its truth value is preserved. If $o'.p_t$ is forced to true by $o.a$, then o' must coincide with o or be one of the objects created by $o.a$, because we assume that $o.a$ acts *locally*, i.e., it may only initialise the proposition symbols of the new objects and update truth values of the proposition symbols of o. For the same reason, a proposition symbol forced to false must be an attribute of o. Finally, all the constants $o.c$ of a created object must be assigned.

We allow simultaneous actions. To handle them, we introduce *events*:

Definition 9. (Events). *An event ϵ is a set $\epsilon = \{o_1.a_1, \ldots, o_k.a_k\}$ of actions. ϵ is admissible in a state $S = (\mathbf{P}, \mathbf{I})$ iff it contains actions of the signature of $\mathbf{P}$ and $o_1, \ldots, o_k$ are different identities.*

We associate with each event ϵ the following sets:

- $\mathcal{E}_\epsilon$ is the conjunction of the enabling conditions of its actions;
- $\mathcal{NO}_\epsilon$ is the set of objects created by its actions;
- $\mathcal{DO}_\epsilon$ is the set of objects deleted by its actions;
- $\mathcal{T}_\epsilon$ is the set of proposition symbols forced to true by its actions;
- $\mathcal{F}_\epsilon$ is the set of all attribute atoms forced to false by its actions, all the assignments implicitly forced to false by its actions, and all the proposition symbols of the objects deleted by its actions.

Events *semantics* is formalised by state transitions, as follows.

We say that ϵ is *enabled* in a state $S = (\mathbf{P}, \mathbf{I})$ iff $S \models \mathcal{E}_\epsilon$ and the objects of $\mathcal{NO}_\epsilon$ are not objects of the current population $\mathbf{P}$, that is, they are new. Moreover, an object can be created by one action. This requirement, together with the locality condition, prevents the possibility of inconsistent updates. If ϵ is enabled in $S = (\mathbf{P}, \mathbf{I})$, then it may fire a transition $(\mathbf{P}, \mathbf{I}) \; \epsilon \mapsto (\mathbf{P}', \mathbf{I}')$:

Definition 10. (OO State Transitions). *For every state $(\mathbf{P}, \mathbf{I})$ and every admissible event ϵ enabled in it, the firing of ϵ produces the state transition*

$$(\mathbf{P}, \mathbf{I}) \; \epsilon \mapsto ((\mathbf{P} \cup \mathcal{NO}_\epsilon) \setminus \mathcal{DO}_\epsilon, (\mathbf{I} \cup \mathcal{T}_\epsilon) \setminus \mathcal{F}_\epsilon)$$

Example 4. The event $\epsilon = \{p1.sells(c1, p0), p0.buys(c1, p1), c1.sold(p1, p0)\}$, containing the actions specified below, represents a contract of purchase.

$$toF(p1.sells(c1, p0), p1.owns(c1)) \leftarrow p1.owns(c1).$$
$$toT(p0.buys(c1, p1), p0.owns(c1)) \leftarrow$$
$$toT(c1.sold(p1, p0), c1.owner \text{ is } p0) \leftarrow$$

Starting from the state with population $c1 : Car$, $p0, p1 : Person$ and interpretation $c1.owner$ is $p1$, $p1.owns(c1)$, the corresponding transition leads to the state with the same population and interpretation $c1.owner$ is $p0$, $p0.owns(c1)$.

3.4 Observation Sequences, Activities, Time and Space

We assume that we can ideally observe the system at successive observation times $t_1, \ldots, t_n, \ldots$, in such a way that no two consecutive actions $o.a_1$ and $o.a_2$ by the same object o occur in a single time interval t_i, t_{i+1}. Under this hypothesis an observation sequence can be modelled as a sequence of state transitions.

Definition 11. (Observation Sequences and Behaviours). *An observation sequence is a sequence $S_0 \ \epsilon_0 \mapsto S_1 \ \epsilon_1 \mapsto S_2 \ldots$ of state transitions such that, if it is finite, then no admissible event is enabled in its final state S_n. A behaviour is a class of observation sequences starting from the same initial state S_0.*

The purpose of a system specification is to define the system behaviour, by specifying *populations, queries, actions and activities.* Informally, an activity is a sequence of actions performed by a group of objects to do something. The enabling conditions may not be sufficient to impose the desired sequence, and a further level of control may be needed. Activities can be modelled as *constraints* on the behaviour. For example, we can model the activity *contract of purchase* considered in Example 4 by the synchronisation constraint imposing that the three actions have to occur simultaneously.

We will come back to the specification issue in Section 5. We conclude this section by considering space and time in an OO system. Time is related to updates, while space is related to the "geometry" of the communication among objects.

Navigability represents one of the space "dimensions". We can use the classical *visibility constraints* like "public" and "private", to constrain navigability.

A second space dimension is the *observes* relation: an object o observes an attribute $o'.A$ of an object o' if o is interested in the updates of $o'.A$. The main reason for observing $o'.A$ is its use in the body of a query or in the enabling condition of an action. However there may be many reasons for observing an attribute, as highlighted for example by the *observer-observable* pattern [9].

To specify dynamic aspects and to reason about them, we introduce time. In an observation sequence $S_0 \ \epsilon_0 \mapsto S_1 \ \epsilon_1 \mapsto S_2 \ldots$, each state S_i $(i \geq 0)$ has time i. We call i the *global time*, since observation sequences represent a global view of the system.

Besides global time, it is useful to consider *local time*, corresponding to the local view of an object or a subsystem. For example we can use $\forall c : Car$. $c@0.km = 0$ to indicate that the odometer of a car is 0 at local time 0, i.e., when it is created, independently from the global time. Local time is also useful when considering single objects or, by a hierarchical organisation of locality, *modules*.

In this paper we do not consider modules, and we introduce local time only for objects, by means of *timed objects*. A timed object with identity o and time t will be indicated by $o@t$. The time of an object *increases* whenever it observes that something is *changed*.

A *timed population* is a set $\mathbf{T}$ of timed objects that does not contain pairs $o@t$, $o@t'$ with the same object and different times. That is, each object has one time. The signature of a timed population $\mathbf{T}$ is that of its objects, where o is an object of $\mathbf{T}$ iff there is t such that $o@t$ belongs to $\mathbf{T}$.

A *timed state* is a pair $(\mathbf{T}, \mathbf{I})$, where $\mathbf{T}$ is a timed population and $\mathbf{I}$ is an interpretation of its propositional symbols. Each timed state $(\mathbf{T}, \mathbf{I})$ has an associated (non-timed) OO state $(\mathbf{P_T}, \mathbf{I})$, where $\mathbf{P_T}$ is obtained from $\mathbf{T}$ by forgetting time.

An object o *observes* an event ϵ if ϵ modifies an attribute observed by o or the population observed by o. Timed transitions trace the observability relation:

Definition 12. (Timed Transitions). *Let $(\mathbf{T}, \mathbf{I})$ and $(\mathbf{T}', \mathbf{I}')$ be two timed states. $(\mathbf{T}, \mathbf{I})$ $\epsilon \mapsto (\mathbf{T}', \mathbf{I}')$ is a timed transition iff $(\mathbf{P_T}, \mathbf{I})$ $\epsilon \mapsto (\mathbf{P_{T'}}, \mathbf{I}')$ is a state transition and for every $o@t \in \mathbf{T}'$ one of the following cases holds: $o@t \in \mathbf{T}$ and o does not observe ϵ, or $o@t - 1 \in \mathbf{T}$ and o observes ϵ, or $t = 0$ and $o \in \mathcal{NO}_\epsilon$.*

A *timed observation sequence* is a sequence of timed transitions, and a *timed behaviour* is a set of timed observation sequences.

In timed observation sequences, the local time of objects implicitly traces the observability relation and is useful for devising independent subsystems, namely subsystems that can be characterised independently from their environment. Independence becomes a central notion when considering modularity aspects. We can also use a local time to trace different independent activities separately.

4   The Meta-level and the Meta-framework

At the meta-level, an OO system $\mathcal{S}$ is represented by a reusable unit $\mathcal{U}(\mathcal{S})$, that we call the *meta-representation* of $\mathcal{S}$. $\mathcal{U}(\mathcal{S})$ is an extension of the *general meta-unit* $\mathcal{U}$ outlined in Fig. 4. $\mathcal{U}$ contains a specification framework $\mathcal{M}$, that we call the *meta-framework*, and an open steadfast program MP, that we call the *meta-program*. The meta-representation $\mathcal{U}(\mathcal{S})$ is obtained by adding suitable *representation axioms* and *clauses*, as we will outline in the next section. Here, we explain the general features of the meta-framework $\mathcal{M}$.

$\mathcal{M}$ axiomatises the general assumptions on OO systems discussed in the previous section, and is the basic component of the general meta-theory in Fig. 1. It contains $\mathcal{OBJ}$, to represent object identities, and $\mathcal{SET}(\text{ACT})$, to axiomatise the defined sort EV of events by finite sets of actions; the subframework $\mathcal{NAT}$ of $\mathcal{SET}(\text{ACT})$ is also used to represent time by natural numbers. The intended

unit $\mathcal{U}$;

MetaFramework $\mathcal{M}$;   IMPORT $\mathcal{OBJ}, \mathcal{SET}(\text{ACT})[set(\text{ACT}) \mapsto \text{EV}]$;

OSORTS: ATBS, ACTS, QRYS, TPLS;

DSORTS: OBJT, ATB, QRY, ACT;

ODECL: dcl : [ATB, TPLS]|[QRY, TPLS]|[ACT, TPLS];

$\quad\quad\quad ini$: [OBJ, TPLS]; $\quad\quad\quad\quad\quad\quad iniT$: [ATB];

$\quad\quad\quad t$: [NAT, QRY]; $\quad\quad\quad\quad\quad\quad toT, toF$: [NAT, ACT, ATB];

$\quad\quad\quad new$: [NAT, ACT, OBJ, TPLS]; $\quad\quad del, obs$: [NAT, ACT, OBJ];

$\quad\quad\quad enb$: [NAT, ACT]; $\quad\quad\quad\quad\quad\quad occ$: [NAT, EV];

DDECL: . : [OBJ, ATBS] $\to$ ATB|[OBJ, QRYS] $\to$ QRY|[OBJ, ACTS] $\to$ ACT;

$\quad\quad\quad$ @ : [OBJ, NAT] $\to$ OBJT; $live$: [NAT, OBJT, TPLS]; t : [NAT, ATB];

CONSTR: for o, o' : OBJ, n : NAT, a, b : ACTS, p : ATBS, e, e' : EV, A, B : ACT :

$\quad occ(n, e) \wedge occ(n, e') \to e = e'$;

$\quad occ(s(n), e) \wedge o.a \in e \to enb(n, o.a) \wedge \exists t. \; live(n, o@t)$;

$\quad occ(n, e) \wedge o.a \in e \wedge o'.b \in e \to \neg o = o'$;

AX1: FreeAx(@ : OBJT, . : ATB, . : QRY, . : ACT);

DEF: for o : OBJ; n : NAT, p : ATBS, a : ACTS, tp : TPLS :

$\quad toNew(n, o, tp) \;\leftrightarrow\; \exists e$: EV. $occ(s(n), e) \wedge \exists a \in e. \; new(n, a, o, tp)$;

$\quad toT(n, o.p) \quad\quad \leftrightarrow \exists e$: EV. $occ(s(n), e) \wedge \exists a \in e. \; toT(n, a, o.p)$;

$\quad notToF(n, o.p) \leftrightarrow \exists e$: EV. $occ(s(n), e) \wedge \forall a \in e. \; \neg toF(n, a, o.p) \wedge \neg del(n, a, o)$;

$\quad obsEv(n, o) \quad\quad \leftrightarrow \exists e$: EV. $occ(s(n), e) \wedge (\exists a \in e. \; obs(n, a, o)) \wedge$

$\quad\quad\quad\quad\quad\quad\quad\quad\quad\quad\quad\quad\quad\quad\quad\quad\quad\quad\quad\quad\quad \forall a \in e. \; \neg del(n, a, o)$;

$\quad notObsEv(n, o) \leftrightarrow \exists e$: EV. $occ(s(n), e) \wedge \forall a \in e. \; \neg del(n, a, o) \wedge \neg obs(n, a, o)$;

AX2: for o : OBJ; n, t : NAT, tp : TPLS :

$\quad live(0, o@t : tp) \quad\quad \leftrightarrow ini(o, tp) \wedge t = 0$;

$\quad live(s(n), o@0 : tp) \quad \leftrightarrow toNew(n, o, tp) \vee notObsEv(n, o) \wedge live(n, o@0 : tp)$;

$\quad live(s(n), o@s(t) : tp) \leftrightarrow obsEv(n, o) \wedge live(n, o@t : tp) \vee$

$\quad\quad\quad\quad\quad\quad\quad\quad\quad\quad\quad\quad\quad notObsEv(n, o) \wedge live(n, o@s(t) : tp)$;

AX3: for n : NAT, p : ATB :

$\quad t(0, p) \quad\quad \leftrightarrow iniT(p)$;

$\quad t(s(n), p) \leftrightarrow toT(n, p) \vee notToF(n, p) \wedge t(n, p)$;

REPR:

$\quad\quad\quad$ Representation axioms and specifications of $\mathcal{S}$;

PROG MP : $live(0, O@0, Templ) \leftarrow ini(O, Templ)$.

$\quad\quad\quad\quad\quad live(s(N), O@0, Templ) \leftarrow toNew(N, O, Templ)$.

$\quad\quad\quad\quad\quad live(s(N), O@0, Templ) \leftarrow notObsEv(s(N), O) \wedge live(N, O@0, Templ)$.

$\quad\quad\quad\quad\quad live(s(N), O@s(T), Templ) \leftarrow obsEv(s(N), O) \wedge live(N, O@T, Templ)$.

$\quad\quad\quad\quad\quad live(s(N), O@s(T), Templ) \leftarrow notObsEv(s(N), O) \wedge$

$\quad\quad\quad\quad\quad\quad\quad\quad\quad\quad\quad\quad\quad\quad\quad\quad\quad\quad\quad live(N, O@s(T), Templ)$.

$\quad\quad\quad\quad t(0, P) \leftarrow iniT(P)$.

$\quad\quad\quad\quad t(s(N), P) \leftarrow toT(N, P)$.

$\quad\quad\quad\quad t(s(N), P) \leftarrow notToF(N, P) \wedge t(N, P)$.

$\quad\quad\quad\quad \ldots$

$\quad\quad\quad\quad$ representation clauses

Fig. 4. General meta unit.

models of $\mathcal{M}$ will be called *meta-models*. The open symbols allow us to *represent* OO systems and OO system specifications, by the representation axioms. We distinguish *population* meta-symbols and the *behavioural* meta-symbols.

The *population meta-symbols* are TPLS, ATBS, ACTS, QRYS (meta-sorts for template identifiers and attribute, action and query signatures) and *dcl* ($dcl(X,T)$ means that X is declared by the template T). They allow us to represent the object-level populations of an OO system $\mathcal{S}$ and their signatures, by adding the suitable representation axioms to $\mathcal{M}$. Since populations depend on signatures, the extension $\mathcal{M}(\Sigma_\mathcal{S})$ obtained in this way will be called the *signature representation* of $\mathcal{S}$. We will assume that it satisfies the following regularity property:

Definition 13. (*Regularity*). *Let $\mathcal{M}(\Sigma_\mathcal{S})$ be the signature representation of a system $\mathcal{S}$, i be a meta-model of $\mathcal{M}(\Sigma_\mathcal{S})$, and n be a natural number. Let $\mathbf{P}_n$ be the population containing the objects $o : tp$ such that $i \models \exists t \centerdot \ live(n, o@t : tp)$, and $\mathbf{I}_n$ be the set containing the ground terms $o.p$ such that $i \models t(n, o.p)$. We say that $\mathcal{M}(\Sigma_\mathcal{S})$ is regular if, for every n, $(\mathbf{P}_n, \mathbf{I}_n)$ is an OO state of $\mathcal{S}$.*

The *behavioural meta-symbols* are introduced to represent queries, actions, events and observation sequences, and are interpreted within a regular signature representation $\mathcal{M}(\Sigma_\mathcal{S})$. The intended correspondence with the object-level observation sequences, i.e., the object-level semantics, is given by the following definition.

Definition 14. (*Correspondence*). *Let $\mathcal{M}(\Sigma_\mathcal{S})$ be a regular representation of the population signatures of an OO system $\mathcal{S}$. A pre-interpretation j of $\mathcal{M}(\Sigma_\mathcal{S})$ corresponds to a timed observation sequence $S_0 \ e_0 \mapsto \ S_1 \ e_1 \mapsto \ \dots \ of \ \mathcal{S}$ iff:*

1. *$j \models toT(n, a, P)$ iff P is forced to true by the action a in S_n;*
2. *$j \models toF(n, a, P)$ iff P is forced to false by the action a in S_n;*
3. *$j \models new(n, a, o, tp)$ iff $o : tp$ is created by the action a in S_n;*
4. *$j \models del(n, a, o)$ iff o is deleted by the action a in S_n;*
5. *$j \models ini(o, tp)$ iff o is an object of $S_0 = (\mathbf{T}_0, \mathbf{I}_0)$, that is, $o@0 : tp \in \mathbf{T}_0$;*
6. *$j \models iniT(P)$ iff P is true in $S_0 = (\mathbf{T}_0, \mathbf{I}_0)$, that is, $P \in \mathbf{I}_0$;*
7. *$j \models enb(n, a)$ iff the enabling condition of a is true in S_n;*
8. *$j \models t(n, Q)$ iff the query Q is true in S_n;*
9. *$j \models obs(n, a, o)$ iff the updates caused by $a \in \epsilon_n$ are observed by o in S_n;*
10. *$j \models occ(s(n), e)$ iff the event e has just occurred at time $s(n)$, i.e., $e = e_n$.*

The constraints CONSTR correspond to the general assumptions on signatures, actions and events discussed in the previous section. For conciseness, we have indicated only the constraints on events. The constraints guarantee that for a regular signature representation $\mathcal{M}(\Sigma_\mathcal{S})$ and a pre-interpretation j that corresponds to an observation sequence Ω, the intended meaning of the defined symbols is axiomatised by the definition axioms as follows.

- AX1 state that the defined sort OBJT is freely generated by @, and ATB, QRY, ACT by ".". A meta-term $o@t$ indicates an object o with local time t. The dot operator $x.\sigma(\dots)$ represents at the meta-level (by the extra-argument approach) the object-level renaming.

- DEF introduce useful abbreviations by explicit definitions.
- AX2 axiomatise the meta-predicate $live(n, o@t, tp)$, with the following intended meaning: at global time n, o is a live object with local time t and template tp. We use the more intuitive syntax $live(n, o@t : tp)$.
- AX3 axiomatise the meta-predicate $t(n, p)$, with the following intended meaning: at global time n, the attribute p is true.

In particular, the defined symbols $live(n, o@t : tp)$ and $t(n, p)$ represent the timed states by the *projection*

$$\mathsf{i} \downarrow n = (\mathbf{T}_n, \mathbf{I}_n)$$

that maps each meta-model i and time n into the timed OO state $(\mathbf{T}_n, \mathbf{I}_n)$ such that $o@t : tp \in \mathbf{T}_n$ iff $\mathsf{i} \models live(n, o@t : tp)$ and $o.p \in \mathbf{I}_n$ iff $\mathsf{i} \models t(n, o.p)$. Thus, once we are able to represent an observation sequence Ω by a corresponding pre-interpretation j, the definition axioms allow us to reconstruct the states of Ω and to reason about them at the meta level. This is what is stated by the next theorem and what will be used in Section 5 to represent object-level properties at the meta level.

Theorem 1. *Let $\mathcal{M}(\Sigma_S)$ be a regular representation of the population signatures of an OO system S. Let j be a pre-interpretation of $\mathcal{M}(\Sigma_S)$ that corresponds to an observation sequence Ω of S and $\mathsf{j}^{\mathcal{M}(\Sigma)}$ be the corresponding j-isoinitial model. Then the sequence $\mathsf{j}^{\mathcal{M}(\Sigma)} \downarrow 0 \ e_0 \mapsto \mathsf{j}^{\mathcal{M}(\Sigma)} \downarrow 1 \ e_1 \mapsto \ \ldots \ such that $j \models occ(j, e_j)$ (for $j = 0, 1, \ldots$) is a timed observation sequence that coincides with Ω.*

Proof. Since j corresponds to Ω, transitions $e_j \mapsto$ are already defined in the right way. We have to show that the axioms of $\mathcal{M}$ define $live(n, o@t : tp)$ and $t(n, o.p)$ (for an attribute symbol p) in such a way that they represent Ω by the projections $\downarrow n$. The sketch of the proof is the following. Each $\mathsf{j}^{\mathcal{M}(\Sigma)} \downarrow n$ is a timed OO state. By induction on n, we can prove that it is the state with global time n of Ω. The basis of the induction follows from the fact that ini and $iniT$ are interpreted according to Definition 14. The induction step follows from the fact that the open symbols $toT, toF, \ldots$ are interpreted according to Definition 14 and from the constraints and the axioms of $\mathcal{M}(\Sigma)$.

5   Representing OO System Specifications

The object and meta levels can be used for representing OO system specifications and for reasoning about them. For lack of space, we will only outline the general approach and illustrate it by some representative examples. The general picture is illustrated in Fig. 5. S is the *system specification*, $\mathcal{O}(S)$ is its *object-level representation*, and $\mathcal{M}(S)$ its *meta-level representation*. $\mathcal{O}(S)$ defines the operational semantics of S as a *behaviour* (Definition 11). $\mathcal{M}(S)$ is an adequate extension of $\mathcal{M}$. It has a model-theoretic (thus declarative) semantics, and observation

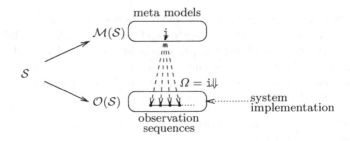

Fig. 5.

sequences are represented by meta-models. The dashed arrows indicate the $\downarrow n$-projections mapping a meta-model i into an observation sequence $\Omega = i\Downarrow$, the solid arrows indicate syntactic maps, and the dotted one an abstraction process, where observation sequences represent ideal observations of the running system at a given granularity.

We distinguish behavioural and correctness specifications.

Behavioural specifications define the system behaviour. The object-level and the meta-level representations have to satisfy the conditions:

(a) $\mathcal{M}(\mathcal{S})$ includes a regular signature representation $\mathcal{M}(\Sigma_\mathcal{S})$ of $\mathcal{S}$.
(b) Let i be a finitary meta-model of $\mathcal{M}(\mathcal{S})$; then $i\Downarrow =_{def} i\downarrow 0\ e_0 \mapsto i\downarrow 1\ e_1 \mapsto$ ..., where $i \models occ(i, e_i)$, is an observation sequence of $\mathcal{O}(\mathcal{S})$.
(c) For every observation sequence Ω of $\mathcal{O}(\mathcal{S})$, there is at least one meta-model i of $\mathcal{M}(\mathcal{S})$ such that $i\Downarrow = \Omega$.

Correctness specifications state properties to be satisfied by the system behaviour, that is, a correctness specification S_P defines a predicate $P : \mathcal{O}(\mathcal{S}) \rightarrow$ *Boolean*. We say that $\mathcal{S}$ *is correct with respect to* S_P iff $P(\Omega) = true$, for every $\Omega \in \mathcal{O}(\mathcal{S})$. A correctness specification S_P can be studied by representing it by a formula $S_P \uparrow$ of $\mathcal{M}(\mathcal{S})$. We will call $S_P \uparrow$ the meta-level representation of S_P. We require that:

(d) for every meta-model i, if $i \models S_P \uparrow$, then $P(i\Downarrow) = true$.

If (a), (b), (c), (d) are satisfied and $S_P \uparrow$ is a theorem of $\mathcal{M}(\mathcal{S})$, then $\mathcal{S}$ is correct with respect to S_P. (a) and (d) must be ensured by the representation of signatures and specifications. Correctness can be treated in $\mathcal{M}(\mathcal{S})$ by *proving* $S_P \uparrow$ and the *steadfastness* of the meta-program. Indeed, (c) and (d) are ensured by the steadfastness of the extension of MP by the representation clauses. Furthermore, MP gives rise to a *reflective environment*, where we can perform meta-level computations.

We conclude this section with some examples that illustrate the approach outlined above.

Example 5. **Representing Signatures, Queries and Actions.** In this example we consider languages where the object-level representation of a specification $\mathcal{S}$ can be formalised as a quadruple $\mathcal{O}(\mathcal{S}) = \langle \mathcal{D}, \mathcal{P}, \mathcal{Q}, \mathcal{A} \rangle$, where: $\mathcal{D}$ is the data type of $\mathcal{S}$, $\mathcal{P}$ is the set of its populations, and $\mathcal{Q}$ and $\mathcal{A}$ are semantic maps that associate every population $\mathbf{P}$ with the queries $\mathcal{Q}(\mathbf{P})$ and the actions $\mathcal{A}(\mathbf{P})$ of $\mathbf{P}$. The specified behaviour $\mathcal{O}(\mathcal{S})$ contains the observation sequences $(\mathbf{P}_1, \mathbf{I}_1)\epsilon_1 \mapsto (\mathbf{P}_2, \mathbf{I}_2)\epsilon_2 \mapsto \ldots$ such that $\mathbf{P}_i$ are populations of $\mathcal{P}$ and the actions and queries of $\mathbf{P}_i$ are given by the maps $\mathcal{A}$ and $\mathcal{Q}$. We will call this behaviour the *free behaviour of* $\mathcal{S}$.

We show a possible Prolog-like specification language of this kind, by means of the following example, where queries and actions are added to the template classes *Car* and *Person* of Example 2.

Class *Car* :
NAVATB : $.owner : [\,] \to$ OBJ;
ATB :　　$.km : [\,] \to Integer$;

QRY :　$self.sameOwner(c) \leftarrow self.owner\,\mathrm{is}(p) \wedge Person(p) \wedge p.owns(c)$;
ACT :　$toT(self.sold(p_1, p_2), self.owner\,\mathrm{is}(p_2)) \leftarrow$
Class *Person* :
NAVATB : $.owns : [\mathrm{OBJ}]$;
ACT :　$toT(self.buys(c, p), self.owns(c)) \leftarrow$;
　　　$toF(self.sells(c, p), self.owns(c)) \leftarrow self.owns(c)$;

A *query clause* is defined in a template T and its atoms may be of the form $self.A$, where A is a query or an attribute of T, or of the form $d.A$, where the *message destination* d (p in the Example) is different from $self$, must be bounded by a *template predicate* $T'(d)$ ($Person(p)$ in the Example) and A must be declared in T'. An action clause has a similar syntax, but now the head is an update atom and the enabling condition must be the same in all the clauses defining the same action.

Now we build the object-level representation $\mathcal{O}(\mathcal{S})$. The data type and populations are defined as in Example 2. We associate each population $\mathbf{P}$ with the actions $\mathcal{A}(\mathbf{P})$ and the queries $\mathcal{Q}(\mathbf{P})$ of $\mathbf{P}$, as follows.

$\mathcal{Q}(\mathbf{P})$ is obtained by grounding each query clause Q by replacing $self$ by the identities o such that $o : T \in \mathbf{P}$, and the (possible) message destinations d by the identities o' such that $o' : T' \in \mathbf{P}$. $\mathcal{A}(\mathbf{P})$ is obtained by the same grounding process. For instance, the query given in Example 3 is the object level semantics of the query clause for *sameOwner* in the population there considered, and the actions in Example 4 are the object-level semantics of the above action clauses.

To build the meta-level representation $\mathcal{M}(\mathcal{S})$, firstly we have to extend $\mathcal{M}$ into a regular signature representation $\mathcal{M}(\Sigma_S)$. For this, we include the data type $\mathcal{INTEGER}$ and we close the population signature by the declarations and axioms[3]:

$$Car, Person : [\,] \to \text{TPLS}\ km\,\mathrm{is} : [Integer] \to \text{ATBS}$$
$$owner\,\mathrm{is} : [Obj] \to \text{ATBS}\ owns : [Obj] \to \text{ATBS}$$

---

[3] The syntax $km\,\mathrm{is}(n)$ has not been considered in Section 4 for conciseness. It can be treated by introducing in $\mathcal{M}$ suitable meta-symbols and constraints.

FreeAx($Car, Person$: TPLS, km is, $owner$ is, $owns$: ATBS, nil : QRYS, nil : $acts$)
$dcl(a, Car) \leftrightarrow (\exists n. \ a = km\,is(n)) \vee (\exists p. \ a = owner\,is(p))$
$dcl(a, Person) \leftrightarrow \exists c. \ a = owns(c))$

We can show that this way of closing the population signature is general and gives rise to regular representations, considering only templates. A suitable meta-theory can be introduced in $\mathcal{M}$, to treat classes and polymorphism.

To complete the meta-level representation $\mathcal{M}(\mathcal{S})$, we add the representation axioms of specifications of queries and actions, according to Example 7.

Finally, to complete the meta-program, we translate the query and action clauses of the specification into meta-clauses defining the open meta-predicates $t, toT, toF, \ldots$. The translation introduces the global time n, replaces $self$ by a fresh variable x, and x is bounded in the body by $live(n, x@t : T)$, where T is the template of $self$. Similarly, the template predicate $T'(d)$ for a destination d is translated by $live(n, d@t' : T')$. The resulting meta-clauses are added to the meta-program MP. For lack of space we omit the details. To give an example, the meta-clauses representing the query and action clauses considered before are:

$$t(n, x.sameOwner(c)) \leftarrow live(n, x@t : Car) \wedge t(n, x.owner\,is(p))$$
$$\wedge \ live(n, p@t : Person) \wedge t(n.p.owns(c));$$
$$toT(n, x.sold(p_1, p_2), x.owner\,is(p_2)) \leftarrow live(n, x@t : Car);$$
$$toT(n, x.buys(c, p), self.owns(c)) \leftarrow live(n, p@t : Person);$$
$$toF(n, x.sells(c, p), self.owns(c)) \leftarrow live(n, p@t : Person) \wedge t(n, x.owns(c)).$$

Example 6. **Activities.** An activity specification is a *behavioural specification*. It is expressed as a constraint on the free behaviour of a system specification. Here we show the example of a possible syntax for expressing synchronisation constraints. The example shows a collaboration of three objects implementing a contract of purchase.

> **Collaboration** p_1, p_2 : *Person*; c : *Car* :
> ACTIVITY *contractOfPurchase* :
> $sync(c.sold(p_1, p_2), [p_1.sells(c, p_2), p_2.buys(c, p_1)]) \leftarrow;$
> $sync(p_1.sells(c, p_2), [c.sold(p_1, p_2), p_2.buys(c, p_1)]) \leftarrow;$
> $sync(p_2.buys(c, p_1), [c.sold(p_1, p_2), p_1.sells(c, p_2)]) \leftarrow;$

The statement $sync(a, l)$ means that action A synchronises the actions in l. The object-level representation of synchronisation clauses is given in the way illustrated for queries and actions. Their semantics is the constraint imposing that an event containing an action A synchronising B must also contain B. This constraint is expressed at the meta level by the meta-axiom:

$$occ(e, n) \wedge a \in e \wedge sync(n, a, s) \wedge b \in s \rightarrow b \in e$$

and we have to add the meta-level representation of the synchronisation clauses.

Example 7. **Correctness Specifications and Invariants.** There are various kinds of correctness specifications. To deal with open correctness (steadfastness) queries and actions must have specifications. Actions are specified by a combined use of pre/post-conditions and invariants. Query specifications can be treated as in [14].

Each kind of specification has a specific meta-level representation. We consider only invariants, for lack of space. Invariants represent properties that must hold in every state, or at least in chosen states, determined for example by the local time or by spy points. An example is the invariant

Context *Car*
INV *zeroKm* : *self*@0.*km* = 0

Like in OCL [22], a constraint is given in the context of a template in a specification. Here the informal correctness property P (see condition (d)) expressed by the invariant is: "for every state S and object $c : Car$, $c.km$ is(0) holds in S if the local time of c is 0". Instead of giving a separate object-level semantics, we can give directly a meta-level representation $S \uparrow$ and assume condition (d) as defining the object-level semantics. In our example $zeroKm \uparrow$ is

$$\forall n, c. \ live(n, c@0 : Car) \rightarrow t(n, c.km \, is(0))$$

We can see that the above formula is true in a meta-model i iff, in the observation sequence $\Omega = i \Downarrow$, $c.km$ is(0) is true in every state S_n with a timed population containing $q@0 : Car$. This formalises the informal predicate P.

Example 8. **General-purpose Specifications**. In general, a separate specification formalism is useful to express specifications in a more compact and natural way, and it is convenient to choose different formalisms for different purposes. There are cases where it is convenient to directly use the meta level as a specification formalism. This choice may be adequate, for instance, to express constraints that are not domain specific. For example, fairness is expressed by the constraint

$$\forall n : \text{NAT}, a : \text{ACT}. \ enb(n, a) \rightarrow \exists m. \ m > n \land occ(m, a)$$

This constraint does not depend on the application domain, but it may be seen as a constraint for the implementations of the programming language. If we assume it, then we require that implementations apply a fair scheduling.

6   Conclusion

We have introduced a three-level formalisation of OO systems, with an object level, a meta level and many possible specification levels, linked by the maps illustrated in Fig. 5. In this context, the specification and meta levels can both be used to write down specifications, while the object-level semantics relates specifications to the corresponding system configurations.

Our approach is very similar, in spirit, to the multi-level approach of UML [19]. In UML, the official specification language is OCL [22]. Various efforts have been made to give a formal semantics to OCL and some Java implementations have been developed [18]. Although we start from a different background, one that is closer to formalising UML by ADTs [3, 8], our multi-level approach has many similarities to the approaches developed in the UML and OCL community. In particular, we have in common the static diagrams, namely class and object diagrams, including invariants, and our behavioural specifications are similar, in a broad sense, to the UML behavioural diagrams. However, our approach is logically based, and is in this regard close to approaches for formalising UML and OCL. A first formalisation of OCL in Isabelle HOL has been proposed in [4]. The approach of [5] is based on the specification language Z. There is a working group on precise UML [21].

Concerning the dynamic aspects, at the object level our model is similar to the approaches based on temporal logic [8]. Indeed, behaviours can be considered as a particular kind of Kripke Transition Systems [16], where each Kripke world has an associated population. Populations allow us to model open systems, in a way similar to [1]. Instead of adding temporal operators to the object level, we have preferred to model time at the meta-level, because this allows us to extend our previous work on open specification frameworks and steadfast open programs [15]. Moreover, temporal logic operators could be introduced at the specification level. That is, our approach is not alternative, but complementary to temporal logic approaches.

In this paper, the main effort has been to extend our previous three-level formalisation of static OO systems by introducing time. The proposed formalisation is the basis for long-term work, involving many related aspects:

(a) *Classes, types and polymorphism.* With a slight extension of the meta-language and of the related constraints, we can define classes and types, together with inheritance and overriding polymorphism.

(b) *Implementing the object and the meta-levels.* It is possible to build a Prolog interpreter for the object level and the meta-level, by introducing a syntax for representing classes, attributes and methods. We are looking for a tool that is useful for understanding specifications (e.g., by animating them), rather than a tool for implementing OO systems.

(c) *Specification languages.* In Section 5, we have shown some examples of specification formalisms, at an intermediate level between the meta- and the object level. The idea is that different aspects are treated in a more natural way by different formalisms (in this, we are in line with the general ideas underlying the UML approach), and that the meta-framework is the unifying framework.

(d) *Correctness.* Correctness can be defined in terms of steadfastness at the meta level, and can be proved using the results of [15]. We have not yet studied specific proof strategies, but we can reasonably expect that different specification languages will underly different proof methods.

(e) *Modules.* We have only some ideas, to be developed further. Essentially, the idea is to formalise modules by enriching the structure of local time.

Our next steps will be (a) and (b), but really all the previous points have to be developed if we want to reach our final goal, which is to model OOD frameworks

[12] by open reusable units. Clearly this paper represents just a step in that direction.

References

1. R. Alur, T.A. Henzinger, O. Kupferman. Alternating-time Temporal Logic. *JACM*, 49(5):672–713, 2002.
2. C. Atkinson *et al. Component-based Product Line Engineering with UML.* Addison-Wesley, 2002.
3. R.H. Bourdeau, B.H.C. Cheng. A formal semantics for object model diagrams. *IEEE Trans. Soft. Eng.*, 21(10):799–821, 1995.
4. A. Brucker, B. Wolf. A proposal for a formal OCL semantics in Isabelle/HOL. *LNCS 2410*, pages 99–114, Springer-Verlag, 2002.
5. T. Clark, A. Evans. Foundations of the Unified Modeling Language. *2nd BCS-FACS Northern Formal Methods Workshop.*
   http://ewic.bcs.org/conferences/1997/papers/paper6.htm
6. Dresden OCL Toolkit. http://dresden-ocl.sourceforge.net
7. D.F. D'Souza, A.C. Wills. *Objects, Components, and Frameworks with UML: The Catalysis Approach.* Addison-Wesley, 1999.
8. H.-D. Ehrich. Object specification. In E. Astesiano, H.-J. Kreowski, and B. Krieg-Brückner, editors, *Algebraic Foundations of Systems Specifications*, chapter 12, pages 435–465. Springer, 1999.
9. E. Gamma, R. Helm, R. Johnson, J. Vlissades. *Design Patterns – Elements of Reusable Object-Oriented Design.* Addison-Wesley, 1994.
10. G. Larsen. Designing component-based frameworks using patterns in the UML. *Comms. ACM*, 42(10):38–45, October 1999.
11. K.-K. Lau, M. Ornaghi. On specification frameworks and deductive synthesis of logic programs. *LNCS 883*, pages 104–121. Springer-Verlag, 1994.
12. K.-K. Lau, M. Ornaghi. OOD frameworks in component-based software development in computational logic. *LNCS 1559*, pages 101–123. Springer-Verlag, 1999.
13. K.-K. Lau, M. Ornaghi. Isoinitial semantics for logic programs. *LNAI 1861*, pages 223–238. Springer-Verlag, 2000.
14. K.-K. Lau, M. Ornaghi. Correct object-oriented systems in computational logic. *LNCS 2372*, pages 168–190. Springer-Verlag, 2002.
15. K.-K. Lau, M. Ornaghi, S.-Å. Tärnlund. Steadfast logic programs. *J. Logic Programming*, 38(3):259–294, March 1999.
16. M. Müller-Olm, D. A. Schmidt, B. Steffen. Model-checking: A tutorial introduction. *LNCS 1694*, pages 330–354. Springer, 1999.
17. Response to the UML 2.0 OCL RfP (ad/2000-09-03). em OMG Document ad/2003-01-07. http://www.omg.org/docs/ad/03-01-07.pdf
18. M. Richters, M. Gogolla. OCL: Syntax, semantics, and tools. *LNCS 2263*, pages 42–68. Springer, 2002.
19. J. Rumbaugh, I. Jacobson, G. Booch. *The Unified Modeling Language Reference Manual.* Addison-Wesley, 1999.
20. J.C. Shepherdson. Negation as failure: a comparison of Clark's completed data base and Reiter's closed world assumption. *J. Logic Programming*, 1:51–79, 1984.
21. The precise UML group http://www.puml.org
22. J. Warmer, A. Kleppe. *The Object Constraint Language.* Addison-Wesley, 1999.
23. M. Wirsing. Algebraic specification. In J. Van Leeuwen, editor, *Handbook of Theoretical Computer Science*, pages 675–788. Elsevier, 1990.

Specification and Synthesis of Hybrid Automata for Physics-Based Animation

Thomas Ellman

Department of Computer Science
Vassar College, Poughkeepsie, NY 12601
ellman@cs.vassar.edu

Physics-based animation programs are useful in a variety of contexts, including science, engineering, education and entertainment. For example, in science, they are used to investigate the behavior of dynamical systems. In engineering, they are used to help design vehicles, machinery and other mechanical devices. In education, they are used to teach basic principles of physics. In entertainment, they are used in games involving cars, planes, spaceships and other moving objects. Such programs are usually constructed by hand, in conventional programming languages, such as C++, possibly augmented with a physics-based animation toolkit. Unfortunately, manual construction of physics-based animation programs is expensive, time-consuming and highly prone to error.

A considerable portion of the difficulty results from the need to track and manage instantaneous changes in the states of objects and the equations and constraints that govern their behavior. For example, when one rigid body collides with another, the objects' states of motion may change instantaneously. If the contact persists for a period of time, the governing equations of motion and constraints may change as well. Similar instantaneous changes occur when an autonomous agent switches from one control mode to another. For example, when the driver of a car depresses or releases the accelerator or brake, the car's acceleration may change instantaneously.

In previous work, the author and his students developed a system for specification and synthesis of numerical simulation programs for physics-based animation applications [2]. The system allows a developer to specify the geometry, shading, lighting and camera angles of a scene in 3D Studio Max(R) and specify the dynamics of the scene in Mathematica(R). A Mathematica program processes these specifications and generates a numerical C++ program that interleaves simulation and rendering to generate a real time animation of the specified scene. This work drew upon the field of analytical dynamics, in which motion is governed by differential equations involving forces and constraints, for modeling physical systems. The equations were assumed to remain fixed over time, resulting in continuous and smooth motion, ignoring the complexities described above.

We have recently extended the system to hybrid automata [3]. A hybrid automaton includes both discrete and continuous dynamical variables. The discrete variables define the automaton's modes of behavior. The continuous variables are governed by mode-dependent differential equations. Hybrid automata are suited

M. Bruynooghe (Ed.): LOPSTR 2004, LNCS 3018, pp. 54–55, 2004.

to modeling physical systems with instantaneous changes in forces, constraints and equations. They are also suited to modeling some types of autonomous behavior by agents operating in a physics-governed environment.

We have defined a family of parameterized specification schemata. Each scheme describes a pattern of behavior as a hybrid automaton passes through a sequence of modes. A developer can specify a program by selecting one or more schemata and supplying application-specific instantiation parameters for each of them. Each scheme has a declarative interpretation, and can be combined with other schemata in an order-independent fashion. We have associated each scheme with a parameterized sentence in a logic of hybrid systems. The sentence serves to document the semantics of the specification scheme. We have also developed sets of rewrite rules that implement each of the specification schemata in a general physics-based animation architecture.

We have tested the system on over a dozen examples. In one example, a ball rolls down a series of steps, repeatedly making transitions between a rolling mode and a bouncing mode. In another example, a robot drives around a track and repeatedly picks up and puts down a ball. In so doing, the robot makes transitions between driving, reaching, carrying and placing modes. In yet another example, two spaceships orbiting a planet are shooting torpedoes at each other. The specifications assert that the torpedoes are launched with initial velocities that cause them to fly along ballistic trajectories to hit their targets. The system automatically synthesizes a numerical shooting method to implement the specification. Experimental results on these and other examples are described in a full length version of this paper[1].

The long-term goal of this research is to develop a specification language and synthesis system that is general enough to handle a wide variety of animation programs, yet restricted enough to permit programs to be synthesized automatically. We are taking an incremental approach in working toward this goal. We intend to expand, generalize and unify the specification schemata and synthesis techniques over time. We expect the process will lead eventually to a logic-based specification language and synthesis system with a combination of expressiveness and automation that makes it useful for developing animation programs in real-life applications.

References

1. T. Ellman, "Specification and Synthesis of Hybrid Automata for Physics-Based Animation", Proceedings of the 18th IEEE International Conference on Automated Software Engineering, 2003, Montreal, Canada.
2. T. Ellman, R. Deak and J. Fotinatos, "Automated Synthesis of Numerical Programs for Simulation of Rigid Mechanical Systems in Physics-Based Animation". Automated Software Engineering, 10, 2003.
3. A. Van Der Schaft and H. Schumacher, "An Introduction to Hybrid Dynamical Systems". Lecture Notes in Control and Information Sciences, 251, Springer, 2000.

Adding Concrete Syntax
to a Prolog-Based Program Synthesis System
(Extended Abstract)

Bernd Fischer[1] and Eelco Visser[2]

[1] RIACS / NASA Ames Research Center, Moffett Field, CA 94035, USA
fisch@email.arc.nasa.gov
[2] Institute of Information and Computing Sciences, Universiteit Utrecht
3508 TB Utrecht, The Netherlands
visser@acm.org

1 Introduction

Program generation and transformation systems work on two language levels, the object-level (i.e., the language of the manipulated programs), and the meta-level (i.e., the implementation language of the system itself). The meta-level representations of object-level program fragments are usually built in an essentially syntax-free fashion using the operations provided by the meta-language. However, syntax matters and a large conceptual distance between the two languages makes it difficult to maintain and extend such systems. Here we describe how an existing Prolog-based system can gradually be retrofitted with concrete object-level syntax using the approach outlined in [5], thus shrinking this distance.

2 AutoBayes

AUTOBAYES [1] is a fully automatic program synthesis system for statistical data analysis problems like the analysis of planetary nebulae images taken by the Hubble space telescope [2]. Its implementation currently comprises about 80,000 lines of SWI-Prolog code. AUTOBAYES derives code from statistical models of the data using a schema-based approach. Schemas consist of parameterized code fragments (i.e., templates) and constraints. The code fragments are written in a sanitized variant of C (e.g., no pointers) that also contains a number of domain-specific extensions (e.g., matrix expressions). The fragments represent the solution methods of the domain, for example statistical algorithms like k-means clustering or numeric optimization algorithms like the Nelder-Mead simplex method. The constraints determine whether a schema is applicable and how the parameters – and thus the code – can be instantiated, either directly by the schema or by AUTOBAYES calling itself recursively with a modified model.

M. Bruynooghe (Ed.): LOPSTR 2004, LNCS 3018, pp. 56–58, 2004.
© Springer-Verlag Berlin Heidelberg 2004

3   Program Generation in Prolog

In the current AUTOBAYES-version, schemas are implemented as simple Prolog-clauses that return a term representing the appropriately instantiated algorithms. The schemas assemble the fragments from many small code pieces that are bound to Prolog-variables acting as meta-variables; otherwise, the abstract syntax would become unreadable. The schemas are also sprinkled with many calls to small meta-programming predicates that for example generate fresh object-level variables or build other constructs of the object language. A particular nuisance is the repeated use of Prolog's built-in =..-operator to construct compound object-level terms with variables as head symbols, which is necessary for second-order term formation. This general style makes it hard to follow and understand the overall structure of the algorithm and thus difficult for a domain expert to modify and write schemas.

4   Migration to Concrete Syntax

Schema migration involves three easy steps. First, terms representing program fragments in abstract syntax are replaced by the equivalent fragments in concrete syntax; these fragments are marked by a quotation operator. Then, calls to meta-programming predicates are replaced by the appropriate object-level constructs. For example, the explicit generation of fresh object variables is expressed *in the object code* by tagging the corresponding meta-variable with a special anti-quotation operator. Finally, the schema is refactored by inlining the program fragments.

The necessary extension of Prolog with concrete syntax relies on the combination of three techniques. (*i*) The syntax definition formalism SDF2 [4] is used to specify the syntax of both languages as well as the embedding (i.e., quotation mechanism and meta-variables). (*ii*) The transformation language Stratego [6] is used to map syntax trees over this combined language back into pure Prolog programs. This eliminates the concrete syntax. (*iii*) Stratego is also used to adapt the resulting schemas into the exact form required to interface them with the remaining AUTOBAYES-system. For example, second-order term formations and fresh variable anti-quotations are hoisted out of the resulting abstract syntax terms and turned back into the original constructors and fresh variable generators provided by the meta-programming kernel.

5   Conclusions

We applied the generalized approach to meta-programming with concrete object-syntax to some of the schemas in AUTOBAYES. In these cases, the introduction of concrete syntax reduces the schema size by about 30% and improves the readability and locality of the schemas. In particular, abstracting out second-order term formation and fresh-variable generation allows the formulation of larger continuous fragments. Moreover, meta-programming with concrete syntax is cheap:

using Stratego and SDF2, the overall effort to develop all supporting tools was less than three weeks, Once the tools were in place, the migration of a schema was a matter of a few hours. Finally, the experiment has also demonstrated that it is possible to introduce concrete syntax support gradually, without forcing a disruptive migration of the entire system to the extended meta-language. The seamless integration with the "legacy" meta-programming kernel is achieved with a few additional transformations, which can be implemented quickly in Stratego.

Acknowledgments

A preliminary version of this paper was presented at LOPSTR 2003; a full version appears as [3]. We thank all reviewers for their comments.

References

1. B. Fischer and J. Schumann. AutoBayes: A system for generating data analysis programs from statistical models. *JFP*, 13(3):483–508, 2003.
2. B. Fischer and J. Schumann. Applying AutoBayes to the analysis of planetary nebulae images. In *ASE-18*, pp. 337–342. IEEE Comp. Soc. Press, 2003.
3. B. Fischer and E. Visser. Retrofitting the AutoBayes Program Synthesis System with Concrete Syntax. Tech. Report UU-CS-2004-012, Utrecht Univ. In [7].
4. E. Visser. *Syntax Definition for Language Prototyping*. PhD thesis, Univ. Amsterdam, 1997.
5. E. Visser. Meta-Programming with Concrete Object Syntax. In *Generative Programming and Component Engineering, LNCS 2487*, pp. 299–315. Springer, 2002.
6. E. Visser. Program transformation with Stratego/XT: rules, strategies, tools, and systems in StrategoXT-0.9. Tech. Report UU-CS-2004-011, Utrecht Univ. In [7].
7. *Domain-Specific Program Generation*. Springer, 2004. To appear.

Formal Development and Verification of Approximation Algorithms Using Auxiliary Variables

Rudolf Berghammer[1] and Markus Müller-Olm[2]

[1] Institut für Informatik und Praktische Mathematik
Universität Kiel
Olshausenstraße 40, D-24098 Kiel, Germany
rub@informatik.uni-kiel.de
[2] Fachbereich 4, Lehrstuhl V
Universität Dortmund
Baroper Straße 301, D-44221 Dortmund, Germany
mmo@ls5.cs.uni-dortmund.de

Abstract. For many intractable optimization problems efficient approximation algorithms have been developed that return near-optimal solutions. We show how such algorithms and worst-case bounds for the quality of their results can be developed and verified as structured programs. The proposed method has two key steps. First, auxiliary variables are introduced that allow a formal analysis of the worst-case behavior. In a second step these variables are eliminated from the program and existential quantifiers are introduced in assertions. We show that the elimination procedure preserves validity of proofs and illustrate the approach by two examples.

1 Introduction

Algorithm design and formal program development and verification are two well established domains in computer science and applied mathematics. Formerly they mostly have been coexisting. However in recent years many computer scientists noticed that the design and verification of efficient algorithms which are not only correct "in principle" but in all details can benefit from techniques of formal program development and verification. Therefore, there is an increasing cooperation between the two fields.

In this paper techniques of formal program development and verification are applied to *approximation algorithms*. Such algorithms (see [11] for an overview) have been developed because a great variety of important optimization problems cannot be solved efficiently (unless $P = NP$). Approximation algorithms are usually very fast but return only near-optimal solutions. Hence, besides feasibility of their results, estimates for the closeness to the optimal solutions are of interest. We show how approximation algorithms and, in particular, their worst-case bounds can formally be derived and verified as structured programs using the well-known assertion method pioneered by Floyd and Hoare [7, 10, 5, 1].

M. Bruynooghe (Ed.): LOPSTR 2004, LNCS 3018, pp. 59–74, 2004.

The proposed method for proving worst-case bounds has two key steps. In the first step, auxiliary variables are added to the program. They are used to collect information that is referred to in the informal proofs but is not present in the algorithm itself. The worst-case behaviour can then be analysed formally by strengthening the assertions used in the feasibility proof. In the second step, the auxiliary variables are removed from the program and existential quantifiers are introduced in assertions. This avoids the inefficient calculation of auxiliary variables at run-time. It also allows to use non-constructive or expensive operations in assignments to auxiliary variables. We show that this elimination procedure preserves validity of partial correctness proofs.

The paper is organized as follows: Section 2 illustrates that auxiliary variables are useful for a formal verification of worst-case behaviour. For this purpose, we recall a well-known approximation algorithm for the minimum vertex cover problem and its proof in the usual semi-formal mathematical way. Afterwards, we show how this proof can be formalized. Proof outlines, which are decisive for our reasoning, are considered in Section 3 and three simple conditions for their validity are presented. In Section 4 we show how auxiliary variables can be eliminated from proof outlines and prove that the resulting proof outline shows the same partial correctness property as the original proof outline. Section 5 applies our method to a second example, an approximation algorithm for the problem of computing an independent set of maximum size. We also discuss some variants of this algorithm. We conclude in Section 6 with some further applications and ideas for future research.

2 An Illustrative Example

Let $g = (V, E)$ be an undirected and loop-free graph with finite (and non-empty) set V of vertices and set E of edges, where each edge is a set $\{x, y\}$ with $x, y \in V$ and $x \neq y$. A *vertex cover* of g is a subset C of V such that every edge in g is incident to some vertex in C, i.e., $e \cap C \neq \emptyset$ for all $e \in E$. To compute a vertex cover of minimum size is an *NP*-hard problem; see [3]. There is a simple greedy approximation algorithm for that problem attributed to Gavril and Yannakakis in [3]. Expressed as a while-program it reads as given below, where we assume that the non-deterministic assignment $e :\in F$ assigns an arbitrary element of $F \neq \emptyset$ to e and the call $inc(e)$ yields the set $\{f \in E \mid e \cap f \neq \emptyset\}$ of all edges incident to edge e:

$$
\begin{aligned}
&C := \emptyset; F := E; \\
&\textbf{while } F \neq \emptyset \textbf{ do} \\
&\quad e :\in F; \\
&\quad C := C \cup e; F := F \setminus inc(e) \textbf{ od} .
\end{aligned}
\qquad (\text{VC}_1)
$$

In [3] it is also shown that this program always returns a vertex cover C of g whose size $|C|$ is guaranteed to be no greater than twice the minimum size c_{opt} of a vertex cover of g. The idea underlying this proof is to consider the set M of all edges that were picked by the statement $e :\in F$ and to show that M is a matching of g with $|C| \leq 2 * |M|$. (A set of edges is a matching if no two different edges are incident.) The estimation $|C| \leq 2 * c_{\text{opt}}$ then follows from the fact that a vertex cover C^* of g of minimum size must include at least one vertex of any edge of M, i.e., $|M| \leq |C^*| = c_{\text{opt}}$.

As is prevalent in the literature on algorithmics, the correctness proof of Gavril and Yannakakis' algorithm in [3] is done in a "free-style" mathematical way without formal problem specification and program verification. Nevertheless it can also be formalized in the assertion approach if the program (VC$_1$) is refined by a pre-condition, a loop invariant, and a post-condition as follows:

$$\{ \textit{true} \}$$
$$C := \emptyset; F := E; M := \emptyset;$$
$$\{ \textit{inv}(C, F, M) \}$$
$$\textbf{while } F \neq \emptyset \textbf{ do} \qquad\qquad (\text{VC}_2)$$
$$e :\in F;$$
$$C := C \cup e; F := F \setminus \textit{inc}(e); M := M \cup \{e\} \textbf{ od}$$
$$\{ \textit{post}(C) \} .$$

The loop invariant $inv(C, F, M)$ is defined as the conjunction of

$$C \text{ vertex cover of } g_F = (V, E \setminus F), \qquad\qquad (1)$$
$$M \text{ matching of } g = (V, E), \qquad\qquad (2)$$
$$|C| \leq 2 * |M|, \qquad\qquad (3)$$
$$\forall\, e \in M, f \in F : e \cap f = \emptyset, \qquad\qquad (4)$$

and the post-condition $post(C)$ as the conjunction of

$$C \text{ vertex cover of } g = (V, E), \qquad\qquad (5)$$
$$|C| \leq 2 * c_{\text{opt}} . \qquad\qquad (6)$$

The annotated program (VC$_2$) terminates regularly since the non-deterministic assignment $e :\in F$ is defined because of the condition $F \neq \emptyset$ of the while-loop and, due to $e \in inc(e)$, the value of F is strictly decreased in every run through the while-loop. To show partial correctness of (VC$_2$) wrt. the pre-condition $true$ and the post-condition $post(C)$, three proof obligations have to be discharged (see Section 3 or [6, 9] for details). First of all, the initialization must establish the loop invariant if the pre-condition holds, i.e.,

$$true \implies inv(\emptyset, E, \emptyset) .$$

Secondly, each execution of the loop's body must maintain the loop invariant, i.e., the implication

$$F \neq \emptyset \wedge inv(C, F, M) \implies inv(C \cup e, F \setminus inc(e), M \cup \{e\})$$

must be shown for all C, F, and M and for any e in F. The proofs of both implications are easy exercises and, therefore, left out. Note, however, that in the second case assertion (4) is necessary to obtain the matching property of $M \cup \{e\}$ from $e \in F$ and the matching property of M. The third and final task is to show that upon termination of the loop the post-condition follows from the loop's exit condition and the loop invariant, which leads to

$$F = \emptyset \wedge inv(C, F, M) \implies post(C)$$

for any C, F and M as last proof obligation. Here (5) follows from (1) and $F = \emptyset$ and (6) is a consequence of (2) and (3), as already shown.

3   Proof Outlines

Proof methods for correctness of programs have been the topic of intense research for more than three decades (see [5] for an overview). Floyd's method [7] of inductive assertions and Hoare logic [10] are particularly well known. In this paper we use proof outlines for proof presentation which combine the strength of both methods. They allow a proof presentation on the level of structured programs but lead to a more compact proof representation as full proof trees. A *proof outline* is a program annotated with assertions as the example (VC$_2$) in Section 2.

An *assertion* is a predicate on the values of the variables used in a program. In practice, assertions are given by predicate-logic formulas. Suppose we have two assertions *pre* and *post*. Then, program π is called *partially correct* with respect to pre-condition *pre* and post-condition *post* if any terminating execution of π from an initial state that satisfies *pre* ends in a state that satisfies *post*; if, in addition π terminates from any state in *pre*, it is called *totally correct* with respect to *pre* and *post*. While we are ultimately interested in total correctness, it is in most cases easier in formal program development and verification to first concentrate on partial correctness and prove termination separately afterwards. Because there is nothing special about termination proofs of approximation algorithms, we focus on partial correctness reasoning in this paper.

A *program element* is a Boolean expression (condition) or an atomic statement. We will discuss the following types of atomic statements in this paper: the "do-nothing" statement **skip**, (deterministic) assignments $x := t$, and nondeterministic assignments $x :\in S$. For simplicity, we assume that t and S are total expressions. The exposition can straightforwardly be extended to other kinds of atomic statements.

Now, let p and q be two assertions in a proof outline. Then a *segment* from p to q is a sequence of program elements that may be traversed successively in an execution of the underlying program on the way from p to q; a segment is not allowed to extend over an assertion. We refrain from a more formal definition but provide an illustrative example. Consider the following simple generic proof outline, where S_1, S_2, S_3, and S_4 are atomic statements, b is a condition, and *pre*, *inv*, and *post* are assertions:

$$\{ \ pre \ \}$$
$$S_1; S_2;$$
$$\{ \ inv \ \}$$
$$\textbf{while } b \textbf{ do}$$
$$S_3; S_4 \textbf{ od}$$
$$\{ \ post \ \}.$$

In it, we have the three segments $\langle S_1, S_2 \rangle$ from *pre* to *inv*, $\langle b, S_3, S_4 \rangle$ from *inv* to *inv*, and $\langle \neg b \rangle$ from *inv* to *post*.

As demonstrated in Section 2, each segment in a proof outline gives rise to a proof obligation: it must be partially correct with respect to the surrounding assertions. This proof obligations is best captured in terms of the weakest liberal pre-condition of the segment, which is inductively defined by

$$
\begin{aligned}
\mathsf{wlp}(\varepsilon, q) &:\Longleftrightarrow q\,, \\
\mathsf{wlp}(e \cdot s, q) &:\Longleftrightarrow \mathsf{wlp}(e, \mathsf{wlp}(s, q))\,.
\end{aligned}
$$

Here ε is the empty sequence (*empty segment*) and $e \cdot s$ is the concatenation of the program element e and the segment s. This definition refers to the weakest liberal pre-condition of program elements, which is given by

$$
\begin{aligned}
\mathsf{wlp}(b, q) &:\Longleftrightarrow b \rightarrow q\,, \\
\mathsf{wlp}(\mathbf{skip}, q) &:\Longleftrightarrow q\,, \\
\mathsf{wlp}(x := e, q) &:\Longleftrightarrow q[e/x]\,, \\
\mathsf{wlp}(x :\in S, q) &:\Longleftrightarrow S \neq \emptyset \wedge (\forall\, s \in S : q[s/x])\,.
\end{aligned}
$$

It is understood that s is a fresh variable in the clause for $x :\in S$, i.e. a variable q is independent of, and $q[s/x]$ is obtained by substituting s for x in q.

Note that the conjunct $S \neq \emptyset$ in the clause for $x :\in S$ puts the obligation on the algorithm designer to prove that S is non-empty. Omitting this conjunct results in an alternative definition in which $\mathsf{wlp}(x :\in S, q)$ holds trivially for all states, in which S evaluates to the empty set. One could argue that this alternative definition would be in accordance with the philosophy of partial correctness: to choose a value from an empty set should result in a run-time error and, like divergent paths, execution paths leading to run-time errors could be ignored in partial correctness. However, without the conjunct $S \neq \emptyset$ we cannot allow non-deterministic assignments to auxiliary variables as otherwise the elimination procedure described in Section 4 would become unsound. Here is a minimal example for the problem: without the conjunct $S \neq \emptyset$, the proof outline $\{true\}\ a :\in \emptyset\ \{false\}$ is valid in the sense defined below. Step (i) of the elimination procedure of Section 4, however, results in $\{true\}\ \mathbf{skip}\ \{false\}$ which is certainly wrong.

Now, a proof outline is *valid* for assertions *pre* and *post* if it satisfies the following three conditions:

(a) Assertion *pre* is placed at the beginning and assertion *post* at the end of the proof outline.
(b) Any loop in the underlying program is broken by an assertion; typically this is achieved by placing a loop invariant right in front of every loop.
(c) For every segment s from an assertion p to another assertion q in the proof outline, p implies $\mathsf{wlp}(s, q)$.

Intuitively, the second condition guarantees that a proof outline induces only a finite number of segments and the last condition says that all segments are partially correct wrt. the surrounding assertions. As every execution of the program is composed of executions of segments, a valid proof outline proves partial correctness of the underlying program π wrt. *pre* and *post*.

4   Auxiliary Variables and Their Elimination

The example in Section 2 illustrates that the enrichment of programs and proof outlines by auxiliary variables often allows a clearer statement of the underlying argument in a formal verification. However if the auxiliary variables are left in the executed version of the program they may lead to inefficiencies caused by additional computations, which in certain cases even forbids the use of the modified programs in practice.

In order to overcome this disadvantage, we show in this section that auxiliary variables can always be eliminated from proof outlines without affecting their validity. From a theoretical point of view, this result proves that auxiliary variables are unnecessary in order to perform a correctness proof. Nevertheless, we recommend their practical use because of the above reason. Note that our result even allows the use of pre-algorithmic constructs (like set comprehension or quantification) in assignments to auxiliary variables. This often simplifies formal reasoning considerably.

In view of our applications, a finite set of variables A is called a *set of auxiliary variables* in a program π if variables $a \in A$ are used only in assignments of the form $x := t$ or $x :\in S$ where $x \in A$. That is: auxiliary variables must not be used in assignments to non-auxiliary variables and in guards of loops or conditionals[1]. Therefore, they can neither influence the control flow nor the values held by non-auxiliary variables Auxiliary variables may be used freely in the assertions of a proof outline. In order to ensure that the specification proved by a proof outline is independent of auxiliary variables, we require, however, that auxiliary variables do not appear freely in the pre- and the post-condition. In the proof outline (VC_2) in Section 2, for instance, M is an auxiliary variable.

In order to eliminate the auxiliary variables $a \in A$ from π, we perform the following simple step; the resulting program is called $\tilde{\pi}$ in the following.

(i) Remove any assignment of the form $a := t$ or $a :\in S$ with $a \in A$ from π.

We can think of this step as a replacement of all these assignments in π by the neutral statement **skip**. Of course, a valid proof outline for π will in general no longer be valid if π is replaced by the modified program $\tilde{\pi}$, as the assertions may use auxiliary variables in an essential way. As we will prove in a moment, however, we can regain a valid proof outline for $\tilde{\pi}$ by the following second step:

(ii) Replace in addition any assertion p in the old proof outline in which auxiliary variables occur freely by the assertion $(\exists\, a_1, \ldots, a_k : p)$, where $a_1, \ldots, a_k \in A$ are the auxiliary variables occurring free in p.

---

[1] Some authors, e.g., [13], use the notion "auxiliary variables" for variables whose appearance is restricted to assertions and whose values may not be changed by programs. Usually, in the literature such variables are called *logical variables*.

Note that this transformation of the proof outline leaves both pre- and post-condition unchanged, as they do not contain free occurrences of auxiliary variables. Hence, the modified proof outline proves, if indeed valid, the same partial correctness property as the original one, but for the modified program $\tilde{\pi}$.

If we apply (i) and (ii) to the valid proof outline (VC$_2$) of Section 2 we get the following valid proof outline (VC$_3$) showing the partial correctness of the original program (VC$_1$) wrt. the pre-condition $true$ and the post-condition $post(C)$:

$$
\begin{aligned}
&\{\ true\ \} \\
&C := \emptyset; F := E; \\
&\{\ \exists\, M : inv(C, F, M)\ \} \\
&\textbf{while}\ F \neq \emptyset\ \textbf{do} \qquad\qquad\qquad\qquad\qquad\text{(VC}_3\text{)} \\
&\quad e :\in F; \\
&\quad C := C \cup e; F := F \setminus inc(e)\ \textbf{od} \\
&\{\ post(C)\ \}\,.
\end{aligned}
$$

Let $\bar{a}$ be a list of variables that contains each variable of A exactly once. We now show that the application of steps (i) and (ii) to a valid proof outline leads always again to a valid proof outline. As the first two conditions (a) and (b) of Section 3 for validity of proof outlines are not affected by the transformation via (i) and (ii), we only have to show that the third condition (c) remains true. Without loss of generality, we can assume that step (ii) replaces *all* assertions p in the proof outline by $(\exists\,\bar{a} : p)$. This assumption which smoothes the proof is justified by the fact that existential quantification over variables a predicate q is independent of results in an equivalent predicate.

As a preparation for the correctness proof, we show an interesting relationship between a program element e in the original program and the program element $\tilde{e}$ which replaces it in the modified program when step (i) is applied:

Lemma 4.1. *Let q be an assertion. Then*

$$(\exists\,\bar{a} : \mathsf{wlp}(e, q)) \quad \Longrightarrow \quad \mathsf{wlp}(\tilde{e}, (\exists\,\bar{a} : q))\,.$$

Proof. The assertions $(\exists\,\bar{a} : \mathsf{wlp}(e, q))$ and $\mathsf{wlp}(\tilde{e}, (\exists\,\bar{a} : q))$ are even equivalent if the program element e is **skip**, a deterministic assignment $x := t$ to a non-auxiliary variable x, or a guard b. For e being **skip** this is obvious: both assertions reduce to $(\exists\,\bar{a} : q)$. For deterministic assignments equivalence is proved by

$$
\begin{aligned}
&\quad\ (\exists\,\bar{a} : \mathsf{wlp}(x := t, q)) \\
&\Longleftrightarrow (\exists\,\bar{a} : q[t/x]) && \text{definition wlp} \\
&\Longleftrightarrow (\exists\,\bar{a} : q)[t/x] && \text{predicate logic} \\
&\Longleftrightarrow \mathsf{wlp}(x := t, (\exists\,\bar{a} : q)) && \text{definition wlp.}
\end{aligned}
$$

The second equivalence exploits that x is a non-auxiliary variable and that t does not depend on auxiliary variables.

The case of guards is shown by

$$
\begin{aligned}
&(\exists\,\bar a : \mathsf{wlp}(b,q))\\
\Longleftrightarrow\ &(\exists\,\bar a : b \to q) && \text{definition wlp}\\
\Longleftrightarrow\ &b \to (\exists\,\bar a : q) && \text{predicate logic}\\
\Longleftrightarrow\ &\mathsf{wlp}(b, (\exists\,\bar a : q)) && \text{definition wlp.}
\end{aligned}
$$

Note that the second equivalence depends on b being independent of auxiliary variables and the fact that the variables of $\bar a$ have a non-empty type, a standard assumption for program variables.

In the case of a non-deterministic assignment $x :\in S$ to a non-auxiliary variable x we calculate as follows, where the second step exploits that S is independent of all the variables in $\bar a$ because $\bar a$ consists of auxiliary variables and the third step that for the fresh variable s the property $s \notin A$ can be assumed:

$$
\begin{aligned}
&(\exists\,\bar a : \mathsf{wlp}(x :\in S, q))\\
\Longleftrightarrow\ &(\exists\,\bar a : S \neq \emptyset \wedge (\forall\, s \in S : q[s/x])) && \text{definition wlp}\\
\Longrightarrow\ &S \neq \emptyset \wedge (\forall\, s \in S : (\exists\,\bar a : q[s/x])) && \text{predicate logic}\\
\Longleftrightarrow\ &S \neq \emptyset \wedge (\forall\, s \in S : (\exists\,\bar a : q)[s/x]) && \text{since } x, s \notin A\\
\Longleftrightarrow\ &\mathsf{wlp}(x :\in S, (\exists\,\bar a : q)). && \text{definition wlp.}
\end{aligned}
$$

For deterministic assignments to an auxiliary variable $a \in A$ the proof looks as follows, where in the fourth step of the derivation s is replaced by a and the two quantifiers are combined.

$$
\begin{aligned}
&(\exists\,\bar a : \mathsf{wlp}(a := t, q))\\
\Longleftrightarrow\ &(\exists\,\bar a : q[t/a]) && \text{definition wlp}\\
\Longleftrightarrow\ &(\exists\,\bar a : (\exists\, s : s = t \wedge q[s/a])) && \text{one-point rule}\\
\Longrightarrow\ &(\exists\,\bar a : (\exists\, s : q[s/a])) && \text{weakening}\\
\Longleftrightarrow\ &(\exists\,\bar a : q) && \text{see above}\\
\Longleftrightarrow\ &\mathsf{wlp}(\mathbf{skip}, (\exists\,\bar a : q)). && \text{definition wlp.}
\end{aligned}
$$

Finally, for a non-deterministic assignment $a :\in S$ to an auxiliary variable we calculate as follows, where in the second step the conjunct $S \neq \emptyset$ ensures that the range of the universal quantification is non-empty such that it can be weakened to an existential quantification:

$$
\begin{aligned}
&(\exists\,\bar a : \mathsf{wlp}(a :\in S, q))\\
\Longleftrightarrow\ &(\exists\,\bar a : S \neq \emptyset \wedge (\forall\, s \in S : q[s/a])) && \text{definition wlp}\\
\Longrightarrow\ &(\exists\,\bar a : S \neq \emptyset \wedge (\exists\, s \in S : q[s/a])) && \text{see above}\\
\Longrightarrow\ &(\exists\,\bar a : (\exists\, s : q[s/a])) && \text{weakening.}
\end{aligned}
$$

The last formula is equivalent to $\mathsf{wlp}(\mathbf{skip}, (\exists\,\bar a : q))$ as we have seen in the proof for deterministic assignments to auxiliary variables.   □

A simple inductive argument shows that the implication in Lemma 4.1 transfers from program elements to segments:

Lemma 4.2. *Suppose s is a segment in the original proof outline, $\tilde{s}$ is the corresponding segment in the modified proof outline, and q is an assertion. Then*

$$(\exists\,\bar{a}:\mathsf{wlp}(s,q)) \implies \mathsf{wlp}(\tilde{s},(\exists\,\bar{a}:q))\,.$$

Proof. The induction base of s being empty is trivial: since $\tilde{s}$ is empty, too, both sides of the implication reduce to $(\exists\,\bar{a}:q)$.

For the induction step of s being of the form $e\cdot r$ we get the derivation

$$
\begin{array}{ll}
& (\exists\,\bar{a}:\mathsf{wlp}(e\cdot r,q)) \\
\Longleftrightarrow & (\exists\,\bar{a}:\mathsf{wlp}(e,\mathsf{wlp}(r,q))) & \text{definition wlp for segments} \\
\Longrightarrow & \mathsf{wlp}(\tilde{e},(\exists\,\bar{a}:\mathsf{wlp}(r,q))) & \text{Lemma 4.1} \\
\Longrightarrow & \mathsf{wlp}(\tilde{e},\mathsf{wlp}(\tilde{r},(\exists\,\bar{a}:q))) & \text{induction hypothesis, monotonicity} \\
\Longleftrightarrow & \mathsf{wlp}(\tilde{e}\cdot\tilde{r},(\exists\,\bar{a}:q)) & \text{definition wlp for segments}
\end{array}
$$

which concludes the proof since the concatenation $e\cdot r$ is modified to $\tilde{e}\cdot\tilde{r}$.   □

After these preparations, it is now easy to show correctness of the elimination procedure.

Theorem 4.1. *The application of steps (i) and (ii) to a valid proof outline leads again to a valid proof outline.*

Proof. As conditions (a) and (b) of Section 3 for validity of proof outlines are not affected by the transformation via (i) and (ii), we only have to show that condition (c) remains true.

For the purpose of proving (c), assume that the original proof outline satisfies condition (c) and suppose we are given a segment t from some assertion $(\exists\,\bar{a}:p)$ to some assertion $(\exists\,\bar{a}:q)$ in the transformed proof outline. As the transformation affects only the form of single statements and assertions but not the global structure of the proof outline, there is a corresponding segment s from p to q in the original proof outline such that the modification $\tilde{s}$ of s equals t. By assumption, the original proof outline satisfies condition (c); thus, p implies $\mathsf{wlp}(s,q)$. We can now show the desired implication by

$$
\begin{array}{ll}
& (\exists\,\bar{a}:p) \\
\Longrightarrow & (\exists\,\bar{a}:\mathsf{wlp}(s,q)) & p \Rightarrow \mathsf{wlp}(s,q),\ \text{monotonicity} \\
\Longrightarrow & \mathsf{wlp}(\tilde{s},(\exists\,\bar{a}:q)) & \text{Lemma 4.2} \\
\Longleftrightarrow & \mathsf{wlp}(t,(\exists\,\bar{a}:q)) & t = \tilde{s}.
\end{array}
$$

   □

5   A Further Example

Let $g = (V, E)$ be an undirected and loop-free graph and assume that the call $ngb(x)$ computes the set $\{y \in V \mid \{x, y\} \in E\}$ of all neighbour vertices of vertex x. A set of vertices of g is called *independent* if no two vertices in it are connected via an edge from E. To derive a program for computing such a set S, we start with the assertion

$$S \text{ independent set of } g = (V, E) \tag{7}$$

as post-condition $post(S)$. Using a new variable X, then we generalize (7) to

$$X \subseteq V \text{ and } S \text{ independent set of } g_X = (X, E_X), \tag{8}$$

where $E_X = \{e \in E \mid e \subseteq X\}$, i.e., g_X is the subgraph of g generated by X. Choosing the conjunction of (8) and the assertion

$$\forall\, x \in V \setminus X, y \in S : \{x, y\} \notin E \tag{9}$$

as loop invariant $inv(S, X)$, it is straightforward to derive the program for computing S shown in the following valid proof outline:

$$
\begin{aligned}
&\{\ true\ \} \\
&S := \emptyset; X := \emptyset; \\
&\{\ inv(S, X)\ \} \\
&\textbf{while } X \neq V \textbf{ do} \qquad\qquad\qquad\qquad (\text{IS}_1) \\
&\quad x :\in V \setminus X; \\
&\quad S := S \cup \{x\}; X := X \cup ngb(x) \cup \{x\} \textbf{ od} \\
&\{\ post(S)\ \}.
\end{aligned}
$$

The definedness of the non-deterministic assignment $x :\in V \setminus X$ in this proof outline follows from the assumption $V \neq \emptyset$, the part $X \subseteq V$ of the loop invariant, and the condition of the while-loop. Termination of the while-loop is obvious.

Like the minimum vertex cover problem of Section 2, the problem of computing an independent set of maximum size is *NP*-hard and the program of the proof outline (IS_1) implements a well-known approximation algorithm proposed and studied by Wei [19].

Now, we formally analyze the worst-case behaviour of Wei's algorithm using our method. To this end, we enrich the program of (IS_1) by an auxiliary variable U, which consists of all the sets $ngb(x) \cup \{x\}$ which are added to X on all iterations of the while loop. This step leads to a first strengthening of the original loop invariant $inv(S, X)$: we add the conjunct

$$X = \bigcup_{u \in U} u. \tag{10}$$

Let $\Delta(g) = \max_{x \in V} |ngb(x)|$ be the so-called *degree* of the graph g. It is obvious that each set in U has at most $\Delta(g) + 1$ elements and we add also the corresponding assertion

$$\forall\, u \in U : |u| \leq \Delta(g) + 1 \tag{11}$$

to the original loop invariant. Finally, we notice that whenever some set $ngb(x) \cup \{x\}$ is added to U, the vertex x is added to S. Due to its choice via the assignment $x :\in V \setminus X$ and assertion (8), x is not yet a member of S. Thus, S cannot be smaller than U. The corresponding estimation

$$|U| \leq |S| \tag{12}$$

is the third addition to the original loop invariant. Altogether, we obtain the following proof outline with auxiliary variable U and a loop invariant $inv(S, X, U)$ given as conjunction of the assertions (8) to (12); its validity proof is rather simple since it contains all necessary information:

$\{\ true\ \}$
$S := \emptyset; X := \emptyset; U := \emptyset;$
$\{\ inv(S, X, U)\ \}$
while $X \neq V$ **do**   (IS$_2$)
$\quad x :\in V \setminus X;$
$\quad S := S \cup \{x\}; X := X \cup ngb(x) \cup \{x\}; U := U \cup \{ngb(x) \cup \{x\}\}$ **od**
$\{\ post(S)\ \}\ .$

Now, we are able to estimate the worst-case behaviour of Wei's algorithm formally. Assume $inv(S, X, U)$ and $X = V$ and let s_{opt} be the size of a maximum independent set of g. Then, we obtain

$$s_{opt} \leq |V| = \left| \bigcup_{u \in U} u \right| \leq \sum_{u \in U} |u| \leq |U| * (\Delta(g) + 1) \leq |S| * (\Delta(g) + 1)\ .$$

Here the second step follows from assertion (10) and the loop's exit condition $X = V$ and the fourth and fifth step use assertions (11) and (12), respectively. Hence, the proof outline (IS$_2$) remains valid if its post-condition $post(S)$ is strengthened to $post'(S)$ by adding the conjunct

$$s_{opt} \leq |S| * (\Delta(g) + 1)\ . \tag{13}$$

Now the auxiliary variable U can be eliminated using steps (i) and (ii) of Section 4 and this, finally, yields the following valid proof outline for Wei's algorithm which includes a worst-case estimation in its post-condition as desired:

$\{\ true\ \}$
$S := \emptyset; X := \emptyset;$
$\{\ \exists U : inv(S, X, U)\ \}$
while $X \neq V$ **do**   (IS$_3$)
$\quad x :\in V \setminus X;$
$\quad S := S \cup \{x\}; X := X \cup ngb(x) \cup \{x\}$ **od**
$\{\ post'(S)\ \}\ .$

We sketch some variants of Wei's algorithm in the remainder of this section. They are based on a slight modification of the above estimation, viz.

$$s_{opt} \leq |V| = \left| \bigcup_{u \in U} u \right| \leq \sum_{u \in U} |u| \leq |U| * \max_{u \in U} |u| \leq |S| * \max_{u \in U} |u|\ .$$

From this property, we get $\max_{u \in U} |u|$ as a worst-case bound of Wei's algorithm which is potentially better than the previous bound $\Delta(g) + 1$. This maximum is not known in advance, but it can easily be computed as a further result. A corresponding modification of the proof outline (IS$_2$) followed by the elimination of the auxiliary variable U leads to

$\{\ true\ \}$
$S := \emptyset; X := \emptyset; s := 0;$
$\{\ \exists\, U : inv(S, X, U, s)\ \}$
while $X \neq V$ **do**   (IS$_4$)
$\quad x :\in V \setminus X;$
$\quad S := S \cup \{x\}; X := X \cup ngb(x) \cup \{x\}; s := max(s, |ngb(x) \cup \{x\}|)$ **od**
$\{\ post(S, s)\ \}.$

Here the maximum $max_{u \in U} |u|$ is stored in the variable s and the postcondition $post(S, s)$ consists of the conjunction of the assertion (7) and the estimation

$$s_{\mathrm{opt}} \leq |S| * s.\tag{14}$$

Furthermore, the assertion $inv(S, X, U, s)$ occurring in the loop invariant is obtained from the assertion $inv(S, X, U)$ in (IS$_3$) by replacing (11) with

$$s = \max_{u \in U} |u|.\tag{15}$$

With this information, it is rather simple to show that (IS$_4$) is indeed a valid proof outline. Of course, the program of (IS$_4$) can slightly be improved by the use of a further variable which avoids the two-fold evaluation of the expression $ngb(x) \cup \{x\}$.

By a little modification of the hitherto derivation, the computed worst-case bound can be improved as follows: instead of collecting all sets $ngb(x) \cup \{x\}$ in U, we only collect their "non-visited parts". That is, we replace the assignment $U := U \cup \{ngb(x) \cup \{x\}\}$ by $U := U \cup \{(ngb(x) \setminus X) \cup \{x\}\}$ in the proof outline (IS$_2$). To minimize the value of $max_{u \in U} |u|$ further, we refine the non-deterministic assignment $x :\in V \setminus X$ of (IS$_2$) and pick now (via a simple loop) the vertex x in such a way from $V \setminus X$ that the size of the set $ngb(x) \setminus X$ is minimal. Obviously, both steps do not affect the invariance property of $inv(S, X, U)$. Hence, the modified proof outline is also valid. Starting with this proof outline, we obtain the desired algorithm following the above derivation of (IS$_4$) from (IS$_2$).

To choose in each iteration a node of minimal degree in the non-visited part of the graph is a common heuristic in connection with Wei's algorithm. The idea, however, to enrich the algorithm by a variable s that computes the resulting worst-case bound and the formal correctness proof seems not to appear in the previous literature.

6   Concluding Remarks

When verifying approximation algorithms, we are particularly interested in estimates for the maximal deviation of their results from optimal solutions of the given problem. While the informal feasibility proofs found in the literature on algorithmics can usually be reformulated as formal assertional proofs straightforwardly, the informal proofs of worst-case bounds often refer to entities that are not present in the program and are thus difficult to formalize. As a solution, we proposed in this paper to collect additional information in auxiliary variables inserted into the program which can be referred to in assertions. These auxiliary variables are introduced solely for the purpose of the formal assertional proof and are not meant to stay in the executed version of the program. Therefore, we showed how they can be eliminated from proof outlines without affecting validity. Their elimination also allows references to non-constructive or expensive operations in assignments to auxiliary variables.

When we develop approximation algorithms in the way proposed in this paper we start from a partial specification (that specifies only feasibility of the result) and strengthen it during the program development (to account for the achieved approximation bound) with the aid of auxiliary variables. There are other application areas where it is natural to proceed in a similar fashion. Examples include development of probabilistic algorithms and reasoning about run-time of programs. Indeed, it is an old idea to use a designated variable in order to model run-time consumption of programs and to reason about it [16, 12, 15].

Our approach can be seen as a particular application of the well-known "invent and verify" technique for program development combined with transformational programming. In doing so, sometimes the specific form of the assignments to auxiliary variables formally can be calculated using, e.g., the postcondition and/or the invariant(s). However, the usual way to introduce auxiliary variables is by an "invent" step. In the latter case only the "verify" step is a formal one. The elimination of auxiliary variables corresponds to the application of a schematic transformation rule.

The approach has been applied to many other, more complex approximation algorithms besides the two examples considered in this paper, in particular, to all approximation algorithms discussed in [17]. This includes e.g., the formal development of a program implementing Chvátal's well-known approximation algorithm for set covering. (A description of this algorithm in the common informal style can be found in [3].)

When investigating the formal development and verification of approximation algorithms we have also discovered a new result viz. an approximation algorithm for the bin packing problem which possesses $\frac{3}{2}$ as absolute worst-case approximation bound and runs in linear time[2]. It follows the Best Fit idea. In contrast with the original approach, however, it works with two partial solutions P_1 and P_2 instead of one and two auxiliary bins B_1 and B_2 – one for each partial solution. Roughly speaking, it proceeds as follows. First, the objects are packed one by

---

[2] As shown in [18], there is no approximation algorithm for the bin packing problem with an absolute approximation factor smaller than $\frac{3}{2}$, unless $P = NP$. But all approximation algorithms with this – in all probability – optimal absolute approximation factor which can be found in the literature are non-linear; the best running time is $\mathcal{O}(n * \log n)$ with n as number of objects. See the overview paper [4].

one into B_1 until its capacity would be exceeded by the insertion of some object u. In this situation the contents of B_1 is inserted into P_1, the bin B_1 is cleared, u is packed into B_2, and the process starts again with the remaining objects. If, however, the insertion of u would lead to an overfilling of B_1 as well as B_2, then additionally the contents of B_2 is inserted into P_2 and u is packed into the cleared B_2. This "book-keeping" in combination with a suitable selection of the next object (based on a partition of the objects into small and large ones at the beginning of the algorithm) allows one to avoid the costly search of a bin the next object will fit in optimally. The decisive idea for proving the bound $\frac{3}{2}$ is to use a function f which yields for a bin B of P_1 the unique object whose insertion into B would lead to an overfilling.

Details of the algorithm can be found in [2], where its correctness (i.e., the feasibility of the result and the absolute approximation factor $\frac{3}{2}$) formally is verified using the assertion technique. In doing so, f is not used as an auxiliary variable but as a logical variable in assertions. It is, however, not hard to develop the algorithm in the style proposed in the current paper using an auxiliary variable that holds the function f. We believe that this development is clearer and, thus, easier to follow than the original one.

Besides their use in approximation algorithms we have investigated also some other applications of auxiliary variables, for instance, their utility for formal termination proofs and for program specialization. We illustrate the latter application by a somewhat academic example. Consider the following proof outline for a program calculating quotient and remainder of two positive integers x and y by iterated subtraction:

$$\{\, x > 0 \wedge y > 0 \,\}$$
$$q := 0; r := x;$$
$$\{\, 0 \leq r \wedge x = q \cdot y + r \,\}$$
$$\textbf{while } r \geq y \textbf{ do}$$
$$q := q + 1; r := r - y \textbf{ od}$$
$$\{\, x = q \cdot y + r \wedge 0 \leq r < y \,\}$$

If we weaken the post-condition to $r = x \bmod y$, then q becomes an auxiliary variable. Subsequently applying elimination leads to the following proof outline:

$$\{\, x > 0 \wedge y > 0 \,\}$$
$$r := x;$$
$$\{\, (\exists q : 0 \leq r \wedge x = q \cdot y + r) \,\}$$
$$\textbf{while } r \geq y \textbf{ do}$$
$$r := r - y \textbf{ od}$$
$$\{\, r = x \bmod y \,\}$$

The underlying program computes just the remainder of integer division, i.e., is a specialization of the program of the first proof outline.

Interestingly, auxiliary variables are of crucial importance for the approach of Owicki aud Gries to verification of concurrent programs: they are necessary for achieving completeness [8]. Therefore, proof rules for elimination of auxiliary variables are found in connection with that method. Rule 17 in [1, p. 193], for instance, reads as follows, where S_0 is the program obtained from program S by deleting all assignments to auxiliary variables.

$$\frac{\{p\}\ S\ \{q\}}{\{p\}\ S_0\ \{q\}}.$$

This rule is usually proved to be correct by referring to an underlying operational semantics; see, e.g., the proof of Lemma 5.17 in [1, p. 196]. We believe that our proof of the correctness of elimination on the level of predicate transformers is much more elegant. Moreover, our result is stronger. We not only show that partial correctness is preserved but validity of whole proof outlines, if auxiliary variables are removed from the programs and existentially quantified in the assertions.

Auxiliary variables can also be used for performing data refinements. In doing so, firstly, concrete variables intended to replace abstract variables are added to the program as auxiliary variables and updated in parallel with the abstract variables such that a coupling invariant is preserved. In a second step then the program is algorithmically refined in such a way that the abstract variables become auxiliary variables. Finally, the abstract variables are eliminated. Morgan [14] investigates this method in the context of predicate transformer semantics. However, he does not describe a systematic transformation for eliminating auxiliary variables from proof outlines as we do here.

To sum up: due to the experiences gained so far, we believe that auxiliary variables in combination with proof outlines and our elimination procedure are a valuable means for formal program development, verification and proof documentation.

Acknowledgments

We gratefully acknowledge discussions with F. Reuter and thank the referees for their valuable comments.

References

1. Apt K.R., Olderog E.-R.: Verification of sequential and concurrent programs. Springer (1991)
2. Berghammer R., Reuter F.: A linear approximation algorithm for bin packing with absolute approximation factor $\frac{3}{2}$. Science of Computer Programming 48, 67-80 (2003)
3. Cormen T.H., Leiserson C.E., Rivest R.L.: Introduction to algorithms. The MIT Press (1990)
4. Coffmann Jr. E.G., Garay M.R., Johnson D.S.: Approximation algorithms for bin packing: A survey. In: Hochbaum D.S. (ed.): Approximation algorithms for NP-hard problems. PWS Publishers, 46-93 (1996)

5. Cousot P.: Methods and logics for proving programs. In: van Leeuwen J. (ed.), Handbook of Theoretical Computer Science, Vol. B, pp. 841-993, Elsevier (1990)
6. Dijkstra E.W.: A discipline of programming. Prentice-Hall (1976)
7. Floyd R.W.: Assigning meanings to programs. In: Schwartz J.T. (ed.), Proc. Symp. on Applied Mathematics 19, American Mathematical Society, pp. 19-32 (1967)
8. Francez N.: Program Verification. Addison-Wesley (1992)
9. Gries D.: The science of computer programming. Springer (1981)
10. Hoare C.A.R.: An axiomatic basis of computer programming. Comm. ACM 12, pp. 576-583 (1969)
11. Hochbaum D.S. (ed.): Approximation algorithms for NP-hard problems. PWS Publishers (1996)
12. Hooman J.: Extending Hoare Logic to Real-Time. Formal Aspects of Computing 6A, 801-825 (1994)
13. Kleymann T.: Hoare logic and auxiliary variables. Formal Aspects of Computing 11, 541-566 (1999)
14. Morgan C.: Auxiliary variables in data refinement. Information Processing Letters 29, pp. 293-296 (1988)
15. Müller-Olm M.: Modular Compiler Verification. LNCS 1283, Springer-Verlag (1997)
16. Nielson H. R.: A Hoare-like Proof System for Run-time Analysis of Programs. Science of Computer Programming 9, 107–136 (1987)
17. Reuter F.: On the formal specification and derivation of approximation algorithms using assertions (in German). Diploma thesis, Inst. für Informatik und Praktische Mathematik, Universität Kiel (2000)
18. Simchi-Levi D.: New worst-case results for the bin packing problem. Naval Research Logistics 41, 479-485 (1994)
19. Wei V.K.: A lower bound for the stability number of a simple graph. Bell Lab. Tech. Memor. 81-11217-9 (1981)

Formal Reasoning about Efficient Data Structures: A Case Study in ACL2*

José Luis Ruiz-Reina, José Antonio Alonso-Jiménez,
María José Hidalgo, and Francisco Jesús Martín-Mateos

Computational Logic Group
Dept. of Computer Science and Artificial Intelligence, University of Seville
E.T.S.I. Informática, Avda. Reina Mercedes, s/n. 41012 Sevilla, Spain
http://www.cs.us.es/{~jruiz,~jalonso,~mjoseh,~fmartin}

Abstract. We describe in this paper the formal verification, using the ACL2 system, of a syntactic unification algorithm where terms are represented as directed acyclic graphs (*dags*) and these graphs are stored in a single-threaded object (*stobj*). The use of stobjs allows destructive operations on data (thus improving the performance of the algorithm), while maintaining the applicative semantics of ACL2. We intend to show how ACL2 provides an environment where execution of algorithms with efficient data structures and formal reasoning about them can be carried out.

1 Introduction

The ACL2 system includes a programming language, a logic for formal reasoning about the properties of the functions defined in the language, and a theorem prover supporting mechanized reasoning in the logic. The ACL2 programming language is an extension of an applicative subset of Common Lisp and the logic is a first-order logic with equality, without quantifiers (all the formulas are implicitly universally quantified).

Since the programming language is applicative, logical arguments about the correctness and termination of algorithms are made as they are in ordinary mathematics, without the complications incured by consideration of state. Notwithstanding, it is possible to declare some objects in the language as single-threaded objects (in the sequel, *stobjs*) and perform destructive updates on them. When an object is declared to be single-threaded, ACL2 enforces certain syntactic restrictions on its use, ensuring that in every moment only one copy of the object is needed. With these restrictions, the destructive updates are consistent with the applicative semantics of ACL2. Using stobjs we can combine efficient imperative implementations with the semantic of functional languages to reason about these implementations.

---

* This work has been supported by project TIC2000-1368-C03-02 (Ministry of Science and Technology, Spain) and FEDER funds.

In this paper we present a case study where we use ACL2 to implement and verify a unification algorithm. A standard approach in the implementation of unification is to represent terms as directed acyclic graphs (*dags* in the following), allowing some amount of structure sharing; in this way, it is not needed to build new terms during the unification process, but merely update (destructively) the graph, thus improving the performance of the algorithm. In our implementation, the dags will be stored using a stobj.

To achieve the formal proof, we follow the well-known methodology of *compositional reasoning*. As a first step, we reason about unification at a very abstract level, without entering in details related to the control of the algorithm or the data structures used. By stepwise-refinement, we finally obtain the proof of the desired properties of our concrete unification algorithm.

Another interesting point in this case study is the use of a new feature in ACL2 (the mbe feature) that associates an "executable body" with a (possibly different) "logical body". This association will be allowed by the system after proving that on the intended domain of the function, the executable body and the logical body are equal. We describe this new feature of ACL2, and explain how it can be used to improve the execution efficiency of the verified unification algorithm.

Although we will not give an introduction to ACL2, we will comment the relevant questions in passing, when needed. An excellent introduction to ACL2 is [5]. A detailed description of the system can be found in the manual, available in [6]. We will assume the reader familiar with Common Lisp. Due to the lack of space, we will not give here details about the proofs obtained and some function definitions will be omitted. We urge the interested reader to consult [11], where the complete development (with a detailed description) is available.

2   Dag Unification

We briefly review some basic concepts about (syntactic) unification, a fundamental process upon which many methods of automated deduction are based. A complete description of the theory of unification can be found in [2].

An *equation* is a pair of first-order terms, denoted as $t_1 \approx t_2$, and a *system of equations* is a finite set of equations. A substitution σ is a *solution* of $t_1 \approx t_2$ if $\sigma(t_1) = \sigma(t_2)$ and it is a solution of a system of equations S if it is a solution of every equation in S. Given two substitutions σ and δ, we say that σ is more general than δ if there exists a substitution γ such that $\delta = \gamma \circ \sigma$, where $\circ$ denotes functional composition. We say that a solution of S is a *most general solution* if it is more general than any other solution of S. Two terms t_1 and t_2 are *unifiable* if there exists a solution (called *unifier*) of the system $\{t_1 \approx t_2\}$. A *most general unifier* (*mgu* in the sequel) of t_1 and t_2 is a most general solution of that system. A *unification algorithm* is an algorithm that decides whether two given terms are unifiable, and in that case it returns a most general unifier.

Essentially, the unification algorithm we have implemented is based on the relation $\Rightarrow_u$ given by the set of transformation rules presented in Figure 1 (known

Delete:	$\{t \approx t\} \cup R; U \Rightarrow_u R; U$
Occur-check:	$\{x \approx t\} \cup R; U \Rightarrow_u \perp$ if $x \in \mathcal{V}(t)$ and $x \neq t$
Eliminate:	$\{x \approx t\} \cup R; U \Rightarrow_u \theta(R); \{x \approx t\} \cup \theta(U)$
	if $x \in X$, $x \notin \mathcal{V}(t)$ and $\theta = \{x \mapsto t\}$
Decompose:	$\{f(s_1, ..., s_n) \approx f(t_1, ..., t_n)\} \cup R; U \Rightarrow_u \{s_1 \approx t_1, ..., s_n \approx t_n\} \cup R; U$
Clash:	$\{f(s_1, ..., s_n) \approx g(t_1, ..., t_m)\} \cup R; U \Rightarrow_u \perp$ if $n \neq m$ or $f \neq g$
Orient:	$\{t \approx x\} \cup R; U \Rightarrow_u \{x \approx t\} \cup R; U$ if $x \in X$, $t \notin X$

Fig. 1. Martelli–Montanari transformation system

as the *Martelli-Montanari transformation system*). This system acts on pairs of systems of equations of the form $S; U$. Intuitively, the system S can be seen as a set of pairs of terms to be unified, and the system U as a (partially) computed unifier[1] (we say that the pair $S; U$ is a *unification problem*). The symbol $\perp$ represents unification failure. Starting with the pair of systems $S; \emptyset$, these rules can be (non-deterministically) applied iteratively, until either a pair of systems of the form $\emptyset; U$ or $\perp$ is obtained. It can be proved that this process must terminate and that S has a solution if and only if $\perp$ is not derived; in that case U is a most general solution of S. Thus, a unification algorithm can be designed choosing an strategy to apply the rules, starting with the pair of systems $\{t_1 \approx t_2\}; \emptyset$, where t_1 and t_2 are two given input terms.

In [10] we had defined and verified a unification algorithm based on this set of transformation rules, as part of an ACL2 library with formal proofs of the lattice-theoretic properties of first-order terms. In that library, terms are represented in prefix notation, using lists (except variables, which are represented by atomic objects). For example, the term $f(x, g(y), h(x))$ is represented by the list (f x (g y) (h x)). Substitutions are represented as association lists, and systems of equations as lists of dotted pairs of terms. In the sequel, this representation of terms and substitutions in prefix form, using lists, will be referred to as *prefix representation* or *prefix notation*.

Using the prefix representation, a unification algorithm may be inefficient in some situations. Consider, for example, the following standard parameterized unification problem, which we will call U_n:

$$p(x_n, \ldots, x_2, x_1) \approx p(f(x_{n-1}, x_{n-1}), \ldots, f(x_1, x_1), f(x_0, x_0))$$

A mgu of this problem is $\{x_1 \mapsto f(x_0, x_0), x_2 \mapsto f(f(x_0, x_0), f(x_0, x_0)), \ldots\}$, which maps each variable x_i to a complete binary tree of height i. This mgu can be obtained by repeatedly applying the **Eliminate** rule of $\Rightarrow_u$. If we use the prefix representation of terms, it will be necessary to reconstruct the instantiated system of equations, each time the rule is applied.

---

[1] We will identify a system of equations of the form $\{x_1 \approx t_1, \ldots, x_n \approx t_n\}$, where the x_i are variables, with the substitution $\{x_1 \mapsto t_1, \ldots, x_n \mapsto t_n\}$. If none of the x_i appear in any of the t_j, we say that the system is in *solved form*. Note that every system in solved form is a mgu of itself.

The standard approach to deal with this problem is to use *term dags* where variables are shared. For example, the following graph represents the equation $f(h(z), g(h(x), h(u))) \approx f(x, g(h(u), v))$. Nodes are labeled with function and variable symbols, and outgoing edges connect every node with dags representing its immediate subterms. We can naturally identify the root node of a term dag with the whole term. Note also that there is a certain amount of *structure sharing*, at least for the repeated variables[2]:

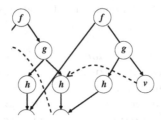

To implement a unification algorithm with this term representation, the main idea is never to build new terms but only create pointers. In particular, the **Eliminate** rule can be implemented adding a pointer linking the variable with the term to which this variable is bound; in that way no reconstruction of the term is required in the application of a substitution. In the graph above, these pointers are represented by dashed arrows. The binding for a variable can be determined by following the pointers traversing the graph depth first, from left to right. In this case, the substitution represented is $\{x \mapsto h(z), u \mapsto h(z), v \mapsto h(h(z))\}$, which is a mgu of $f(h(z), g(h(x), h(u)))$ and $f(x, g(h(u), v))$.

3   An ACL2 Implementation

The implementation described here is based on the Pascal implementation given in section 4.8 of [1]. The main difference is that instead of a record with pointers, we use a single-threaded object. This stobj is a structure called **terms-dag** with only one field: an array called **dag** (whose size can be modified dynamically). This array is used to store the unification problem in dag form:

```
(defstobj terms-dag
  (dag :type (array t (0)) :resizable t))
```

The effect of this ACL2 event is to introduce the stobj **terms-dag** and its associated recognizers, creator, accessors, updaters, and length and resize functions of the array field. In particular, given an index i (a natural number) corresponding to a cell of the **dag** array, the expressions (**dagi** i **terms-dag**) and (**update-dagi** i v **terms-dag**) access and update (with value v) respectively the i-th cell of the **dag** array. These operations are done in constant time and the

---

[2] It should be remarked that this is simply one possible representation in which only variables are shared; this is not the most compact representation, but the one that serves as the basis of the verified unification algorithm.

update is destructive. Nevertheless, from the logical point of view, the array can be thought as a list, with an applicative semantic (that is, as if in every update a new object were created) . This is possible due to the fact that in ACL2, the use of stobjs is syntactically restricted, ensuring that in every moment only one copy of the object is needed. Roughly speaking, these syntactic restrictions enforce that the only references to the stobj are done via its name (terms-dag, in this case). See [4, 6] for further information about *stobjs* in ACL2 and the restrictions on its use.

Each node in the graph is represented by a cell in the dag array of the stobj. Thus, a node in the graph can be identified with an array index. Each cell stores the label and the successors of one node, in the following way:

- If node i represents an unbound variable x, then (dagi i terms-dag) contains a dotted pair of the form (x . t).
- If node i represents a bound variable, then (dagi i terms-dag) contains an index n pointing to the root node of the term to which the variable is bound.
- If node i is the root node of a non-variable term $f(t_1, \ldots, t_n)$, then (dagi i terms-dag) is a dotted pair of the form (f . l), where l is the list of the indices corresponding to the root nodes of $t_1, \ldots, t_n$.

In this way, we can store a unification problem using the terms-dag stobj. For example, if we store the term $equ(f(h(z), g(h(x), h(u))), f(x, g(h(u), v)))$ the significant cells of the dag array are:

0	1	2	3	4	5	6
(EQU . (1 9))	(F . (2 4))	(H . (3))	(Z . T)	(G . (5 7))	(H . (6))	(X . T)
(H . (8))	(U . T)	(F . (10 11))	6	(G . (12 14))	(H . (13))	8	(V . T)
7	8	9	10	11	12	13	14

We can naturally identify an array index with the term whose root node is stored in the corresponding array cell. Taking advantage of this idea, we can define a function (called dag-transform-mm-st, figure 2) that applies one step of the transformation relation $\Rightarrow_u$ to a unification problem stored in terms-dag.

Let us precise about the behavior of dag-transform-mm-st. In addition to the stobj, this function receives as input a (non-empty) system of equations S to be unified and a partially computed substitution U. The key point here is that S and U *only contain indices* pointing to the terms stored in terms-dag. In particular, S is a list of pairs of indices, and U is a list of pairs of the form (x . n) where x is a variable symbol and n is the index of the node for which the variable is bound (we say that S is an *indices system* and U an *indices substitution*). Depending on the pair of terms pointed to by the first equation of S[3], one of the rules of $\Rightarrow_u$ is applied. The function returns a multivalue with the following components, obtained as a result of the application of one step of transformation: the resulting indices system of equations to be solved, the

---

[3] Note that the indices of the selected equation are *dereferenced* using the function dag-deref-st, which follows a chain of instantiations until it reaches an unbound variable or non-variable node.

```
(defun dag-transform-mm-st (S U terms-dag)
  (declare (xargs :stobjs terms-dag))
  (let* ((ecu (car S))
         (t1 (dag-deref-st (car ecu) terms-dag))
         (t2 (dag-deref-st (cdr ecu) terms-dag))
         (R (cdr S))
         (p1 (dagi t1 terms-dag))
         (p2 (dagi t2 terms-dag)))
    (cond
     ((= t1 t2) (mv R U t terms-dag))
     ((dag-variable-p p1)
      (if (occur-check-st t t1 t2 terms-dag)
          (mv nil nil nil terms-dag)
        (let ((terms-dag (update-dagi t1 t2 terms-dag)))
          (mv R (cons (cons (dag-symbol p1) t2) U) t terms-dag))))
     ((dag-variable-p p2)
      (mv (cons (cons t2 t1) R) U t terms-dag))
     ((not (eql (dag-symbol p1)
                (dag-symbol p2)))
      (mv nil nil nil terms-dag))
     (t (mv-let (pair-args bool)
               (pair-args (dag-args p1) (dag-args p2))
               (if bool
                   (mv (append pair-args R) U t terms-dag)
                 (mv nil nil nil terms-dag)))))))))
```

Fig. 2. One step of transformation

resulting indices substitution, a boolean (if $\bot$ is obtained, this value is `nil`) and the stobj `terms-dag`. Note that only when **Eliminate** is applied, the stobj is updated, causing the corresponding variable to point to the corresponding term.

With `dag-transform-mm-st` as its main component, we can define the unification algorithm. In short, this function, called `dag-mgu`, receives as input two terms in prefix form; after storing these terms as directed acyclic graphs in the stobj (previously resizing the `dag` array properly), it iteratively applies the function `dag-transform-mm-st` until either non-unifiability is detected or there are no more equations to be solved. In this last case, the returned substitution (in prefix form) is built from the final contents of `dag`, following the pointers of the instantiated variables. The following are two examples obtained with `dag-mgu`. Note that the function returns two values: the first one is a boolean indicating whether the terms are unifiable or not, and, in case of unifiability, the second is the mgu.

```
ACL2 !>(dag-mgu '(f (h z) (g (h x) (h u))) '(f x (g (h u) v)))
(T ((V . (H (H Z))) (U . (H Z)) (X . (H Z))))
ACL2 !>(dag-mgu '(f y x) '(f (k x) y))
(NIL NIL)
```

It is worth pointing out that the syntactic requirements needed to ensure the single-threadedness of the ACL2 functions that use stobjs are naturally met in this algorithm. See [11] for the definitions of all the auxiliary functions used. Since the ACL2 language is a subset of Common Lisp (and we have verified guards[4]), the defined algorithm can be compiled and executed in every compliant Common Lisp, with the appropriate ACL2 files loaded.

4   The Formal Properties of the Unification Algorithm

Once defined the function dag-mgu, we use the ACL2 logic and its theorem prover to formally establish that it computes the most general unifier of two terms if and only if the terms are unifiable:

```
(defthm dag-mgu-completeness
  (implies (and (term-p t1) (term-p t2)
                (equal (instance t1 sigma) (instance t2 sigma)))
           (first (dag-mgu t1 t2))))

(defthm dag-mgu-soundness
  (implies (and (term-p t1) (term-p t2)
                (first (dag-mgu t1 t2)))
           (equal (instance t1 (second (dag-mgu t1 t2)))
                  (instance t2 (second (dag-mgu t1 t2))))))

(defthm dag-mgu-most-general-solution
  (implies (and (term-p t1) (term-p t2)
                (equal (instance t1 sigma) (instance t2 sigma)))
           (subs-subst (second (dag-mgu t1 t2)) sigma)))
```

The function instance defines the application of a substitution to a term, and the predicate subs-subst defines the relation "more general than" between substitutions. The predicate term-p recognizes those ACL2 objects that represent first-order terms in prefix notation. Note that the basic theory used to state the properties is built on the terms represented in prefix notation. For a detailed description of this theory, see [10]. Also the input and the output of the function dag-mgu are terms and substitutions in prefix notation. But it has to be emphasized that internally, the main process is carried out on term dags.

The first theorem, dag-mgu-completeness, establishes that the algorithm returns t (as its first value) if the input terms are unifiable[5]. The theorem dag--mgu-soundness establishes that in that case it returns (as its second value) a unifier of both terms. Finally, the theorem dag-mgu-most-general-solution establishes that the returned substitution is more general than any other unifier of both terms. These three proved theorems constitute a formal proof of the correctness of the algorithm.

---

[4] The notion of *guard* of a function will be explained in section 6.

[5] Note that the variable sigma, although implicitly universally quantified, can be seen as existentially quantified, since it only appears in the hypothesis of the theorem.

5   Comments about the Proof

In this section, we give an overview of the proof process. To emphasize the "compositional reasoning" methodology followed, we have structured it in subsections. First we begin with the subsections describing properties of the algorithm at a more abstract level. These abstract properties can be gradually concretized to finally obtain the theorems shown in the previous section.

5.1   Reasoning about the Reduction $\Rightarrow_u$

One step of transformation of $\Rightarrow_u$ is determined by the rule applied and the equation selected. To formalize this intuitive idea in ACL2, we define $\Rightarrow_u$ by means of *operators*. In this context, an operator is a dotted pair of the form ($name$. i) where $name$ is one of the rule names in figure 1 and i is a natural number, corresponding to the i-th equation of the system. Thus, the transformation $\Rightarrow_u$ can be seen as applying one operator to a unification problem. This operator can be applied whenever the conditions of the particular rule applied are met. For example, the operator (`eliminate` . 3) can be applied to a unification problem if its third equation is of the form $x \approx t$ and x does not occur in t. The following two functions formalize this idea in ACL2:

- (`unif-legal-pr upl op`), checking the conditions needed to apply a given operator `op` to a unification problem `upl` (in prefix notation).
- (`unif-reduce-one-step-pr upl op`), returning the transformed unification problem (in prefix notation) after applying `op` to `upl`.

With this operator-based representation we proved in ACL2 the main properties of $\Rightarrow_u$. That is: a) the set of solutions of a unification problem is preserved in each step, b) if the second system of a unification problem is in solved form, then the transformed unification problem has its second system in solved form, and c) the transformation relation is terminating. These properties are more naturally proved with terms represented in prefix form, and this allows us to reuse part of the theory developed in [10] for the verification of the applicative unification algorithm.

Having proved the main properties of one-step transformations, we can easily extend these properties to finite sequences of transformations. In particular we prove that if $\{t_1 \approx t_2\}; \emptyset \stackrel{*}{\Rightarrow}_u \emptyset; \sigma$, then σ is a *mgu* of t_1 and t_2, and if $\{t_1 \approx t_2\}; \emptyset \stackrel{*}{\Rightarrow}_u \perp$, then t_1 and t_2 are not unifiable. Note that in our formalization, a sequence of transformation can be identified with a list of (legal) operators.

It is remarkable that these results do not deal with control or data structures issues: to prove the correctness of a concrete unification algorithm, it suffices to show that the actions of the algorithm can be simulated by a finite sequence of transformations w.r.t. $\Rightarrow_u$. That is the main advantage of rule-based specifications: they allow to prove the essential properties of the procedure without the burden of technical implementation issues.

5.2   Dags and Well-Formedness Conditions

In order to translate the main properties of $\Rightarrow_u$ to our implemented algorithm, we have to relate the information stored in the `terms-dag` stobj with the terms in prefix notation it may represent. In general, not every possible contents of the `dag` array represent first-order terms. The main reason is that the graph could contain cycles, and in that case, no first-order term is represented by the cells of the array.

This means that we have to define predicates to recognize the properties needed to ensure that the array contents represent a first-order term; the main of those properties is acyclicness, ensuring that the graph stored in the `dag` array is actually a dag. Some other well-formedness properties are also needed (for instance the sharing of variables).

Another important reason why these well-formedness conditions are needed has to do with the restrictions imposed by the ACL2 logic in its principle of definition: new function definitions are admitted as axioms in the logic only if there exists a measure in which the arguments of each recursive call decrease with respect to a well-founded relation, ensuring in this way that the function terminates on all inputs (and consequently no inconsistencies are introduced by new function definitions). For example, a function implementing "occur-check" (looking for the occurrence of a given variable in a term) may not terminate if the graph stored in the array contains cycles. The same happens with dereferencing or even with the function that iteratively applies `dag-transform-mm-st`. Thus, these functions require an explicit check to verify that the stobj does indeed represent an acyclic graph, ensuring their termination. We will comment more about this point in section 6.

For these reasons, we have developed a library of results about directed acyclic graphs. For example, this library contains the definition of the function `dag-p`; this function checks that a given graph (stored following the conventions described in section 3) does not contain cycles. It is implemented as a standard depth-first search algorithm, looking for cycles in the graph. The following theorems establish that a graph g verifies the `dag-p` condition if and only if does not contain cycles:

```
(defthm dag-p-soundeness
  (implies (not (dag-p g))
           (cycle-p (one-cyclic-path g) g)))
```

```
(defthm dag-p-completeness
  (implies (cycle-p p g)
           (not (dag-p g))))
```

Some other general definitions and results about dags are part of this library. See [11] for details. Having `dag-p` as its main auxiliary function, we can define a function checking the well-formedness conditions of a unification problem given in dag form: (`well-formed-upl dag-upl`) is true if and only if `dag-upl` is a three-element list such that its first element is an indices system, the second is an indices substitution and the third is an acyclic term graph with shared variables. In the following, by *well-formed dag unification problem* we mean an ACL2 object that satisfies `well-formed-upl`. Every well-formed dag unification problem has a unification problem in prefix notation associated.

One technical issue is worth pointing out. The main advantage in the reasoning about stobjs is that from the logical point of view, an array field of a stobj is like a list whose elements are the contents of the array[6]. For this, we can reason about dags as if the graph were a list, instead of an array field of a stobj. For example, the function `dag-p` above is defined on lists. In addition to simplifying the formulation of the theorems, this allows to define some properties about graphs following the usual "`car-cdr`" recursion style. This style would not be allowed if the definition were on the stobj, due to the syntactic restrictions imposed by ACL2 on stobjs. Of course, those functions that are going to be executed have to be defined on the stobj; but we define a "list version" for reasoning and then translate the main properties proved to the "stobj version" (for example, we define a function `dag-p-st` on the `terms-dag` stobj, logically equivalent to `dag-p`).

5.3   Compositional Reasoning

Since our implemented algorithm acts on terms represented as dags, we must now define in ACL2 the behavior of the relation $\Rightarrow_u$ acting on well-formed dag unification problems. As in subsection 5.1, we adopt an operator based approach. That is, we define the following two functions:

- (`unif-legal-d dag-upl op`), checking the conditions needed to apply a given operator `op` to a dag unification problem `dag-upl`. These conditions are similar, for each rule, to the conditions checked by the function `dag-transform-mm-st` (figure 2) before applying a transformation.
- (`unif-reduce-one-step-d dag-upl op`), returning the transformed dag unification problem obtained after applying `op` to `dag-upl`. These transformations are similar, for each rule, to the transformations performed by the function `dag-transform-mm-st`.

Instead of proving the properties of these transformations reasoning directly with the definitions of the above functions (which can be difficult due to the more sophisticated data structures used), we can translate the properties proved for the transformations on the prefix representation, using compositional reasoning. More precisely, denoting as UPL_p the set of unification problems represented in prefix form, and as UPL_d the set of well-formed dag unification problems, the key point is to prove that the following diagram commutes:

---

[6] For example, the accessors and updaters are logically equivalent to the list functions `nth` and `update-nth` which, respectively, access and update the contents of a list.

$$UPL_p \xrightarrow{\Rightarrow_{u,p}} UPL_p$$
$$dp \uparrow \qquad dp \uparrow$$
$$UPL_d \xrightarrow{\Rightarrow_{u,d}} UPL_d$$

Here dp is a function such that given a well-formed dag unification problem, it returns the corresponding unification problem in prefix form; $\Rightarrow_{u,p}$ and $\Rightarrow_{u,d}$ denote, respectively, the relation $\Rightarrow_u$ defined on the prefix representation and on the dag representation. The commutativity of the above diagram is formally established in ACL2 by the following theorem (the function upl-as-pair-of-systems plays the role of the function dp in the diagram):

```
(defthm conmutativity-of-diagram-prefix-dag
  (implies (and (well-formed-upl dag-upl)
                (unif-legal-d dag-upl op))
    (and (well-formed-upl (unif-reduce-one-step-d dag-upl op))
         (unif-legal-pr (upl-as-pair-of-systems dag-upl) op)
         (equal (upl-as-pair-of-systems
                    (unif-reduce-one-step-d dag-upl op))
                (unif-reduce-one-step-pr
                    (upl-as-pair-of-systems dag-upl) op)))))
```

This theorem establishes that:

- The well-formedness property of dag unification problems is preserved by the transformation rules.
- If the conditions needed to apply a rule to a well-formed dag unification problem are met, then the conditions required to apply the same rule to the corresponding unification problem in prefix form are also met.
- In that case, the transformed unification problem obtained applying the rule to the prefix representation is the same as the unification problem in prefix form corresponding to the dag unification problem obtained applying the same rule to the dag representation.

These properties allow us to easily translate the main properties described in subsection 5.1 to this more efficient data structure. In particular, it can be proved that we can obtain a most general unifier of two terms by exhaustively applying the rules of transformation on its dag representation.

5.4   Final Steps

Now that we have all the main pieces needed for the verification of the algorithm, we proceed as follows:

- First, we define a function that, given two terms in prefix form, returns the corresponding dag unification problem. We must prove that this dag unification problem is well-formed. This result turned out to be one of the hardest part of all the verification process.

- Second, we show that the transformations performed by our unification algorithm can be simulated by a sequence of transformations of $\Rightarrow_{u,d}$. That is, we deal with the specific control (or selection strategy) of the algorithm. In our case, we always select the first equation, but any other strategy could work. In terms of operators, this means that we have to explicitly give a sequence of operators that, iteratively applied to the initial dag unification problem, obtains the same final dag unification problem as the implemented algorithm. Note that even though operators are used for defining the transformation relation, these are an intermediate concept used for reasoning, but not used by the unification algorithm.

- Finally, since the above properties are established for the "dag-list version" of the algorithm, we translate the properties to the executable "dag-stobj version", finally proving the formal properties presented in section 4.

5.5 Quantifying the Proof Effort

The ACL2 theorem prover supports mechanized reasoning in the ACL2 logic, being particularly well-suited for obtaining automated proofs based on induction and simplification. The prover is automatic in the sense that once `defthm` is invoked, the user can no longer interact with the system. However, in a deeper sense, the system is interactive: usually, when proving non-trivial theorems, the user has to guide the prover by adding lemmas and definitions (used in subsequent proofs as rewrite rules during the simplification process), or giving some hints to the `defthm` command, such as the scheme for a induction proof.

A typical ACL2 proof effort consists of formalizing the problem in the logic and helping the prover to find a preconceived proof by means of a suitable set of rewrite rules. These rules can be found by inspecting the failed proofs: when the proof attempt deviates from the expected proof, usually a lemma is needed to deal with that part of the proof by simplification. This methodology produces a collection of lemmas (and definitions) leading the prover to the proof of the main result. Some of these lemmas are interesting by themselves and can be reused later in other parts of the development. This way of interacting with the system is called "The Method" by the authors of the system and it is explained in detail in [5]. We followed "The Method" in this case study.

The table below shows some quantitative information about the proof effort, the number of definitions and theorems needed during the different stages of the verification process (we have not included in the table data of the basic theory about first-order terms):

Phase	Definitions	Theorems
Properties on the prefix representation	24	81
Acyclic graphs	37	95
Diagram commutativity	39	66
Storing the initial terms in the graph	34	208
Properties of the implemented algorithm	43	76
Total	177	703

These numbers may give an idea of the complexity of the formalized theories and the degree of automation of the proofs obtained. We should say that most of the lemmas needed during the first phase were already proved in [10]. It is also remarkable (and somewhat surprising) the number of theorems needed to prove the properties of a function that stores the initial terms as directed acyclic graphs.

6 Execution of the Algorithm

As we have already said, ACL2 is a logic of total functions. That is, a proof of the termination of the function on all possible inputs is required for the definition to be accepted by the prover. In some cases, this means that a definition must include in its body an explicit check on their arguments, ensuring its termination. This check may seriously affect the execution performance of the function. Until the current ACL2 version 2.7, this was a weakness of the system that appeared when dealing with functions that only terminate on their intended domain, but not for every possible input. In the next ACL2 release, the new mbe feature (which stands for "must be equal") overcomes that weakness: it allows to assign to a function an alternate "executable body" to that provided for the logic.

We use mbe in this work, avoiding (for execution) the expensive well-formed-ness checks that are needed in the logical definitions of some of the functions of the dag unification algorithm. We explain this with an example. The following is the definition of the function dag-solve-upl-st, which iteratively applies steps of transformation to a given unification problem, until either there are no equations to be solved or unsolvability is detected:

```
(defun dag-solve-upl-st (S U bool terms-dag)
  (declare
   (xargs :stobjs terms-dag
          :guard (well-formed-upl-st S U terms-dag)
          ...)
  (MBE
   :logic
   (if (well-formed-upl-st S U terms-dag)
       (if (or (not bool) (endp S))
           (mv S U bool terms-dag)
         (mv-let (S1 U1 bool1 terms-dag)
                 (dag-transform-mm-st S U terms-dag)
                 (dag-solve-upl-st S1 U1 bool1 terms-dag)))
     (mv nil nil nil terms-dag))
   :exec
   (if (or (not bool) (endp S))
       (mv S U bool terms-dag)
     (mv-let (S1 U1 bool1 terms-dag)
             (dag-transform-mm-st S U terms-dag)
             (dag-solve-upl-st S1 U1 bool1 terms-dag)))))
```

This **defun** defines the function in the logic using the body given by the :**logic** key argument, but when the function is evaluated on arguments of its intended domain (this intended domain is given by the :**guard** key) then the body given by the :**exec** key argument is used. The logical body needs an explicit check performed by the function **well-formed-upl-st**[7], in order to ensure its termination (which it is not trivial to prove). This condition is expensive, since acyclicness is checked; moreover, if we use this logic body for execution, this expensive check would be evaluated *in every recursive call*, making execution of the function impractical.

From the logical point of view (mbe :**logic** *logicbody* :**exec** *execbody*) is equal to *logicbody*, so *execbody* is ignored for reasoning. But when the function is evaluated on its intended domain, the underlying Common Lisp uses the (hopefully) more efficient *execbody*. The "intended domain" is specified in ACL2 by its *guard*, and the proof obligations generated by the guard verification mechanism ensure the soundness of using the executable body instead of the logic body.

Guards in ACL2 are used to specify the intended domain of a function. Although this specification is actually ignored by the logic, the guard verification mechanism allows to evaluate the function directly in Common Lisp. If the guards of a function are verified, then it is ensured that when the function is evaluated on arguments satisfying its guard, then all subsequent function calls during that evaluation will be on arguments satisfying the guard of the called function. The proof obligations generated by the guard verification mechanism ensure this property. Since the primitive Common Lisp functions of ACL2 has guards consistent with the Common Lisp specification, an ACL2 function with its guards verified is Common Lisp compliant and can be evaluated, on arguments satisfying its guard, directly in the underlying Common Lisp.

The guard of the function **mbe** specifies that its two arguments are equal. Thus, when a function that uses **mbe** has its guard verified, then it is sound to use the executable body for execution, whenever the input arguments are in the intended domain specified by the guard.

In addition to the above function, some of the auxiliary functions used by the implemented algorithm **dag-mgu** are defined in a similar way, using **mbe** (for example, occur checking or dereferencing). Since we have verified the guards of **dag-mgu** (and therefore the guards of all the functions used by the algorithm), all the expensive well-formedness checks are ignored when calling the function **dag-mgu** on two ACL2 objects representing terms in prefix form (the guard of **dag-mgu**). Note that the guard of the main top level function is very simple, and since guards are verified, it is not needed to evaluate the more expensive guards of its auxiliary functions in subsequent calls.

We have tested the verified unification algorithm using the parameterized unification problem U_n (presented in section 2). We compare its performance with the applicative algorithm defined in [10]. The problem U_n is particularly well suited for the dag unification algorithm, since it is already in *dag solved*

---

[7] This function is the "dag-stobj version" of the function **well-formed-upl** described in subsection 5.2.

form. For that reason we also test the algorithm on the problem U_n^{-1}, where the equations of U_n are processed in reverse order. The following table summarizes the results obtained[8]:

	Pref. U_n		Dag U_n		Pref. U_n^{-1}		Dag U_n^{-1}		Quadratic U_n^{-1}	
n	Time	Space	Time	Space	Time	Space	Time	Space	Time	Space
20	19	376839	ϵ	3	7	49160	4	10	ϵ	20
22	78	1638409	ϵ	4	21	196654	18	11	ϵ	22
24	–	–	ϵ	5	90	786444	72	12	ϵ	26
1000	–	–	0.2	151	–	–	–	–	15	195
5000	–	–	2	781	–	–	–	–	61	945

It can be observed that the space complexity is much better in the dag implementation than in the applicative implementation in all cases. The time performance it is also much better with U_n, and about 25% faster with U_n^{-1}. Note that the definition of the algorithm using mbe is essential for obtaining this time performance, since, as we have said, the logical definition of the algorithm is impractical for execution.

The column labeled Dag U_n^{-1} reveals that the implemented algorithm has still exponential time complexity. The problem is that some operations, like the occur check, may traverse terms exponential in size. Nevertheless, the implemented algorithm is the most often used in practice, since that exponential behavior is not usual. Anyway, we have implemented a quadratic version of the dag unification algorithm, introducing a few technical modifications to the verified algorithm. We also include in the table the tests for this improved version, which it is much faster, being able to solve U_n^{-1} for $n = 5000$. For the moment, this quadratic implementation is not formally verified.

7   Conclusions

We have presented a case study in ACL2, where we verify a unification algorithm acting on term dags, implemented using ACL2 single-threaded objects. We urge the interested reader to consult the complete development in [11]. The main features of this case study are:

- The formal verification of an executable algorithm that uses efficient data structures.
- The methodology used: from a rule-based specification of the algorithm, we prove its more abstract properties. The final properties of the algorithm can be seen as an optimization process, using compositional reasoning.
- The use of the new mbe feature of ACL2, that permits to associate to a function some "executable body" that can be different from its "logical body".

---

[8] Tested on an AMD© 2200XP processor, with 512Mb RAM. The data are obtained with the function time of Clisp. The dash denotes that either an output is not obtained in reasonable time, or that a stack overflow occurs. ϵ stands for a quantity less than 0.01. Numbers bigger than 1 are rounded to the nearest integer.

The intuitive idea that algorithms employing more complex data structures or more sophisticated control structures require more effort in verification is supported by the table of subsection 5.5. These data contrast with the effort needed in the verification of the same algorithm using a prefix representation of terms [10]. In that work, we needed 19 definitions and 129 theorems, and in this case we needed 177 definitions and 703 theorems. Anyway, this additional verification effort has resulted in the development of a number of ACL2 files that could be used in other formalizations (for example, the theory about directed acyclic graphs).

As for related works, unification algorithms have been the center of several formalizations. In particular, formal proofs of the correctness of a unification algorithm have been given in LCF [8], Coq [9] and ALF [3]. Although these works are related to ours, the logic used is quite different and, more important, their main concern is not efficiency or the data structures used.

Other related work is done by Mehta and Nipkow [7], who have recently developed in Isabelle/HOL a general framework for reasoning about programs that use pointers. As a non-trivial case study, they present a proof of the correctness of the Schorr–Waite graph marking algorithm. This work is more general than ours, since all the reasoning about pointers that we do is especifically devoted to the results needed by the algorithm. Moreover, the logics used are different: in [7], a Hoare logic for pointer programs is embedded in Isabelle/HOL, whereas we are using the ACL2 logic for reasoning about ACL2 functions that can be directly executed in any compliant Common Lisp. Nevertheless, some of the techniques used in [7] are similar to ours: for example, what they call abstraction (mapping low level structures in the heap to higher level concepts) is similar to what we do when we first reason about the main properties of the algorithm using the prefix representation of terms (a higher level representation) and then we translate them to the algorithm that uses dags (a lower level representation).

As for further work, we already pointed out at the end of subsection 6 that we can introduce some technical improvements in order to make the verified algorithm run in quadratic time. We also plan to verify this improved algorithm.

Finally, note that although our main concern is an efficient and formally verified algorithm, we do not prove theorems about the efficiency of the algorithm. Although reasoning about complexity of algorithms in the ACL2 logic is (in principle) possible, we think that it could be much more difficult than reasoning about the correctness of the algorithm, mainly due to the need of formalizing the "big-O notation" (and its asymptotic character) in the ACL2 logic.

Acknowledgments

Part of this work was done during a visit of the first author to the Computer Science Department of the University of Texas at Austin. We would like to thank the ACL2 group in Austin, especially to J Moore and Matt Kaufmann, for their support, and for introducing mbe in ACL2.

References

1. BAADER, F. AND NIPKOW, T. *Term Rewriting and All That.* Cambridge University Press, 1998.
2. BAADER, F. AND SNYDER, W. Unification theory. *Handbook of Automated Reasoning*, Elsevier Science Publishers, 2001.
3. BOVE, A. Programming in Martin-Lf Type Theory: Unification - A non-trivial Example. *Licentiate Thesis*, Department of Computer Science, Chalmers University of Technology, 1999.
4. BOYER R.S. AND MOORE J S. Single-threaded objects in ACL2. In *Practical Aspects of Declarative Languages*, LNCS 2257, pages 9–27, Springer–Verlag, 2002.
5. KAUFMANN, M., MANOLIOS, P. AND MOORE, J S. *Computer-Aided Reasoning: An Approach.* Kluwer Academic Publishers, 2000.
6. KAUFMANN, M. AND MOORE, J S. ACL2 Version 2.7, 2002.
   Homepage: `http://www.cs.utexas.edu/users/moore/acl2/`
7. MEHTA, F. AND NIPKOW, T. Proving Pointer Programs in Higher-Order Logic . to be presented at *CADE-19*, 2003.
8. PAULSON, L. Verifying the unification algorithm in LCF. *Science of Computer Programming*, 5, 1985.
9. ROUYER, J. Dveloppement de l'algorithme d'unification dans le calcul des constructions avec types inductifs. Tech. Rep. 1795, INRIA Lorraine, 1992 (in french).
10. RUIZ–REINA, J.L., ALONSO, J.A., HIDALGO, M.J. AND MARTÍN, F.J. A theory about first–order terms in ACL2 In *Third ACL2 Workshop*, Grenoble, 2002.
11. RUIZ–REINA, J.L., ALONSO, J.A., HIDALGO, M.J. AND MARTÍN, F.J. A verified dag unification algorithm in ACL2, 2002.
    Available at `http://www.cs.us.es/~jruiz/unificacion-dag`

A Program Transformation
for Backwards Analysis of Logic Programs

John P. Gallagher[*]

Roskilde University, Computer Science, Building 42.1
DK-4000 Roskilde, Denmark
jpg@ruc.dk

Abstract. The input to backwards analysis is a program together with properties that are required to hold at given program points. The purpose of the analysis is to derive initial goals or pre-conditions that guarantee that, when the program is executed, the given properties hold. The solution for logic programs presented here is based on a transformation of the input program, which makes explicit the dependencies of the given program points on the initial goals. The transformation is derived from the *resultants* semantics of logic programs. The transformed program is then analysed using a standard abstract interpretation. The required pre-conditions on initial goals can be deduced from the analysis results without a further fixpoint computation. For the modes backwards analysis problem, this approach gives the same results as previous work, but requires only a standard abstract interpretation framework and no special properties of the abstract domain.

1 Introduction

The input to backwards analysis is a program together with properties that are required to hold at given program points. The purpose of the analysis is to derive initial goals or pre-conditions that guarantee that, when the program is executed, the given properties hold. Discussion of the motivation for backwards analysis is given by King and Lu [KL02] and Genaim and Codish [GC01]. For example, in a logic program, it is useful to know which instantiation modes of goals will definitely not produce run-time instantiation errors caused by calls to built-in predicates with insufficiently instantiated arguments [KL02], and which goals are sufficiently instantiated to ensure termination [GC01]. By contrast, program analysis frameworks usually start with given goals, and derive properties that hold at various program points, when those goals are executed.

An essential aspect of static analysis using abstractions or approximations is that the analysis results are *safe*. Backwards analysis algorithms have distinctive characteristics in this regard. The final result, namely (a description of) the set of initial goals that guarantee the establishment of the given properties, should be an *under* approximation of the actual set of goals that satisfy the requirements. Analyses usually yield an *over* approximation, this has led investigators to develop special abstract interpretations that give an under approximation.

---

[*] Supported by European Framework 5 Project ASAP (IST-2001-38059).

M. Bruynooghe (Ed.): LOPSTR 2004, LNCS 3018, pp. 92–105, 2004.

In this paper we develop a method for using standard abstraction and over-approximation techniques, and still obtain valid results for backwards analysis. This is achieved by analysing not the original program, but rather a transformed program that makes explicit the dependencies between the given properties and initial goals.

The method is presented in terms of (constraint) logic programs. The essential idea is to transform a given program P into another program (or rather meta-program) whose semantics is a *dependency* relation $\langle A, B \rangle$, where B is a call at some specified program point, and A is an atomic goal for P. Analysis of this transformed program yields an over-approximation of the set of dependencies between A and B, which can then be examined to find goals A that guarantee some required property of B.

1.1   Making Derivations Observable

The transformation to be presented in Section 2 makes explicit the dependencies of program points on initial goals. The transformation can be viewed as the implementation of a more expressive semantics than usual. Standard semantics (such as least Herbrand models, c-semantics, s-semantics, call and success patterns for atomic goals, and so on) do not record explicitly the relationship between initial goals and specific program points. The *resultants semantics* [GLM96,GG94] provides a sufficiently expressive framework.

Resultants Semantics. A *resultant* is a formula $Q_1 \leftarrow Q_2$ where Q_1, Q_2 are conjunctions of atoms[1]. If Q_1 is an atom the resultant is a *clause*. Variables occurring in Q_2 but not in Q_1 are implicitly existentially quantified. All other variables are free in the resultant.

Definition 1. $\mathcal{O}_L(P)$
 Given a definite program P, the resultants semantics $\mathcal{O}_L(P)$ is the set of all resultants[2] $p(\bar{X})\theta \leftarrow R$ such that $p(\bar{X})$ is a "most general" atom (that is, an atom of the form $p(x_1, \ldots, x_n)$ where $x_1, \ldots, x_n$ are distinct variables) for some predicate in P, and $\leftarrow p(\bar{X}), \ldots, \leftarrow R$ is an SLD- derivation (with a computation rule selecting the leftmost atom) of $P \cup \{\leftarrow p(\bar{X})\}$ with computed answer θ. Such a resultant represents a partial computation of the goal $p(\bar{X})$. We include the zero-length derivations of form $p(\bar{X}) \leftarrow p(\bar{X})$.

From here on the leftmost computation rule is assumed and the subscript L in $\mathcal{O}_L(P)$ is omitted. There is also a fixpoint definition of $\mathcal{O}(P)$; abstract interpretation of the resultants and related semantics was considered in [CLM01].

Other standard semantics can be derived as abstractions of $\mathcal{O}(P)$. The subset of elements $p(\bar{X})\theta \leftarrow R \in \mathcal{O}(P)$ where $R = \mathsf{true}$ is isomorphic to the s-semantics

---

[1] Standard terminology and notation for logic programming is used [Llo87].
[2] Strictly speaking $\mathcal{O}_L(P)$ contains equivalence classes of resultants with respect to variable renaming, rather than resultants themselves.

[BGLM94], from which in turn the c-semantics [Cla79] and the least Herbrand model [Llo87] can be derived by computing all instances and ground instances respectively. Calls generated by a given goal can also be derived from $\mathcal{O}(P)$. The set of calls that arise from a given atomic goal A in a leftmost SLD derivation is given by the set $\text{calls}(P, A) = \{B_1\theta \mid H \leftarrow B_1, \ldots, B_n \in \mathcal{O}(P), \text{mgu}(A, H) = \theta\}$. We assume as usual that A is standardised apart from the elements of $\mathcal{O}(P)$.

1.2   Backwards Analysis Based on the Resultants Semantics

The possibility of using the resultants semantics for backwards analysis does not seem to have been considered previously. The relation $B \in \text{calls}(P, A)$ can be read backwards; given B, A is a goal that invokes a call B.

We can capture the essential information about the dependencies between calls and goals using the *downwards closure* of $\mathcal{O}(P)$, denoted $\mathcal{O}^+(P)$. That is, $\mathcal{O}^+(P)$ is $\mathcal{O}(P)$ extended with all the instances obtained by substitutions for free variables, which are variables occurring in the resultants' heads. Then define a relation $\mathcal{D}$, called the *goal dependency* relation for P.

$$\mathcal{D}(A, B) \equiv (A \leftarrow B, \ldots, B_n \in \mathcal{O}^+(P))$$

The goal dependency relation for a program is closely related to the binary clause semantics of Codish and Taboch [CT99] (but is downwards closed with respect to the free variables).

Proposition 1. *Let P be a program, and $\mathcal{D}$ be the goal dependency relation for P. Then (i) if $\mathcal{D}(A, B)$ then $B \in \text{calls}(P, A)$, and (ii) for all goals A and $B \in \text{calls}(P, A)$, there exists a substitution σ such that $\mathcal{D}(A\sigma, B)$.*

Proof. (i). If $\mathcal{D}(A, B)$ then $\mathcal{O}(P)$ contains $A' \leftarrow B'_1, \ldots, B'_n$ such that $A \leftarrow B, \ldots, B_n$ is an instance obtained by a substitution, say θ, for the variables in A'. Hence $\text{mgu}(A, A') = \theta$ and $B = B'_1\theta$, and so $B \in \text{calls}(P, A)$ (ii) If $B \in \text{calls}(P, A)$ then $\mathcal{O}(P)$ contains $A' \leftarrow B'_1, \ldots, B'_n$, $\text{mgu}(A, A') = \sigma$ and $B = B'_1\sigma$. The instance $A\sigma \leftarrow B, \ldots, B'_n\sigma$ is thus contained in the downwards closure $\mathcal{O}^+(P)$ and hence $\mathcal{D}(A\sigma, B)$ holds.

Definition 2. *Let P be a program and $\mathcal{D}$ be the goal dependency relation for P. Let Θ and Φ be properties of atoms; that is, for every atom A, $\Theta(A)$ and $\Phi(A)$ are either true or false. We say that a call-dependency $\Theta \rightarrow \Phi$ follows from $\mathcal{D}$ if there does not exist $\mathcal{D}(A, B)$ such that $\Theta(A) \wedge \neg\Phi(B)$.*

Definition 3. *A property Θ is called downwards closed if, whenever $\Theta(A)$ holds, $\Theta(A\varphi)$ holds for all substitutions φ.*

Proposition 2. *Let P be a program, and $\mathcal{D}$ be the goal dependency relation for P. Suppose $\Theta \rightarrow \Phi$ follows from $\mathcal{D}$, and that Θ is a downwards closed property. Then for all goals A, and $B \in \text{calls}(P, A)$, $\Theta(A) \rightarrow \Phi(B)$.*

Proof. Let A be a goal, such that $\Theta(A)$ holds. For all $B \in \text{calls}(P, A)$, we must establish that $\Phi(B)$ holds. For each such B there exists some instance $A\sigma$ such that $\mathcal{D}(A\sigma, B)$ by Proposition 1. $\Theta(A\sigma)$ holds since Θ is a downwards closed property. Hence $\Phi(B)$ holds since $\Theta \rightarrow \Phi$ follows from $\mathcal{D}$.

Proposition 2 establishes that we can use the goal dependency relation of a program in order to establish dependencies between goals and calls, provided that the properties on goals are downwards closed. The next proposition shows that we can use over-approximations of the goal dependency relation to deduce dependencies.

Proposition 3. *Let S be a goal dependency relation and let S' be a relation including S. Then, if the call-dependency $\Theta \to \Phi$ follows from S', it also follows from S.*

Proof. Suppose that $\Theta \to \Phi$ follows from S'. Then there does not exist $\mathcal{D}(A, B) \in S'$ such that $\Theta(A) \wedge \neg\Phi(B)$. Hence such a pair does not exist in S either, and so $\Theta \to \Phi$ follows from S.

We can also explain how our approach achieves the "under-approximations" of the conditions on initial goals discussed earlier. Given a call property Φ, suppose $\Theta \to \Phi$ follows from the goal dependency relation $\mathcal{D}$. In an over-approximation of $\mathcal{D}$, we will in general be able to establish dependencies $\Theta' \to \Phi$, such that $\Theta' \to \Theta$. Put another way, the larger the approximation is, the more chance there is of finding a counterexample $\mathcal{D}(A, B)$ such that $\Theta(A) \wedge \neg\Phi(B)$. The greater the over-approximation, the more restrictive are the properties Θ' for which $\Theta' \to \Phi$ can be shown.

The backwards analysis method can now be summarised in the following way. The concrete semantics on which we define properties is the goal dependency relation $\mathcal{D}$ for a given program. Given a program P we define a transformed program containing a predicate whose logical consequences contain the goal dependency relation $\mathcal{D}$. Using abstract interpretation of the transformed program, we compute approximations of $\mathcal{D}$, which can be used to establish dependencies between goals and calls, as proved in Propositions 2 and 3.

We shall also define an even more refined transformed program, whose semantics is restricted to a subset of the goal dependency relation $\mathcal{D}$, containing tuples $\mathcal{D}(A, B)$ where B is a call occurring at one of a specified set of program points.

Basing our approach on a downwards closed semantics allows a straightforward approach to implementation, using for example the framework presented in [GBS95]. Our analyses are based on the c-semantics [Cla79], which is the set of atomic logical consequences of a program. Given a program P, let $\mathcal{C}(P)$ be the c-semantics of P. As shown in [GBS95], $\mathcal{C}(P)$ can be given a least fixpoint form.

2 The Program Transformation

First, the resultants semantics is formulated as a program transformation.

2.1 Resultants Semantics by Program Transformation

A resultant $A \leftarrow Q$ is represented as a meta-predicate $\mathcal{R}(A, Q)$. Let P be a program. For each program clause $H \leftarrow D_1, \ldots, D_n$ $(n > 0)$ in P we produce n clauses.

$$\mathcal{R}(H, (Q, D_2, \ldots, D_n)) \leftarrow \mathcal{R}(D_1, Q)$$
$$\mathcal{R}(H, (Q, D_3, \ldots, D_n)) \leftarrow D_1, \mathcal{R}(D_2, Q)$$
$$\ldots$$
$$\mathcal{R}(H, Q) \leftarrow D_1, \ldots, D_{n-1}, \mathcal{R}(D_n, Q)$$

For each unit clause $H \leftarrow$ true produce a single clause $\mathcal{R}(H, \text{true}) \leftarrow$ true. Finally, for each predicate p we add a clause $\mathcal{R}(p(\bar{x}), p(\bar{x}))$ where $p(\bar{x})$ is a most general call to p.

In the bodies of the clauses for $\mathcal{R}$ there are calls to the original program atoms D_1, D_2 and so on, so it is assumed that the clauses for P are included in the transformed program. These object program calls could have been written $\mathcal{R}(D_1, \text{true}), \mathcal{R}(D_2, \text{true})$ respectively since A is in the minimal model of the program iff there is a ground instance of a resultant $A \leftarrow$ true in the resultants semantics of the program. If this modification were made, the transformation corresponds closely to the fixpoint definition of the resultants semantics [GLM96]. We denote by Res_P the collection of clauses defining the predicate $\mathcal{R}$ as shown above, together with P itself.

Example 1. Let P be the "naive reverse" program. The transformed program is shown in Figure 1. The meta-predicate $\mathcal{R}$ is denoted res in the program.

```
res(rev([],[]),true) :- true.                rev([],[]).
res(rev([X|Xs],Zs),(Q,app(Ys,[X],Zs))) :-    rev([X|Xs],Zs) :-
   res(rev(Xs,Ys),Q).                            rev(Xs,Ys),
res(rev([X|Xs],Zs),Q) :-                         app(Ys,[X],Zs).
   rev(Xs,Ys), res(app(Ys,[X],Zs),Q).        app([],Ys,Ys).
res(app([],Ys,Ys),true) :- true.             app([X|Xs],Ys,[X|Zs]) :-
res(app([X|Xs],Ys,[X|Zs]),Q) :-                 app(Xs,Ys,Zs).
   res(app(Xs,Ys,Zs),Q).
res(rev(X,Y),rev(X,Y)) :- true.
res(app(X,Y,Z),app(X,Y,Z)) :- true.
```

Fig. 1. Res_P where P is the naive reverse program

Proposition 4. *Let P be a program. Then for all resultants $A \leftarrow G \in \mathcal{O}^+(P)$, $\mathcal{R}(A, G) \in \mathcal{C}(\text{Res}_P)$.*

Proof. (Outline). A derivation corresponding to a resultant can be represented as an AND-OR proof tree. The proof is by induction on the depth of AND-OR trees.

Note that $\mathcal{C}(\text{Res}_P)$ contains more instances of resultants than does $\mathcal{O}^+(P)$. Specifically, local variables in resultants are also instantiated, as well as head variables. The transformed program thus represents an approximation of the dependency relation. In practice this is not a loss in precision, since clearly no dependencies will be derived between local variables in resultants and head variables.

2.2   From Resultants to Binary Clauses

The program above can be modified to yield (the downwards closure of) binary clauses [CT99]. Only the first call in the right-hand-side of the resultants is recorded, rather than the whole resultant. A resultant $A_1 \leftarrow A_2$ in which both A_1 and A_2 are atoms is called a *binary clause*. In the binary clause semantics, a resultant $A \leftarrow B_1, \ldots, B_n$ is abstracted to $A \leftarrow B_1$.

The transformed program corresponding to the binary clauses is as follows. A meta-predicate $\mathcal{B}(A_1, A_2)$ represents the binary resultant $A_1 \leftarrow A_2$.

$$\mathcal{B}(H, Q) \leftarrow \mathcal{B}(D_1, Q).$$
$$\mathcal{B}(H, Q) \leftarrow D_1, \mathcal{B}(D_2, Q).$$
$$\cdots$$
$$\mathcal{B}(H, Q) \leftarrow D_1, \ldots, D_{n-1}, \mathcal{B}(D_n, Q).$$

As before, we add a clause $\mathcal{B}(p(\bar{x}), p(\bar{x}))$ for each predicate p where $p(\bar{x})$ is a most general atom for p. Note that a unit clause in P produces no clauses for $\mathcal{B}$. Let Bin_P be the transformed program consisting of P together with the clauses defining the predicate $\mathcal{B}$ as shown above.

Example 2. Let P be the "naive reverse" program. The transformed program is shown in Figure 2. The meta-predicate $\mathcal{B}$ is denoted bin in the program.

```
bin(rev([X|Xs],Zs),Q) :-          rev([],[]).
  bin(rev(Xs,Ys),Q).               rev([X|Xs],Zs) :-
bin(rev([X|Xs],Zs),Q) :-            rev(Xs,Ys),
  rev(Xs,Ys), bin(app(Ys,[X],Zs),Q).    app(Ys,[X],Zs).
bin(app([X|Xs],Ys,[X|Zs]),Q) :-    app([],Ys,Ys).
  bin(app(Xs,Ys,Zs),Q).            app([X|Xs],Ys,[X|Zs]) :-
bin(rev(X,Y),rev(X,Y)) :- true.      app(Xs,Ys,Zs).
bin(app(X,Y,Z),app(X,Y,Z)) :- true.
```

Fig. 2. Bin_P where P is the naive reverse program

Proposition 5. *Let P be a program. Then for all resultants $A \leftarrow B_1, \ldots, B_n \in \mathcal{O}^+(P)$, $\mathcal{B}(A, B_1) \in \mathcal{C}(\mathsf{Bin}_P)$.*

$\mathcal{C}(\mathsf{Bin}_P)$ is an over approximation of the goal dependency relation for P. As was the case for the resultants program Res_P, the downwards closure of local variables is included in the relation $\mathcal{B}$ in $\mathcal{C}(\mathsf{Bin}_P)$.

2.3   Transforming with Respect to Program Points

Next, a further simplification is made, when calls at specified program points are to be observed, rather than all calls. We may if required observe only a specific argument of a call at some program point. A meta-predicate $\mathsf{Dep}(A_1, A_2)$ is defined, whose meaning is that there is a clause $A_1 \leftarrow A_2$ in the binary clause semantics, and A_2 is a call, or some argument of a call, at one of the specified program points to be observed.

Let $H \leftarrow B_1, \ldots, B_j, \ldots, B_n$ be a clause in a program P. Suppose that we wish to observe calls to B_j in this clause body, and determine some property of initial goals which establish some property of B_j. In the semantics, only the binary clauses of the form $A \leftarrow B_j$ are to be observed: no other calls other than those to B_j need be recorded.

To achieve this, we simply modify the binary clause transformation shown above. Specifically, instead of the clauses of form $\mathcal{B}(p(\bar{x}), p(\bar{x}))$, we create base case clauses for the given program points.

For instance, for the clause $H \leftarrow D_1, \ldots, D_j, \ldots, D_n$ with one point D_j to be observed, the following clauses for Dep are generated.

$$\mathsf{Dep}(H, D_j) \leftarrow D_1 \ldots, D_{j-1} \quad \mathsf{Dep}(H, Q) \leftarrow \mathsf{Dep}(D_1, Q).$$
$$\mathsf{Dep}(H, Q) \leftarrow D_1, \mathsf{Dep}(D_2, Q).$$
$$\ldots$$
$$\mathsf{Dep}(H, Q) \leftarrow D_1, \ldots, D_{n-1}, \mathsf{Dep}(D_n, Q).$$

For each body atom to be observed, we add one clause similar to the one for D_j above. We can see that the only atoms that can appear in the second argument of Dep are instances of D_j. Denote by Dep_P the transformed program consisting of P together with the clauses defining Dep as shown above.

Proposition 6. *Let P be a program, and $\{D_{j_1}, \ldots, D_{j_k}\}$ be a set of body atoms from clauses in P. Let Dep_P be the transformed program consisting of P together with the clauses defining Dep as shown above. Then for all resultants $A \leftarrow D_{j_i}, \ldots \in \mathcal{O}^+(P)$, where D_{j_i} is an instance of one of the specified atoms, $\mathsf{Dep}(A, D_{j_i}) \in \mathcal{C}(\mathsf{Dep}_P)$.*

The transformation can be refined (with respect to computational efficiency) by having a separate Dep predicate corresponding to each predicate in P. That is, each occurrence of $\mathsf{Dep}(p(\bar{t}), Q)$ in the transformed program is replaced by $\mathsf{Dep}_p(\bar{t}, Q)$.

The transformation can be varied by observing in the second argument of Dep not the actual call, but simply one or more variables from the call. This is illustrated in the next example.

Example 3. Let P be the "naive reverse" program. Suppose the call that we wish to observe is app(Ys, [X], Zs) in the recursive clause for rev as shown in Figure 3. For example, we suppose that we require that integer(X) holds whenever this call is encountered. We need observe only the variable X in app(Ys, [X], Zs). However, the transformation is independent of the actual property. The transformed program, shown in Figure 3, consists of P together with the clauses defining drev/2 and dapp/3 (representing the meta-predicates Dep_{rev} and Dep_{app}). In place of the call app(Ys, [X], Zs) in the final argument, we observe only the variable X.

Next, we apply standard static analysis techniques to the transformed program.

```
drev([X|Xs],Zs,X) :-           rev([],[]).
  rev(Xs,Ys).                  rev([X|Xs],Zs) :-
drev([X|Xs],Zs,Q) :-             rev(Xs,Ys),app(Ys,[X],Zs).
  drev(Xs,Ys,Q).               app([],Ys,Ys).
drev([X|Xs],Zs,Q) :-           app([X|Xs],Ys,[X|Zs]) :-
  rev(Xs,Ys), dapp(Ys,[X],Zs,Q).   app(Xs,Ys,Zs).
dapp([X|Xs],Ys,[X|Zs],Q) :-
  dapp(Xs,Ys,Zs,Q).
```

Fig. 3. Transformed Naive Reverse Program for Backwards Analysis

2.4 Analysis of the Transformed Programs

The transformed program can be input to an abstract interpretation framework. In the experiments carried out so far, analysis was based on the c-semantics abstracted using pre-interpretations [GBS95]. A pre-interpretation is a mapping from terms into a (finite) domain D, defined by a pre-interpretation function J. For each n-ary function symbol f, J contains a function $D^n \to D$, written $J(f(d_1, \ldots, d_n)) = d$ for $d_1, \ldots, d_n, d \in D$. A mapping α is defined inductively as $\alpha(c) = d$ where $J(c) = d$, for 0-ary functions c, and $\alpha(f(t_1, \ldots, t_n)) = J(f(\alpha(t_1), \ldots, \alpha(t_n)))$ for terms with functions of arity greater than 0. An abstract "domain program" is generated by abstract compilation, in the style introduced by Codish and Demoen [CD93]. A bottom-up analysis of the domain program yields its c-semantics. Let P be a program and $\mathcal{C}(P)$ its minimal model, which is identical to the c-semantics in this case. Let P^J be the abstract domain program for some pre-interpretation J. The safety result is that for all atoms $p(t_1, \ldots, t_n) \in \mathcal{C}(P)$, $p(\alpha(t_1), \ldots, \alpha(t_n)) \in \mathcal{C}(P^J)$.

Example 4. We analyse the above example where we wish to establish the property app(Ys,[X],Zs) $\leftrightarrow$integer(X), for the occurrence of app(Ys,[X],Zs) in the recursive clause for rev/2. A simple type domain could be used, consisting of the types int, listint, other. We construct an abstract "domain program" as described in [GBS95], based on the pre-interpretation constructed from the program's function symbols and the given types.

[] $\longrightarrow$ listint	[int | other] $\longrightarrow$ other	[other | other] $\longrightarrow$ other
[listint | other] $\longrightarrow$ other	[int | int] $\longrightarrow$ other	[listint | int] $\longrightarrow$ other
[other | int] $\longrightarrow$ other	[int | listint] $\longrightarrow$ listint	[listint | listint] $\longrightarrow$ other
[other | listint] $\longrightarrow$ other		

The pre-interpretation is encoded as a predicate $\to$/2 corresponding to the pre-interpretation, that is, for each mapping $f(d_1, \ldots, d_n) \to d$ in the pre-interpretation, we write an atomic clause $f(d_1, \ldots, d_n) \to d : -$true. The domain program is shown in Figure 4. Its least model over the pre-interpretation for the domain of simple types is shown in Figure 5.

```
rev(X1,X2):-
   []→X1,[]→X2.
rev(X1,X2):-
   rev(X3,X4),app(X4,X5,X2),
   [X6|X3]→X1,[]→X7,[X6|X7]→X5.
app(X1,X2,X2):-
   []→X1.
app(X1,X2,X3):-
   app(X4,X2,X5),[X6|X4]→X1,[X6|X5]→X3.
drev(X1,X2,X3):-
   rev(X4,X5),[X3|X4]→X1.
drev(X1,X2,X3):-
   rev(X4,X5),dapp(X5,X6,X2,X3),
   [X7|X4]→X1,[]→X8,[X7|X8]→X6.
drev(X1,X2,X3):-
   drev(X4,X5,X3),[X6|X4]→X1.
dapp(X1,X2,X3,X4):-
   dapp(X5,X2,X6,X4),[X7|X5]→X1,[X7|X6]→X3.
```

Fig. 4. Domain Program for Backwards Analysis of Naive Reverse

```
app(listint,X1,X1)       rev(listint,listint)  drev(listint,X1,int)
app(listint,int,other)   rev(other,other)      drev(other,X1,int)
app(other,other,other)                         drev(other,X1,listint)
app(other,int,other)                           drev(other,X,other)
app(other,listint,other)
```

Fig. 5. Least model of program in Figure 4, over domain of simple types

2.5   Interpretation of the Analysis Result

Examining the results in Figure 5, we see a number of abstract facts for drev. (There are no results for dapp derived since no call to app affects the given program point.) The results show that whenever rev/2 is called with its first argument a list of integers, then X is an integer at the given program point. This is indicated by the fact that drev(listint, X1, int) is in the model of the abstract program, and there are no other tuples drev(listint, X1, Y) where Y ≠ int. By contrast, there is a tuple drev(other, X1, int) but there is also a tuple drev(other, X1, listint), so although goals of the form rev(other, Y) *might* establish the property, they are not *guaranteed* to establish it.

In terms of the discussion in Section 1.2, the goal dependency $\Theta \rightarrow \Phi$ follows from the abstract relation, where $\Theta(\text{rev}(X, Y))$ is true if X is a list of integers, and $\Phi(\text{app}(Ys, [X], Zs))$ is true is this call arises from the specified program point, and X is an integer.

Example 5. Let P be the *quicksort* program, shown in Figure 6. Backwards analysis was considered for this program in [KL02]. Suppose we wish to check the calls to the built-in predicates ≥ and <. The intention is that these predicates

```
qsort([],Ys,Ys).                      dqsort([X|Xs],Ys,Zs,Q) :-
qsort([X|Xs],Ys,Zs) :-                   dpartition(Xs,X,Us,Vs,Q).
  partition(Xs,X,Us,Vs),              dqsort([X|Xs],Ys,Zs,Q) :-
  qsort(Us,Ys,[X|Ws]),                   partition(Xs,X,Us,Vs),
  qsort(Vs,Ws,Zs).                       dqsort(Us,Ys,[X|Ws],Q).
partition([],Z,[],[]).                dqsort([X|Xs],Ys,Zs,Q) :-
partition([X|Xs],Z,Ys,[X|Zs]) :-         partition(Xs,X,Us,Vs),
  X ≥ Z, partition(Xs,Z,Ys,Zs).          qsort(Us,Ys,[X|Ws]),
partition([X|Xs],Z,[X|Ys],Zs) :-         dqsort(Us,Ys,[X|Ws],Q).
  X < Z, partition(Xs,Z,Ys,Zs).     dpartition([X|Xs],Z,Ys,[X|Zs],X ≥ Z).
                                      dpartition([X|Xs],Z,Ys,[X|Zs],Q) :-
                                         X ≥ Z, dpartition(Xs,Z,Ys,Zs,Q).
                                      dpartition([X|Xs],Z,[X|Ys],Zs,X<Z).
                                      dpartition([X|Xs],Z,[X|Ys],Zs,Q) :-
                                         X < Z, dpartition(Xs,Z,Ys,Zs,Q).
```

Fig. 6. Transformed Quicksort Program for Backwards Analysis

require their argument to be ground when called in order to prevent run-time instantiation errors. The transformed *quicksort* program is included in Figure 6.

2.6 Analysis of Quicksort

We perform groundness analysis on the program in Figure 6. A pre-interpretation over the domain elements g and ng (standing for *ground* and *non-ground*) is constructed. This is equivalent to the Pos boolean domain.

$$[] \longrightarrow g \quad [g \mid g] \longrightarrow g \quad [g \mid ng] \longrightarrow ng \quad [ng \mid g] \longrightarrow ng \quad [ng \mid ng] \longrightarrow ng$$

After generating the domain program, the least model is computed and is shown in Figure 7. (When computing the minimal model we assign the success modes g≥g and g<g to the built-ins).

Examining the results via the relation dqsort, we see that the only calls to qsort(X,Y,Z) that guarantee that the required groundness properties g≥g and g<g are those in which X is ground. The arguments Y and Z are completely independent of the property. For dpartition, note that a variable X1 occurs in both the final argument of dpartition and in the second argument of partition. This variable can be instantiated by g or ng. Thus the second argument of partition has to be ground to establish g≥g and g<g. In addition, the arguments of ≥ and < are ground if either the first argument of partition or the third and fourth are ground. These are the same results reported by King and Lu [KL02], summarised as $X_2 \land (X_1 \lor (X_3 \land X_4))$ in the notation of Pos, where $X_1, \ldots, X_4$ are the arguments of partition.

2.7 Computing the Goal Conditions

For examples such as the ones discussed above, the required properties of the input goals that guarantee the observed property were derived informally by examining the abstract tuples. We now explain how to do this systematically.

```
partition(g,X1,g,g)                qsort(g,X1,X1)
                                   qsort(ng,ng,g)
                                   qsort(ng,ng,ng)


dpartition(ng,X1,ng,X2,g<X1)       dqsort(ng,X1,X2,ng≥ng)
dpartition(ng,X1,g,X2,g<X1)        dqsort(ng,X1,X2,ng≥g)
dpartition(ng,X1,ng,X2,ng<X1)      dqsort(ng,X1,X2,g≥ng)
dpartition(g,X1,ng,X2,g<X1)        dqsort(ng,X1,X2,ng<ng)
dpartition(g,X1,g,X2,g<X1)         dqsort(ng,X1,X2,ng<g)
dpartition(ng,X1,X2,ng,g≥X1)       dqsort(ng,X1,X2,g<ng)
dpartition(ng,X1,X2,g,g≥X1)        dqsort(g,X1,X2,g≥g)
dpartition(ng,X1,X2,ng,ng≥X1)      dqsort(g,X1,X2,g<g)
dpartition(g,X1,X2,ng,g≥X1)        dqsort(ng,X1,X2,g≥g)
dpartition(g,X1,X2,g,g≥X1)         dqsort(ng,X1,X2,g<g)
```

Fig. 7. Least model of program in Figure 6, over groundness domain

Let $\mathsf{Dep}(A, B)$ be the abstract dependency relation returned by the analysis, which is a finite set of tuples. Let Φ be the property required in the call; that is, we seek calls B where $\Phi(B)$ is true. Consider the set $S = \{A \mid \mathsf{Dep}(A, B) \wedge \Phi(B)\}$. S is the set of calls that *possibly* establishes $\Phi(B)$. Now consider candidate properties Θ that hold for all elements of S. For each such property, check whether there exists $\mathsf{Dep}(A, B)$ such that $\Theta(A)$ and $\neg\Phi(B)$. If there is, the candidate property is eliminated. For all other candidate properties, we have established that $\Theta \to \Phi$ follows from the abstract dependency relation.

We illustrate this process for the *quicksort* example. Consider the relation dqsort shown in Figure 7. The required property is that $\Phi(g \geq g)$ and $\Phi(g < g)$ are true and Φ is false for all other arguments of $\geq$ and $<$. The tuples in the abstract dqsort relation in which Φ holds are the following.

dqsort(g, X1, X2, g≥g)
dqsort(g, X1, X2, g<g)
dqsort(ng, X1, X2, g≥g)
dqsort(ng, X1, X2, g<g)

A candidate property is then that the first argument of qsort can be either g or ng, to establish the required property. However, we can search the relation to find a counterexample to the candidate property that the first argument is ng, such as dqsort(ng,X1,X2,ng<g). However we can find no counterexample to the property that the first argument is g. Hence we have established that qsort(g,X1,X2) $\to \Phi$.

2.8   The Relative Pseudo-complement

Domains which possess a relative pseudo-complement allow a more direct method. Giacobazzi and Scozzari [GS98] identified a property of abstract domains that allows analyses to be reversible. This property is central to the approach of King and Lu [KL02,KL03]. The key property is that the domain possesses a *relative pseudo-complement* operator. We quote the definition as given by King and Lu. Let D be an abstract domain with meet and join operations $\sqcap$ and $\sqcup$. Let d_1, d_2 be elements of D. The pseudo-complement of d_1 relative to d_2, denoted $d_1 \Rightarrow d_2$ is the greatest element whose meet with d_1 is less than d_2: that is, $d_1 \Rightarrow d_2 = \sqcup \{d \in D \mid d \sqcap d_1 \sqsubseteq d_2\}$.

To take Example 5 again, treat g and ng as true and false respectively. The set of abstract tuples for say, dpartition in Figure 7, can be rewritten as the following boolean expression, in the domain Pos, which possesses a relative pseudo-complement operation (here $q(X, Y)$ means $X \geq Y \wedge X < Y$).

$$
\begin{aligned}
&\texttt{dpartition}(X_1, X_2, X_3, X_4, q(X_5, X_6)) \equiv \\
&(X_2 \leftrightarrow X_6) \wedge ((\bar{X}_1 \wedge \bar{X}_3 \wedge X_5) \vee (\bar{X}_1 \wedge X_3 \wedge X_5) \vee (\bar{X}_1 \wedge \bar{X}_3 \wedge \bar{X}_5) \vee \\
&(X_1 \wedge \bar{X}_3 \wedge X_5) \vee (X_1 \wedge X_3 \wedge X_5) \vee (\bar{X}_1 \wedge \bar{X}_4 \wedge X_5) \vee (\bar{X}_1 \wedge X_4 \wedge X_5) \vee \\
&(\bar{X}_1 \wedge \bar{X}_4 \wedge \bar{X}_5) \vee (X_1 \wedge \bar{X}_4 \wedge X_5) \vee (X_1 \wedge X_4 \wedge X_5))
\end{aligned}
$$

The pseudo-complement of the above boolean expression relative to the desired property $X_5 \wedge X_6$ gives $X_2 \wedge (X_1 \vee (X_3 \wedge X_4))$, which is equivalent to the result derived in Example 5, and the same as that reported by King and Lu [KL02] for this predicate.

3   Related Work

The most closely related work is that of King and Lu [KL02,KL03], who describe a method for backwards analysis of logic programs, and report results for the domain of ground and non-ground modes. Their results have all been reproduced by the technique shown above, but a formal proof of equivalence has not yet been constructed. Their approach requires the construction of an abstract interpretation which under-approximates the concrete semantics. This requires the definition of a universal projection operator, and requires a condensing domain possessing a relative pseudo-complement operator. The fixpoint computation uses a greatest fixpoint rather than the standard least fixpoint. Our approach appears to be more flexible in the sense that a wide variety of domains can be used for the analysis, not only condensing domains. The relative pseudo-complement, if it exists, can be used in our approach to extract the result from the abstract program, but is not essential.

Mesnard et al. [Mes96,MN01] have also performed termination inference, which is a form of backwards analysis. Their approach uses a greatest fixpoint, and in this respect seems to align more with the approach of King and Lu.

The binary clause semantics of Codish and Taboch [CT99] was used to make loops observable, by deriving an explicit relationship between a calls and its successor calls. The transformation presented here can be targeted to observe any program points of interest, not only loops, but the spirit of the approach is the same. In later work based on binary clause semantics, Genaim and Codish [GC01] perform termination inference which involves backwards analysis. However, they use the framework of King and Lu for the backwards analysis, rather than the binary clause semantics.

Binary clause semantics is derived from the more general and expressive resultants semantics [GLM96,GG94]. We do not know of any implemented applications of resultants semantics, apart from the present work and that of [CT99,GC01], nor any previous suggestion that resultants semantics could form the basis for backwards analysis.

The approach of transforming programs to realise non-standard semantics is also followed in the *query-answer* transformations, which include magic-set transformations and its relations [DR94,BMSU86]. There, the aim is to simulate a top-down goal-directed computation, in a bottom-up semantic framework. A related approach is advocated by Codish and Søndergaard [CS02]. Different semantics for logic programs can be represented by meta-interpreters, which are also written as logic programs. Codish and Genaim's implementation of the binary semantics [GC01] follows this style.

4   Conclusion

A method for backwards analysis of logic programs has been presented. Given a program, and one or more specified body calls, a program transformation is performed. In the transformed program, the dependencies between the selected calls and initial goals is made explicit. Analysis of the transformed program using abstract interpretation yields an over-approximation of the dependency relation, and it was proved that dependencies could safely be derived from the approximation.

In contrast to previous work on backwards analysis, our approach requires no special properties of the abstract domain, nor any non-standard operations such as universal projection, or a greatest fixpoint computation. This is put forward as an advantage of our approach, since implementations can be based on existing abstract interpretation tools.

Experimental results carried out so far indicate that this method is of similar complexity to other reported work on backwards analysis, and gives equivalent precision at least over the Boolean domain POS. A detailed analytical comparison is difficult due to the great differences between the two approaches. It is indeed quite surprising that two such different algorithms yield the same results in experiments carried out so far.

Our use of downwards closed semantics does not seem to be essential to our general approach, but does allow a simpler analysis and implementation.

Acknowledgements. Thanks to Andy King and Mike Codish for introduction to, and discussions on backwards analysis, and to Maurice Bruynooghe and the LOPSTR'03 referees for valuable comments on an earlier draft. Roberto Giacobazzi, Samir Genaim and Maurizio Gabbrielli also provided useful feedback on the version appearing in the LOPSTR'03 Pre-proceedings. This research is supported in part by the IT-University of Copenhagen.

References

[BGLM94]   Annalisa Bossi, Maurizio Gabbrielli, Giorgio Levi, and Maurizio Martelli. The s-semantics approach: Theory and applications. *Journal of Logic Programming*, 19/20:149–197, 1994.

[BMSU86]   F. Bancilhon, D. Maier, Y. Sagiv, and J. Ullman. Magic sets and other strange ways to implement logic programs. In *Proceedings of the 5th ACM SIGMOD-SIGACT Symposium on Principles of Database Systems*, 1986.

[CD93]   M. Codish and B. Demoen. Analysing logic programs using "Prop"-ositional logic programs and a magic wand. In D. Miller, editor, *Proceedings of the 1993 International Symposium on Logic Programming, Vancouver*. MIT Press, 1993.

[Cla79]   K. Clark. Predicate logic as a computational formalism. Technical Report DOC 79/59, Imperial College, London, Department of Computing, 1979.

[CLM01]   Marco Comini, Giorgio Levi, and Maria Chiara Meo. A theory of observables for logic programs. *Information and Computation*, 169(1):23–80, 2001.

[CS02]   Michael Codish and Harald Søndergaard. Meta-circular abstract interpretation in prolog. In Torben Mogensen, David Schmidt, and I. Hal Sudburough, editors, *The Essence of Computation: Complexity, Analysis, Transformation*, volume 2566 of *Lecture Notes in Computer Science*, pages 109–134. Springer-Verlag, 2002.

[CT99]   Michael Codish and Cohavit Taboch. A semantic basic for the termination analysis of logic programs. *The Journal of Logic Programming*, 41(1):103–123, 1999.

[DR94]   S. Debray and R. Ramakrishnan. Abstract Interpretation of Logic Programs Using Magic Transformations. *Journal of Logic Programming*, 18:149–176, 1994.

[GBS95]   J. Gallagher, D. Boulanger, and H. Sağlam. Practical model-based static analysis for definite logic programs. In J. W. Lloyd, editor, *Proc. of International Logic Programming Symposium*, pages 351–365, 1995.

[GC01]   S. Genaim and M. Codish. Inferring termination conditions of logic programs by backwards analysis. In *International Conference on Logic for Programming, Artificial intelligence and reasoning*, volume 2250 of *Springer Lecture Notes in Artificial Intelligence*, pages 681–690, 2001.

[GG94]   Maurizio Gabbrielli and Roberto Giacobazzi. Goal independency and call patterns in the analysis of logic programs. In *Proceedings of the 1994 ACM Symposium on Applied Computing, SAC 1994*, pages 394 – 399, 1994.

[GLM96]   Maurizio Gabbrielli, Giorgio Levi, and Maria Chiara Meo. Resultants semantics for Prolog. *Journal of Logic and Computation*, 6(4):491–521, 1996.

[GS98]   R. Giacobazzi and F Scozzari. A logical model for relational abstract domains. *ACM Transactions on Programming Languages and Systems*, 20(5):1067–1109, 1998.

[KL02]   Andy King and Lunjin Lu. A backward analysis for constraint logic programs. *Theory and Practice of Logic Programming*, 2(4-5):514–547, 2002.

[KL03]   Andy King and Lunjin Lu. Forward versus backward verification of logic programs. In *ICLP'2003 (to appear)*, 2003.

[Llo87]   J.W. Lloyd. *Foundations of Logic Programming: 2nd Edition*. Springer-Verlag, 1987.

[Mes96]   F. Mesnard. Inferring left-terminating classes of queries for constraint logic programs. In M. J. Maher, editor, *Joint International Conference and Symposium on Logic Programming*, pages 7–21. MIT Press, 1996.

[MN01]   F. Mesnard and U. Neumerkel. Applying static analysis techniques for inferring termination conditions of logic programs. In *Static Analysis Symposium*, volume 2126 of *LNCS*, pages 93–110, 2001.

An Efficient Staging Algorithm
for Binding-Time Analysis

Takuma Murakami[1], Zhenjiang Hu[1,2],
Kazuhiko Kakehi[1], and Masato Takeichi[1]

[1] Department of Mathematical Informatics,
Graduate School of Information Science and Technology, University of Tokyo,
7-3-1 Hongo, Bunkyo-ku, Tokyo 113-8656, Japan
{murakami,kaz}@ipl.t.u-tokyo.ac.jp
{hu,takeichi}@mist.i.u-tokyo.ac.jp
[2] PRESTO 21, Japan Science and Technology Agency

Binding-Time Analysis (BTA) is one of the compile-time program analyses which is a general framework for program optimization and program generation [1]. The task of BTA is to divide a source program into two parts according to a given binding-time specification [2]. A binding-time specification gives information about availability of data: *static* data are available at compile-time while *dynamic* data are available at run time. BTA determines, from a binding-time specification of the input, on which parts computation can take place by propagating information on static data. Partial evaluators specialize the program for the static data by using the information from BTA to generate a more efficient program than the original.

By now several algorithms for BTA has been developed, such as abstract interpretation [3], type inference [4], constraint solving [5] or type based search [6]. Looking at the type directed searching approach proposed by Tim Sheard and Nathan Linger [6], we found two unclear points. First, it is not obvious how the algorithm can cut off the searching space, and the precise running time is left unestimated. The second concerns the accuracy of the solution. The result obtained by the algorithm is good, but may not be the best. These two kinds of uncertainty are due to the existence of heuristics.

We developed a new algorithm for BTA which makes use of an established method of program transformation, *the optimization theorem* for the maximum marking problem [7,8]. This is a technique to derive an efficient program based on dynamic programming. Since it formally gives the estimation of computation complexity and guarantees optimality of solutions with respect to given weight functions, the obtained BTA naturally inherits these characteristics.

The main contribution of our algorithm is to avoid iterations in BTA. Finiteness of binding-time enables us to compute all possible binding-time annotations by only one traversal over the given program. The naive algorithm in this approach obviously requires a large table to memoize intermediate results; we address the problem by applying the optimization theorem. The theorem drastically reduces the intermediate table if a problem is in a suitable form in which we are to formalize the original BTA problem.

M. Bruynooghe (Ed.): LOPSTR 2004, LNCS 3018, pp. 106–107, 2004.
© Springer-Verlag Berlin Heidelberg 2004

Moreover, our algorithm computes the optimal solution under given measurements of optimality. Generally an expression has multiple ways of binding-time annotations that conform to given binding-time specification. In such cases we want to select the optimal one as the result. Though the measurement of optimality is up to users, a result which computes more parts in static is normally better than the others. Our algorithm allows users to define their own measurement, and it derives the optimal solution under the measurement.

It is true that the derived BTA algorithm is rather traditional one, namely a simple monovariant algorithm which gives one binding-time specification for each function, but the proposed framework is of much use: Since marks, predicates and weight functions are parameterized in our algorithm, we can devise new strategies for BTA and their implementations follow directly. Furthermore, the optimization theorem guarantees that the all algorithms derived via our framework run in linear time with respect to the size of the analyzed program.

Acknowledgments

We are grateful to Robert Glück for his valuable suggestions. We also thank the reviewers and participants in the conference for their worthful comments.

References

1. Jones, N.D., Gomard, C.K., Sestoft, P.: Partial Evaluation and Automatic Program Generation. Prentice Hall (1993)
2. Jones, N.D.: An Introduction to Partial Evaluation. ACM Computing Surveys **28** (1996) 480–503
3. Consel, C.: Binding Time Analysis for Higher Order Untyped Functional Languages. In: Proceedings of the 1990 ACM conference on LISP and functional programming, ACM Press (1990) 264–272
4. Henglein, F.: Efficient Type Inference for Higher-Order Binding-Time Analysis. In: Proceedings of the Fifth International Conference on Functional Programming Languages and Computer Architecture. Volume 523 of Lecture Notes in Computer Science., Cambridge, USA, Springer-Verlag (1991) 448–472 Lecture Notes in Computer Science, Vol. 523.
5. Glück, R., Jørgensen, J.: Fast Binding-Time Analysis for Multi-Level Specialization. In: Proceedings of Perspectives of System Informatics. (1996) 261–272
6. Sheard, T., Linger, N.: Search-Based Binding Time Analysis using Type-Directed Pruning. In: Proceedings of the ACM SIGPLAN Asian Symposium on Partial Evaluation and Semantics-Based Program Manipulation, Aizu, Japan (2002) 20–31
7. Sasano, I., Hu, Z., Takeichi, M., Ogawa, M.: Make it Practical: A Generic Linear-Time Algorithm for Solving Maximum-Weightsum Problems. In: Proceedings of the Fifth ACM SIGPLAN International Conference on Functional Programming, Montreal, Canada (2000) 137–149
8. Sasano, I., Hu, Z., Takeichi, M.: Generation of Efficient Programs for Solving Maximum Multi-Marking Problems. In: Workshop on the Semantics, Applications, and Implementation of Program Generation. Volume 2196 of Lecture Notes in Computer Science. Springer-Verlag, Firenze, Italy (2001) 72–91

Proving Termination with Adornments

Alexander Serebrenik and Danny De Schreye

Department of Computer Science, K.U. Leuven
Celestijnenlaan 200A, B-3001, Heverlee, Belgium
{Alexander.Serebrenik,Danny.DeSchreye}@cs.kuleuven.ac.be

Termination is well-known to be one of the important aspects of program correctness. Logic programming provides a framework with a strong theoretical basis for tackling this problem. However, due to the declarative formulation of programs, the danger of non-termination may increase. As a result, termination analysis received considerable attention in logic programming. Recently, the study of termination of numerical programs led to the emerging of the *adorning technique* [7]. This technique implements the well-known *"divide et impera"* strategy by distinguishing between different subsets of values for variables, and deriving termination proofs based on these subsets. In this paper we generalise this technique and discuss its applicability to the domain of terms (the Herbrand domain).

A set of adornments is derived from the program itself. As a basis for a set of adornments one can use types [1], sets of integers [7]. Given a program and a set of adornments, the program can be transformed such that a predicate p^a in the transformed program P^a is called if and only if the corresponding predicate p is called in the original program P and the arguments of the call are in the segment a. One can show that under certain conditions this transformation preserves termination. In this way (implicit) information on the domain is made explicit in the transformed program. It should be observed, that instead of one level mapping required for P that is supposed to decrease along all possible computations, in order to prove termination of P^a one can find a number of potentially less sophisticated different level mappings for each one of the "cases". In the examples we have considered, such level-mappings can be constructed automatically, and thus, they play a key role in automation of the approach. It should be noted that the transformation we performed can be seen as a form of multiple specialisation [8]. After the transformation step is performed, existing termination analysers can be applied to infer termination of the transformed program. Since the transformation above preserved termination, termination of the original program is implied as well.

The contributions of this work are twofold. First of all, it leads us to an entirely new understanding of the relationship between partial deduction and termination analysis. While so far termination has been brought together with partial deduction only in the context of terminating the deduction process [2, 5], i.e., of using termination analysis techniques for program specialisation, we suggest a complementary approach of using program specialisation techniques for termination analysis. On a practical note, this relationship implies that tools like ECCE [4] or Mixtus [6] can be used to generate specialised programs to be

M. Bruynooghe (Ed.): LOPSTR 2004, LNCS 3018, pp. 108–109, 2004.
© Springer-Verlag Berlin Heidelberg 2004

fed to termination analysers. Alternatively, one can design specialisation techniques specifically for termination analysis. Our adornments methodology can be considered as an example of such technique. The main advantage of our results is the uniform approach to different kinds of computations: numerical (integer and floating-point) and symbolic (unification-based and interargument relations-based).

The practical importance of the transformation can be illustrated by observing that for such examples as *dist* [3], none of the termination analysers available is powerful enough to prove termination of the original program, while all of them succeed in proving termination of the transformed one.

References

1. M. Bruynooghe, M. Codish, S. Genaim, and W. Vanhoof. Reuse of results in termination analysis of typed logic programs. In M. V. Hermenegildo and G. Puebla, editors, *Static Analysis, 9th International Symposium*, volume 2477 of *Lecture Notes in Computer Science*, pages 477–492. Springer Verlag, 2002.
2. M. Bruynooghe, D. De Schreye, and B. Martens. A general criterion for avoiding infinite unfolding during partial deduction. *New Generation Computing*, 11(1):47–79, 1992.
3. N. Dershowitz and C. Hoot. Topics in termination. In C. Kirchner, editor, *Rewriting Techniques and Applications, 5th International Conference*, volume 690 of *Lecture Notes in Computer Science*, pages 198–212. Springer Verlag, 1993.
4. M. Leuschel. The ECCE partial deduction system. In G. Puebla, editor, *Proceedings of the ILPS'97 Workshop on Tools and Environments for (Constraint) Logic Programming*, Universidad Politécnica de Madrid, Tech. Rep. CLIP7/97.1, Port Jefferson, USA, October 1997.
5. M. Leuschel, B. Martens, and K. Sagonas. Preserving termination of tabled logic programs while unfolding. In N. Fuchs, editor, *Proceedings of the 7th International Workshop on Logic Program Synthesis and Transformation*, volume 1463 of *Lecture Notes in Computer Science*, pages 189–205. Springer Verlag, 1998.
6. D. Sahlin. Mixtus: An automatic partial evaluator for full Prolog. *New Generation Computing*, 12(1):7–51, 1993.
7. A. Serebrenik and D. De Schreye. Inference of termination conditions for numerical loops in Prolog. In R. Nieuwenhuis and A. Voronkov, editors, *Logic for Programming, Artificial Intelligence, and Reasoning, 8th International Conferencerence, Proceedings*, volume 2250 of *Lecture Notes in Computer Science*, pages 654–668. Springer Verlag, 2001.
8. W. Winsborough. Multiple specialization using minimal-function graph semantics. *Journal of Logic Programming*, 13(2/3):259–290, 1992.

Constructively Characterizing Fold and Unfold*

Tjark Weber[1] and James Caldwell[2]

[1] Institut für Informatik, Technische Universität München
Boltzmannstr. 3, D-85748 Garching b. München, Germany
webertj@in.tum.de
[2] Department of Computer Science, University of Wyoming
Laramie, Wyoming 82071-3315
jlc@cs.uwyo.edu

Abstract. In this paper we formally state and prove theorems characterizing when a function can be constructively reformulated using the recursion operators fold and unfold, *i.e.* given a function h, when can a function g be constructed such that $h = $ fold g or $h = $ unfold g? These results are refinements of the classical characterization of fold and unfold given by Gibbons, Hutton and Altenkirch in [6]. The proofs presented here have been formalized in Nuprl's constructive type theory [5] and thereby yield program transformations which map a function h (accompanied by the evidence that h satisfies the required conditions), to a function g such that $h = $ fold g or, as the case may be, $h = $ unfold g.

1   Introduction

Under the proofs-as-programs interpretation, constructive proofs of theorems relating programs yield "correct-by-construction" program transformations. In this paper we formally prove constructive theorems characterizing when a function can be formulated using the recursion operators fold and unfold, *i.e.* given a function h, when does there exist (constructively) a function g such that $h = $ fold g or $h = $ unfold g? The proofs have been formalized in Nuprl's constructive type theory [5] and thereby yield program transformations which map a function h – accompanied by the evidence that h satisfies the required conditions – to a function g such that $h = $ fold g or, as the case may be, $h = $ unfold g.

The results presented here are refinements of the classical characterization of fold / unfold given by Gibbons, Hutton and Altenkirch in [6]. As they remark, their characterization is set theoretic and makes essential use of classical logic and the Axiom of Choice. A constructive characterization of fold was given by Weber in [15] and a counter-example showing that indeed, under the characterization given in [6], there are constructive functions h that can be written in the form fold g where g is necessarily incomputable. We extend those results here and

---

* This work was supported by NSF grant CCR-9985239, a DoD Multidisciplinary University Research Initiative (MURI) program administered by the Office of Naval Research under grant N00014-01-1-0765, and by the PhD program Logic in Computer Science of the German Research Foundation.

M. Bruynooghe (Ed.): LOPSTR 2004, LNCS 3018, pp. 110–127, 2004.

present a constructive characterization for both fold and unfold. Following [6] our results are presented in the context of a category-theoretic framework, also formalized in Nuprl.

In the next section we describe the definitions of the Nuprl formalization of category theory required later in the paper resisting elaboration. We do not state or prove any theorems in this section. A description of the Nuprl formalization of category theory can be found in [15]. In following sections we define catamorphisms and anamorphisms and, relying on their universal property, give formal Nuprl definitions of fold and unfold. We present the statements of the theorems which classically characterize fold and unfold from [6]. It turns out that one direction of the classical theorems is constructively provable. For the other direction, we refine the conditions on the antecedents to obtain characterizations of fold and unfold which hold constructively. The constructive content of the proof of these theorems are the desired program transformations.

2   Category Theory in Nuprl

The Nuprl type theory and proof system have previously been described in this conference [4], a recent and comprehensive reference for Nuprl's constructive type theory is available on-line [1]. In short, Nuprl draws heavily on Martin-Löf type theory [12], which uses an open-ended sequence of universes $\mathbb{U}_1, \mathbb{U}_2, \mathbb{U}_3, \ldots$ to stratify the concept of type.

The formal Nuprl definition of the type *category* (up through universe level i) is shown in Fig. 1. This definition follows the standard definition, as found in say [10]. In the definition: `Obj` is the type of objects in the category; `A` is the type of arrows; `dom` and `cod` are the functions mapping arrows to their domains and codomains; `o` is the type of the composition operator (which is constrained to be defined only on arrows whose domains and codomains align properly and is associative); and the final component of the product, `id`, specifies the function which maps objects to arrows preserving the unit law.

```
Cat{i} ≝
   Obj:𝕌ᵢ
 × A:𝕌ᵢ
 × dom:(A ⟶ Obj)
 × cod:(A ⟶ Obj)
 × o:{o:(g:A ⟶ f:{f:A| cod f = dom g} ⟶
                       {h:A| dom h = dom f ∧ cod h = cod g}) |
        ∀f,g,h:A. cod f = dom g ∧ cod g = dom h ⇒
                     (h o g) o f = h o (g o f)
     }
 × {id:(p:Obj ⟶ {f:A| dom f = p ∧ cod f = p}) |
        ∀f:A. (id(cod f)) o f = f ∧ f o (id(dom f)) = f}
```

Fig. 1. Abstraction: `category`

For a category `C` we use selectors `C_Obj`, `C_Arr`, `C_dom`, `C_cod`, `C_op` and `C_id` to refer to the components of `C`.

The analog of the large category of sets in our type theoretic formulation is the category of types whose universe level is bounded by some $i \in \mathbb{N}$. The arrows in this category are triples of the form $\langle A, B, f \rangle$ where $A, B \in \mathbb{U}_i$ and $f \in A \to B$. The category of types is defined in Fig. 2.

```
large_category{i} def
                    ≝
  <𝕌ᵢ,
    (A:𝕌ᵢ × B:𝕌ᵢ × (A → B)),
    λf. f.1,
    λf. f.2.1,
    λg,f. <f.1, g.2.1, g.2.2 o f.2.2>,
    λp. <p, p, λx.x>>
```

Fig. 2. Abstraction: `large_category`

The well-formedness goal is stated as: `large_category{i}` $\in$ `Cat{i'}`, *i.e.* it says that the category of types below universe level i inhabits the type category at level $i + 1$.

A miscellany of defined notions used later in the paper are displayed in Fig. 3.

```
C-composable(f,g) def
                   ≝   C_cod f = C_dom g
Mor[C](p,q)       def
                   ≝   {f:C_Arr| C_dom f = p ∧ C_cod f = q}
C-initial(p)      def
                   ≝   ∀q:C_Obj. ∃!f:C_Arr. C_dom f = p ∧ C_cod f = q
C-terminal(p)     def
                   ≝   ∀q:C_Obj. ∃!f:C_Arr. C_dom f = q ∧ C_cod f = p
```

Fig. 3. Abstractions: `composable`, `morphism`, `initial` and `terminal`

Functors are arrows between categories. A functor from $\mathcal{C}$ to $\mathcal{D}$, where $\mathcal{C}$ and $\mathcal{D}$ are categories, maps objects in $\mathcal{C}$ to objects in $\mathcal{D}$ and arrows in $\mathcal{C}$ to arrows in $\mathcal{D}$ such that these maps preserve structure, *i.e.* they are compatible with the categories' domain and codomain operators, preserve identity elements and respect composition of arrows. The formal definition is given in Fig. 4.

```
Functor{i}(C,D) def
                 ≝
  {C:Cat{i}}
  × {D:Cat{i}}
  × O:(C_Obj → D_Obj)
  × {M:C_Arr → D_Arr|
        (∀f:C_Arr. D_dom (M f) = O (C_dom f)
                  ∧ D_cod (M f) = O (C_cod f))
        c∧ ((∀f:C_Arr. ∀g:{g:C_Arr| C_dom g = C_cod f}
              M (g C_op f) = (M g) D_op (M f))
          ∧ (∀p:C_Obj. M (C_id p) = D_id (O p)))}
F_dom def
       ≝F.1
F_cod def
       ≝F.2.1
```

Fig. 4. Abstractions: `functor`, `functor_dom` and `functor_cod`

Given a category $\mathcal{C}$ and a functor $F : \mathcal{C} \to \mathcal{C}$, an *algebra* over F is a pair $\langle A, f \rangle$, where A is an object and $f : FA \to A$ is an arrow in $\mathcal{C}$. The formal definitions are given in Fig. 5.

```
Algebra(F) ≝
  p:F_dom_Obj × {f:F_dom_Arr| F_dom_dom f = F_O p ∧ F_dom_cod f = p}
Hom(F) ≝
  A:Algebra(F)
    × B:Algebra(F)
    × {f:F_dom_Arr| (F_dom_dom f = A_obj) c∧ (F_dom_cod f = B_obj)
                    c∧ (f F_dom_op A_arr = B_arr F_dom_op (F_M f))}
algebra_category(F) ≝<Algebra(F), Hom(F), λh.h_dom, λh.h_cod,
                      λh,g.h o_hom[F] g, λA.id_hom[F](A)>
```

Fig. 5. Abstractions: `algebra`, `homomorphism` and `algebra_category`

A *coalgebra* is a pair $\langle A', f' \rangle$, where A' is an object and $f' : A' \to FA'$ is an arrow in $\mathcal{C}$. Thus, coalgebras are algebras over the dual category. The formal definitions are given in Fig. 6.

```
Coalgebra(F) ≝
  p:F_dom_Obj × {f:F_dom_Arr| F_dom_dom f = p ∧ F_dom_cod f = F_O p}
Cohom(F) ≝
  A:Coalgebra(F)
    × B:Coalgebra(F)
    × {f:F_dom_Arr| (F_dom_dom f = A_obj) c∧ (F_dom_cod f = B_obj)
                    c∧ ((F_M f) F_dom_op A_arr = B_arr F_dom_op f)}
coalgebra_category(F) ≝<Coalgebra(F), Cohom(F), λh.h_dom, λh.h_cod,
                        λh,g.h o_cohom[F] g, λA.id_cohom[F](A)>
```

Fig. 6. Abstractions: `coalgebra`, `cohomomorphism` and `coalgebra_category`

3 Catamorphisms and Anamorphisms

Catamorphisms ('folds') and anamorphisms ('unfolds') can be formalized as certain arrows in the category of algebras and in the category of coalgebras, respectively. Significantly, they serve as a basis for a transformational approach to functional programming [3] and a wide variety of transformations, optimizations and proof techniques are known for algorithms that are expressed as combinations of folds and unfolds [14,2,8,7,9,15].

Catamorphisms are homomorphisms from an initial algebra in the category of algebras, *anamorphisms* are defined as cohomomorphisms to a terminal coalgebra in the category of coalgebras.

An algebra $\langle \mu F, in \rangle$ is *initial* if and only if it is an initial object (see Fig. 3) in the category of algebras; that is, for every algebra $\langle A, f \rangle$, there exists a unique homomorphism $h : \langle \mu F, in \rangle \to \langle A, f \rangle$. A coalgebra $\langle \nu F, out \rangle$ is *terminal* if and only if it is a terminal object in the category of coalgebras; *i.e.*, for every coalgebra $\langle A, f \rangle$, there exists a unique cohomomorphism $h : \langle A, f \rangle \to \langle \nu F, out \rangle$.

Definition 1 (fold) *Suppose $\mathcal{C}$ is a category, $F : \mathcal{C} \to \mathcal{C}$ is a functor and $\langle \mu F, in \rangle$ is an initial algebra. Then for every algebra $\langle A, f \rangle$, fold f is defined as the unique homomorphism from $\langle \mu F, in \rangle$ to $\langle A, f \rangle$.*

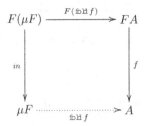

Fig. 7. $(\text{fold } f) \cdot in = f \cdot F(\text{fold } f)$

We say an arrow h is a *catamorphism* if and only if it can be written as fold f for some arrow f.

Definition 2 (unfold) *Suppose $\mathcal{C}$ is a category, $F : \mathcal{C} \rightarrow \mathcal{C}$ is a functor and $\langle \nu F, out \rangle$ is a terminal coalgebra. Then for every coalgebra $\langle A, f \rangle$, unfold f is defined as the unique cohomomorphism from $\langle A, f \rangle$ to $\langle \nu F, out \rangle$.*

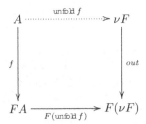

Fig. 8. $F(\text{unfold } f) \cdot f = out \cdot (\text{unfold } f)$

Figure 8 illustrates this situation. We say an arrow h is an *anamorphism* if and only if it can be written as unfold f for some arrow f. These definitions imply the following *universal properties* for fold and unfold [11].

Theorem 1 (Universal Property: fold). *Let $\mathcal{C}$ be a category, $F : \mathcal{C} \rightarrow \mathcal{C}$ a functor and $\langle \mu F, in \rangle$ an initial algebra. Furthermore, suppose that $\langle A, f \rangle$ is an algebra and that $h : \mu F \rightarrow A$. Then*

$$h = \text{fold } f \iff h \cdot in = f \cdot Fh.$$

Theorem 2 (Universal Property: unfold). *Let $\mathcal{C}$ be a category, $F : \mathcal{C} \rightarrow \mathcal{C}$ a functor and $\langle \nu F, out \rangle$ a terminal coalgebra. Furthermore, suppose that $\langle A, f \rangle$ is a coalgebra and that $h : A \rightarrow \nu F$. Then*

$$h = \text{unfold } f \iff Fh \cdot f = out \cdot h.$$

Based on their universal properties, formalize `fold` and `unfold` as relations (shown in Fig. 9). The well-formedness theorems state that they inhabit $\mathbb{P}$, Nuprl's type of propositions. We remark that h is unique when $h = \text{unfold } f$ or $h = \text{fold } f$.

```
h=fold[C,F,I](f) ≝(F_dom_dom h = I_obj) c∧ (F_dom_cod h = f_obj)
                    c∧ (h F_dom_op I_arr = f_arr F_dom_op (F_M h))
h=unfold[C,F,T](f) ≝(F_dom_dom h = f_obj) c∧ (F_dom_cod h = T_obj)
                     c∧ ((F_M h) F_dom_op f_arr = T_arr F_dom_op h)
```

Fig. 9. Abstractions: `fold` and `unfold`

4 When Is an Arrow a Catamorphism or an Anamorphism?

The universal properties for fold and unfold provide technically complete answers to this question. An arrow $h : \mu F \to A$ is a catamorphism if and only if $h \cdot in = f \cdot Fh$ for some arrow $f : FA \to A$. However, usually only the arrow h is given – how would we know if an arrow f exists such that the above equation holds? And more importantly, how would we construct f from h? Dually, an arrow $h : A \to \nu F$ is an anamorphism if and only if $Fh \cdot f = out \cdot h$ for some arrow $f : A \to FA$. Again, to show that f exists or methods to construct it are not given.

E. Meijer, M. Fokkinga, and R. Paterson [13] give the following results regarding left and right invertible arrows.

Definition 3 (Left and Right Invertible) *Let C be a category and f an arrow in C.*

1.) *We say f is left-invertible (in C) if and only if there exists an arrow g in C such that $g \cdot f = id(dom(f))$.*

2.) *We say f is right-invertible (in C) if and only if there exists an arrow g in C such that $f \cdot g = id(cod(f))$.*

The corresponding Nuprl abstractions are shown in Fig. 10. Their well-formedness theorems simply state that these abstractions are propositions.

```
left-invertible[C](f) ≝
  ∃g:{g:C_Arr| C-composable(f,g)} . g C_op f = C_id (C_dom f)
right-invertible[C](f) ≝
  ∃g:{g:C_Arr| C-composable(g,f)} . f C_op g = C_id (C_cod f)
```

Fig. 10. Abstractions: `left_invertible` and `right_invertible`

The following theorems provide tools to show when f exists.

Theorem 3. *If C is a category, $F : C \to C$ is a functor with an initial algebra $\langle \mu F, in \rangle$, and $h : \mu F \to A$ is a left-invertible arrow in C, then, for some arrow $f : FA \to A$, $h = fold\,f$.*

Theorem 4. *If C is a category, $F : C \to C$ is a functor with a terminal coalgebra $\langle \nu F, out \rangle$, and $h : A \to \nu F$ is a right-invertible arrow in C, then, for some arrow $f : A \to FA$, $h = unfold\,f$.*

The Nuprl theorems formalizing these results are shown in Fig. 11. Proofs in Nuprl are created in an interactive fashion. In each proof step, instances of (one or more) proof rules are chosen by the user and applied to the current sequent. Both theorems above are proved in about 70 steps each.

```
∀C:Cat{i}. ∀F:Functor{i}(C,C).
 ∀I:{I:Algebra(F)| algebra_category(F)-initial(I)} .
  ∀h:{h:F_dom_Arr| F_dom_dom h = I_obj} .
   left-invertible[F_dom](h) ⇒ (∃f:Algebra(F). h=fold[C,F,I](f) )
∀C:Cat{i}. ∀F:Functor{i}(C,C)
 ∀T:{T:Coalgebra(F)| coalgebra_category(F)-terminal(T)}
  ∀h:{h:F_dom_Arr| F_dom_cod h = T_obj}
   right-invertible[F_dom](h) ⇒ ∃f:Coalgebra(F). h=unfold[C,F,T](f)
```

Fig. 11. Thms: `left_invertible_implies_fold` `right_invertible_implies_unfold`

Figure 12 shows the extract[1] of the proof of `right_invertible_implies_unfold`. We can clearly see the witness term in Nuprl notation: The witness term is given by the coalgebra `<F_dom_dom h, (F_M g) F_dom_op (T_arr F_dom_op h)>`. A similar extract results from the proof of the theorem `left_invertible_implies_fold`.

```
λC,F,T,h,p.
 let <g,_> = p in
  <<F_dom_dom h, (F_M g) F_dom_op (T_arr F_dom_op h)>, Ax, Ax, Ax>
```

Fig. 12. Simplified Extract of `right_invertible_implies_unfold`

5   Classically Characterizing **fold** and **unfold**

For the special case of the category $\mathcal{SET}$, with sets as objects and functions as arrows, J. Gibbons, G. Hutton, and T. Altenkirch [6] proved the following theorems characterizing when an arrow is a catamorphism or an anamorphism.

Theorem 5 (Gibbons, Hutton, Altenkirch: fold). *Let $F : \mathcal{SET} \to \mathcal{SET}$ be a functor with an initial algebra $\langle \mu F, in \rangle$, A be a set, and $h : \mu F \to A$. Then $(\exists g : FA \to A.\quad h = fold\, g) \iff ker(Fh) \subseteq ker(h \cdot in)$.*

Here, $ker\, f$, the *kernel* of a function $f : A \to B$, is defined as a binary relation on A containing all pairs of elements in A that are mapped to the same element in B. It is formalized in Fig. 13.

We remark here that this theorem of classical set theory is too strong in the following sense: there exists a function h such that h is computable and such that $ker(Fh) \subseteq ker(h \cdot in)$ but where g, which exists by Thm. 5, is necessarily incomputable [15].

The following theorem characterizes the dual unfold.

---

[1] The extract has been simplified by unfolding definitions, performing β-reductions and α-renaming selected variables to make the code more readable.

Theorem 6 (Gibbons, Hutton, Altenkirch: unfold). *Let* $F : \mathcal{SET} \to \mathcal{SET}$ *be a functor with a terminal coalgebra* $\langle \nu F, out \rangle$, A *be a set, and* $h : A \to \nu F$. *Then* $(\exists g : A \to FA. \quad h = unfold\, g) \iff img(out \cdot h) \subseteq img(Fh)$.

The *image* of a function $f : A \to B$, img f, is the dual notion to the kernel of f (see Fig. 13).

```
ker[A,B] f ≝ {aa:A × A| f aa.1 = f aa.2}
img[A,B] f ≝ {b:B| ∃a:A. b = f a}
```

Fig. 13. Abstractions: `kernel` and `image`

6 A Constructive Characterization of **fold** and **unfold**

Translating the statements of Thms. 5 and 6 so that the category $\mathcal{SET}$ is replaced by the large category of types result in theorems that are constructively provable in the ($\Rightarrow$) direction [15]. However, the ($\Leftarrow$) direction contains the computationally interesting parts of these theorems; it claims existence for the function g we are interested in.

6.1 Characterizing **fold**

Analyzing the proof of Thm. 5 led us to identify additional constraints that in fact allow a constructive proof of a modified version of the ($\Leftarrow$) direction. Before we state these conditions, we must address an issue that is not raised by differences between classical and constructive mathematics, but by the inherent differences between set theory and type theory.

Thus far, while considering the constructive interpretation of the classical results we have interpreted types *mutatis mutandis* as sets. Up to this point this informal practice has proved harmless, but at this point our naïve identification of sets and types fails. Consider the analogue of the empty set, *i.e.* types having no inhabitants. Equality on types in Nuprl is not extensional as it is for sets. Hence, unlike set theory, where every set containing no elements is identified with $\emptyset$, there is no canonical representative for the empty type; *e.g.* neither *Void* nor $\{x : \mathbb{Z}| \ x < x\}$ are inhabited and yet they are distinguished as types. The identification of empty sets with *the* empty set is a crucial step in the ($\Leftarrow$) direction of the classical proof.

Here is the statement of the refined theorem (still in terms of the category $\mathcal{SET}$) corresponding to the ($\Leftarrow$) part of Thm. 5.

Theorem 7. *Let* $F : \mathcal{SET} \to \mathcal{SET}$ *be a functor with an initial algebra* $\langle \mu F, in \rangle$, *and let* A *be a set such that we can decide whether* A *is empty, and* $h : \mu F \to A$. *Furthermore, suppose that for every* $b \in FA$ *we can decide whether* $b = (Fh)(a)$ *for some* $a \in F(\mu F)$. *Then* $(\exists g : FA \to A.h = fold\, g) \Longleftarrow ker(Fh) \subseteq ker(h \cdot in)$.

Figure 14 shows a type-theoretic formalization of this theorem in Nuprl. `Dec(P)` is used to abbreviate $P \vee \neg P$. The proof depends on two lemmata, namely that the inclusion of kernels implies the existence of postfactors, and that the existence of a function $h : \mu F \to A$ implies the existence of a function $g : FA \to A$. We say $g : B \to C$ is a *postfactor* of $f : A \to B$ for $h : A \to C$ if and only if $h = g \cdot f$. We will use the notation $A \to B \neq \emptyset$ to mean that there is a function inhabiting $A \to B$.

We state and prove the former lemma first.

```
∀F:Functor{i'}(large_category{i},large_category{i}).
 ∀I:{I:Algebra(F)| algebra_category(F)-initial(I)} .
  ∀A:large_category{i}_Obj. ∀h:Mor[large_category{i}](I_obj,A).
   Dec(A) ⇒ (∀b:F_O A. Dec(∃a:F_O I_obj. b = (F_M h).2.2 a)) ⇒
    ((∃g:Algebra(F). h=fold[large_category{i},F,I](g) )
       ⇐ ker[F_O I_obj,large_category{i}_cod (F_M h)] (F_M h).2.2
          ⊆ ker[F_O I_obj,large_category{i}_cod (h F_dom_op I_arr)]
            (h F_dom_op I_arr).2.2)
```

Fig. 14. Theorem: `kernel_inclusion_implies_fold`

Lemma 1. *Let $f : A \to B$ and $h : A \to C$. Furthermore, suppose we can decide whether C is empty, and for every $b \in B$ we can decide whether $b = f(a)$ for some $a \in A$. Then $(\exists g : B \to C. \quad h = g \cdot f) \Longleftarrow (\ker f \subseteq \ker h \wedge B \to C \neq \emptyset)$.*

Proof. Assume $\ker f \subseteq \ker h$ and $B \to C \neq \emptyset$.

If $C = \emptyset$, then $B = \emptyset$ since $B \to C \neq \emptyset$, and $A = \emptyset$ since $f : A \to B$. Therefore $f = h = id(\emptyset)$, and if we choose $g = id(\emptyset)$, clearly $g : B \to C$ and $h = g \cdot f$.

If $C \neq \emptyset$, let c be an arbitrary element in C. Let $choice : \{b \in B \mid \exists a \in A. b = f(a)\} \to A$ be a function with $f(choice(b)) = b$ for all $b \in \{b \in B \mid \exists a \in A. b = f(a)\}$ [2]. For $b \in B$ define $g(b) \in C$ as follows: If $b = f(a)$ for some $a \in A$, then $g(b) = h(choice(b))$. Otherwise, $g(b) = c$.

Now let $a \in A$. Since $f(choice(f(a))) = f(a)$ by definition of $choice$, we have $(choice(f(a)), a) \in \ker f \subseteq \ker h$. Hence $g(f(a)) = h(choice(f(a))) = h(a)$, and therefore $h = g \cdot f$. □

```
∀A,B,C:𝕌ᵢ. ∀f:A → B. ∀h:A → C.
 Dec(C) ⇒ (∀b:B. Dec(∃a:A. b = f a)) ⇒
  ((∃g:B → C. h = g o f) ⇐ ker[A,B]f ⊆ ker[A,C]h ∧ B → C)
```

Fig. 15. Theorem: `kernel_inclusion_implies_postfactor`

To give a constructive proof that the inclusion of kernels implies the existence of postfactors, we made two additional assumptions compared to the statement of this lemma in [6]: *i.*) that we can decide whether the codomain of h is empty, and *ii.*) that we can decide whether an element in the codomain of f is in the image of f. The Nuprl theorem `kernel_inclusion_implies_postfactor` is shown in Figure 15. The formal proof is about 43 steps long.

---

[2] To prove that such a function *choice* exists, we use the Axiom of Choice which is provable in constructive type theory [12] and is a theorem in the Nuprl standard library.

Figure 16 shows a "lifted" version of the lemma for arrows in the category of types. Despite the use of the original lemma in the proof of the lifted version, the proof is about 71 steps long.

```
∀A,B,C:large_category{i}_Obj. ∀f:Mor[large_category{i}](A,B).
 ∀h:Mor[large_category{i}](A,C).
   Dec(C) ⇒ (∀b:B. Dec(∃a:A. b = f.2.2 a)) ⇒
     ((∃g:Mor[large_category{i}](B,C). h = g large_category{i}_op f)
       ⇐ ker[A,B]f.2.2 ⊆ ker[A,C]h.2.2 ∧ Mor[large_category{i}](B,C))
```

Fig. 16. Theorem: `kernel_inclusion_implies_postfactor_cat`

The second lemma required for the proof of Thm. 7 is stated below.

Lemma 2. *If $F : \mathcal{SET} \to \mathcal{SET}$ is a functor with an initial algebra $\langle \mu F, in \rangle$, and A is a set such that we can decide whether A is empty, then*

$$\mu F \to A \neq \emptyset \implies FA \to A \neq \emptyset.$$

Proof. If $A \neq \emptyset$, then trivially $FA \to A \neq \emptyset$.

If $A = \emptyset$, then the embedding $g : A \hookrightarrow \mu F$ is a function from A to μF. Thus $Fg : FA \to F(\mu F)$ by the properties of functors. Hence $h \cdot in \cdot Fg : FA \to A$.

Therefore $FA \to A \neq \emptyset$ in either case. □

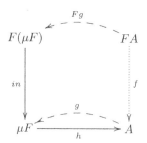

Fig. 17. $\mu F \to A \neq \emptyset \implies FA \to A \neq \emptyset$.

Figure 17 illustrates the situation: Given a function $h : \mu F \to A$, we can find a function $f : FA \to A$. The functions $g : A \to \mu F$ and $Fg : FA \to F(\mu F)$ are needed only in the case $A = \emptyset$. If $A \neq \emptyset$, they may not exist – but we can construct a function $f : FA \to A$ directly then. Note that the lemma is not true for arbitrary categories. The proof of the lemma given above is different from the proof that was given in [6][3], but the theorem `hom_fun_implies_algebra_fun` (which is shown in Figure 18) is proved along the same lines. The formal proof is about 49 steps long.

---

[3] The differences between our proofs can be attributed to the empty type issue mentioned earlier, but also because we avoided the form of contrapositive used there, $(\neg p \Rightarrow \neg q) \Rightarrow (q \Rightarrow p)$, which is not constructively valid.

```
∀F:Functor{i'}(large_category{i},large_category{i}).
  ∀I:{I:Algebra(F)| algebra_category(F)-initial(I)} .
    ∀A:large_category{i}_Obj. Dec(A) ⇒
    Mor[large_category{i}](I_obj,A) ⇒Mor[large_category{i}](F_0 A,A)
```

Fig. 18. Theorem: `hom_fun_implies_algebra_fun`

We are now ready to prove Theorem 7.

Proof.

$$\ker(Fh) \subseteq \ker(h \cdot in)$$
$$\Longleftarrow \quad \{ \text{ Lemma 2}, h : \mu F \to A \}$$
$$\ker(Fh) \subseteq \ker(h \cdot in) \land FA \to A \neq \emptyset$$
$$\Longrightarrow \quad \{ \text{ Lemma 1 } \}$$
$$\exists g : FA \to A. \quad h \cdot in = g \cdot Fh$$
$$\Longleftarrow \quad \{ \text{ universal property } \}$$
$$\exists g : FA \to A. \quad h = \text{fold } g.$$

$\square$

Clearly we can decide whether an element in FA is in the image of Fh when Fh is surjective (onto). We will show that Fh is surjective if h is. Therefore every surjective function that satisfies the condition of kernel inclusion is a catamorphism if we can decide whether its codomain A is empty[4]. We could relatively easily prove this as a corollary to Theorem 7. Closer inspection of the proof of Theorem 7 however shows that when h is surjective, we do not need the additional assumption that we can decide whether A is empty.

Theorem 8. *Suppose $F : \mathcal{SET} \to \mathcal{SET}$ is a functor with an initial algebra $\langle \mu F, in \rangle$, and $h : \mu F \to A$ is surjective. Then*

$$(\exists g : FA \to A. \quad h = \text{fold } g) \Longleftarrow \ker(Fh) \subseteq \ker(h \cdot in).$$

We first prove that a function is surjective if and only if it is right-invertible in $\mathcal{SET}$.

Lemma 3. *Suppose $f : A \to B$. Then*

$$f \text{ is surjective} \Longleftrightarrow f \text{ is right-invertible in } \mathcal{SET}.$$

Proof. For the ($\Rightarrow$) direction, suppose f is surjective. Then there exists a function $g : B \to A$ such that $f(g(b)) = b$ for all $b \in B$ (by the Axiom of Choice). Hence $f \cdot g = id(B)$, so f is right-invertible.

For the ($\Leftarrow$) direction, suppose f is right-invertible in $\mathcal{SET}$. Then $f \cdot g = id(B)$ for some function $g : B \to A$. Now let $b \in B$. Then $f(g(b)) = (f \cdot g)(b) = (id(B))(b) = b$. Therefore f is surjective. $\square$

---

[4] Note that every injective (one-to-one) function is a catamorphism by Theorem 3.

Figure 19 shows a formalization of the lemma in Nuprl. The formal proof is about 33 steps long and makes use of the `ax_choice` lemma from the Nuprl standard library.

```
∀A,B:U_i. ∀f:A → B.
    Surj(A;B;f) ⟺ right-invertible[large_category{i}](<A, B, f>)
```

Fig. 19. Theorem: `surjective_iff_right_invertible`

We also state and prove a lifted version of the lemma for arrows in the category of types. This lifted version is shown in Figure 20. Lifting the lemma requires about 11 proof steps using the lemma `surjective_iff_right_invertible`.

```
∀f:large_category{i}_Arr
    Surj(large_category{i}_dom f;large_category{i}_cod f;f.2.2)
    ⟺ right-invertible[large_category{i}](f)
```

Fig. 20. Theorem `surjective_iff_right_invertible_cat`

We now prove a lemma similar to Lemma 1, but for surjective functions.

Lemma 4. *Suppose $f : A \to B$ is surjective, and suppose $h : A \to C$. Then*

$$(\exists g : B \to C. \quad h = g \cdot f) \Longleftarrow \ker f \subseteq \ker h.$$

Proof. Assume $\ker f \subseteq \ker h$.

Let *choice* $: B \to A$ be a function with $f(choice(b)) = b$ for all $b \in B$ (such a function *choice* exists by the Axiom of Choice since f is surjective). Define $g : B \to C$ by $g(b) = h(choice(b))$ for every $b \in B$.

Now $h = g \cdot f$ by construction of g: Let $a \in A$. Since $f(choice(f(a))) = f(a)$ by definition of *choice*, $(choice(f(a)), a) \in \ker f \subseteq \ker h$. Therefore $g(f(a)) = h(choice(f(a))) = h(a)$. □

Figure 21 shows a formalization of this lemma in Nuprl. The formal proof requires about 14 steps. It is similar to the proof of `kernel_inclusion_implies_postfactor`, but slightly simpler – just like the informal proof.

```
∀A,B,C:U_i. ∀f:A → B. ∀h:A → C. Surj(A;B;f) ⇒
 ((∃g:B → C. h = g o f) ⟸ ker[A,B] f ⊆ ker[A,C] h)
```

Fig. 21. Theorem: `kernel_inclusion_implies_postfactor_surjective`

As for the `kernel_inclusion_implies_postfactor` lemma above, we prove a lifted version of this lemma for arrows in the category of types. The lifted version is shown in Figure 22. Its proof is similar to the proof of the lifted lemma for functions with a decidable image (see Figure 16) and requires about 47 steps.

```
∀A,B,C:large_category{i}_Obj. ∀f:Mor[large_category{i}](A,B).
 ∀h:Mor[large_category{i}](A,C). Surj(A;B;f.2.2) ⇒
  ((∃g:Mor[large_category{i}](B,C). h = g large_category{i}_op f)
      ⟸ ker[A,B] f.2.2 ⊆ ker[A,C] h.2.2)
```

Fig. 22. Theorem: `kernel_inclusion_implies_postfactor_surjective_cat`

Using the two Lemmata 3 and 4, we can now prove Theorem 8.

Proof. We first show that $Fh : F(\mu F) \to FA$ is surjective. Since h is surjective, h is right-invertible by Lemma 3. Let $g : A \to \mu F$ be a function with $h \cdot g = id(A)$. Then

$$Fh \cdot Fg$$
$$= \quad \{ \text{ functors } \}$$
$$F(h \cdot g)$$
$$= \quad \{ \text{ assumption } \}$$
$$F(id(A))$$
$$= \quad \{ \text{ functors } \}$$
$$id(FA).$$

Hence Fh is right-invertible, and therefore surjective (again by Lemma 3). Now

$$\ker(Fh) \subseteq \ker(h \cdot in)$$
$$\Longrightarrow \quad \{ \text{ Lemma 4 } \}$$
$$\exists g : FA \to A. \quad h \cdot in = g \cdot Fh$$
$$\Longleftrightarrow \quad \{ \text{ universal property } \}$$
$$\exists g : FA \to A. \quad h = \mathsf{fold}\, g$$

completing the proof.   □

See Figure 23 for a statement of this theorem in Nuprl. We use the lemma `kernel_inclusion_implies_postfactor_surjective_cat` to prove the existence of g, and `surjective_iff_right_invertible_cat` to prove that Fh is surjective. Altogether the formal proof requires about 145 steps.

```
∀F:Functor{i'}(large_category{i},large_category{i}).
 ∀I:{I:Algebra(F)| algebra_category(F)-initial(I)} .
  ∀A:large_category{i}_Obj. ∀h:Mor[large_category{i}](I_obj,A).
   Surj(I_obj;A;h.2.2) ⇒
     ((∃g:Algebra(F). h=fold[large_category{i},F,I](g) )
        ⇐ ker[F_O I_obj,large_category{i}_cod (F_M h)] (F_M h).2.2
           ⊆ ker[F_O I_obj,large_category{i}_cod (h F_dom_op I_arr)]
              (h F_dom_op I_arr).2.2)
```

Fig. 23. Theorem: `kernel_inclusion_implies_fold_surjective`

We now have two simple conditions for when a constructive function h that satisfies the condition of kernel inclusion is a catamorphism: h is a catamorphism if the image of Fh is decidable and we can decide whether the codomain of h is empty, and h is a catamorphism if h is surjective.

6.2   A Small Example

Embedded in the constructive proof of Thm. 7 is an algorithm to compute a function g such that $h = \mathsf{fold}\, g$. As an example, we want to apply this algorithm to the function `all`, defined by `all p L = and (map p L)`. Here L is a list over some type T, and $p : T \to \mathbb{B}$. This function computes whether all elements in L satisfy the predicate p. To do so however, the implementation first iterates over L to compute an intermediate list of boolean values, and then it iterates over the list of booleans to compute their conjunction. Writing `all` directly as a catamorphism would eliminate the need for an intermediate list.

Before we can prove that `all` can be written as a catamorphism, we have to show that $List(T)$ is the object of an initial algebra. Consider the functor $\mathcal{L}_T : \mathcal{SET} \to \mathcal{SET}$, defined by $\mathcal{L}_T(A) = \mathbf{1} + (T \times A)$ and $\mathcal{L}_T(f) = id(\mathbf{1}) + (id(T) \times f)$. Formally verifying that this is in fact a functor takes about 54 proof steps in Nuprl. This functor has an initial algebra $(\mu\mathcal{L}_T, in) = (List(T), nil + cons)$. To verify initiality, we have to show that for every other algebra (A, f) there exists a unique homomorphism h from $(List(T), nil + cons)$ to (A, f). Since h is a homomorphism, $h([]) = f(inl \cdot)$ and $h(u :: v) = f(inr (u, h(v)))$ for all $u \in T$, $v \in List(T)$. Both that h is a homomorphism and that h is unique can then be proved by structural induction on lists. The formal proof is quite technical, and complicated by our inevitable formalization of algebras, homomorphisms and arrows in the category of types as tuples. With approximately 211 proof steps, it is the longest proof in this paper. About 140 of those steps are required only to show uniqueness of h. However, initiality only needs to be proven once for each data-type. Having proven initiality of $List(T)$, we can treat any list-consuming function, not just `all`.

Using the `kernel_inclusion_implies_fold` theorem, we can now prove that the composition of `map` and `and` is a catamorphism. We need just one more assumption: that we can decide for all $b \in \mathbb{B}$ whether there exists a list $L \in List(T)$ with $b = and(map(p; L))$. Since $and(map(p; [])) = $ true, it is sufficient if we can decide whether $p(t) = $ false for some $t \in T$. (If there is such a t, false $= and(map(p; t :: []))$. Otherwise $and(map(p; L)) = $ true for all $L \in List(T)$. This argument is reflected in the structure of the resulting program.) Figure 24 shows the Nuprl theorem `list_and_2_map_is_fold`.

```
* THM list_and_2_map_is_fold
∀T:U. ∀p:T → B.
Dec(∃t:T. p t = false)
⇒ (∃g:Algebra(ListF{i}(T))
    <T List, B, λL.∧ᵦ(map(p;L))> =
    fold[large_category{i},ListF{i}(T),InitialAlgebra(ListF(T))](g) )
```

Fig. 24. Theorem `list_and_2_map_is_fold`

We can unfold its extract (and the extracts of other lemmata that were used in its proof) to obtain the actual function g with $and(map(p; \cdot)) = $ fold g. This function (with a few simplifications made by hand) is shown in Figure 25. The first and second component of the triple are the function's domain and codomain, respectively. The `if-then-else` statement is used to determine whether $x \in \mathbf{1} + (T \times \mathbb{B})$ is in the image of $\mathcal{L}_T(and(map(p; \cdot)))$. Three cases need to be distinguished: $x = inl \cdot$, $x = inr (y1, true)$, and $x = inr (y1, false)$. The latter can only occur if $p(t) = $ false for some $t \in T$; whether such a t exists is determined by the value of ϕ. If x is in the image of $\mathcal{L}_T(and(map(p;\cdot)))$, the **then** part is used to apply $and(map(p;\cdot)) \cdot (nil + cons)$ to an element $z \in 1 + (T \times List(T))$ with $(\mathcal{L}_T(and(map(p;\cdot))))(z) = x$. Otherwise, an arbitrary boolean (in this case true) is returned in the **else** part.

```
< (ListF{i}(T)_0 B)
, B
, λx.if case x
     of inl(_) => true
     | inr(<y1,y2>) => case y2
                of inl(_) => true
                | inr(_) => case φ
                     of inl(_) => true
                     | inr(_) => false
   then (<T List, B, λL.∧b(map(p;L))> ListF{i}(T)_dom_op
     InitialAlgebra(ListF(T))_arr).2.2
     (case x
     of inl(_) => <inl ·, Ax>
     | inr(<y1,y2>) => case y2
                of inl(_) => <inr <y1, []> , Ax>
                | inr(_) => case φ
                     of inl(<t,_>) => <inr <y1, t::[]>, Ax>
                     | inr(_) => arbitrary)
     else true
fi >
```

Fig. 25. A function g with $and(map(p;\cdot)) = \mathsf{fold}\ g$

The function shown in Figure 25 is unlikely to be more efficient than the initial composition of **and** and **map**, due to the increased overhead associated with each list element. However, we could further simplify the function by using $and(map(p;[])) = \text{true}$ and $and(map(p;t :: [])) = \text{false}$ and combining the two outermost **case** constructs (which have identical structure).

6.3 Constructively Characterizing unfold

Now we consider reformulating the ($\Leftarrow$) direction of Theorem 6. To prove it, we identify additional assumptions under which the inclusion of images constructively implies the existence of prefactors. Dualizing our results for kernels and postfactors, one could suspect that (among other things) we need to be able to decide whether the domain of h is empty. However, it turns out that the classical proof of the ($\Leftarrow$) direction of Theorem 6 given in [6] can be simplified significantly. In particular, the dual of Lemma 2, although easily provable in Nuprl (see Fig. 26), turns out not to be needed.

```
∀F:Functor{i'}(large_category{i},large_category{i}).
  ∀T:{T:Coalgebra(F)| coalgebra_category(F)-terminal(T)} .
    ∀A:large_category{i}_Obj. Dec(A) ⇒
      Mor[large_category{i}](A,T_obj) ⇒ Mor[large_category{i}](A,F_0 A)
```

Fig. 26. Theorem: `cohom_fun_implies_coalgebra_fun`

Therefore it is sufficient to replace the precondition $\text{img}(out \cdot h) \subseteq \text{img}(Fh)$ by the (classically equivalent) condition $\forall c \in \text{img}(out \cdot h). \exists b \in FA. \quad c = (Fh)(b)$ to give a constructive proof. We first prove that the latter condition implies the existence of prefactors.

Lemma 5. *Suppose that $f : B \to C$ and $h : A \to C$, where A, B, C are sets. Then $(\exists g : A \to B. \quad h = f \cdot g) \Longleftarrow (\forall c \in \text{img}\, h. \exists b \in B. \quad c = f(b))$.*

Proof. Assume $\forall c \in \text{img}\, h. \exists b \in B. \quad c = f(b)$. Let $choice : \text{img}\, h \to B$ be a function with $f(choice(c)) = c$ for all $c \in \text{img}\, h$. Now define $g = choice \cdot h$. Then $(f \cdot g)(a) = f(choice(h(a))) = h(a)$ for every $a \in A$, hence $h = f \cdot g$. $\qquad\square$

Note the difference between Lemma 5 and [6, Lemma 5.3]: our proof does not need $A \to B \neq \emptyset$ as an additional assumption. Figure 27 shows the corresponding Nuprl theorem, which is proved in 19 steps. As usual, we prove a lifted version for arrows in the category of types. This lifted version is shown in Fig. 28; using the `image_inv_fun_implies_prefactor` lemma, it is proved in 45 steps.

```
∀A,B,C:𝕌ᵢ. ∀f:B → C. ∀h:A → C. (∃g:A → B. h = f o g)
  ⇐ (∀c:img[A,C] h. ∃b:B. c = f b)
```

Fig. 27. Theorem: `image_inv_fun_implies_prefactor`

```
∀A,B,C:large_category{i}_Obj. ∀f:Mor[large_category{i}](B,C).
  ∀h:Mor[large_category{i}](A,C).
   (∃g:Mor[large_category{i}](A,B). h = f large_category{i}_op g)
     ⇐ (∀c:img[A,C] h.2.2 ∃b:B. c = f.2.2 b)
```

Fig. 28. Theorem: `image_inv_fun_implies_prefactor_cat`

Our main result for anamorphisms is now immediate.

Theorem 9. *Suppose $F : \mathcal{SET} \to \mathcal{SET}$ is a functor with a terminal coalgebra $\langle \nu F, out \rangle$, A is a set, and $h : A \to \nu F$. Then*

$$(\exists g : A \to FA. \quad h = unfold\, g) \Longleftarrow (\forall c \in \text{img}(out \cdot h). \exists b \in FA. \quad c = (Fh)(b)).$$

Proof.

$$\forall c \in \text{img}(out \cdot h). \exists b \in FA. \quad c = (Fh)(b)$$
$$\Longrightarrow \quad \{\text{ Lemma 5 }\}$$
$$\exists g : A \to FA. \quad out \cdot h = Fh \cdot g$$
$$\Longleftrightarrow \quad \{\text{ universal property }\}$$
$$\exists g : A \to FA. \quad h = unfold\, g.$$

$\qquad\square$

Theorem `image_inv_fun_implies_unfold`, shown in Fig. 29, is the corresponding Nuprl theorem. Again mostly due to well-formedness goals, the formal proof requires about 91 steps.

```
∀F:Functor{i'}(large_category{i},large_category{i}).
 ∀T:{T:Coalgebra(F)| coalgebra_category(F)-terminal(T)} .
  ∀A:large_category{i}_Obj. ∀h:Mor[large_category{i}](A,T_obj).
   (∃g:Coalgebra(F). h=unfold[large_category{i},F,T](g))
      ⇐ (∀c:img[A,F_O T_obj] (T_arr F_dom_op h).2.2
           ∃b:F_O A. c = (F_M h).2.2 b)
```

Fig. 29. Theorem: `image_inv_fun_implies_unfold`

7   Conclusions

We have presented a constructive characterization of fold and unfold which we believe is of interest, independent of the formalizations presented here. However, we *have* completely formalized these results in Nuprl. The extract of Thm. 7 was applied to a small example involving the reformulation of the program `all p L = and (map p L)` as a fold. The hardest part of that proof was to show that the inductive type $List(T)$ is in fact the object of an initial algebra. However, proofs of initiality or finality only need be done once for each data-type. We have also proven finality for the coinductive type $Stream(T)$ and exercised the extract of Thm. 9 on a simple stream-generating function.

The presented program transformations could be used in an optimizing compiler to transform any function that meets certain (rather simple) semantic criteria into a fold or unfold. No knowledge of the function's implementation is required. Of course this generality comes at a price: the semantic properties that must be verified are, like all non-trivial semantic properties, not decidable in general. The compiler could analyze the function in question to try and prove these properties automatically, it could rely on human guidance, or it could use a combination of both approaches.

In the longer term, we hope to incorporate a wide variety of program transformations into the framework outlined here.

References

1. Stuart Allen. *NuprlPrimitives - Explanations of Nuprl Primitives and Conventions.* Department of Computer Science, Cornell University, Ithaca, NY, 2003. http://www.cs.cornell.edu/Info/People/sfa/Nuprl/NuprlPrimitives/.
2. Richard S. Bird. Functional algorithm design. In Bernhard Moller, editor, *Mathematics of Program Construction '95*, volume 947 of *Lecture Notes in Computer Science*, pages 2–17. Springer-Verlag, 1995.
3. Rod M. Burstall and John Darlington. A transformation system for developing recursive programs. *Journal of the ACM*, 24(1):44–67, January 1977.
4. James Caldwell. Extracting recursion operators in Nuprl's type-theory. In A. Pettorossi, editor, *Eleventh International Workshop on Logic-based Program Synthesis, LOPSTR-02*, volume 2372 of *LNCS*, pages 124–131. Springer, 2002.

5. Robert L. Constable, Stuart F. Allen, H. M. Bromley, W. R. Cleaveland, J. F. Cremer, R. W. Harper, Douglas J. Howe, T. B. Knoblock, N. P. Mendler, P. Panangaden, James T. Sasaki, and Scott F. Smith. *Implementing Mathematics with the Nuprl Proof Development System*. Prentice-Hall, NJ, 1986.

6. Jeremy Gibbons, Graham Hutton, and Thorsten Altenkirch. When is a function a fold or an unfold? In Andrea Corradini, Marina Lenisa, and Ugo Montanari, editors, *Proceedings 4th Workshop on Coalgebraic Methods in Computer Science, CMCS'01, Genova, Italy, 6–7 Apr. 2001*, volume 44(1). Elsevier, Amsterdam, 2001.

7. Jeremy Gibbons and Geraint Jones. The under-appreciated unfold. In *Proceedings 3rd ACM SIGPLAN Int. Conf. on Functional Programming, ICFP'98, Baltimore, MD, USA, 26–29 Sept. 1998*, volume 34(1), pages 273–279. ACM Press, New York, 1998.

8. Graham Hutton. Fold and unfold for program semantics. In *Proceedings 3rd ACM SIGPLAN Int. Conf. on Functional Programming, ICFP'98, Baltimore, MD, USA, 26–29 Sept. 1998*, volume 34(1), pages 280–288. ACM Press, New York, 1998.

9. Graham Hutton. A tutorial on the universality and expressiveness of fold. *Journal of Functional Programming*, 9(4):355–372, 1999.

10. Saunders MacLane. *Categories for the Working Mathematician*, volume 5 of *Graduate Texts in Mathematics*. Springer-Verlag, New York, 2nd edition, 1997. (1st ed., 1971).

11. G. Malcolm. Algebraic data types and program transformation. *Science of Computer Programming*, 14(2–3):255–280, 1990.

12. Per Martin-Löf. Constructive mathematics and computer programming. In *Sixth International Congress for Logic, Methodology, and Philosophy of Science*, pages 153–175, 1982.

13. Erik Meijer, Maarten Fokkinga, and Ross Paterson. Functional programming with bananas, lenses, envelopes and barbed wire. In J. Hughes, editor, *Proceedings 5th ACM Conf. on Functional Programming Languages and Computer Architecture, FPCA'91, Cambridge, MA, USA, 26–30 Aug 1991*, volume 523, pages 124–144. Springer-Verlag, Berlin, 1991.

14. P. Wadler. Deforestation: Transforming programs to eliminate trees. In *ESOP '88. European Symposium on Programming, Nancy, France, 1988*, volume 300 of *Lecture Notes in Computer Science*, pages 344–358. Berlin: Springer-Verlag, 1988.

15. Tjark Weber. Program transformations in Nuprl. Master's thesis, University of Wyoming, Laramie, WY, August 2002.

Deterministic Higher-Order Patterns
for Program Transformation

Tetsuo Yokoyama[1], Zhenjiang Hu[1,2], and Masato Takeichi[1]

[1] Department of Mathematical Informatics,
Graduate School of Information Science and Technology,
University of Tokyo,
7-3-1 Hongo, Bunkyo-ku, Tokyo 113-8656, Japan
{tetsuo_yokoyama,hu,takeichi}@mist.i.u-tokyo.ac.jp
[2] PRESTO21, Japan Science and Technology Agency

Abstract. Higher-order patterns, together with higher-order matching, enable concise specification of program transformation, and have been implemented in several program transformation systems. However, higher-order matching in general is nondeterministic, and the matching algorithm is so expensive that even second-order matching is NP-complete. It is orthodox to impose constraint on the form of patterns to obtain the desirable matches satisfying certain properties such as decidability and finiteness. In the context of unification, Miller's *higher-order patterns* have a single most general unifier. We relax the restrictions in his patterns without changing determinism within the context of matching instead of unification. As a consequence, the new class of patterns covers a wide class of useful patterns for program transformation. The time-complexity of the matching algorithm is linear for the size of a term for a fixed pattern.

Keywords: Higher-order pattern matching; Functional programming; Program derivation; Program transformation; Fusion transformation

1 Introduction

Patterns, together with pattern matching algorithms, play an important role in the specification of transformation rules as well as the implementation of transformation systems. Usually, the more flexible the patterns are, the more difficult it is to design efficient matching algorithms. Although first-order patterns are simple and first-order matching algorithms are cheap and deterministic, these patterns lack descriptive power. In contrast, although the second- (or higher-) order patterns [1–3] are flexible enabling powerful transformation to be concisely specified, second-order matching algorithms are expensive and nondeterministic.

Consider, for example, fusion transformation [4, 5], which is used to optimize programs by eliminating the unnecessary intermediate data structures that are passed between functions. The basic fusion transformation rule (in Haskell-like notation [6]) is:

$$\frac{\forall x, y.\, x \otimes f\ y = f(x \oplus y)}{f\ .\ foldr\ (\oplus)\ e = foldr\ (\otimes)\ (f\ e)},$$

M. Bruynooghe (Ed.): LOPSTR 2004, LNCS 3018, pp. 128–142, 2004.

which states that a composition of function f with a *foldr* can be fused into a single *foldr*, provided one can find function $\otimes$ satisfying the side condition, i.e.,

$$x \otimes f\ y = f\ (x \oplus y)\ .$$

Note that the key step in fusion transformation is to find function $\otimes$ meeting the side condition. This is actually a higher-order matching problem: matching higher-order pattern $\lambda x\,y.\,x \otimes f\ y$ with term[1] $\lambda x\,y.\,f\ (x \otimes y)$ to obtain a substitution (definition) for pattern variable $\otimes$. To be more concrete, let us look at the fusion of the following program to compute the sum of squares of each element of a list[2].

$$
\begin{aligned}
sumsq\ &=\ sum\ .\ foldr\ (\lambda x\,y.\,x * x : y)\ [\,] \\
\textbf{where}\ sum\ [\,] \quad\ \ &=\ 0 \\
sum\ (x : xs)\ &=\ x + sum\ x
\end{aligned}
$$

Expanding the right-hand side of the fusion condition, we get

$$
\begin{aligned}
&\lambda x\,y.\,f\ (x \oplus y) \\
=\quad &\{\ \text{instanciating } \oplus\ \} \\
&\lambda x\,y.\,sum\ (x * x : y) \\
=\quad &\{\ \text{definition of } sum\ \} \\
&\lambda x\,y.\,x * x + sum\ y
\end{aligned}
$$

We then obtain $\otimes$ by matching the resulting term, $\lambda x\,y.\,x * x + sum\ y$, with pattern $\lambda x\,y.\,x \otimes sum\ y$. This pattern is beyond Miller's higher-order pattern, and match

$$\{\otimes \mapsto \lambda y_1\,y_2.\,y_1 * y_1 + y_2\}$$

cannot be obtained by first-order matching. Our approach, on the other hand, can deal with such patterns and guarantee a unique match.

Despite the attractive power of higher-order patterns and higher-order matching, there have been several significant objections to the use of higher-order matching for implementing program transformation, particularly in functional languages.

- First, higher-order matching is known to be so expensive that even second-order is NP-complete [7]. Therefore, really efficient implementation is out of the question.
- Second, higher-order matching algorithms are generally nondeterministic, resulting in more than one solution. Unlike logic languages such as Prolog, which deal with this sort of nondeterminism by means of backtracking, it cannot be directly handled by functional languages.
- Last, although solutions to the matching problem can clearly be specified, nondeterminism makes the semantics complex and it is often difficult to explain why a particular match was not produced.

---

[1] Strictly speaking, the term should be normalized before being matched with a pattern.

[2] Here binary operators (.), (*), (:), and (+) are constants.

Fortunately, experience in implementing program transformation systems tells that it is not really necessary to have fully flexible higher-order patterns and higher-order matching in practice. We may, therefore, think of imposing reasonable restrictions on the form of patterns to generate desirable higher-order matching that is both *deterministic* and *efficient*. It is known that by restricting the form of patterns, one can make possibly undecidable fifth-order matching decidable [8], and infinite third-order matching finite [2].

Within the context of unification, Miller defined a class of *higher-order patterns* [9]. In his higher-order patterns, each occurrence of free variables should be applied to a sequence of distinct bound variables. For example, the pattern

$$\lambda x\, y.\, p\, y\, x$$

is valid, since free variable p appears at the head of application $p\, y\, x$ and the arguments of p, namely x and y, are distinct bound variables. However, the patterns of $\lambda x.\, p\, x\, x$ where p has the same bound variable x, $\lambda x.\, p\, (x+x)$ where the argument $(x+x)$ of p is not a variable, and $p\, q$ where the argument q of p is not a bound variable, are all invalid. It has been proved that general higher-order unification (matching) with respect to Miller's patterns is deterministic, and this has been implemented [10]. Miller's patterns are, however, too restrictive to describe program transformation rules. For instance, the arguments of free variables in a pattern may be complicated terms instead of variables, as can be seen in the fusion law where the arguments of free variable $\otimes$ in the pattern are x and $f\, y$.

In this paper, we relax the restriction of Miller's higher-order patterns by allowing the arguments to be terms, and propose new class $\mathcal{A}$ of patterns, with the following features.

- Class $\mathcal{A}$ covers a wider class of patterns that are often used in specifying program transformation and program calculation. It enables the fusion law to be concisely described. This is very important, as fusion law plays an essential role in program transformation and calculation [11, 12] and many other transformations can be formalized using this law.
- The higher-order matching algorithm for any patterns in class $\mathcal{A}$ is as simple and efficient as a first-order matching algorithm.

The organization of the paper is as follows. Section 2 gives a formal definition for class $\mathcal{A}$. In Section 3, we prove the determinism of our matching algorithm with respect to patterns in class $\mathcal{A}$. In Section 4, we present an efficient algorithm, and prove its soundness and efficiency. We briefly explain related work in Section 6 and conclude the paper in Section 7.

2   Deterministic Higher-Order Patterns

We consider simply typed lambda *terms* recursively defined by constants, variables, applications, and λ-abstractions as follows.

$$T \;=\; c \mid v \mid T\,T \mid \lambda x\,.\,T$$

Let FV be a function mapping from a term to a set of free variables in the term. For example, $FV(\lambda x.\, p\, x)$ returns p. We call term E *closed* if $FV(E) = \{\,\}$. For readability, we sometimes use the infix notation, so $x + y$ denotes term $(+)\, x\, y$. A β-redex is an expression of the form $(\lambda x.\, B)\, E$; a β-reduction replaces a β-redex with *body* B where every occurrence of bound variables x is replaced by argument E. An η-redex is an expression of form $\lambda x.\, E\, x$ where E does not contain x, which is η-reduced into E. We call a term β-*normal* if the term does not contain any β-redex, and similarly we call term η-*normal* if the term does not contain any η-redex. We call $\beta\eta$-normal *normal*. We sometimes write $\lambda \bar{x}.\, p\, \bar{E}$ for $\lambda x_1 \cdots \lambda x_l.\, p\, E_1 \cdots E_m$.

We say that a term E_1 is a *subterm* of E_2, denoted by $E_1 \trianglelefteq E_2$, if $E_1 \in subTerm(E_2)$ (here α-renaming is implicitly assumed), where $subTerm$ is defined below:

$$
\begin{aligned}
subTerm(c) &= \{c\} \\
subTerm(v) &= \{v\} \\
subTerm(E_1\, E_2) &= \{E_1\, E_2\} \cup subTerm(E_1) \cup subTerm(E_2) \\
subTerm(\lambda x.\, E) &= \{\lambda x.\, E\} \cup subTerm(E)
\end{aligned}
$$

We call terms $E_i (1 \leq i \leq m)$ *distinct* iff each E_i is not a subterm of the others. Let $v\, T_1\, \cdots\, T_n$ a subterm and v a variable. We call $T_1, \ldots, T_n$ *arguments* of v, and call v the *head* of the subterm.

We call a term *flexible* iff the head of the term is a free variable, otherwise we call it *rigid*.

A *context* $C[]$ is a term with some holes in it. Note that a free variable in T may become bound in $C[T]$.

A *substitution* (or *match*) is mapping from variables to closed terms and denoted

$$
\phi = \{p \mapsto \lambda x.\, x\, b\}\ .
$$

We denote the domain of substitution ϕ as $dom(\phi)$. The composition of substitutions ϕ and ψ is defined if the substitutions are *compatible*, i.e., the same variables in domains have the same ranges:

$$
\forall v \in dom(\phi) \cap dom(\psi)\,.\, \phi\, v =_{\alpha\beta\eta} \psi\, v\ ,
$$

where the equality operator $(=_{\alpha\beta\eta})$ is modulo $\alpha\beta\eta$-conversion. Otherwise, it will return the special match *fail*. Note that *fail* is the zero of match composition, i.e.,

$$
fail \circ m = m \circ fail = fail\ .
$$

For example, the composition of substitutions $\{p \mapsto c\} \circ \{p \mapsto \lambda x.\, x\}$ is *fail*.

Types are constructed in the usual way in simply typed lambda calculus. Let T_0 be a set of base types. Type set T is defined as follows.

$$
\begin{aligned}
\alpha \in T_0 &\Rightarrow \alpha \in T \\
\alpha, \beta \in T &\Rightarrow \alpha \to \beta \in T
\end{aligned}
$$

The *order* of type τ $ord(\tau)$ is defined as follows.

$$
\begin{aligned}
ord(\alpha) &= 1, \quad \textbf{if } \alpha \in T_0 \\
ord(\alpha \to \beta) &= max\{ord(\alpha) + 1, ord(\beta)\}
\end{aligned}
$$

The order of any base type is 1. The order of function types is a maximum of one plus the order of the argument type and the order of the result type. The order of a term is defined as the order of its type.

Given term P and closed term T where P and T are normal, a *matching pair* is a pair of terms written as $P \to T$. We call P the *pattern* for the matching pair. The order of a pattern is the maximum order of free variables in the pattern.

The general *matching problem* is defined as follows. Given matching pair $P \to T$, find all substitutions ϕ such that $\phi P =_{\alpha\beta\eta} T$. We call this substitution *match*, and write $\phi \vdash P \to T$ to indicate that ϕ is a match of matching pair $P \to T$. If matching produces at most one ϕ such that $\phi \vdash P \to T$, i.e.,

$$
\forall\phi_1 \forall\phi_2. \phi_1 \vdash P \to T \ \wedge \ \phi_2 \vdash P \to T \Rightarrow \phi_1 =_{\alpha\beta\eta} \phi_2 \ ,
$$

we say it is *deterministic*, or simply say that $\phi \vdash P \to T$ is deterministic. We call a class of higher-order patterns *deterministic higher-order patterns* ($\mathcal{DHP}$) iff matching a pattern in this class with a closed term will give at most one match. The order of the matching problem is the order of the pattern. We call more than a first-order matching problem a *higher-order matching problem*.

In this paper, we use the following notational convention. We use a, b, c, and d, strings starting from small letters, and binary operators $(+)$ and $(*)$ to represent constants, and use other small letters such as e, p, v, x, and operators $\oplus$ and $\otimes$ to represent variables. We will use p, q, and r to denote the free variables and w, x, y, and z to denote bound variables to distinguish these in a pattern. We use the Greek identifiers ϕ, ψ, and σ to represent matches, and capital letters such as B, E, P, T to represent patterns and terms.

We are now ready to define class $\mathcal{A}$ of patterns. We will see later that patterns in this class are $\mathcal{DHP}$, i.e., matching a pattern in this class with a closed term will give at most one match. The class of patterns is a simple extension of Miller's higher-order patterns, which has at most single most-general unification; the arguments of every free variable in the pattern must be distinct and be bound variables.

Definition 1. *Term P is class $\mathcal{A}$, iff arguments $E_1, \ldots, E_m$ of any free variable occurring in a normalized term of P satisfy the following conditions.*

   (i) $\forall i. FV(E_i) \neq \{\}$,
   (ii) $\forall i, j. i \neq j \Rightarrow E_i \not\trianglelefteq E_j$,
   (iii) $\forall i. (v \in FV(E_i) \Rightarrow v \notin FV(P))$, *and*
   (iv) *For all i, E_i is not a λ-abstraction.* □

The conditions for arguments are a relaxation of Miller's idea from "distinct and bound variables" to "non-mutually embedded terms containing bound variables": (i) E_i should not be a closed term. For example, term $p\ 1$ is not of class

$\mathcal{A}$ because argument 1 is closed. (ii) For all $i,j(i \neq j)$, E_i is not a subterm of E_j. Therefore, $\lambda x.\, p\, x\, (x+1)$ is not of class $\mathcal{A}$ since argument x is a subterm of another argument $x+1$. (iii) Free variables in E_i should be bounded in pattern P. As a result, $p\, q$ is not of class $\mathcal{A}$. (iv) For example, $p\, (\lambda x.\, x)$ is not of class $\mathcal{A}$ because argument $(\lambda x.\, x)$ is a λ-abstraction.

Class $\mathcal{A}$ covers a wide class of useful patterns for describing transformation rules. Pattern $\lambda x\, y.\, x \otimes f\, y$ in the fusion law discussed in the introduction is of class $\mathcal{A}$. Another example is, the following pattern of a class $\mathcal{A}$

$$\lambda w\, x.\, \textbf{if } p\, x \textbf{ then } q\, x \textbf{ else } r\, (car\, x)\, (w\, (cdr\, x))\ ,$$

which is used to extract a specific program structure. This pattern is beyond Miller's higher-order patterns since the arguments of free variable r are not variables. Matching this pattern with the program

$$\begin{aligned}\lambda reverse\, x.\, &\textbf{if } null\, x \textbf{ then } x \textbf{ else}\\ &append\, (reverse\, (cdr\, x))\, (cons\, (car\, x)\, nil)\end{aligned}$$

gives the unique match

$$\{p \mapsto null, q \mapsto \lambda x.\, x, r \mapsto \lambda z\, w.\, append\, w\, (cons\, z\, nil)\}\ ,$$

and matching the pattern with the program

$$\begin{aligned}\lambda mapsquare\, x.\, &\textbf{if } null\, x \textbf{ then } x \textbf{ else}\\ &cons\, (square\, (car\, x))\, (mapsquare\, (cdr\, x))\end{aligned}$$

gives another unique match

$$\{p \mapsto null, q \mapsto \lambda x.\, x, r \mapsto \lambda z\, w.\, cons\, (square\, z)\, w\}\ .$$

We will discuss the matching algorithm later.

3   Deterministic Higher-Order Matching

Thus far, we have given the definition of class $\mathcal{A}$ of patterns, where matching a term with one of these patterns is guaranteed to produce a unique match if one exists. We prove this in this section, and in Section 4 describe an efficient algorithm to obtain the match.

To begin with, let us introduce the important concept of discharging subterms. Discharging $E_1, \ldots, E_m$ by $y_1, \ldots, y_m$ in T means replacing all occurrences of $E_1, \ldots, E_m$ with fresh variables $y_1, \ldots, y_m$ respectively in T. One possible implementation is given in Fig. 1. Intuitively, the function

$$discharge\, [(y_1, E_1), \ldots, (y_m, E_m)]\, T$$

replaces all occurrences of $E_1, \ldots, E_m$ with fresh variables $y_1, \ldots, y_m$ respectively in T. That is

$$\begin{aligned}B = discharge\, &[(y_1, E_1), \ldots, (y_m, E_m)]\, T\ \wedge\ \forall i.\, E_i \text{ is not a } \lambda\text{-abstraction}\\ &\Rightarrow (\lambda \bar{y}.\, B)\, \bar{E} =_{\alpha\beta\eta} T\ \wedge\ \forall i.\, E_i \not\leq B\ .\end{aligned}$$

$discharge\ s\ c\ =\ c$
$discharge\ s\ v\ =\ replace\ s\ v$
$discharge\ s\ (\lambda x.\ T_1)\ =$
   let $T' = replace\ s\ (\lambda x.\ T_1)$
   in if $T' = (\lambda x.\ T_1)$ **then** $\lambda x.\ (discharge\ s\ T_1)$ **else** T'
$discharge\ s\ (T_1\ T_2)\ =$
   let $T' = replace\ s\ (T_1\ T_2)$
   in if $T' = (T_1\ T_2)$
      then $((discharge\ s\ T_1)\ (discharge\ s\ T_2))$
      else T'

$replace\ []\ T\ =\ T$
$replace\ ((y, E) : s)\ T\ =$
   if $E = T$ **then** y **else** $replace\ s\ T$

Fig. 1. Discharging Algorithm

Redundant traversing of equality check in function *discharge* in Fig. 1 can be removed by tupling transformation.

Lemma 2. *If* $P = \lambda \bar{x}.\ p\ \bar{E}$ *is of class* $\mathcal{A}$ *where* p *is a free variable, then there is at most single match* ϕ *such that* $\phi \vdash P \to T$.

Proof. We assume that P, T, and $\bar{E}$ are all in normal form. There is no match if T is not transformed into $\lambda \bar{x}.\ T'$ by $\alpha\eta$-conversion. The match of matching pair $p\ \bar{E} \to T'$ should have the form $\{p \mapsto \lambda \bar{y}.\ B\}$. There is no loss of generality if we assume B is in normal form. Since free variables in each E_i are bounded in P by Definition 1.(iii), due to the definition of matching, equation $(\lambda \bar{y}.\ B)\ \bar{E} =_{\alpha\beta\eta} T'$ should be satisfied. Therefore, term B is the result of replacing $\bar{E}$ with $\bar{y}$ in T', since B is in normal form and E_i is not a λ-abstraction. Through Definition 1.(i), subterms E_i $(1 \leq i \leq m)$ contain free variables and if we leave any occurrences of E_i in B, then $\lambda \bar{y}.\ B$ will contain free variables. This generates an illegal substitution containing free variables. Instead, term B should be obtained through full discharging; replacing all occurrences of $\bar{E}$ with $\bar{y}$ in T', i.e, $(\lambda \bar{y}.\ B)\ \bar{E} =_{\alpha\beta\eta} T'\ \wedge\ \forall i.\ E_i \not\trianglelefteq B$. If some free variables still occur in B after discharging, this results in illegal substitution. Otherwise, since one argument is not a subterm of another argument by Definition 1.(ii), the order of replacing does not affect the result of the match. Thus, the match is obtained deterministically. $\square$

Note that similar to the proof, we can use any discharging function satisfying the condition

$$(\lambda \bar{y}.\ B)\ \bar{E} =_{\alpha\beta\eta} T'\ \wedge\ \forall i.\ E_i \not\trianglelefteq B\ ,$$

for discharging arguments of free variables in class $\mathcal{A}$. In the following, we use the function *discharge* for discharging arguments from a term. Our main theorem is given below.

Theorem 3 (Deterministic Higher-order Matching). *If P is of class $\mathcal{A}$, there is at most single match ϕ such that $\phi \vdash P \to T$.*

Proof. We use mathematical induction on the structure of the pattern.

Case ($P = \lambda\bar{x}.\ c\ \bar{E}$). There is no match if the corresponding term cannot be transformed into $\lambda\bar{x}.\ c\ \bar{F}$ by $\alpha\eta$-conversion where the lengths of $\bar{E}$ and $\bar{F}$ are equal. Otherwise, matching can be decomposed into m matchings $\phi_i \vdash \lambda\bar{x}.\ E_i \to \lambda\bar{x}.\ F_i$ for $i = 1 \ldots m$. By induction hypothesis, each match $\phi_i \vdash \lambda\bar{x}.\ E_i \to \lambda\bar{x}.\ F_i$ is unique or there is no match in which case $\phi_i = fail$. Therefore $\phi' \vdash P \to T$ is a unique match or there is no match if ϕ' is a *fail* where $\phi' = \phi_1 \circ \cdots \circ \phi_m$.

Case ($P = \lambda\bar{x}.\ v\ \bar{E} \wedge v \notin FV(P)$). Similar to the first case.

Case ($P = \lambda\bar{x}.\ v\ \bar{E} \wedge v \in FV(P)$). Through Lemma 2, the match generated by the pattern is unique or there is no match. $\quad\square$

For example, consider $P = \lambda x.\ p\ (c\ x)\ (d\ x)$ and term $T = \lambda x.\ a\ (c\ x)\ (b\ (d\ x))$ where a, b, c and d are constants, p and x are variables, and p occurs freely in P. To match P against T, we replace $c\ x$ and $d\ x$ with fresh variables y_1 and y_2 in T resulting in the unique match $\{p \mapsto \lambda y_1\ y_2.\ a\ y_1\ (b\ y_2)\}$.

4 Efficient Deterministic Higher-Order Matching Algorithm

Given matching pair $P \to T$ where P is of class $\mathcal{A}$, algorithm $\mathcal{M}[\![\ P \to T\ ]\!]$, defined in Fig. 2 computes a unique match if one exists. Otherwise, it returns the special match *fail*. For example, $\mathcal{M}[\![\ c \to \lambda x.\ d\ ]\!]$ returns *fail*. In Fig. 2, the first case acts as η-expansion, so, $\mathcal{M}[\![\ \lambda x.\ p\ (c\ x) \to c\ ]\!]$ returns $\mathcal{M}[\![\ \lambda x.\ p\ (c\ x) \to \lambda x.\ c\ x\ ]\!]$. The second and third cases correspond to ones in our proof of Theorem 3. If the heads of the pattern and the term are equal and the lengths of their arguments are the same, the matching pair is decomposed into smaller ones. The fourth case which calls the function *discharge* for exhaustive discharging corresponds to Lemma 2. An example of this is

$$\mathcal{M}[\![\ \lambda a\ r.\ a \otimes sum\ r \to \lambda a\ r.\ a * a + sum\ r\ ]\!]\ ,$$

which computes the following match

$$\{\otimes \mapsto \lambda x\ y.\ (discharge\ [(y_1, a), (y_2, sum\ r)]\ (a * a + sum\ r))\}\ .$$

Formally, we can prove the soundness of algorithm $\mathcal{M}$, i.e., $\mathcal{M}$ will return a unique match if there is one. Here, $\exists! x.\ P$ means that there is exactly one x such that P.

Theorem 4 (Soundness). *If P is of class $\mathcal{A}$, then*

$$\forall T \exists! \phi.\ \phi \vdash P \to T \Leftrightarrow \phi = \mathcal{M}[\![\ P \to T\ ]\!]\ \wedge\ \phi \neq fail\ .$$

$$\mathcal{M}[\![\, \lambda x_1 \cdots x_l.\, P_1 \rightarrow \lambda x_1 \cdots x_o.\, T_1 \,]\!] =$$
$$\mathcal{M}[\![\, \lambda x_1 \cdots x_l.\, P_1 \rightarrow \lambda x_1 \cdots x_l.\, T_1\, x_{o+1} \cdots x_l \,]\!]$$
$$\textbf{if } o < l \ \wedge\ P_1 \text{ and } T_1 \text{ are not } \lambda\text{-abstraction}$$
$$\mathcal{M}[\![\, \lambda \bar{x}.\, c\ E_1\ \cdots\ E_m \rightarrow \lambda \bar{x}.\, d\ T_1\ \cdots\ T_m \,]\!] =$$
$$\mathcal{M}[\![\, \lambda \bar{x}.\, E_1 \rightarrow \lambda \bar{x}.\, T_1 \,]\!] \circ \cdots \circ \mathcal{M}[\![\, \lambda \bar{x}.\, E_m \rightarrow \lambda \bar{x}.\, T_m \,]\!]$$
$$\textbf{if } c = d$$
$$\mathcal{M}[\![\, \lambda \bar{x}.\, x_i\ E_1\ \cdots\ E_m \rightarrow \lambda \bar{x}.\, x_j\ T_1\ \cdots\ T_m \,]\!] =$$
$$\mathcal{M}[\![\, \lambda \bar{x}.\, E_1 \rightarrow \lambda \bar{x}.\, T_1 \,]\!] \circ \cdots \circ \mathcal{M}[\![\, \lambda \bar{x}.\, E_m \rightarrow \lambda \bar{x}.\, T_m \,]\!]$$
$$\textbf{if } i = j$$
$$\mathcal{M}[\![\, \lambda \bar{x}.\, p\ E_1\ \cdots\ E_m \rightarrow \lambda \bar{x}.\, T_1 \,]\!] =$$
$$\{ p \mapsto \lambda y_1 \cdots y_m.\, B \}$$
$$\textbf{if } \lambda y_1 \cdots y_m.\, B \text{ is closed}$$
$$\textbf{where}$$
$$y_1, \ldots, y_m \text{ are fresh variables}$$
$$B = discharge\ [(y_1, E_1), \ldots, (y_m, E_m)]\ T_1$$
$$\mathcal{M}[\![\, \_ \,]\!] = fail$$

Fig. 2. Matching Algorithm

Proof. We prove this through this induction on the structure of the pattern. We calculate as follows for the first case of matching algorithm $\mathcal{M}$,

$$\exists!\phi.\ \phi = \mathcal{M}[\![\, \lambda x_1 \cdots x_l.\, P_1 \rightarrow \lambda x_1 \cdots x_o.\, T_1 \,]\!]$$
$$\Leftrightarrow\quad \{\ \eta\text{-conversion}\ \}$$
$$\exists!\phi.\ \phi = \mathcal{M}[\![\, \lambda x_1 \cdots x_l.\, P_1 \rightarrow \lambda x_1 \cdots x_l.\, T_1\, x_{o+1} \cdots x_l \,]\!]$$
$$\Leftrightarrow\quad \{\ \text{induction hypothesis}\ \}$$
$$\phi \vdash \lambda x_1 \cdots x_l.\, P_1 \rightarrow \lambda x_1 \cdots x_l.\, T_1\, x_{o+1} \cdots x_l\ \wedge\ \phi \neq fail$$
$$\Leftrightarrow\quad \{\ \eta\text{-conversion}\ \}$$
$$\phi \vdash \lambda x_1 \cdots x_l.\, P_1 \rightarrow \lambda x_1 \cdots x_o.\, T_1\ \wedge\ \phi \neq fail$$

For the second case, we assume

$$\phi = \phi_1 \circ \cdots \circ \phi_m$$

and we derive the outcome in Fig. 3. Since the third case is similar to the second case, we have omitted the proof.

Since the fourth case is rather complex, we prove sufficient and necessity conditions separately.

($\Leftarrow$) For the case, a matching pair is

$$\lambda x_1 \cdots x_l.\, p\ E_1\ \cdots\ E_m \rightarrow \lambda x_1 \cdots x_l.\, T_1\ .$$

Let

$$B = discharge\ [(y_1, E_1), \ldots, (y_m, E_m)]\ T_1\ .$$

Since *discharge* satisfies the property

$$(\lambda y_1 \cdots y_m.\, B)\ E_1 \cdots E_m = T_1\ ,$$

the matching property holds as follows:

$$\{ p \rightarrow \lambda y_1 \cdots y_m.\, B \} \vdash \lambda x_1 \cdots x_l.\, p\ E_1\ \cdots\ E_m \rightarrow \lambda x_1 \cdots x_l.\, T_1\ .$$

$$\phi = \mathcal{M}[\![\, \lambda \bar{x}.\, c\ E_1\ \cdots\ E_m \to \lambda \bar{x}.\, d\ T_1\ \cdots\ T_m \,]\!] \ \wedge\ c = d\ \wedge\ \phi \neq fail$$
$$\Leftrightarrow\ \{\ \text{definition of } \mathcal{M}\ \}$$
$$\phi = \mathcal{M}[\![\, \lambda \bar{x}.\, E_1 \to \lambda \bar{x}.\, T_1 \,]\!] \circ \cdots \circ \mathcal{M}[\![\, \lambda \bar{x}.\, E_m \to \lambda \bar{x}.\, T_m \,]\!] \ \wedge\ c = d\ \wedge\ \phi \neq fail$$
$$\Leftrightarrow\ \{\ \phi \neq fail\ \}$$
$$\phi = \mathcal{M}[\![\, \lambda \bar{x}.\, E_1 \to \lambda \bar{x}.\, T_1 \,]\!] . \cdots . \mathcal{M}[\![\, \lambda \bar{x}.\, E_m \to \lambda \bar{x}.\, T_m \,]\!] \ \wedge\ c = d\ \wedge\ \phi \neq fail$$
$$\Leftrightarrow\ \{\ \text{assumption}\ \}$$
$$\forall i \exists \phi_i.\, \phi_i = \mathcal{M}[\![\, \lambda \bar{x}.\, E_i \to \lambda \bar{x}.\, T_i \,]\!] \ \wedge\ c = d\ \wedge\ \phi \neq fail\ \wedge\ \phi = \phi_1 \circ \cdots \circ \phi_m$$
$$\Leftrightarrow\ \{\ \text{induction hypothesis}\ \}$$
$$\forall i \exists! \phi_i \vdash \lambda \bar{x}.\, E_i \to \lambda \bar{x}.\, T_i \ \wedge\ c = d\ \wedge\ \phi \neq fail\ \wedge\ \phi = \phi_1 \circ \cdots \circ \phi_m$$
$$\Leftrightarrow\ \{\ \text{definition of } \vdash\ \}$$
$$\forall i \exists! \phi_i.\, \phi_i(\lambda \bar{x}.\, E_i) =_{\alpha\beta\eta} \lambda \bar{x}.\, T_i \ \wedge\ c = d\ \wedge\ \phi \neq fail\ \wedge\ \phi = \phi_1 \circ \cdots \circ \phi_m$$
$$\Leftrightarrow\ \{\ \text{property of } (.)\ \}$$
$$\exists! \phi.\, \phi\ (\lambda \bar{x}.\, c\ E_1 \cdots E_m) =_{\alpha\beta\eta} \lambda \bar{x}.\, d\ T_1 \cdots T_m \ \wedge\ c = d\ \wedge\ \phi \neq fail$$
$$\Leftrightarrow\ \{\ \text{definition of match}\ \}$$
$$\exists! \phi.\, \phi \vdash \lambda \bar{x}.\, c\ E_1 \cdots E_m \to \lambda \bar{x}.\, d\ T_1 \cdots T_m \ \wedge\ c = d$$

Fig. 3. The derivation

$(\Rightarrow)$ Through Theorem 3, there is at most a single match ϕ such that

$$\phi \vdash \lambda \bar{x}.\, p\ E_1\ \cdots\ E_m \to \lambda \bar{x}.\, T_1 \ .$$

The form of the match should be $\phi = \{p \mapsto \lambda y_1 \cdots y_m.\, B\}$ where

$$\{y_1 \mapsto E_1, \ldots, y_m \mapsto E_m\}\, B =_{\alpha\beta\eta} T_1 \ .$$

Term B should be prepared by replacing some E_i with y_i from T_1. Through the Definition 1.(i), E_i contains free variables. Thus if B contains E_i, then ϕ is an illegal match. Therefore, term B should be prepared by replacing all occurrences of E_i with y_i from T_1. This operation matches

$$B = discharge\ [(y_1, E_1), \ldots, (y_m, E_m)]\ T_1 \ .$$

$\square$

The complexity of our matching algorithm can be summarized in the following theorem. Let $size(t)$ be a function to compute a size of the term t.

$$
\begin{aligned}
size\ c\ \ &= 1 \\
size\ v\ \ &= 1 \\
size\ (t_1\ t_2) &= 1 + size\ t_1 + size\ t_2 \\
size\ (\lambda x.\, t) &= 1 + size\ t
\end{aligned}
$$

Theorem 5 (Efficiency). *Let P be of class $\mathcal{A}$, n be the size of term T, and m be the size of pattern P. The time complexity of $\mathcal{M}[\![\, P \to T \,]\!]$ is $O(m^2 n)$.*

Proof. Except for the second last case, the time complexity of $\mathcal{M}$ is straightforwardly linear in the size of the pattern. For the second last case, the function *discharge* traverses the term and the function *replace* checks for each argument E_i. Since equality check in *replace* needs $O(m)$, that *replace* costs $O(m^2)$. Traversing cost of *discharge* is $O(n)$. Therefore, *discharge* costs $O(m^2 n)$. $\square$

Since m is quite small and bounded and patterns are much smaller than terms in practice, the algorithm is almost $O(n)$. For fixed patterns, the algorithm is $O(n)$.

5   Application to Program Transformation

Class $\mathcal{A}$ covers a wider class of patterns than Miller's higher-order patterns as we saw in fusion transformation in Section 1 and Section 2. In this section, we demonstrate how our matching algorithm can be useful in mechanizing tupling transformation.

Tupling [15] is program transformation where several results are returned from a single traversal of a data structure. For example, a function for computing the average of a list

```
average1 xs = sum xs / length xs
```

is transformed into

```
average2 xs = s/l
   where (s,l) = sumLength xs
```

where s stores the summation and l stores the length of the list xs.

The definition of sumLength is defined as

```
sumLength [] = (0, 0)
sumLength (x:xs) = (x + s, 1 + l)
   where (s,l) = sumLength xs
```

which is derived as follows. The base case is trivial.

```
  sumLength []
= { spec. of sumLength }
  (sum [], length [])
= { unfolding sum and length }
  (0, 0)
```

The recursive case of sumLength is derived by

```
  sumLength (x:xs)
= { spec. of sumLength }
  (sum (x:xs), length (x:xs))
= { unfolding sum and length }
  (x + sum xs, 1 + length xs)
= { introducing new function p }
  p x (sum xs) (length xs)
= { introducing new function p'
    s.t. p' = \x (y,z) -> p x y z }
  p' x (sumLength xs)
```

In fact, finding p is a matching problem

$$\lambda x\, xs.\, p\; x\; (sum\; xs)\; (length\; xs) \to (x + sum\; xs, 1 + length\; xs)\ ,$$

which is resolved with our matching algorithm and the substitution

$$\{p \mapsto \lambda y_1\, y_2\, y_3.\, (y_1 + y_2, 1 + y_3)\}$$

can be automatically obtained. Substituting this into the definition of p', we obtain the definition of sumLength as

```
sumLength (x:xs)
   = (\y1 (y2,y3) -> (y1+y2,1+y3)) x (sumLength xs)
```

As another example, to avoid repeated evaluations where a function generates several identical calls to itself, function fib defined as

```
fib 0     = 1
fib 1     = 1
fib (n+2) = fib (n+1) + fib n
```

is transformed into

```
fastfib n = v where (_,v) = fibt n
fibt 0     = (1,1)
fibt (n+1) = (u+v,u) where (u,v) = fibt n
```

The derivation is reduced into a matching problem for matching pair

$$\lambda n.\, p\; (fib\; n)\; (fib\; (n+1)) \to \lambda n.\, (fib\; (n+1) + fib\; n, fib\; (n+1))\ ,$$

which is resolved with the following match.

$$\{p \mapsto \lambda x\, y.\, (y + x, y)\}$$

6   Related Work and Discussion

Higher-order matching problems in general are complicated to apply its patterns to program transformation, since second-order matching is nondeterministic, third- or fourth-order matching is infinite, and a part of more than fifth-order matching is undecidable. For time complexity, higher-order matching in general is expensive; even second-order matching algorithm is NP-complete [7]. Its implementations are also expensive [1, 16].

To generate desirable higher-order matching, a classical approach is to restrict the form of patterns. For example, under some restrictions, possibly undecidable fifth-order matching is decidable [8], and infinite third-order matches are finite [2]. There are many research on time complexity of restricted patterns. Second-order pure matching (even unification) with a bounded number of variables is PTIME [17]. Hirata, Yamada and Harao [18] studied the complexity of various second-order matching problems. According to their classification, a pattern in class $\mathcal{A}$ is a *predicate*, i.e., any arguments of free variables have no function variables. The matching problem of a predicate is polynomial if it is *binary function-free*, i.e., any function variables are at most 2-ary and have no function constants. *Linear context matching*, a restricted form of linear higher-order matching, is $O(n^3)$ [19]. It solves the problem through dynamic programming with a table of size $O(n^2)$ building from the bottom up.

Pattern matching play an important role in program transformations. Many systems use first-order patterns [20–22] and most of these use first-order matching [14, 23–25]. Exceptions are MAG [26], KORSO [3], and TrafoLa [13]; they use higher-order matching, which enables program transformation to be concisely specified, and makes transformation more abstract and more reusable. To make it $\mathcal{DHP}$s, we restricted class of patterns, and, therefore, the matching algorithm for them is deterministic. As a result, many patterns are excluded. For example, One of the matching algorithms used in MAG is one-step matching [2, 27] which returns at least complete second-order match for arbitrary polymorphically second-order patterns; our matching algorithm covers only a restricted class of polymorphic second-order patterns in class $\mathcal{A}$. Nevertheless, for descriptive power of patterns, our restriction is not restrictive for program transformation. Class $\mathcal{A}$ is a simple and natural extension of Miller's higher-order patterns [9], which has a single most-general unifier. As we saw in the previous section, patterns in this class cover wide class of patterns. It enabled the fusion law to be concisely described, which plays important roles in program transformations.

Consider the extension of class $\mathcal{A}$. Patterns in class $\mathcal{A}$ are not sufficient for $\mathcal{DHP}$s; many deterministic higher-order patterns are not included in class $\mathcal{A}$ such as a non-linear pattern $\lambda x. p\ (p\ x)$, a pattern where the argument of free variable contains free variables $\lambda x. p\ (c\ x\ q)$, a pattern where one argument of free variable contains the other argument for subterms $\lambda x. p\ (c\ x)\ (c\ x\ x)$, and a pattern where the argument of free variable is λ-abstraction $\lambda x. p\ (\lambda y.c\ y\ x)$, we have not specified the syntactical class of patterns useful in program transformation that is easy to understand and whose matching algorithm is efficient. Can we use patterns in class $\mathcal{A}$ as extension of Miller's patterns in the context of unification? In the context of unification, patterns in class $\mathcal{A}$ are not deterministic. For example, given terms $\lambda x\, y. p\ (c\ x)\ (c\ y)$ and $\lambda x\, y. c\ (q\ y\ x)$ from a class $\mathcal{A}$, there are at least three most-general unifiers

$$\{\, p \mapsto \lambda x\, y.\, x,\ q \mapsto \lambda x\, y.\, y\,\}\ ,$$
$$\{\, p \mapsto \lambda x\, y.\, y,\ q \mapsto \lambda x\, y.\, x\,\}\ , and$$
$$\{\, p \mapsto \lambda x\, y.\, c\ (r\ x\ y),\ q \mapsto \lambda y\, x.\, r\ (c\ x)\ (c\ y)\}\ .$$

7   Conclusion

We proposed class $\mathcal{A}$ for $\mathcal{DHP}$s that has at most a single higher-order match. Our restriction on patterns made our matching algorithm fast; given a fixed pattern, the time complexity of our deterministic matching algorithm is linear for the size of the term being matched.

There is a trade-off between completeness and efficiency in the matching algorithm. Since pattern types are statically distinguished in program transformation to some extent, we might want to choose an algorithm for each patterns. As we saw in Section 5, class $\mathcal{A}$ cover a wide class of patterns often used in important parts of program transformation.

Our main idea with $\mathcal{DHP}$ was the deterministic choice of *discharging*, where the higher-order matching was boiled down to a first-order problem. It is our hope that our approach can provide a new and effective way of incorporating higher-order patterns into functional languages [13].

References

1. Huet, G.P., Lang, B.: Proving and applying program transformations expressed with second-order patterns. Acta Informatica **11** (1978) 31–55
2. de Moor, O., Sittampalam, G.: Higher-order matching for program transformation. Theoretical Computer Science **269** (2001) 135–162
3. Krieg-Brückner, B., Liu, J., Shi, H., Wolff, B.: Towards correct, efficient and reusable transformational developments. In Broy, M., Jähnichen, S., eds.: KORSO – Methods, Languages, and Tools for the Construction of Correct Software. Volume 1009 of LNCS., Springer-Verlag (1995) 270–284
4. Gill, A., Launchbury, J., Jones, S.L.P.: A short cut to deforestation. In: Proceedings of the 6th International Conference on Functional Programming Languages and Computer Architecture (FPCA'93), Copenhagen, Denmark, ACM Press (1993) 223–232
5. Sheard, T., Launchbury, J.: Warm fusion: Deriving build-catas from recursive definitions. In: Conference on Functional Programming Languages and Computer Architecture, La Jolla, CA, USA, ACM (1995) 314–323
6. Bird, R.: Introduction to Functional Programming using Haskell (second edition). Prentice Hall (1998)
7. Baxter, L.: The complexity of unification. PhD thesis, Department of Computer Science, University of Waterloo (1977)
8. Schubert, A.: Linear interpolation for the higher-order matching problem. In Bidoit, M., Dauchet, M., eds.: Theory and Practice of Software Development, 7th International Joint Conference CAAP/FASE. Volume 1214., Lille, France, Springer (1997) 441–452
9. Miller, D.: A logic programming language with lambda-abstraction, function variables, and simple unification. Journal of Logic and Computation **1** (1991) 497–536
10. Nipkow, T.: Functional unification of higher-order patterns. In: 8th IEEE Symposium on Logic in Computer Science, IEEE Computer Society Press (1993) 64–74
11. Meijer, E., Fokkinga, M., Paterson, R.: Functional programming with bananas, lenses, envelopes and barbed wire. In: Proceedings of the 5th International Conference on Functional Programming Languages and Computer Architecture (FPCA'91). Volume 523 of LNCS., Cambridge, Massachusetts, Springer-Verlag (1991) 124–144
12. Sheard, T., Fegaras, L.: A fold for all seasons. In: Conference on Functional Programming Languages and Computer Architecture. (1993) 233–242
13. Heckmann, R.: A functional language for the specification of complex tree transformation. In: Proc. ESOP. Volume 300 of LNCS. (1988) 175–190

14. Sheard, T., Peyton Jones, S.L.: Template metaprogramming for Haskell. In: Haskell Workshop, Pittsburgh, Pennsylvania (2002) 1–16
15. Hu, Z., Iwasaki, H., Takeichi, M., Takano, A.: Tupling calculation eliminates multiple data traversals. In: Proceedings of the 2nd ACM SIGPLAN International Conference on Functional Programming (ICFP'97), Amsterdam, The Netherlands, ACM Press (1997) 164–175
16. Curien, R., Qian, Z., Shi, H.: Efficient second-order matching. In Ganzinger, H., ed.: Rewriting Techniques and Applications. Volume 1103 of LNCS., New Brunswick, New Jersey, USA, Springer (1996) 317–331
17. Wierzbicki, T.: Complexity of the higher order matching. In Ganzinger, H., ed.: Automated Deduction. Volume 1632 of LNCS., Trento, Italy, Springer (1999) 82–96
18. Hirata, K., Yamada, K., Harao, M.: Tractable and intractable second-order matching problems. In Asano, T., Imai, H., Lee, D.T., Nakano, S., Tokuyama, T., eds.: Computing and Combinatorics, 5th Annual International Conference. Volume 1627 of LNCS., Tokyo, Japan, Springer (1999) 432–441
19. Schmidt-Schauß, M., Stuber, J.: On the complexity of linear and stratified context matching problems. Rapport de Recherche RR-4923, Institut National de Recherche en Informatique et en Automatique (2003)
20. Guttmann, W., Partsch, H., Schulte, W., Vullinghs, T.: Tool support for the interactive derivation of formally correct functional programs. In: Journal of Universal Computer Science. Volume 9. (2003) 173–188
21. Peyton Jones, S.L., Tolmach, A., Hoare, T.: Playing by the rules: rewriting as a practical optimisation technique in ghc. In: Haskell Workshop. (2001)
22. Visser, E.: Stratego: A language for program transformation based on rewriting strategies. system description of stratego 0.5. In Middeldorp, A., ed.: Rewriting Techniques and Applications. Volume 2051 of LNCS., Springer-Verlag (2001) 357–362
23. Bauer, F., Ehler, H., Horsch, B., Möller, B., Partsch, H., Paukner, O., Pepper, P., eds.: The Munich Project CIP – Volume II: The Program Transformation System CIP-S. Volume 292 of LNCS. Springer-Verlag (1987)
24. Taha, W., Sheard, T.: Multi-stage programming with explicit annotations. In: Proc. Conference on Partial Evaluation and Program Manipulation, Amsterdam, ACM Press (1997) 203–217
25. Tullsen, M., Hudak, P.: An intermediate meta-language for program transformation. Research report yaleu/dcs/rr-1154, Department of Computer Science, Yale University (1998)
26. de Moor, O., Sittampalam, G.: Generic program transformation. In: Third International Summer School on Advanced Functional Programming. Volume 1608 of LNCS., Braga, Portugal, Springer-Verlag (1998) 116–149
27. Sittampalam, G.: Higher-order matching for program transformation. PhD thesis, University of Oxford (2001)

From Interpreter to Logic Engine by Defunctionalization

Dariusz Biernacki and Olivier Danvy

BRICS*
Department of Computer Science
University of Aarhus
IT-parken, Aabogade 34, DK-8200 Aarhus N, Denmark
{dabi,danvy}@brics.dk
http://www.brics.dk/~{dabi,danvy}

Abstract. Starting from a continuation-based interpreter for a simple logic programming language, propositional Prolog with cut, we derive the corresponding logic engine in the form of an abstract machine. The derivation originates in previous work (our article at PPDP 2003) where it was applied to the lambda-calculus. The key transformation here is Reynolds's defunctionalization that transforms a tail-recursive, continuation-passing interpreter into a transition system, i.e., an abstract machine. Similar denotational and operational semantics were studied by de Bruin and de Vink (their article at TAPSOFT 1989), and we compare their study with our derivation. Additionally, we present a direct-style interpreter of propositional Prolog expressed with control operators for delimited continuations.

1 Introduction

In previous work [2], we presented a derivation from interpreter to abstract machine that makes it possible to connect known λ-calculus interpreters to known abstract machines for the λ-calculus, as well as to discover new ones. The goal of this work is to test this derivation on a programming language other than the λ-calculus. Our pick here is a simple logic programming language, propositional Prolog with cut (Section 2). We present its abstract syntax, informal semantics, and computational model, which we base on success and failure continuations (Section 3). We then specify an interpreter for propositional Prolog in a generic and parameterized way that leads us to a logic engine. This logic engine is a transition system that we obtain by defunctionalizing the success and failure continuations (Section 4). We also present and analyze a direct-style interpreter for propositional Prolog (Appendix A).

The abstract machines we consider are models of computation rather than devices for high performance, and the transformations we consider are changes of representation rather than optimizations.

---

* Basic Research in Computer Science (http://www.brics.dk), funded by the Danish National Research Foundation.

M. Bruynooghe (Ed.): LOPSTR 2004, LNCS 3018, pp. 143–159, 2004.

Prerequisites: We expect a passing familiarity with the notions of success and failure continuations as well as with Standard ML and its module language.

As for defunctionalization, it originates in Reynolds's seminal article on definitional interpreters for higher-order programming languages [27]. The point of defunctionalization is to transform a higher-order program into a first-order program by replacing its function types by sum types. Before defunctionalization, the inhabitants of each function type are instances of anonymous λ-abstractions. Defunctionalizing a program amounts to enumerating these λ-abstractions in a sum type: each function introduction (i.e., λ-abstraction) is replaced by the corresponding constructor holding the values of the free variables of this λ-abstraction, and each function elimination (i.e., application) is replaced by a case dispatch. After defunctionalization, the inhabitants of each function type are represented by elements of a corresponding sum type.

Danvy and Nielsen's study of defunctionalization contains many examples [14], but to make the present article self-contained, let us consider two concrete cases.

1.1   A Simple Example of Defunctionalization

The following (trivial) program is higher-order because of the auxiliary function `aux`, which is passed a function of type `int -> int` as argument:

```
(*  aux : int * (int -> int) -> int  *)
fun aux (x, f)
    = (f 10) + (f x)

(*  main : int * int * int -> int  *)
fun main (a, b, c)
    = (aux (a, fn x => x + b)) * (aux (c, fn x => x * x))
```

The inhabitants of the function space `int -> int` are instances of the two anonymous λ-abstractions declared in `main`, `fn x => x + b` and `fn x => x * x`. The first one has one free variable (`b`, of type `int`), and the second one is closed, i.e., it has no free variables.

To defunctionalize this program, we enumerate these λ-abstractions in a sum type `lam`, and we define the corresponding apply function to interpret each of the summands:

```
datatype lam = LAM1 of int
             | LAM2

(*  apply_lam : lam * int -> int  *)
fun apply_lam (LAM1 b, x)
    = x + b
  | apply_lam (LAM2, x)
    = x * x
```

In the defunctionalized program, each λ-abstraction is replaced by the corresponding constructor, and each application is replaced by a call to the apply function:

```
(*  aux : int * lam -> int  *)
fun aux (x, f)
    = (apply_lam (f, 10)) + (apply_lam (f, x))

(*  main : int * int * int -> int  *)
fun main (a, b, c)
    = (aux (a, LAM1 b)) * (aux (c, LAM2))
```

The resulting program is first order.

1.2   A More Advanced Example: The Factorial Function

Let us defunctionalize the following continuation-passing version of the factorial function:

```
(*  fac_c : int * (int -> 'a) -> 'a  *)
fun fac_c (0, k)
    = k 1
  | fac_c (n, k)
    = fac_c (n - 1, fn v => k (n * v))

(*  main : int -> int  *)
fun main n
    = fac_c (n, fn v => v)
```

We consider the whole program (i.e., both main and fac_c). Therefore the polymorphic type 'a, i.e., the domain of answers, is instantiated to int. The candidate function space for defunctionalization is that of the continuation, int -> int. Its inhabitants are instances of two λ-abstractions: the initial continuation in main with no free variables, and the intermediate continuation in the induction case of fac_c with two free variables: n and k. The corresponding data type has therefore two constructors:

```
datatype cont = CONT0
              | CONT1 of int * cont

(*  apply_cont : cont * int -> int  *)
fun apply_cont (CONT0, v)
    = v
  | apply_cont (CONT1 (n, k), v)
    = apply_cont (k, n * v)
```

Correspondingly, the apply function associated to the data type interprets each of these constructors according to the initial continuation and the intermediate continuation.

We observe that cont is isomorphic to the data type of lists of integers. We therefore adopt this simpler representation of defunctionalized continuations:

```
type cont = int list

(*  apply_cont : cont * int -> int  *)
fun apply_cont (nil, v)
     = v
  | apply_cont (n :: k, v)
     = apply_cont (k, n * v)
```

In the defunctionalized program, the continuations are replaced by the constructors, and the applications of the continuations are replaced by a call to apply_cont:

```
(*  fac_c : int * cont -> int  *)
fun fac_c (0, k)
     = apply_cont (k, 1)
  | fac_c (n, k)
     = fac_c (n - 1, n :: k)

(*  main : int -> int  *)
fun main n
     = fac_c (n, nil)
```

The resulting program is first-order, all its calls are tail calls, and all computations in the actual parameters are elementary. It is therefore a transition system in the sense of automata and formal languages [23]. Both main and fac_c, together with their actual parameters, form configurations and their ML definitions specify a transition relation, as expressed in the following table. The top transition specifies the initial state and the bottom transition specifies the terminating configurations. The machine consists of two mutually recursive transition functions; the first one operates over pairs of integers, and the second one operates over a stack of integers and an integer:

$$n \Rightarrow \langle n,\ nil \rangle_{fac}$$

$$\langle 0,\ k \rangle_{fac} \Rightarrow \langle k,\ 1 \rangle_{app}$$

$$\langle n,\ k \rangle_{fac} \Rightarrow \langle n-1,\ n :: k \rangle_{fac}$$

$$\langle n :: k,\ v \rangle_{app} \Rightarrow \langle k,\ n \times v \rangle_{app}$$

$$\langle nil,\ v \rangle_{app} \Rightarrow v$$

Accordingly, the result of defunctionalizing a continuation-passing interpreter is also a transition system, i.e., an abstract machine in the sense of automata and formal languages [23]. We used this property in our work on the λ-calculus [2], and we use it here for propositional Prolog.

2   Propositional Prolog

The abstract syntax of propositional Prolog reads as follows:

```
structure Source
= struct
    type ide = string
    datatype atom = IDE of ide
                  | OR of goal * goal
                  | CUT
                  | FAIL
    withtype goal = atom list
    type clause = ide * goal
    datatype program = PROGRAM of clause list
    datatype top_level_goal = GOAL of goal
  end
```

A program consists of a list of clauses. A clause consists of an identifier (the head of the clause) and a goal (the body of the clause). A goal is a list of atoms; an empty list represents the logical value 'true' and a non-empty list of atoms represents their conjunction. Each atom is either an identifier, the disjunction of two goals, the cut operator, or the fail operator.

The intuitive semantics of the language is standard. Given a Prolog program and a goal, we try to verify whether the goal follows from the program in the sense of propositional logic, i.e., in terms of logic programming, whether the SLD-resolution algorithm for this goal and this program stops with the empty clause. If it does, then the answer is positive; if it stops with one or more subgoals still waiting resolution, then the answer is negative. Here the unification algorithm consists in looking up the clause with a specified head in the program.

An atom can be a disjunction of two goals, and therefore if a chosen body does not lead to the positive answer, the other disjunct is tried, using backtracking. Backtracking can also be used to find all possible solutions in the resolution tree, which in case of propositional Prolog amounts to counting the positive answers. Two operators provide additional control over the traversal of the resolution tree: the cut operator removes some of the potential paths and the fail operator makes the current goal unsatisfiable, which triggers backtracking.

3   A Generic Interpreter for Propositional Prolog

To account for the backtracking necessary to implement resolution, we use success and failure continuations [13]. A failure continuation is a parameterless function (i.e., a thunk) yielding a final answer. A success continuation maps a failure continuation to a final answer. The initial success continuation is applied if a solution has been found. The initial failure continuation is applied if no solution has been found. In addition, to account for the cut operator, we pass a cut continuation, i.e., a cached failure continuation. As usual with continuations, the domain of answers is left unspecified.

3.1   A Generic Notion of Answers and Results

We specify answers with an ML signature. The type of answers comes together with an initial success continuation and an initial failure continuation. The signature also declares a type of results and an extraction function mapping a (generic) answer to a (specific) result.

```
signature ANSWER
= sig
    type answer
    val sc_init : (unit -> answer) -> answer
    val fc_init : unit -> answer

    type result
    val extract : answer -> result
  end
```

3.2   Specific Answers and Results

We consider two kinds of answers: the first solution, if any, and the total number of solutions.

The first solution: This notion of answer is the simplest to define. Both `answer` and `result` are defined as the type of booleans and `extract` is the identity function. The initial success continuation ignores the failure continuation and yields `true`, whereas the initial failure continuation yields `false`.

```
structure Answer_first : ANSWER
= struct
    type answer = bool
    fun sc_init fc = true
    fun fc_init () = false

    type result = bool
    fun extract a = a
  end
```

The number of solutions: This notion of answer is more delicate. One could be tempted to define `answer` as the type of integers, but the resulting implementation would no longer be tail recursive[1]. Instead, we use an extra layer of continuations: We define `answer` as the type of functions from integers to integers, `result` as the type of integers, and `extract` as a function triggering the whole resolution by applying an answer to the initial count, 0. The initial success continuation takes note of an intermediate success by incrementing the current count and activating the failure continuation. The initial failure continuation is passed the final count and returns it.

---

[1] In "`fun sc_init fc = 1 + (fc ())`", the call to `fc` is not a tail call.

```
structure Answer_how_many : ANSWER
= struct
     type answer = int -> int
     fun sc_init fc = (fn m => fc () (m+1))
     fun fc_init () = (fn m => m)

     type result = int
     fun extract a = a 0
   end
```

3.3   The Generic Interpreter, Semi-compositionally

We define a generic interpreter for propositional Prolog, displayed in Figure 1, as a recursive descent over the source syntax, parameterized by a notion of answers, and implementing the following signature:

```
signature INTERPRETER
= sig
      type result
      val main : Source.top_level_goal * Source.program -> result
    end
```

In `run_goal`, an empty list of atoms is interpreted as 'true', and accordingly, the success continuation is activated. A non-empty list of atoms is sequentially interpreted by `run_seq` by extending the success continuation; this interpretation singles out the last atom in a properly tail-recursive manner. An identifier is interpreted either by failing if it is not the head of any clause in the program, or by resolving the corresponding goal with the cut continuation replaced with the current failure continuation. The function `lookup` searching for a clause with a given head reads as follows:

```
(*  lookup : Source.ide * Source.clause list -> Source.goal option  *)
fun lookup (i, p)
    = let fun walk nil
               = NONE
           | walk ((i', g) :: p)
               = if i = i'
                 then SOME g
                 else walk p
      in walk p
      end
```

A disjunction of two goals is interpreted by extending the failure continuation. The cut operator is interpreted by replacing the failure continuation with the cut continuation. The fail operator is interpreted as 'false', and accordingly, the failure continuation is activated.

This interpreter is not compositional (in the sense of denotational semantics) because g, in the interpretation of identifiers, does not denote a proper subpart

```
functor mkInterpreter (structure A : ANSWER) : INTERPRETER =
struct
  open Source
  type answer = A.answer
  type result = A.result
  type fcont = unit -> answer
  type scont = fcont -> answer
  type ccont = fcont

  (*  run_goal : goal * clause list * scont * fcont * ccont -> answer  *)
  fun run_goal (nil, p, sc, fc, cc)
      = sc fc
    | run_goal (a :: g, p, sc, fc, cc)
      = run_seq (a, g, p, sc, fc, cc)

  (*  run_seq : atom * goal * clause list * scont * fcont * ccont  *)
  (*                  -> answer                                    *)
  and run_seq (a, nil, p, sc, fc, cc)
      = run_atom (a, p, sc, fc, cc)
    | run_seq (a, a' :: g, p, sc, fc, cc)
      = run_atom (a, p, fn fc' => run_seq (a', g, p, sc, fc', cc), fc, cc)

  (*  run_atom : atom * clause list * scont * fcont * ccont -> answer  *)
  and run_atom (IDE i, p, sc, fc, cc)
      = (case lookup (i, p)
           of NONE
              => fc ()
            | (SOME g)
              => run_goal (g, p, sc, fc, fc))
    | run_atom (OR (g1, g2), p, sc, fc, cc)
      = run_goal (g1, p, sc, fn () => run_goal (g2, p, sc, fc, cc), cc)
    | run_atom (CUT, p, sc, fc, cc)
      = sc cc
    | run_atom (FAIL, p, sc, fc, cc)
      = fc ()

  (*  main : top_level_goal * program -> result  *)
  fun main (GOAL g, PROGRAM p)
      = let val a = run_goal (g, p, A.sc_init, A.fc_init, A.fc_init)
        in A.extract a
        end
end
```

Fig. 1. A generic interpreter for propositional Prolog

of the denotation of 1. The interpreter, however, is semi-compositional in Jones's sense [19, 20], i.e., g denotes a proper subpart of the source program. (To make the interpreter compositional, one can follow the tradition of denotational semantics and use an environment mapping an identifier to a function that either evaluates the goal denoted by the identifier or calls the failure continuation. The environment is threaded in the interpreter instead of the program. The resulting ML interpreter represents the valuation function of a denotational semantics of propositional Prolog.)

3.4   Specific Interpreters

A specific interpreter computing the first solution: A specific interpreter computing the first solution, if any, is obtained by instantiating `mkInterpreter` with the corresponding notion of answers:

```
structure Prolog_first = mkInterpreter (structure A = Answer_first)
```

A specific interpreter computing the number of solutions: A specific interpreter computing the number of solutions is also obtained by instantiating `mkInterpreter` with the corresponding notion of answers:

```
structure Prolog_how_many = mkInterpreter (structure A = Answer_how_many)
```

Appendix A contains a direct-style counterpart of the interpreter (uncurried and without cut) computing the number of solutions.

4   Two Abstract Machines for Propositional Prolog

We successively consider each of the specific Prolog interpreters of Section 3.4 and we defunctionalize their continuations. As already illustrated in Section 1 with the factorial program, in each case, the result is an abstract machine. Indeed the interpreters are in continuation-passing style, and thus:

- all their calls are tail calls, and therefore they can run iteratively; and
- all their subcomputations (i.e., the computation of their actual parameters) are elementary.

In both cases the types of the defunctionalized success and failure continuations read as follows:

```
datatype scont = SCONT0
               | SCONT1 of atom * goal * clause list * scont * ccont
     and fcont = FCONT0
               | FCONT1 of goal * clause list * scont * fcont * ccont
withtype ccont = fcont
```

As in Section 1.2, since both data types are isomorphic to the data type of lists, we represent them as such when presenting the abstract machines.

- Atoms, goals and programs:

$$a ::= \mathtt{IDE}\, i \mid \mathtt{OR}\,(g_1,\, g_2) \mid \mathtt{CUT} \mid \mathtt{FAIL}$$
$$g ::= a^*$$
$$p ::= (i,\, g)^*$$

- Control stacks:

$$sc ::= nil \mid (a,\, g,\, p,\, cc) :: sc$$
$$fc ::= nil \mid (g,\, p,\, sc,\, cc) :: fc$$
$$cc ::= fc$$

- Initial transition, transition rules and final transition:

$\langle g,\, p \rangle \Rightarrow \langle g,\, p,\, nil,\, nil,\, nil \rangle_{goal}$
$\langle nil,\, p,\, (a,\, g,\, p',\, cc') :: sc,\, fc,\, cc \rangle_{goal} \Rightarrow \langle a,\, g,\, p',\, sc,\, fc,\, cc' \rangle_{seq}$ $\langle a :: g,\, p,\, sc,\, fc,\, cc \rangle_{goal} \Rightarrow \langle a,\, g,\, p,\, sc,\, fc,\, cc \rangle_{seq}$
$\langle a,\, nil,\, p,\, sc,\, fc,\, cc \rangle_{seq} \Rightarrow \langle a,\, p,\, sc,\, fc,\, cc \rangle_{atom}$ $\langle a,\, a' :: g,\, p,\, sc,\, fc,\, cc \rangle_{seq} \Rightarrow \langle a,\, p,\, (a',\, g,\, p,\, cc) :: sc,\, fc,\, cc \rangle_{atom}$
$\langle \mathtt{IDE}\, i,\, p,\, sc,\, fc,\, cc \rangle_{atom} \Rightarrow \langle g,\, p,\, sc,\, fc,\, fc \rangle_{goal}$ $\qquad if\ lookup\,(i)\ succeeds\ with\ g$ $\langle \mathtt{IDE}\, i,\, p,\, sc,\, (g,\, p,\, sc',\, cc') :: fc,\, cc \rangle_{atom} \Rightarrow \langle g,\, p',\, sc',\, fc,\, cc' \rangle_{goal}$ $\qquad if\ lookup\,(i)\ fails$ $\langle \mathtt{OR}\,(g_1,\, g_2),\, p,\, sc,\, fc,\, cc \rangle_{atom} \Rightarrow \langle g_1,\, p,\, sc,\, (g_2,\, p,\, sc,\, cc) :: fc,\, cc \rangle_{goal}$ $\langle \mathtt{CUT},\, p,\, (a,\, g,\, p',\, cc') :: sc,\, fc,\, cc \rangle_{atom} \Rightarrow \langle a,\, g,\, p',\, sc,\, fc,\, cc' \rangle_{seq}$ $\langle \mathtt{FAIL},\, p,\, sc,\, (g,\, p',\, sc',\, cc') :: fc,\, cc \rangle_{atom} \Rightarrow \langle g,\, p',\, sc',\, fc,\, cc' \rangle_{goal}$
$\langle nil,\, p,\, nil,\, fc,\, cc \rangle_{goal} \Rightarrow true$ $\langle \mathtt{IDE}\, i,\, p,\, sc,\, nil,\, cc \rangle_{atom} \Rightarrow false,\ if\ lookup\,(i)\ fails$ $\langle \mathtt{FAIL},\, p,\, sc,\, nil,\, cc \rangle_{atom} \Rightarrow false$ $\langle \mathtt{CUT},\, p,\, nil,\, fc,\, cc \rangle_{atom} \Rightarrow true$

Fig. 2. An abstract machine computing the first solution

The first solution: The abstract machine is defined as the transition system shown in Figure 2. The top part specifies the initial state and the bottom part specifies the terminating configurations. The machine consists of three mutually recursive transition functions, two of which operate over a quintuple and one over a six-element tuple. The quintuple consists of the goal, the program, the (defunctionalized) success continuation, the (defunctionalized) failure continuation and the cut continuation (a register caching a previous failure continuation). The six-element tuple additionally has the first atom of the goal as its first element.

- Atoms, goals and programs:

$$a ::= \text{IDE}\,i \mid \text{OR}\,(g_1,\,g_2) \mid \text{CUT} \mid \text{FAIL}$$
$$g ::= a^*$$
$$p ::= (i,\,g)^*$$

- Control stacks:

$$sc ::= nil \mid (a,\,g,\,p,\,cc) :: sc$$
$$fc ::= nil \mid (g,\,p,\,sc,\,cc) :: fc$$
$$cc ::= fc$$

- Initial transition, transition rules and final transition:

$\langle g,\,p \rangle \Rightarrow \langle g,\,p,\,nil,\,nil,\,nil,\,0 \rangle_{goal}$
$\langle nil,\,p,\,nil,\,(g,\,p',\,sc,\,cc') :: fc,\,cc,\,m \rangle_{goal} \Rightarrow \langle g,\,p',\,sc,\,fc,\,cc',\,m+1 \rangle_{goal}$
$\langle nil,\,p,\,(a,\,g,\,p',\,cc') :: sc,\,fc,\,cc,\,m \rangle_{goal} \Rightarrow \langle a,\,g,\,p',\,sc,\,fc,\,cc',\,m \rangle_{seq}$
$\langle a :: g,\,p,\,sc,\,fc,\,cc,\,m \rangle_{goal} \Rightarrow \langle a,\,g,\,p,\,sc,\,fc,\,cc,\,m \rangle_{seq}$
$\langle a,\,nil,\,p,\,sc,\,fc,\,cc,\,m \rangle_{seq} \Rightarrow \langle a,\,p,\,sc,\,fc,\,cc,\,m \rangle_{atom}$
$\langle a,\,a' :: g,\,p,\,sc,\,fc,\,cc,\,m \rangle_{seq} \Rightarrow \langle a,\,p,\,(a',\,g,\,p,\,cc) :: sc,\,fc,\,cc,\,m \rangle_{atom}$
$\langle \text{IDE}\,i,\,p,\,sc,\,fc,\,cc,\,m \rangle_{atom} \Rightarrow \langle g,\,p,\,sc,\,fc,\,fc,\,m \rangle_{goal}$ $\quad$ *if lookup* (i) *succeeds with* g
$\langle \text{IDE}\,i,\,p,\,sc,\,(g,\,p,\,sc',\,cc') :: fc,\,cc,\,m \rangle_{atom} \Rightarrow \langle g,\,p',\,sc',\,fc,\,cc',\,m \rangle_{goal}$ $\quad$ *if lookup* (i) *fails*
$\langle \text{OR}\,(g_1,\,g_2),\,p,\,sc,\,fc,\,cc,\,m \rangle_{atom} \Rightarrow \langle g_1,\,p,\,sc,\,(g_2,\,p,\,sc,\,cc) :: fc,\,cc,\,m \rangle_{goal}$
$\langle \text{CUT},\,p,\,(a,\,g,\,p',\,cc') :: sc,\,fc,\,cc,\,m \rangle_{atom} \Rightarrow \langle a,\,g,\,p',\,sc,\,fc,\,cc',\,m \rangle_{seq}$
$\langle \text{CUT},\,p,\,nil,\,(g,\,p',\,sc,\,cc') :: fc,\,cc,\,m \rangle_{atom} \Rightarrow \langle g,\,p',\,sc,\,fc,\,cc',\,m+1 \rangle_{goal}$
$\langle \text{FAIL},\,p,\,sc,\,(g,\,p',\,sc',\,cc') :: fc,\,cc,\,m \rangle_{atom} \Rightarrow \langle g,\,p',\,sc',\,fc,\,cc',\,m \rangle_{goal}$
$\langle nil,\,p,\,nil,\,nil,\,cc,\,m \rangle_{goal} \Rightarrow m+1$
$\langle \text{FAIL},\,p,\,sc,\,nil,\,cc,\,m \rangle_{atom} \Rightarrow m$
$\langle \text{CUT},\,p,\,nil,\,nil,\,cc,\,m \rangle_{atom} \Rightarrow m+1$
$\langle \text{IDE}\,i,\,p,\,sc,\,nil,\,cc,\,m \rangle_{atom} \Rightarrow m,\ \text{if lookup}\ (i)\ \text{fails}$

Fig. 3. An abstract machine computing the number of solutions

The number of solutions: This abstract machine is displayed in Figure 3 and is similar to the previous one, but operates over a six- and seven-element tuples. The extra component is the counter.

Both machines are deterministic because they were derived from (deterministic) functions.

5   Related Work and Conclusion

In previous work [2, 3, 10], we presented a derivation from interpreter to abstract machine, and we were curious to see it applied to something else than a functional programming language. The present paper reports its application to a logic programming language, propositional Prolog. In its entirety, the derivation consists of closure conversion, transformation into continuation-passing style (CPS), and defunctionalization. Closure conversion ensures that any higher-order values are made first-order[2]. The CPS transformation makes the flow of control of the interpreter manifest as a continuation. Defunctionalization materializes the flow of control as a first-order data structure. In the present case, propositional Prolog is a first-order language and the interpreter we consider is already in continuation-passing style (cf. Appendix A). Therefore the derivation reduces to defunctionalization. The result is a simple logic engine, i.e., mutually recursive and first-order transition functions. It was derived, not invented, and so, for example, its two stacks arise as defunctionalized continuations. Similarly, it is properly tail recursive since the interpreter is already properly tail recursive.

Since the correctness of defunctionalization has been established [5, 26], the correctness of the logic engine is a corollary of the correctness of the original interpreter.

Prolog has both been specified and formalized functionally. For example, Carlsson has shown how to implement Prolog in a functional language [7]. Continuation-based semantics of Prolog have been studied by de Bruin and de Vink [15] as well as by Nicholson and Foo [25]. Our closest related work is de Bruin and de Vink's continuation semantics for Prolog with cut:

- de Bruin and de Vink present a denotational semantics with success and failure continuations; their semantics is (of course) compositional, and comparable to the compositional interpreter outlined in Section 3.3. The only difference is that their success continuations expect both a failure continuation and a cut continuation, whereas our success continuations expect only a failure continuation. Analyzing the control flow of the corresponding interpreter, we have observed that the cut continuation is the same at the definition point and at the use point of a success continuation. Therefore, there is actually no need to pass cut continuations to success continuations.
- de Bruin and de Vink also present an operational semantics, and prove it equivalent to their denotational semantics. In contrast, we defunctionalized the interpreter corresponding to a denotational semantics into an interpreter corresponding to an operational semantics. We also "refunctionalized" the interpreter corresponding to de Bruin and de Vink's operational semantics, and we observed that in the resulting interpreter (which corresponds to a denotational semantics), success continuations are not passed cut continuations.

Designing abstract machines is a favorite among functional programmers [16]. Unsurprisingly, this is also the case among logic programmers, for example, with

---

[2] Closures, for example, are used to implement higher-order logic programming [8].

Warren's abstract machine [4], which incidentally is more of a device for high performance than a model of computation. Just as unsurprisingly, functional programmers use functional programming languages as their meta-language and logic programmers use logic programming languages as their meta-language. For example, Kursawe showed how to "invent" Prolog machines out of logic-programming considerations [22]. The goal of our work here was more modest: we simply aimed to test an interpreter-to-abstract-machine derivation that works well for the λ-calculus. The logic engine we obtained is basic but plausible. Its chief illustrative virtue is to show that the representation of a denotational semantics can be mechanically defunctionalized into the representation of an operational semantics (and, actually, vice versa). It also shows that proper tail recursion and the two control stacks did not need to be invented – they were already present in the original interpreter.

An alternative to deriving an abstract machine from an interpreter is to factor this interpreter into a compiler and a virtual machine, using, e.g., Wand's combinator-based compiler derivation [29], Jørring and Scherlis's staging transformations [21], Hannan's pass-separation approach [18], or more generally the binding-time separation techniques of partial evaluation [20, 24]. We are currently experimenting with a such a factorization to stage our Prolog interpreter into a byte-code compiler and a virtual machine executing this byte code [1].

Acknowledgments

We are grateful to Mads Sig Ager, Małgorzata Biernacka, Jan Midtgaard, and the anonymous referees for their comments. This work is supported by the ESPRIT Working Group APPSEM II (http://www.appsem.org) and by the Danish Natural Science Research Council, Grant no. 21-03-0545.

A   A Direct-Style Interpreter for Prolog

The interpreter of Section 3 is in continuation-passing style to account for the backtracking necessary to implement resolution. Therefore, our derivation method which in its entirety consists of three steps – closure conversion, CPS transformation, and defunctionalization [2] – was reduced to only the last step. Less natural, but making the derivation closer to its original specification, would be to start it with an interpreter in direct style. The failure continuation could be eliminated by transforming the interpreter into direct style [9]. The success continuation, however, would remain. Because it is used non tail-recursively in the clause for disjunctions, it is what is technically called a *delimited* continuation (in contrast to the usual unlimited continuations of denotational semantics [28]). Transforming the interpreter into direct style requires control operators for delimited continuations that are compatible with continuation-passing style, e.g., shift and reset [11, 12, 17].

Figure 4 presents such a direct-style interpreter for Propositional Prolog without cut, counting the number of solutions. CPS-transforming this interpreter

```
structure Prolog_how_many_DS : INTERPRETER
= struct
    open Source
    type result = int
    (*  run_goal : goal * clause list * int -> int  *)
    fun run_goal (nil, p, m)
          = m
      | run_goal (a :: g, p, m)
          = run_seq (a, g, p, m)
    (*  run_seq : atom * goal * clause list * int -> int  *)
    and run_seq (a, nil, p, m)
          = run_atom (a, p, m)
      | run_seq (a, a' :: g, p, m)
          = let val m' = run_atom (a, p, m)
            in run_seq (a', g, p, m')
            end
    (*  run_atom : atom * clause list * int -> int  *)
    and run_atom (FAIL, p, m)
          = shift (fn sc => m)
      | run_atom (IDE i, p, m)
          = (case lookup (i, p)
               of NONE
                    => shift (fn sc => m)
                | (SOME g)
                    => run_goal (g, p, m))
      | run_atom (OR (g1, g2), p, m)
          = shift (fn sc => let val m' = sc (run_goal (g1, p, m))
                            in sc (run_goal (g2, p, m'))
                            end)
    (*  main : top_level_goal * program -> int  *)
    fun main (GOAL g, PROGRAM p)
          = reset (fn () => let val m = run_goal (g, p, 0)
                            in m + 1
                            end)
end
```

Fig. 4. A direct-style interpreter for propositional Prolog

once makes the success continuation appear. CPS-transforming the result makes the failure continuation appear, and yields the interpreter of Section 3.4 (minus cut). Defunctionalizing this interpreter yields the abstract machine of Section 4 (minus cut).

The reset control operator delimits control. Any subsequent use of the shift control operator will capture a delimited continuation that can be composed; this delimited continuation is the success continuation. Conjunction, in run_seq, is implemented by function composition. Failure, in `run_atom`, is implemented by capturing the current success continuation and not applying it. Disjunction, in `run_atom`, is implemented by capturing the current success continuation and applying it twice. This interpreter is properly tail recursive, which is achieved by the two functions `run_goal` and `run_seq` that single out the last atom in a goal.

The interpreter is a new example of nondeterministic programming in direct style with control operators for the first level of the CPS hierarchy [6, 11]. In order to interpret the cut operator we would have to use the control operators of the second level, $shift_2$ and $reset_2$.

References

1. Mads Sig Ager, Dariusz Biernacki, Olivier Danvy, and Jan Midtgaard. From interpreter to compiler and virtual machine: a functional derivation. Technical Report BRICS RS-03-14, DAIMI, Department of Computer Science, University of Aarhus, Aarhus, Denmark, March 2003.
2. Mads Sig Ager, Dariusz Biernacki, Olivier Danvy, and Jan Midtgaard. A functional correspondence between evaluators and abstract machines. In Dale Miller, editor, *Proceedings of the Fifth ACM-SIGPLAN International Conference on Principles and Practice of Declarative Programming (PPDP'03)*, pages 8–19. ACM Press, August 2003.
3. Mads Sig Ager, Olivier Danvy, and Jan Midtgaard. A functional correspondence between call-by-need evaluators and lazy abstract machines. Technical Report BRICS RS-04-03, DAIMI, Department of Computer Science, University of Aarhus, Aarhus, Denmark, February 2004. Extended version of an article to appear in Information Processing Letters.
4. Hassan Aït-Kaci. *Warren's Abstract Machine: A Tutorial Reconstruction*. The MIT Press, 1991.
5. Anindya Banerjee, Nevin Heintze, and Jon G. Riecke. Design and correctness of program transformations based on control-flow analysis. In Naoki Kobayashi and Benjamin C. Pierce, editors, *Theoretical Aspects of Computer Software, 4th International Symposium, TACS 2001*, number 2215 in Lecture Notes in Computer Science, pages 420–447, Sendai, Japan, October 2001. Springer-Verlag.
6. Małgorzata Biernacka, Dariusz Biernacki, and Olivier Danvy. An operational foundation for delimited continuations. In Hayo Thielecke, editor, *Proceedings of the Fourth ACM SIGPLAN Workshop on Continuations*, Technical report CSR-04-1, Department of Computer Science, Queen Mary's College, pages 25–33, Venice, Italy, January 2004.
7. Mats Carlsson. On implementing Prolog in functional programming. *New Generation Computing*, 2(4):347–359, 1984.
8. Weidong Chen, Michael Kifer, and David S. Warren. Hilog: A foundation for higher-order logic programming. *The Journal of Logic Programming*, 15(3):187–230, February 1993.
9. Olivier Danvy. Back to direct style. *Science of Computer Programming*, 22(3):183–195, 1994.
10. Olivier Danvy. A rational deconstruction of Landin's SECD machine. Technical Report BRICS RS-03-33, DAIMI, Department of Computer Science, University of Aarhus, Aarhus, Denmark, October 2003.

11. Olivier Danvy and Andrzej Filinski. Abstracting control. In Mitchell Wand, editor, *Proceedings of the 1990 ACM Conference on Lisp and Functional Programming*, pages 151–160, Nice, France, June 1990. ACM Press.

12. Olivier Danvy and Andrzej Filinski. Representing control, a study of the CPS transformation. *Mathematical Structures in Computer Science*, 2(4):361–391, 1992.

13. Olivier Danvy, Bernd Grobauer, and Morten Rhiger. A unifying approach to goal-directed evaluation. *New Generation Computing*, 20(1):53–73, 2002. Extended version available as the technical report BRICS RS-01-29.

14. Olivier Danvy and Lasse R. Nielsen. Defunctionalization at work. In Harald Søndergaard, editor, *Proceedings of the Third International ACM SIGPLAN Conference on Principles and Practice of Declarative Programming (PPDP'01)*, pages 162–174, Firenze, Italy, September 2001. ACM Press.

15. Arie de Bruin and Erik P. de Vink. Continuation semantics for Prolog with cut. In Josep Díaz and Fernando Orejas, editors, *TAPSOFT'89: Proceedings of the International Joint Conference on Theory and Practice of Software Development*, number 351 in Lecture Notes in Computer Science, pages 178–192, Barcelona, Spain, March 1989. Springer-Verlag.

16. Stephan Diehl, Pieter Hartel, and Peter Sestoft. Abstract machines for programming language implementation. *Future Generation Computer Systems*, 16:739–751, 2000.

17. Andrzej Filinski. Representing monads. In Hans-J. Boehm, editor, *Proceedings of the Twenty-First Annual ACM Symposium on Principles of Programming Languages*, pages 446–457, Portland, Oregon, January 1994. ACM Press.

18. John Hannan. Operational semantics directed machine architecture. *ACM Transactions on Programming Languages and Systems*, 16(4):1215–1247, 1994.

19. Neil D. Jones. *Computability and Complexity from a Programming Perspective*. Foundations of Computing. The MIT Press, 1997.

20. Neil D. Jones, Carsten K. Gomard, and Peter Sestoft. *Partial Evaluation and Automatic Program Generation*. Prentice-Hall International, London, UK, 1993. Available online at http://www.dina.kvl.dk/~sestoft/pebook/.

21. Ulrik Jørring and William L. Scherlis. Compilers and staging transformations. In Mark Scott Johnson and Ravi Sethi, editors, *Proceedings of the Thirteenth Annual ACM Symposium on Principles of Programming Languages*, pages 86–96, St. Petersburg, Florida, January 1986. ACM Press.

22. Peter Kursawe. How to invent a Prolog machine. *New Generation Computing*, 5(1):97–114, 1987.

23. John C. Martin. *Introduction to Languages and the Theory of Computation*. McGraw-Hill, 1991.

24. Torben Æ. Mogensen. Separating binding times in language specifications. In Joseph E. Stoy, editor, *Proceedings of the Fourth International Conference on Functional Programming and Computer Architecture*, pages 14–25, London, England, September 1989. ACM Press.

25. Tim Nicholson and Norman Y. Foo. A denotational semantics for Prolog. *ACM Transactions on Programming Languages and Systems*, 11(4):650–665, 1989.

26. Lasse R. Nielsen. A denotational investigation of defunctionalization. Technical Report BRICS RS-00-47, DAIMI, Department of Computer Science, University of Aarhus, Aarhus, Denmark, December 2000.

27. John C. Reynolds. Definitional interpreters for higher-order programming languages. *Higher-Order and Symbolic Computation*, 11(4):363–397, 1998. Reprinted from the proceedings of the 25th ACM National Conference (1972), with a foreword.

28. Christopher Strachey and Christopher P. Wadsworth. Continuations: A mathematical semantics for handling full jumps. *Higher-Order and Symbolic Computation*, 13(1/2):135–152, 2000. Reprint of the technical monograph PRG-11, Oxford University Computing Laboratory (1974), with a foreword.

29. Mitchell Wand. Semantics-directed machine architecture. In Richard DeMillo, editor, *Proceedings of the Ninth Annual ACM Symposium on Principles of Programming Languages*, pages 234–241. ACM Press, January 1982.

Linearization by Program Transformation

Sandra Alves and Mário Florido

University of Porto
Department of Computer Science & LIACC
R. do Campo Alegre 823, 4150-180 Porto, Portugal
{sandra,amf}@ncc.up.pt

Abstract. We identify a restricted class of terms of the lambda calculus, here called weak linear, that includes the linear lambda-terms keeping their good properties of strong normalization, non-duplicating reductions and typability in polynomial time. The advantage of this class over the linear lambda-calculus is the possibility of transforming general terms into weak linear terms with the same normal form. We present such transformation and prove its correctness by showing that it preserves normal forms.

1 Introduction

Linear programs are simple. Concerning implementation issues, for linear programs one may safely inline the term bound to any variable, or safely update structures in place. Every linear term in the λ-calculus is β-strongly normalizing (i.e., there is no infinite β-reduction sequence starting from M), every β-reduction of a linear term is non-duplicating and every closed linear term is typable in the simple type system [10], thus it is typable in polynomial time.

The language we use in this paper is the lambda-calculus, because it can be viewed simultaneously as a simple programming language in which computations can be described, and as a mathematical object about which rigorous statements can be proved. Thus linear programs are modeled by *linear* λ-terms: λ-terms M such that for each subterm $\lambda x.P$ of M, x occurs free in P at most once.

Consider the following question: is there a way of simulating the standard λ-calculus by the linear λ-calculus? If simulation means transforming the original standard term into a linear term with the same normal form then it is not possible, in general, to define such transformation. This is shown by the next simple example: it is not possible to transform the term (in normal form) $\lambda x.xx$ into a linear term with the same normal form. This happens for any non-linear normal form.

In this paper we address the following problem: is there a restricted class of λ-terms, with the same nice properties of the linear λ-calculus and such that we can simulate the standard λ-calculus by terms of that class?

We show that there is a restriction with these properties, which we here call the *weak linear* λ-*calculus*. A λ-term M is *weak linear* if in any reduction sequence of M, when there is a contraction of a β-redex $(\lambda x.P)Q$, then x occurs

M. Bruynooghe (Ed.): LOPSTR 2004, LNCS 3018, pp. 160–175, 2004.

free in P at most once, i.e., when a function $\lambda x.P$ is applied, its formal parameter x must occur at most once in the function body. For example the term $\lambda x.xx$ is weak linear because it is a non-linear λ-abstraction which is never applied. The term $(\lambda x.xx)I$ is not weak linear because it has a redex where the function is not linear. For weak linear terms, only functions that can be applied to an argument in the reduction process are required to be linear.

Notice that our definition does not refer only to β-redexes $(\lambda x.P)Q$ that are subterms of the original term M, but to abstractions $\lambda x.P$ that are going to be the function part of a β-redex in the reduction of M. For example the term $M \equiv ((\lambda x.x)(\lambda x.xx))k$ is not weak linear although it does not have any subterm of the form $(\lambda x.P)Q$ with x occurring more than once in P. The problem is that there is a redex of this form (in this case, $(\lambda x.xx)k$), in a reduction sequence from M.

The main contributions of this paper are the following:

- A restricted class of λ-terms, here called the *weak linear λ-calculus* with the same basic properties of the linear λ-calculus. Here we show that weak linear terms are strong normalizing and typable in polynomial time.
- A transformation of general terms into weak linear terms preserving normal forms. To deal with transformation of redexes which will appear during the reduction process (the *virtual redexes*) our transformation uses *legal paths*, [3, 4], because this notion provides a formal characterization of the intuitive notion of *virtual redex*. This contribution is also significant for the methodology it develops. What we set up is a new use of legal paths for complex term transformation.

Let us quickly review the existing literature on the question. A linearization of the λ-calculus was made by Kfoury [12]. He embedded the λ-calculus into a larger calculus, denoted $\Lambda^\wedge$ with a new notion of reduction, denoted $\beta^\wedge$. In the new calculus $\Lambda^\wedge$, in every function application, an argument is used at most once. He also defined the notion of *contraction* of a term in the new calculus, giving a λ-term. This last notion gives a way of transforming terms in the new calculus into terms of the λ-calculus, however, it was not presented a direct definition of a transformation of λ-terms into terms of the new calculus. The relation between the two calculus was made indirectly saying that the *well-formed* terms of the new calculus are the ones for which there is a *contraction* in the λ-calculus. Our algorithm is defined directly as a transformation from λ-terms to *weak linear* terms and simulating the λ-calculus by a subset of the λ-calculus and not by a non-standard calculus. The problem was also discussed in [8] where it was established a relation, not a transformation, between terms typable in an intersection type system and linear terms. Types played a central role is the definition of this relation and, because the mapping was on the linear λ-calculus, β-normal forms were not preserved.

The type system used in our paper was used (with minor differences) before in [13] and [1], as a restricted form of intersection type inference for terms resulting from a simplification process of arbitrary terms. Finally we remark that our definition of *linear* term follows [12], but some people call this class of terms *affine*, and use the word *linear* for terms $\lambda x.M$ where x occurs free exactly once in M.

In the rest of the paper we assume that the reader is familiar with the λ-calculus. A standard reference for this area is [5]. A good survey on the application of λ-calculus to programming language technology can be found in [6].

We start in Section 2 with the definition of weak linear lambda terms. In section 3 we present a type system and a type inference algorithm for the weak linear calculus. In section 4 we present a transformation from λ-terms into weak linear λ-terms, and prove that it is correct in the sense that it preserves normal forms. Finally we conclude and outline some future work in section 5.

2   The Weak Linear Lambda Calculus

We start this section by giving some brief notions on λ-calculus.

Definition 1. *Let x range over an infinite set of variables. The set of λ-terms, Λ is defined as:*

$$M, N \in \Lambda ::= x \mid \lambda x.M \mid MN$$

As usual the set of λ-terms is quotiented by α-conversion. We use the usual notation of reduction

$$(\lambda x.M)N \to_\beta M[N/x]$$

As usual, $FV(M)$ denotes the set of free variables of M. In the rest of the paper we assume that no variable is bound more than once, and that it is impossible for a variable to occur both free and bound in a term.

Definition 2. *The length of a term M is defined as follows:*

- *$length(x) = 1$;*
- *$length(MN) = length(M) + length(N) + 1$;*
- *$length(\lambda x.M) = length(M) + 1$.*

Definition 3 (Weak linear terms). *A λ-term M is* weak linear *iff every redex $(\lambda x.P)Q$, in the reduction graph of M (consisting of every reduction sequence from M), is such that x occurs at most once in P.*

Definition 4. *If M is strongly normalizable, the maximal length of a derivation from M is called the reduction depth of M, and denoted $depth(M)$.*

Lemma 1. *For weak linear λ-terms, contracting a redex reduces the length of a term.*

Proof. The redex $((\lambda x.M)N)$ is longer than $M[N/x]$ if x occurs free at most once in M.   □

Corollary 1 (Strong normalization). *If M is a weak linear λ-term, then a β-reduction sequence starting at M cannot have more reduction steps than the length of M. Hence, every weak linear λ-term has a normal form.*

3   Type Inference for the Weak Linear Lambda Calculus

Here we present a type system that types every weak linear term. Note that closed linear terms are typed in the Simple Type System [11], but the same does not happen with weak linear terms. In this case functions which are never applied may not be linear. For example the term $\lambda x.xx$ is weak linear and it is not typable in the Simple Type System. The type system described in this section, here called T_W type system, is based on intersection types [7]. Note that the previous term, $\lambda x.xx$, is typed by intersection types with type $((\alpha \to \beta) \cap \alpha) \to \beta$. We use intersections only to type abstractions, and when typing applications the function part cannot have a domain denoted by an intersection. This is enough to type every weak linear term keeping the decidability of the type inference problem.

3.1   A Type System for Weak Linear Terms

Definition 5. *An infinite sequence of type-variables is assumed to be given. Intersection types are expressions defined thus:*

1. *each type-variable is a type;*
2. *if σ and $\tau_1 \ldots \tau_n$ are types (for $n \geq 1$) then $(\tau_1 \cap \cdots \cap \tau_n \to \sigma)$ is a type.*

In the previous definition $\cap$ is assumed to be an associative, commutative and idempotent operator.

Definition 6. *A type environment is a finite set of pairs of the form $x : \tau$, where x is a term variable (called the* subject*) and τ is a type.*

Notation: The set of subjects of a type environment B will be called $Subjects(B)$. The set of types associated to a variable x in an environment B will be called $B(x)$.

Definition 7. *The T_W system is defined by:*

$$VAR \qquad \{x : \sigma\} \vdash x : \sigma$$

$$ABS\text{-}I \quad \frac{A \cup \{x : \tau_1, \ldots, x : \tau_n\} \vdash M : \sigma}{A \vdash \lambda x.M : \tau_1 \cap \cdots \cap \tau_n \to \sigma} \quad if \ x \in FV(M) \ \ (a)$$

$$ABS\text{-}K \qquad \frac{A \vdash M : \sigma}{A \vdash \lambda x.M : \tau \to \sigma} \qquad if \ x \notin FV(M)$$

$$APP \quad \frac{A_1 \vdash M : \tau \to \sigma \quad A_2 \vdash N : \tau}{A_1 \cup A_2 \vdash MN : \sigma}$$

(a) If $x : \tau_1, \ldots, x : \tau_n$ are all and nothing but statements about x on which $A \cup \{x : \tau_1, \ldots, x : \tau_n\} \vdash M : \sigma$ depends.

$M : \sigma$ is derivable from an environment A in the T_W type system, notation $A \vdash M : \sigma$, if and only if it is obtained using the previous rules. Note that in T_W intersections only appear in the *ABS-I* rule, thus in type derivations, intersection types can only appear in the types of abstractions which are not applied.

Example 1. In system T_W we have $\vdash (\lambda x.xx) : (\alpha \cap (\alpha \to \beta)) \to \beta$ but $(\lambda x.xx)(\lambda x.x)$ is not typable.

Lemma 2. *For any term M, if $A \vdash M : \sigma$, then $Subjects(A) = FV(M)$.*

Proof. By a straightforward structural induction on M. $\square$

Lemma 3. *Let M be a weak linear λ-term of the form $M \equiv (\lambda x.P)Q$ and $M^* \equiv P[Q/x]$. Let $B \vdash M^* : \sigma$. Then:*

1. *If x occurs free in P, then $\exists_{B'}.B' \vdash M : \sigma$;*
2. *If x does not occur free in P, and $\exists_{B'',\tau}.B'' \vdash Q : \tau$ then $\exists_{B'}.B' \vdash M : \sigma$.*

Proof.

1. By lemma 2, $B = B' \cup B''$ and
   - $B' \cup B'' \vdash P[Q/x] : \sigma$ (1)

   where $Subjects(B') = FV(P) \setminus \{x\}$ and $Subjects(B'') = FV(Q)$. This derivation contains a sub-derivation of the form:
   - $B'' \vdash Q : \theta$ (2)

   In (1), the assumption $Q : \theta$ is only used once, since P only contains one x. If we replace Q by x through (1), we get the deduction
   $$B' \cup \{x : \theta\} \vdash P : \sigma$$ (3)
   Rule (ABS) can be applied to (3) to get
   $$B' \vdash \lambda x.P : \theta \to \sigma$$ (4)
   and then by (2) and rule (APP) we have $M : \sigma$.
2. Argue as in 1, but use the assumed-to-be-given type derivation for Q instead of (2). $\square$

Theorem 1. *Every weak linear term M is typable in system T_W.*

Proof. By induction on $(depth(M), length(M))$, using lemma 3. $\square$

3.2   A Type Inference Algorithm

The type inference algorithm presented here is a generalization of the Hindley's algorithm for Simple Types ([9], [11]). A brief sketch of a similar system was presented before in [13]. The main difference to the Simple Type System is that type declarations for the same variable in the environment may not be unique, and abstractions are typable even when types of their formal parameter do not unify.

Definition 8. *Let UNIFY be Robinson's unification algorithm [15]. Given a λ term M, we define the function $\mathcal{I}(M) = (\Gamma, \tau)$, where Γ is a type environment and τ is a type, thus:*

1. *If $M = x$ then $\mathcal{I}(M) = (\{x : \alpha\}, \alpha)$ where α is a type variable.*
2. *If $M = \lambda x.N$ then:*
   - *If $\mathcal{I}(N) = (\Gamma', \tau)$ and $x \notin Subjects(\Gamma')$, then $\mathcal{I}(\lambda x.N) = (\Gamma', \alpha \to \tau)$ where α is a new type variable.*

- If $\mathcal{I}(N) = (\Gamma', \tau)$ and $\Gamma'(x) = \{\tau_1, \ldots, \tau_n\}$, then $\mathcal{I}(\lambda x.N) = (\Gamma'_x, \tau_1 \cap \cdots \cap \tau_n \to \tau)$.

3. If $M = M_1 M_2$ then $\mathcal{I}(M) = (S(\Gamma_1 \cup \Gamma_2), S(\alpha))$ where:
   - $\mathcal{I}(M_1) = (\Gamma_1, \tau_1)$;
   - $\mathcal{I}(M_2) = (\Gamma_2, \tau_2)$;
   - $S = UNIFY(\tau_1, \tau_2 \to \alpha)$ (α is a new type variable).

Theorem 2.
1. $\mathcal{I}(M) = (\Gamma, \sigma)$ if and only if M is typable in system T_W.
2. $\mathcal{I}(M)$ terminates in time polynomial in the size of M.

Proof. (sketch) For the first part we must show that $\mathcal{I}(M) = (\Gamma, \sigma) \Rightarrow M$ is typable in system T_W and $B \vdash M : \tau \Rightarrow \exists_{A,\sigma}.\mathcal{I}(M) = (A, \sigma)$. The first point is proved by induction on the structure of M. In the proof of the second point we claim that if $B \vdash M : \tau$, then there is an environment A, type σ and substitution S such that $\mathcal{I}(M) = (A, \sigma)$ and $(B, \tau) = (SA, S\sigma)$. Our claim is proved by induction on the structure of M.

The second part of the theorem follows noticing that unification is PTIME-complete and that the inference algorithm analyses each subterm at most once. □

4   Transformation into Weak Linear Terms

Let us see what means to transform a λ-term into a *weak linear* term. Consider the following example: suppose one wants to define the weak linear version of the term $(\lambda xy.xy)(\lambda z.zz)(\lambda w.w)$. In this term the only variable which occurs more than once is z. Thus we must linearize $(\lambda z.zz)$ to get the term $(\lambda z_1 z_2.z_1 z_2)$. But $(\lambda z.zz)$ will have y as an argument after one reduction step. Thus y in $(\lambda xy.xy)$ has to be copied and we get the term:

$$(\lambda xy.xyy)(\lambda z_1 z_2.z_1 z_2)(\lambda w.w)$$

Now, a variable which occurred once in the original term occurs twice in the new term, thus the linearization process has to go on, linearizing $(\lambda xy.xyy)$ to obtain $(\lambda xy_1 y_2.xy_1 y_2)$. Notice that y will be replaced by $\lambda w.w$ in the original version of the term, thus, as y was replaced by two new parameters, we have to duplicate $(\lambda w.w)$ in the resulting term to get the final term:

$$(\lambda xy_1 y_2.xy_1 y_2)(\lambda z_1 z_2.z_1 z_2)(\lambda w.w)(\lambda w.w)$$

Notice that y will be replaced by $\lambda w.w$ after one reduction step. Thus the transformation algorithm has to know in advance that subterms of the form $(\lambda x.M)$ and N are going to be the function and argument part of a redex in the future, i.e. $(\lambda x.M)N$ is a *virtual redex*. To deal with this complicated issue we make use of *legal paths*. Legal paths were introduced by Asperti and Laneve [4] as a characterization based on paths of Lévy's redex families in the context of optimal reductions for the λ-calculus. They provide a static characterization of virtual redexes and revealed to be quite useful for program transformation. As far as we know this is the first work relating the two subjects.

4.1   The Labeled λ-Calculus and Legal Paths

The Labeled λ-Calculus. The labeled λ-calculus is an extension of the λ-calculus, proposed by Lévy in [14]. In the rest of the paper, we will use $x, y, z, \ldots$ to range over variables, $a, b, c, \ldots, l, m, k, \ldots$ to range over labels, and $\varphi, \psi, \phi, \ldots$ to range over paths.

Definition 9. *Let x range over an infinite set of variables $\mathcal{V}$, and l over an infinite set of labels L. The set of labelled λ-terms, $\Lambda_{\mathcal{V}}^L$ is defined as:*

$$M, N \in \Lambda_{\mathcal{V}}^L ::= x^l \mid (MN)^l \mid (\lambda x.M)^l$$

We make the same assumptions regarding free and bound variables, as in the λ-calculus, and we also assume that all the labels in a labeled λ-term are pairwise distinct.

Labeled β-reduction is the following rule (note that $l_0 \cdot (T)^{l_1} = (T)^{l_0 l_1}$):

$$((\lambda x.M)^{l_0} N)^{l_1} \rightarrow l_1 \cdot \overline{l_0} \cdot M[\underline{l_0} \cdot N/x]$$

where the label l_0 is the *degree* of the redex $((\lambda x.M)^{l_0} N)^{l_1}$

Labels provide an approach to the notion of computation as a travel along a path. Note that every label trivially defines a path in the syntactic tree of the term.

Example 2. $M = ((\lambda x.((x^e(\lambda y.(y^h y^i)^g)^f)^d v^j)^c)^b(\lambda w.(\lambda z.(w^n(w^p z^q)^o)^m)^l)^k)^a$ has the graph representation given by Figure 1.

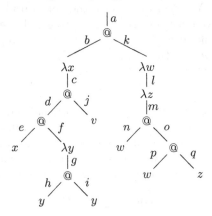

Fig. 1. Labeled λ-term

Definition 10. *If l is a label of an edge generated along some reduction from M, the* path *of l in M is inductively defined as follows:*

$$\begin{aligned}
path(a) &= a \\
path(l_1 l_2) &= path(l_1) \cdot path(l_2) \\
path(\overline{l}) &= path(l) \\
path(\underline{l}) &= (path(l))^r
\end{aligned}$$

where $\varphi_1 \cdot \varphi_2$ means concatenation of the two paths (in the following we will sometimes omit $\cdot$), and φ^r is the path obtained by reversing φ.

Legal Paths. Different degrees of redexes correspond to different paths in the original term. Legal paths are a characterization of paths yield by degrees. Legal paths are obtained by suitably constraining another type of paths which are the well balanced paths (wbp). (All the definitions and results concerning legal paths, presented in this sub-section, can be found in [4].)

Definition 11. *Well balanced paths are inductively defined in the following way (see Figure 2):*

- (***base case***) *The function edge of any application, is a* well balanced path.
- (λ-***composition***) *Let ψ be a wbp of type @-x whose ending variable is bound to a λ-node **c** and φ be a wbp of type @-λ coming into **c**. Then $\psi.(\varphi)^r.u$ is a wbp, where u is the argument edge of the initial node of φ;*
- (@-***composition***) *Let ψ be a wbp of type @-@ ending into a node **d** and φ be of type @-λ leading from **d** to some λ-node **c**. Then $\psi.\varphi.u$ is a wbp, where u outgoes **c** towards its body.*

The type @-? where ? can be λ, @ or x (variable) is determined by the type of the node where the wbp ends.

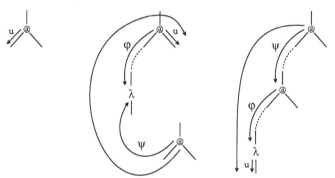

Fig. 2. Well balanced paths

Example 3. The set of wbp (of the form *path : type*) of the λ-term M of Figure 1 is given by:
Initial paths:

$$\{b : @\text{-}\lambda, d : @\text{-}@, e : @\text{-}x, h : @\text{-}x, n : @\text{-}x, p : @\text{-}x\}$$

Applying (λ-*composition*) to the initial paths, and (@-*composition*) to the new paths we get,

$$\{e \cdot b \cdot k : @\text{-}\lambda, d \cdot e\, b\, k \cdot l : @\text{-}\lambda\}$$

Again by (λ-*composition*) and (@-*composition*) we get

$$\{n \cdot k\, b\, e \cdot f : @\text{-}\lambda, p \cdot k\, b\, e \cdot f : @\text{-}\lambda\}$$

After one more iteration

$$\{h \cdot f\,e\,b\,k\,n \cdot o : @\text{-}x, h \cdot f\,e\,b\,k\,p \cdot q : @\text{-}x\}$$

Finally

$$\{h\,f\,e\,b\,k\,p\,q \cdot l\,k\,b\,e\,d \cdot j : @\text{-}x\}$$

Thus, the set of wbp of type $@\text{-}\lambda$ is given by:

$$\{b : @\text{-}\lambda, e \cdot b \cdot k : @\text{-}\lambda, d \cdot e\,b\,k \cdot l : @\text{-}\lambda, n \cdot k\,b\,e \cdot f : @\text{-}\lambda, p \cdot k\,b\,e \cdot f : @\text{-}\lambda\}$$

Note that, if we imagine that bound variables (x) are explicitly connected to their binders (λx), these paths are actual paths in the graph representation of M.

We now present two other kinds of paths in a term needed to define legal paths.

Definition 12. *Let φ be a wbp.*

- *(v-**cycles**) Let v be the label of a variable edge. A v-cycle (over v) is a cyclic subpath of the form $v\lambda(\varphi)^r@\psi@\varphi\lambda v$ where φ is a wbp and ψ is a @-cycle.*
- *(@-**cycles**) A @-cycle, over an @ node with argument subterm N, is a sub-path ψ that starts and ends with the argument edge of the @-node, and composed of subpaths internal to the argument N and v-cycles over free variables of N. A particular case of @-cycle is a cycle starting from and ending to the argument edge p of a @-node (the negative auxiliary port), and internal to the argument N of the application (i.e. not traversing variables which are free in N).*

Example 4. The wbp $h\,f\,e\,b\,k\,p\,q\,l\,k\,b\,e\,d\,j$ of type $@\text{-}x$ of example 3 has a v-cycle $e\lambda b@k\,p\,q\,l\,k@b\lambda e$ and a @-cycle $@k\,p\,q\,l\,k@$.

Proposition 1. *Let φ be a wbp with a @-cycle $@\psi@$. Then φ can be uniquely decomposed as*

$$\zeta_1\lambda\zeta_2@\psi@(\zeta_3)^r\lambda\zeta_4$$

where both ζ_2 and ζ_3 are wbp's. The paths ζ_2 and ζ_3 are called the call *and* return *paths of the @-cycle ψ. The last label of ζ_1 and the first label of ζ_4 are named the* discriminants *of the call and return paths, respectively.*

Definition 13. *A wbp is a* legal path *if and only the call and return paths of any @-cycle are one the reversed of the other and their discriminants are equal.*

Example 5. The wbp's of example 3 are all legal. Notice that in the only path having a @-cycle $h\,f\,e\,b\,k\,p\,q\,l\,k\,b\,e\,d\,j$, the call and return paths of the cycle are both b (thus one is the reversed of the other), and the discriminants are both e.

Theorem 3. *Every path yield by the degree of a redex is a legal path.*

Theorem 4. *For any legal path φ of type $@\text{-}\lambda$ in a term M, there exists a degree l of a redex originated along some reduction of M such that $path(l) = \varphi$.*

Example 6. Consider the labeled λ-term of Figure 1. Let $\Delta' = (\lambda y.(y^h y^i)^g)^f$ and $P = (\lambda w.(\lambda z.(w^n (w^p z^q)^o)^m)^l)$. After one labeled reduction we get the λ-term $((P^{e\,\overline{b}\,k}\Delta')^d v^j)^{a\,\overline{b}\,c}$. The path yield by degree $e\,\overline{b}\,k$ of the redex $(P^{e\,\overline{b}\,k}\Delta')^d$, is $e\,b\,k$ and it is the legal path of type @-λ starting in the application node having Δ' as argument subterm and ending in P. Also note that $e\,b\,k$ is an actual path in the graph in Figure 1 when we assume that bound variables (x) are explicitly connected to their binders (λx).

4.2   Term Transformation

Here we present a transformation from arbitrary λ-terms into weak linear terms. We first prove some lemmas which are going to be used in the proof of the correctness of the transformation.

Lemma 4. *M is a strongly normalizable term, iff the set $\mathcal{LP}$ of legal paths of type @-λ in M is a finite set.*

Proof. We prove the two directions separately.
$\Leftarrow$ Suppose that the set of legal paths of M is not finite. By theorem 4 there is an infinite number of paths yield by degrees of redexes. Thus, there is an infinite reduction of M, which means that M is not strongly normalizable.
$\Rightarrow$ Suppose that M isn't strongly normalizable. Let us choose a reduction of M that doesn't stop. That reduction will cause an infinite number of paths yield by degrees of redexes. Thus, by theorem 3, an infinite number of legal paths.   □

Definition 14. *Let M be a λ-term, $\mathcal{LP}$ be the set of legal paths of M, and S_1 the paths corresponding to redexes in M. We define the chain of dependences between legal paths of type @-λ in $\mathcal{LP}$ as $S_1 \gg S_2 \gg \cdots \gg S_n \gg \cdots$ such that the legal paths in S_i are build by λ-composition from the paths in the sets $S_1, \ldots, S_{i-1}$ and @-composition from the paths in S_i.*

Definition 15. *Let M be a λ-term, and $\mathcal{LP}$ be the set of legal paths of M. The function next_non_linear(M) returns a pair of labels (l, k), where l is the abstraction node where the next non linear legal path, of type @-λ, in the chain of legal paths built from $\mathcal{LP}$, ends and k is the function edge of the application node where it starts. If every legal path is linear, next_non_linear(M) $= \perp$.*

Basically this function returns the labels which identify the next non-linear virtual redex.

Example 7. For the λ-term M in Figure 1, with the set $\mathcal{LP}$, of legal paths of type @-λ, given in example 3 the chain of legal paths is

$$\{b\} \gg \{e \cdot b \cdot k, \; d \cdot e\,b\,k \cdot l\} \gg \{n \cdot k\,b\,e \cdot f, \; p \cdot k\,b\,e \cdot f\}$$

thus the result of next_non_linear($\mathcal{LP}$) is (k, e).

Lemma 5. *If M is a λ-term and $(l, k) = $ next_non_linear(M), then the only application node such that there is a legal path φ of type @-λ ending in l is the application with function edge, labeled k.*

Proof. Suppose there are legal paths φ_1 and φ_2 both finishing in the abstraction $(\lambda x.P)^l$ and starting in two diferent application nodes. Thus there are two diferent degrees l_1 l_2 of redexes (having the abstraction labeled l as left side) originated along some reduction of M such that $path(l_i) = \varphi_i$ ($i = 1, 2$). If $(\lambda x.P)^l$ appears as the left side of two different redexes, then $(\lambda x.P)^l$ was duplicated by some reduction previous to l_1 and l_2. Thus, there is a non linear legal path previous to φ_1 and φ_2, in which case l would not be the result of *next_non_linear*(M).   □

Example 8. Consider the chain of legal paths of type @-λ in example 7. We have *next_non_linear*(M) $= (k, e)$, and the application node whose function edge is e is the only application node for which there is a legal path φ ending in k.

Definition 16 (one step of the transformation). *Let M be a λ-term. We define the term $\mathcal{L}(M)$, that results from linearizing the next non linear abstraction $(\lambda x.P)^l$ of M. Let n be the number of occurrences of x in P:*

$$\mathcal{L}(M) = \begin{cases} M & \textit{if next\_non\_linear}(M) = \perp \\ M_l & \textit{otherwise} \end{cases}$$

where

- *$(l, k) = $ next_non_linear(M);*
- *$M' = $ replace(l, M), where replace(l, M) replaces the abstraction $(\lambda x.P)^l$ in M by $(\lambda x_1. \ldots. (\lambda x_n.P^*)^{l_n} \cdots)^{l_1}$, and P^* results from replacing the ith occurrence of x in P by the fresh variable x_i ($i = 1, \ldots, n$).*
- *$M_l = $ replace_n(k, n, M'), where replace_n(k, n, M') is the function that replaces the term $(Q^k N^m)^j$ by $((\cdots (Q^{k_1} \underbrace{N^{m_1}) \cdots)^{k_n} N^{m_n})^j}_{n \; times}$ (see Figure 3).*

Remark: Note that the labels in each copy of N are such that, if N has a label c in M, there is a label c_i in the ith copy of N in M_l.

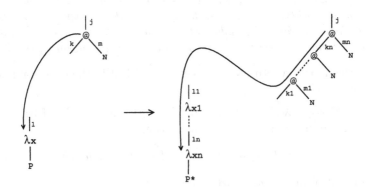

Fig. 3. Expansion of an abstraction

Example 9. Let M be the λ-term in Figure 1. The term that results from expanding the first non linear path $(e \cdot b \cdot k)$ in M, $\mathcal{L}(M)$ is given by Figure 4.

Definition 17 (Transformation into weak linear terms). *Let M be a λ-term, and $\mathcal{LP}$ the set of legal paths in M. We define the following function:*

$$\mathcal{T}(M) = \begin{cases} M & \text{if all\_linear}(M) \\ \mathcal{T}(\mathcal{L}(M)) & \text{otherwise} \end{cases}$$

The function all_linear(M) returns true *if all the legal paths of type @-λ in M, end in a linear abstraction, and* false *otherwise.*

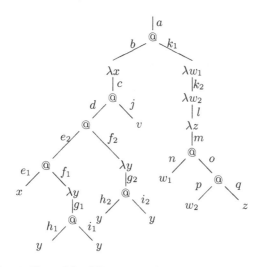

Fig. 4. Term M, of Figure 1, after one step of transformation

Example 10. Let $\Delta = \lambda y.yy$ and $D = \lambda y_1 y_2.y_1 y_2$. Let $M = (\lambda x.x \Delta v)$ $(\lambda wz.w(wz))$ be the term represented in Figure 1. Let us follow the transformation in some detail. We will omit the labels of the terms, except the ones needed to follow the example. We first linearize the abstraction $(\lambda wz.w(wz))^k$ and duplicate the argument of x^e corresponding to the first non-linear abstraction on the chain of paths in example 7, $(e \cdot b \cdot k)$, to get the term in Figure 4.

$$\mathcal{T}(M) = \mathcal{T}((\lambda x.x \Delta^{f_1} \Delta^{f_2} v)(\lambda w_1.(\lambda w_2 z.w_1 (w_2 z))^{k_2})^{k_1})$$

After one more step, linearizing Δ^{f_1}, we get:

$$\mathcal{T}((\lambda x.x D \Delta v)(\lambda w_1 w_2 z.w_1 (w_2 z)(w_2 z)))$$

Now the abstractions labeled by k_2 and l in $(\lambda w_2.(\lambda z.w_1 (w_2 z)(w_2 z))^l)^{k_2}$ which were linear, became non-linear thus, after a one more step we get:

$$\mathcal{T}((\lambda x.x D \Delta \Delta v)(\lambda w_1 w_2 w_3 z.w_1 (w_2 z)(w_3 z)))$$

Linearizing $\lambda z.w_1(w_2 z)(w_3 z)$ we get

$$T((\lambda x.x D^{f_1} \Delta^{f_{21}} \Delta^{f_{22}} vv)(\lambda w_1 w_2 w_3 z_1 z_2.w_1(w_2 z_1)(w_3 z_2)))$$

The next non-linear abstraction is the copy of Δ labeled by f_{21}, thus we get:

$$T((\lambda x.x DD \Delta vv)(\lambda w_1 w_2 w_3 z_1 z_2.w_1(w_2 z_1 z_1)(w_3 z_2)))$$

The abstraction $(\lambda z_1 z_2.w_1(w_2 z_1 z_1)(w_3 z_2)))$ becomes non-linear, thus, after a few more steps, we get:

$$
\begin{aligned}
&= T((\lambda x.x DD \Delta vvv)(\lambda w_1 w_2 w_3 z_1 z_3 z_2.w_1(w_2 z_1 z_3)(w_3 z_2))) \\
&= T((\lambda x.x DDD vvvv)(\lambda w_1 w_2 w_3 z_1 z_3 z_2 z_4.w_1(w_2 z_1 z_3)(w_3 z_2 z_4))) \\
&= (\lambda x.x DDD vvvv)(\lambda w_1 w_2 w_3 z_1 z_2 z_3 z_4.w_1(w_2 z_1 z_2)(w_3 z_3 z_4))
\end{aligned}
$$

Now all the legal paths of type @-λ are linear, thus the transformation terminates. Note that $nf(M) = (vv)(vv) = nf(T(M))$. As we shall prove latter, this happens for every term.

4.3   Correctness

Here we show that the transformation preserves normal forms. The proof relies in the next lemma, which basically, relates the legal paths of the original term and of the transformed term.

Lemma 6. *If $\mathcal{L}(M) = M_{\mathcal{L}}$, let $(l, k) = next\_non\_linear(M)$ and N the subterm argument of the application node having k as function edge, then the set $P_{\mathcal{L}}$ of legal paths of $M_{\mathcal{L}}$ is such that:*

1. *If φ is a legal path internal to N, then φ_i ($i = 1 \ldots n$) is a legal path in the ith copy of N in $M_{\mathcal{L}}$;*
2. *If φ is a legal path with a @-cycle in N (starting and ending outside N), then φ' is a legal path with a cycle in a copy of N in $M_{\mathcal{L}}$;*
3. *If φ is a legal path not internal but starting and ending in N, then φ' is a legal path starting and ending in a copy of N in $M_{\mathcal{L}}$;*
4. *If φ is a legal path starting/ending in N, then φ' is a legal path starting/ending in a copy of N in $M_{\mathcal{L}}$, and ending/starting in the same edge;*
5. *If $\varphi = k\psi l$ is the legal path in M of type @-λ ending in $(\lambda x.P)^l$, then in $M_{\mathcal{L}}$, there are n paths of type @-λ ending respectively in $(\lambda x_1 \ldots x_n.P^*)^{l_1}$, $(\lambda x_2 \ldots x_n.P^*)^{l_2}, \ldots, (\lambda x_n.P^*)^{l_n}$, and starting respectively in $k_1, k_2, \ldots, k_n$, $(n \geq 1)$;*
6. *If φ is a legal path in M of any type, external to N, then there is a legal path of the same type in $M_{\mathcal{L}}$, starting and ending in the same edges.*

Proof. The proof follows by induction on the number of recursive calls of the algorithm for building legal paths. This is a tedious case analysis. Details are in the Appendix of the full report of this paper [2].

Example 11. Let M be the labeled term in Figure 1, and $M_{\mathcal{L}}$ (the term obtained from M after one step of transformation) in Figure 4.

Given the legal path of M, h, we have the corresponding legal paths h_1 and h_2 in $M_{\mathcal{L}}$. This illustrates point 1 of lemma 6.

For point 5 of the same lemma, notice that given the legal path $e\,b\,k$ of M, we have two legal paths $e_1\,b\,k_1$ and $e_2\,e_1\,b\,k_1\,k_2$ is $M_{\mathcal{L}}$.

Theorem 5. *If $T(M) = N$, then N is weak linear.*

Proof. If $T(M)$ terminates then the set of legal paths (of type @-λ) in N, is a finite set of linear legal paths. Since only the abstraction nodes which are the end of a legal path appear as the left side of a redex along a reduction of N (that follows from theorem 3), and being all those abstractions linear, then no reduction starting from N duplicates arguments. Thus N is weak linear.   □

Lemma 7. *Let r be a reduction sequence from a term M using the normal order reduction strategy (i.e., at each step do the leftmost outermost β-reduction). Let Δ be a β-redex reduced in another reduction sequence of M and such that Δ is not reduced in r. Then there exists a β-redex Δ' reduced in r such that*

$$\Delta' \equiv (\lambda x.P)\Delta \text{ and } x \notin FV(P)$$

Proof. Suppose that Δ is not reduced in r and that Δ is not erased in r (by a redex of the form Δ'). Then Δ must be a subterm of the normal form of M, which is absurd, because it is a β-redex, thus it cannot be a subterm of a term in β-normal form.   □

Lemma 8. *If $\mathcal{L}(M) = N$, and both N and M have a normal form, then $nf(M) = nf(N)$.*

Proof. Notice that the normal order reduction strategy is normalizing, i.e., if there is a normal form of M then it can be reached using the normal order strategy of reduction. Now let $(\lambda x.P)$ be the abstraction labeled l, where $l = next\_non\_linear(M)$, and choose the normal order reduction of M. We then have two cases:

1. The expanded abstraction appears in the normal reduction sequence:

$$M \to \cdots \to (\lambda x.P)Q \to [Q/x]P \to \cdots \to nf(M)$$

By lemma 6, we have

$$N \to \cdots \to (\lambda x_1 \ldots x_n.P^*)\underbrace{Q \ldots Q}_{n \text{ times}} \to_* [Q/x_1, \ldots, Q/x_n]P^*.$$

But $[Q/x_1, \ldots, Q/x_n]P^* = [Q/x]P$, thus $[Q/x_1, \ldots, Q/x_n]P^* \to \cdots \to nf(M)$. Thus $nf(N) = nf(M)$.

2. If the expanded abstraction does not appear in the normal reduction sequence of M then, use lemma 7 to get a similar result.   □

Theorem 6. *If* $T(M) = N$, *then* $nf(M) = nf(N)$.

Proof. By induction on the number of recursive calls of T.
− Base case : $all\_linear(M)$. Then $T(M) = M$ in which case $nf(M)$ is trivially equal to $nf(N)$;
− Induction step : $T(M) = T(M_l)$, where $M_l = \mathcal{L}(M)$. By the induction hypothesis, $nf(M_l) = nf(N)$, and by lemma 8 $nf(M_l) = nf(M)$, thus $nf(N) = nf(M)$.□

Theorem 7. *If* $T(M) = N$, *then* M *is strongly normalizable.*

Proof. If $T(M)$ terminates then the set of legal paths of N is finite. By lemma 6, it is easy to verify that the number of legal paths in $T(M)$ is greater or equal to the number of legal paths in M, thus the set of legal paths of M is finite, which means, by lemma 4, that M is strongly normalizable.   □

Note that the transformation may not terminate. In every example tested, the non-termination of $T(M)$ arises when the reduction of M itself may not terminate.

Example 12. Let $\Delta = \lambda x.xx$, $D = \lambda x_1 x_2.x_1 x_2$, and $\Omega = \Delta\Delta$. We have:
$T(\Omega) = T(D\Delta\Delta) = T(\lambda x_1 x_2.x_1 x_2 x_2)D\Delta) =$
$= T(\lambda x_1 x_2 x_3.x_1 x_2 x_3)D\Delta\Delta) = T(\lambda x_1 x_2 x_3.x_1 x_2 x_3 x_3)DD\Delta) =$
$= T(\lambda x_1 x_2 x_3 x_4.x_1 x_2 x_3 x_4)DD\Delta\Delta) = \cdots$
Since the set of legal paths of Ω is not finite, $T(\Omega)$ never terminates.

5   Final Remarks

Using linearization in practice. This work is carried out in the context of a larger project to explore the implications of linearization for programming language implementation. A number of practical concerns need to be addressed to make the technology presented in this paper usable in the overall project. In particular, the following tasks are important:

1. Restrict the domain of application of our transformation to typable terms. This will decrease the lookahead needed to find out virtual redexes, and thus the complexity of the problem.
2. Add support for built-in constructors such as booleans, conditionals, arithmetic and recursive definitions (a fixpoint operator or letrec bindings). One way to go is considering an initial linearization environment for built-ins.

Theoretical concerns. In this paper we present a transformation of general terms into weak linear terms. In the presence of nontermination of reductions starting at the initial term, our transformation may not terminate (see example 12). It is necessary to find out sufficient conditions for the initial terms, under which we can guarantee that the transformation terminates. For every example tested non-termination of the transformation coincides with the existence of a non-terminating path in the reduction graph of the term. This is somehow expected since, apparently, the only cause of non-termination of the transformation process is the existence of an infinite number of legal paths (which can only happen when the term is not strongly normalizable). Based on this we conjecture that our transformation terminates if and only if the term is strongly normalizable. The left-to-right implication is proved in Theorem 7. The right-to-left implication requires a more detailed analysis of the interaction between reductions of the initial term and of the transformed term, and it is left for future work.

Acknowledgements. We thank Laurent Regnier for his helpful comments on some aspects of legal paths. We also would like to thank the anonymous referees for their comments on a preliminary version of this paper. The work presented in this paper has been partially supported by funds granted to *LIACC* through the *Programa de Financiamento Plurianual, Fundação para a Ciência e Tecnologia* and *Programa POSI*.

References

1. Sandra Alves and Mario Florido. On the relation between rank 2 intersection types and simple types. In *Joint Conference on Declarative Programming (AGP'2002)*, 2002.
2. Sandra Alves and Mario Florido. Linearization by program transformation. Technical report, DCC-FC, LIACC, University of Porto, 2003. (available from www.dcc.fc.up.pt/~sandra/papers/report2003.ps).
3. Andrea Asperti, Vincent Danos, Cosimo Laneve, and Laurent Regnier. Paths in the lambda-calculus. In *Logic in Computer Science*, pages 426–436, 1994.
4. Andrea Asperti and Cosimo Laneve. Paths, computations and labels in the lambda-calculus. *Theoretical Computer Science*, 142(2):277–297, 1995.
5. Henk Barendregt. *The Lambda Calculus. Its Syntax and Semantics*, volume 103 of *Studies in Logic and the Foundations of Mathematics*. North-Holland, 1984.
6. Henk Barendregt. The impact of the lambda calculus. *Bulletin of Symbolic Logic*, 3(2):181–215, 1997.
7. M. Coppo and M. Dezani-Ciancaglini. An extension of the basic functionality theory for the λ-calculus. *Notre Dame Journal of Formal Logic*, 21(4):685–693, 1980.
8. Mario Florido and Luis Damas. Linearization of the lambda-calculus and its relation with intersection type systems. *To appear in Journal of Functional Programming*, 2004.
9. J. R. Hindley. The principal type-scheme of an object in combinatory logic. *Trans. American Math. Soc.*, 146:29–60, 1969.
10. J. R. Hindley. BCK-Combinators and linear lambda-terms have types. *Theoretical Computer Science*, 64(1):97–105, 1989.
11. J. R. Hindley. *Basic Simple Type Theory*. Cambridge University Press, 1997.
12. Assaf J. Kfoury. A linearization of the lambda-calculus. *Journal of Logic and Computation*, 10(3), 2000.
13. Assaf J. Kfoury, Harry G. Mairson, Franklyn A. Turbak, and J. B. Wells. Relating typability and expressiveness in finite-rank intersection type systems. In *International Conference on Functional Programming*, pages 90–101, 1999.
14. J.J. Lévy. *Réductions correctes et optimales dans le lambda calcul*. PhD thesis, Université Paris VII, 1978.
15. J. A. Robinson. A machine-oriented logic based on the resolution principle. *J. Assoc. for Computing Machinery*, 12:23–41, 1965.

Continuation Semantics as Horn Clauses*

Qian Wang and Gopal Gupta

Applied Logic, Programming-Languages and Systems (ALPS) Laboratory
Department of Computer Science
University of Texas at Dallas

Abstract. Provably correct compilation is an important aspect in development of high assurance software systems. In this paper we further
develop our approach to provably correct compilation based on *Horn
logical semantics* of programming languages and partial evaluation. We
show that the definite clause grammar (DCG) notation can be used for
specifying both the syntax and semantics of imperative languages. We
next show that continuation semantics can also be expressed in the Horn
logical framework. Our approach has been applied for developing the semantics of the SCR specification language, the semantics is then used to
(automatically) generate target code in a provably correct manner.

In [2] we developed an approach for generating code in a provably correct manner
based on partial evaluation and a type of semantics called *Horn logical semantics*.
This approach is similar in spirit to semantics-based approaches, however, its
basis is Horn-logical semantics [2] which possesses both an operational as well
as a denotational (declarative) flavor. In the Horn logical semantics approach,
both the syntax and semantics of a language is specified using Horn clause logic
statements (or pure Prolog). The semantics can be viewed dually as operational
or denotational [7]. Taking an operational view, one immediately obtains an
interpreter of the language $\mathcal{L}$ from the Horn-logical semantic description of the
language $\mathcal{L}$. Given a program $\mathcal{P}$ written in language $\mathcal{L}$, the interpreter obtained
for $\mathcal{L}$ can be used to execute the program. Moreover, given a partial evaluator for
pure Prolog, such as Mixtus [6], the interpreter can be *partially evaluated* w.r.t.
the program $\mathcal{P}$ to obtain compiled code for $\mathcal{P}$ [1, 3]. Since the compiled code
is obtained automatically via partial evaluation of the interpreter, it is faithful
to the source of $\mathcal{P}$, provided the partial evaluator is correct. The correctness
of the partial evaluator, however, has to be proven only once. The correctness
of the code generation process for *any* language can be certified, provided the
compiled code is obtained via partial evaluation. Given that efficient execution
engines have been developed for Horn Logic (pure Prolog), partial evaluation is
relatively fast. Also, the declarative nature of the Horn logical semantics allows
for language semantics to be rapidly obtained.

---

* The authors have been partially supported by NSF grants CCR 9900320, CCR
9820852, INT 9904063, by the Department of Education and the Environmental
Protection Agency.

M. Bruynooghe (Ed.): LOPSTR 2004, LNCS 3018, pp. 176–177, 2004.

We have further developed the Horn logical semantics approach; we show that in Horn logical semantics not only the syntax but also the semantics can be expressed using the definite clause grammar notation. The semantics expressed in the DCG notation allows for the store argument to be naturally (syntactically) hidden. As a result, code generated via partial evaluation does not have the store argument threading through. Moreover, we also show that continuation semantics can be expressed in Horn clause logic using the DCG notation. Continuation semantics model the semantics of imperative constructs such as *goto statements, exception handling mechanisms, abort*, and *catch/throw constructs* more naturally. This continuation semantics views the program as a sequence of commands – a command is viewed as the *difference* between the current program and the command's continuation. The semantic function maps a command represented as a difference to the the difference of two stores. We also show that continuation semantics expressed as DCGs can be partially evaluated w.r.t. a source program to obtain target code in a provably correct manner, even in the presence of imperative features such as the goto statements, abort commands, catch/throw, etc.

The extensions have been applied to the SCR [4] (software cost reduction) method for specifying embedded real-time systems. Our approach based on partial evaluation is considerably faster than approaches based on generic program transformation systems [5].

References

1. Y. Futamura. Partial Evaluation of Computer Programs: An approach to compiler-compiler. *J. Inst. Electronics and Comm. Engineers, Japan.* 1971.
2. G. Gupta "Horn Logic Denotations and Their Applications," *The Logic Programming Paradigm: A 25 year perspective.* Springer Verlag. 1999:127-160.
3. N. Jones. Introduction to Partial Evaluation. In *ACM Computing Surveys.* 28(3):480-503.
4. C. L. Heitmeyer, R. D. Jeffords, and B. G. Labaw. Automated Consistency Checking of Requirements Specifications. ACM Trans. Software Eng. and Methodology 5, 3, July 1996.
5. E. I. Leonard and C. L. Heitmeyer. Program Synthesis from Requirements Specifications Using APTS. Kluwer Academic Publishers, 2002.
6. D. Sahlin. An Automatic Partial Evaluator for Full Prolog. Ph.D. Thesis. 1994. Royal Institute of Tech., Sweden. (available at www.sics.se)
7. D. Schmidt. *Denotational Semantics: a Methodology for Language Development.* W.C. Brown Publishers, 1986.

Simplification of Database Integrity Constraints Revisited: A Transformational Approach

Henning Christiansen and Davide Martinenghi

Roskilde University, Computer Science Dept.
P.O.Box 260, DK-4000 Roskilde, Denmark
{henning,dm}@ruc.dk

Abstract. Complete checks of database integrity constraints may be prohibitively time consuming, and several methods have been suggested for producing simplified checks for each update. The present approach introduces a set of transformation operators that apply to database integrity constraints with each operator representing a concise, semantics-preserving operation. These operators are applied in a procedure producing simplified constraints for parametric transaction patterns, which then can be instantiated and checked for consistency at run-time but before any transaction is executed. The operators provide a flexibility for other database enhancements and the work may also be seen as more systematic and general when compared with other approaches. The framework is formulated with first-order clause logic but with the perspective of being applied with present-day database technology.

1   Introduction

Simplification of integrity constraints is a principle that has been recognized for more than two decades, dating back to at least [20], and elaborated by several other authors. Despite a general recognition, it has not gained ground in standard databases. Our work is an attempt to reconcile and generalize such ideas in a systematic way that may promote practical applications with current database management technology.

An integrity constraint is a logical formula, typically depending on the nature of the application domain, that must hold for any database state for it to represent a meaningful set of data. Integrity constraints often concern the entire database and require linear or worse time complexity for a complete check, which is prohibitive in any non-trivial case. Simplification in this context means to derive specialized versions of the integrity constraints that can be checked more efficiently at each update, employing the hypothesis that the database is consistent before the update itself. Ideally, the simplified constraint should be a test that can be generated at database design time and that can be executed before a potentially offensive update is performed, so that rollback operations become unnecessary.

This paper introduces a framework providing a set of semantics-preserving program transformations by means of which an effective simplification procedure

M. Bruynooghe (Ed.): LOPSTR 2004, LNCS 3018, pp. 178–197, 2004.

as well as other optimizations and database enhancements can be defined. Integrity constraints, here in the form of denial clauses, are considered as programs in the sense that they can be executed as Prolog queries that must fail or, more in the line with present-day database technologies, as SQL queries that must return the empty answer. Unlike some previous approaches, which only consider single updates, our simplification procedure (and the individual transformations) applies to transaction patterns. Once a specific transaction is proposed, and *before* it is executed, the simplified formulas can be evaluated as pieces of code integrated in database application programs so that only consistency-preserving transactions are eventually given to the database.

We also illustrate other applications of our framework combined with other techniques such as data mining, abductive reasoning and data integration.

The paper is organized as follows. In section 2 we review existing literature in the field. The notation and theoretical setting are introduced in section 3, while in section 4 the program transformations and the simplification procedure are formally defined. Other applications are discussed in section 5 and concluding remarks are provided in section 6.

2   Motivation and Related Works

Simplification of integrity constraints, is highly relevant for optimizations in database integrity checking. Typically it gives a speed-up of a linear factor (in the size of the database state) for singleton updates but for certain transactions an even higher speed-up can be gained. We find crucial the ability to check consistency of a possibly updated database *before* execution of the transaction under consideration so that inconsistent states are completely avoided. Several approaches to simplification first require the transaction to be performed, and *then* the resulting state to be checked for consistency [20, 18, 23, 8, 11].

The proposal of [14] presents many analogies with our method, although the referenced paper does not present a fully developed method. A series of tests is generated from an integrity constraint C and an update U; if one of these tests succeeds, then U is legal with respect to C. This method is based on *resolution* and *transition axioms*, which provide an effect similar to our After operator (introduced in section 4 below). Updates are limited to be single actions, but can contain so-called dummy constants, very similar to our notion of parameters. The main disadvantage of this approach is that once the set of tests is generated, strategies have to be employed to decide which specific tests to execute and in which order. Furthermore, failure of all tests does not necessarily imply inconsistency. Our simplification algorithm is more straightforward in that it generates a single test whose result is a necessary and sufficient condition for determining consistency of the database if the update were performed.

Grant and Minker [11] introduce a principle called partial subsumption applied among other things to produce simplified integrity constraints. This method applies to singleton additions or deletions and produces conditions to be applied *after* the update; it also handles parametric updates expressed using logical variables. For compound updates (transactions) the principle is explained in terms of examples, but no general procedure is described. Partial subsumption applies also to semantic query optimization; see [12, 10] for an overview.

Qian [22] observes the relationship between Hoare's logic [13, 9] for imperative languages and integrity checking, identifying a simplified integrity constraint as a weakest precondition for having a consistent updated state. This notion is enforced by assuming the consistency of the database before the update. We give a more detailed discussion of this issue in section 3. Qian's method works for a variety of SQL-like ways of updating relations but with the impractical limitation that it does not allow more than one update action in a transaction to operate on the same relation; furthermore, no mechanism corresponding to parameters is present, thus requiring to execute the procedure for each update. We have no such restrictions.

Another problematic issue inherent in most work in the field is the lack of a characterization of what it means for a formula to be simplified; this is traditionally defined in terms of a semantic criterion. Our view is that a transformed integrity constraint, in order to qualify as "simplified", must represent a minimum in some ordering that reflects the effort of actually evaluating it. We propose a simple ordering based on the number of literals but we have no proof that our own algorithm hits a minimum in all cases.

Standard ways of translating integrity constraints into SQL exist. In a recent paper [7], Decker shows how to implement integrity constraint checking by translating first-order logic specifications into SQL triggers. In this way the advantages of declarativity are combined with the efficiency of execution. It is interesting to note that the result of our transformations can be combined with similar translation techniques and thus integrated in a database system. An extension of trigger syntax is proposed in [7] that allows the specification of the positions of the arguments of a relation that are relevant for an update. Our approach using parameters clearly subsumes this one.

The use of constraint techniques for abduction in logic programming may display an incremental evaluation of integrity constraints without an explicit simplification algorithm: each time an abducible atomic update a arises, the current representation of the integrity constraints wakes up, checks a's dependencies and, in case of success, delays a specialized version of the integrity constraints waiting for the next update. This principle is applied in the DemoII system [2, 5] and in the approach of [1] using Constraint Handling Rules for abduction; [3] is an attempt to relate such methods to database applications. However, a common drawback of these techniques is that the delayed constraints typically unroll to a size proportional to the database and that, occasionally, an unsatisfiable set of constraints is delayed where a failure should be reported.

With few exceptions (e.g., [17, 16, 15, 4]), little attention has been devoted to the problem of checking the integrity of a database containing recursive views, although recursion is now part of the current SQL standard. Consider, for example, a directed graph in which a path between two nodes is recursively expressed as the transitive closure of the edge relation and suppose that the graph is acyclic. If a new edge $a \mapsto b$ is added, the optimal way to check whether the new graph still is acyclic is to verify that there is currently no path connecting b to a. None of the methods we are aware of is able to provide such a simplified check. When recursive rules are present, the methods described in [17, 4] produce a set of constraints which is typically the same as the original one, i.e., no actual simplification takes place during the application of the procedure. In [16], low-cost pre-tests are generated which are sufficient conditions that guarantee the integrity of the database; however, these pre-tests typically fail in the presence of recursion, so nothing can be concluded about consistency. In [15], partial evaluation is applied to a general integrity checker to generate logic programs that correspond to simplified constraints. Generally, it is difficult to evaluate the method described in [15], as it depends on a number of heuristics in the partial evaluator as well as in the general checker; furthermore, no results are reported for recursive databases. The method we present here applies to non-recursive databases only.

Technical difficulties related to undecidability may also hinder the realization of a perfect simplification method (see subsection 4.4).

We are not aware of any other approach that reduces simplification into a combination of well-defined program transformations, which furthermore serve as an "algebra" in which different optimizations and interesting transformations can be described (see section 5). An experimental prototype [19] implementing a simplified version of these transformations is available on the World Wide Web.

Finally, we emphasize that we only consider integrity constraints expressed relative to all states; constraints that compare successive states, by some authors called dynamic or transactional integrity constraints, are not considered.

3   Preliminaries

Assume a function-free first-order language equipped with negation and predicates for equality ($\doteq$) and inequality ($\neq$), called *predefined predicates*. *Terms* are either *variables* ($x, y, \ldots$) or *constants* ($a, b, \ldots$). However, special constants called *parameters* are written in boldface ($\mathbf{a}, \mathbf{b}, \ldots$); constants that are not parameters are called *ground* constants. *Predicates* ($p, q, \ldots$) are used to build *atoms*, i.e. expressions of the form $p(t_1, \ldots, t_n)$, where the t_i's are terms and $n \geq 0$. A predicate that is not predefined is called a *database predicate*. *Formulas* are formed as usual from the atoms and the logical connectives. A formula is ground if its terms are only ground constants. A *literal* is either an atom A or a negated atom $\neg A$; whenever $\neg\neg A$ appears, it should be read as A and $\neg s \doteq t$ as $s \neq t$ and $\neg s \neq t$ as $s \doteq t$. *Clauses* are written in the form *Head ← Body* where the head is an atom and the body a (perhaps empty) conjunction of literals; the head may be left out, understood as *false*, in which case the clause is a *denial*; the body may be left out, understood as *true*, in which case the clause is a *fact*; any other clause is a *rule*. (In)equalities are not allowed in the head and are assumed with their usual meaning of syntactic (in)equality, but the order in which the arguments of $\doteq$ and $\neq$ are written does not matter. Logical equivalence between parameter-free formulas is denoted by $\equiv$. The notation $\vec{t}$ indicates a sequence of terms $t_1, \ldots, t_n$ and $p(\vec{t})$ an atom whose arguments are $t_1, \ldots, t_n$. The expression $\vec{t} \doteq \vec{s}$ is a shorthand for $t_1 \doteq s_1 \wedge \ldots \wedge t_n \doteq s_n$ where t_i's and s_i's are the terms of the two sequences; in a similar way, $\vec{t} \neq \vec{s}$ refers to the disjunction of individual inequalities.

Definition 1 (Parametric instance and equivalence). *For any expression E with parameters $\vec{a}$ and sequence of constants $\vec{c}$ of the same length as $\vec{a}$, the notation $E_{\vec{a}/\vec{c}}$ refers to the expression that arises from E when each element of $\vec{a}$ is replaced consistently by the matching element of $\vec{c}$; $E_{\vec{a}/\vec{c}}$ is called a (parametric) instance of E.*

Two formulas F and G are equivalent up to instantiation of parameters, written $F \cong G$, whenever $F' \equiv G'$ for all parametric instances (F', G') of (F, G).

Clearly $\cong$ is symmetric, reflexive and transitive. Note that name uniqueness is assumed for all ground constants but not for parameters, as different parameters may be instantiated by the same ground constant.

Example 1. Let $\mathbf{a}$, $\mathbf{b}$ be two parameters and c, d two ground constants. Then both $p(c, d, c)$ and $p(c, c, c)$ are instances of $p(\mathbf{a}, \mathbf{b}, \mathbf{a})$, whereas $p(c, c, d)$ is not. We have $c \doteq d \cong false$ but neither $\mathbf{a} \doteq \mathbf{b} \cong false$ nor $\mathbf{a} \doteq \mathbf{b} \cong true$. Note that two formulas being parametrically equivalent does not necessarily indicate that they contain the same parameters, e.g. $\mathbf{a} \doteq \mathbf{a} \cong true$. □

We further assume that all clauses are *range restricted*, as defined below.

Definition 2 (Range restriction). *A variable in a clause is* range bound *if it appears in a positive database literal in the body. A clause is* range restricted *if all variables in it are range bound.*

Notice that parameters in this definition are treated in the same way as ground constants. As already stated, we do not allow recursion, but our method is relevant for all database environments in which range restricted queries produce a finite set of ground tuples. The notion of *subsumption* is applied repeatedly in this paper.

Definition 3 (Subsumption). *A clause C_1 subsumes another C_2 iff there is a substitution σ such that each literal in the body of $C_1\sigma$ occurs in the body of C_2 and similarly for the heads.*

Example 2. The clause $\leftarrow p(x, y) \wedge a \neq x$ subsumes $\leftarrow p(x, b) \wedge x \neq a \wedge q(b)$. □

The definition of subsumption is syntactic but has the semantic property that the subsuming clause implies the subsumed one.

Complying with [10], a *database* is characterized by three components:

- a set of facts, called the *extensional database*;
- a set of rules (the *intensional database*);
- a set of integrity constraints (here denials), known as the *constraint theory*.

Parameters cannot occur in a database but the transformation operators may produce integrity constraints that contain parameters. We call these *parameterized* integrity constraints. In a recursion-free language, we can limit our attention, without any loss of generality, to integrity constraints that refer to extensional predicates only, as intensional predicates can be (repeatedly) replaced with their definitions, that will eventually only be extensional. We will therefore keep this assumption throughout the rest of the paper. By *database state* we refer to the union of the extensional and the intensional parts only.

As semantics of a database state D, with default negation for negative literals, we take its *standard model*, denoted $\mathcal{M}_D$, as D is here recursion-free and thus *stratified*. The truth value of a closed formula F, relative to D, is defined as its valuation in $\mathcal{M}_D$ and denoted $D(F)$. (See e.g. [21] for exact definitions.) The meaning of a formula that includes parameters can be thought of as an operator taking instantiations of the parameters and producing a truth value. In the following, the overloaded notation $D_1(F_1) \cong D_2(F_2)$ will indicate that $D_1(F_1') = D_2(F_2')$ holds for all parametric instances (F_1', F_2') of (F_1, F_2), where D_1 and D_2 are database states and F_1 and F_2 are formulas. Consistency of the integrity constraints can be defined in different ways; we follow [10] arguing that the following is the most natural choice.

Definition 4 (Consistency). *A database state D is consistent with a constraint theory Γ iff $D(\Gamma) = true$.*

Definition 5 (Update and update pattern). *An* update $U = U^+ \cup U^-$ *is a non-empty set of additions U^+ and deletions U^-, both consisting of ground facts, with the deletions indicated by a $\neg$ sign. The reverse of an update U, denoted $\neg U$, contains the same elements as U but with the roles of additions and deletions interchanged. The additions and deletions of an update are required to be disjoint, i.e. $U^+ \cap \neg U^- = \emptyset$. The notation $D \cup U$, where D is a database state, is a shorthand for $(D \cup U^+) \setminus \neg U^-$. An update pattern is an expression whose parametric instances are updates.*

This definition of update fits with all cases where the additions and deletions are known independently of the database state. This is not always the case. For example, given the statement "delete all records of computer science books from the library", which is easily expressible in SQL, the set of tuples that will be deleted depends on the actual database state. Our method can be generalized to such more general updates including also SQL's `UPDATE`, but for reasons of space this is omitted in the present version of the paper.

As already emphasized, it is important to be able to test that a prospective database update does not violate the integrity constraints – without actually executing the update, i.e., a test is needed that can be checked in the present state but indicating properties of the prospective new state. A semantic correctness criterion for such a test is given by the notion of weakest precondition.

Definition 6 (Weakest precondition, strongest postcondition). *Let Γ and Γ' be constraint theories and U an update pattern. Γ' is a weakest precondition of Γ with respect to U and Γ is a strongest postcondition of Γ' with respect to U whenever $D(\Gamma') \cong (D \cup U)(\Gamma)$ for any database state D.*

As also noticed by Qian [22], this definition is similar to the standard axiom for defining assignment statements in a programming language [9], whose side effects are analogous to a database update. Hoare's [13] original version of the axiom used only implication from pre- to postcondition; the notion of *weakest* precondition that we need is due to Dijkstra [9].

The concept of strongest postcondition is not used for simplification but is useful for other purposes. It characterizes how questions concerning the previous state may be answered by considering transformed questions in the updated state. The essence of simplification is the optimization of a weakest precondition based on the invariant that the constraint theory holds in the present state. The semantic characterization of this property is defined as follows.

Definition 7 (Conditional weakest precondition). *Let Γ be a constraint theory and U an update pattern. A constraint theory Γ' is a* conditional weakest precondition *of Γ with respect to U whenever $D(\Gamma') \cong (D \cup U)(\Gamma)$ for any database state D consistent with Γ.*

A weakest precondition is also a conditional weakest precondition but not necessarily the other way round. All other known definitions of simplification are based solely on this or similar semantic notions, but this is not sufficient: a characterization should be given of the sense in which the resulting formula is actually "simpler" than the original one. In example 3 we show that a criterion based on semantic weakness does not capture the intuition behind simplicity.

Example 3. In case a theory Γ_1 holds in more states that another Γ_2, we say that Γ_1 is weaker than Γ_2 and that Γ_2 is stronger that Γ_1. Consider the constraint theory $\Gamma = \{\leftarrow p(a) \wedge q(a), \leftarrow r(a)\}$ and the update $U = \{p(a)\}$. The strongest, intuitively simplest, and weakest conditional weakest preconditions of Γ with respect to U are shown in the following table.

Strongest	Simplest	Weakest
$\{\leftarrow q(a), \leftarrow r(a)\}$	$\{\leftarrow q(a)\}$	$\{\leftarrow q(a) \wedge \neg p(a) \wedge \neg r(a)\}$

□

We shall use a syntactic selection criterion instead, as discussed in detail in section 4.2.

4   Transformations on Integrity Constraints

In the following, we define four syntactic transformation operators, each performing a well-defined function that satisfies straightforward semantic conditions. With these, we can compose a simplification procedure and, as shown in section 5, other useful transformations of integrity constraints.

4.1   Translation of Integrity Constraints Back and Forth between Different States

To consider whether a given property holds after a prospective update means to reason about the truth of a formula in a future state, but arguing in the present state.

The following After operator translates a constraint theory into a weakest precondition with respect to a given update pattern in a straightforward way; it does not assume consistency of the present state and is, thus, applicable for other things than plain simplification. By means of it, we define also a dual operator Before that translates a constraint theory Γ into another theory that can be used after the update to test whether Γ held before the update; it is not used in the simplification procedure, but it proves useful for other purposes, as shown in section 5.

Definition 8. *Consider an update pattern U:*

$$U = \{\, p_1(\vec{a}_{1,1}), p_1(\vec{a}_{1,2}), \ldots, p_1(\vec{a}_{1,n_1}),$$
$$p_2(\vec{a}_{2,1}), p_2(\vec{a}_{2,2}), \ldots, p_2(\vec{a}_{2,n_2}),$$
$$\cdots$$
$$p_k(\vec{a}_{k,1}), p_k(\vec{a}_{k,2}), \ldots, p_k(\vec{a}_{k,n_k}),$$
$$\neg p_1(\vec{b}_{1,1}), \neg p_1(\vec{b}_{1,2}), \ldots, \neg p_1(\vec{b}_{1,m_1}),$$
$$\neg p_2(\vec{b}_{2,1}), \neg p_2(\vec{b}_{2,2}), \ldots, \neg p_2(\vec{b}_{2,m_2}),$$
$$\cdots$$
$$\neg p_k(\vec{b}_{k,1}), \neg p_k(\vec{b}_{k,2}), \ldots, \neg p_k(\vec{b}_{k,m_k})\,\},$$

where the p_i's are distinct predicates and the $\vec{a}_{i,j}$'s and $\vec{b}_{i,j}$'s are sequences of constants. For a constraint theory Γ, the notation $\mathsf{After}^U(\Gamma)$ refers to the set of denials Γ' obtained as follows.

1. *Let Γ' consist of a copy of Γ in which all occurrences of an atom of the form $p_i(\vec{t})$ have been simultaneously replaced by*

$$(p_i(\vec{t}) \wedge \vec{t} \neq \vec{b}_{i,1} \wedge \cdots \wedge \vec{t} \neq \vec{b}_{i,m_i}) \vee \vec{t} \doteq \vec{a}_{i,1} \vee \cdots \vee \vec{t} \doteq \vec{a}_{i,n_i}.$$

2. *Do the following in Γ' as long as possible (A, B_1, B_2 and C are formulas):*
   - *Replace any formula in Γ' of the form $\leftarrow A \wedge (B_1 \vee B_2) \wedge C$ by the two formulas $\leftarrow A \wedge B_1 \wedge C$ and $\leftarrow A \wedge B_2 \wedge C$.*
   - *Replace any formula in Γ' of the form $\leftarrow A \wedge \neg(B_1 \vee B_2) \wedge C$ by the formula $\leftarrow A \wedge \neg B_1 \wedge \neg B_2 \wedge C$.*
   - *Replace any formula in Γ' of the form $\leftarrow A \wedge \neg(B_1 \wedge B_2) \wedge C$ by the two formulas $\leftarrow A \wedge \neg B_1 \wedge C$ and $\leftarrow A \wedge \neg B_2 \wedge C$.*

The notation $\mathsf{Before}^U(\Gamma)$ refers to the set of denials $\mathsf{After}^{\neg U}(\Gamma)$.

The intermediary formulas with disjunctions resulting from step 1 may not be clauses, but step 2 takes care of restoring the clausal form. The following properties follow immediately from the definition of After and are stated without proof.

Proposition 1 (Composition of After over denials). *For any update U and constraint theories Γ_1 and Γ_2 the following property holds:*

$$\mathsf{After}^U(\Gamma_1 \cup \Gamma_2) \quad = \quad \mathsf{After}^U(\Gamma_1) \cup \mathsf{After}^U(\Gamma_2).$$

Proposition 2 (Composition of After over updates). *For any constraint theory Γ and updates U, U_1, U_2, with $U = U_1 \cup U_2$ and U_1 and U_2 disjoint, we have*

$$\mathsf{After}^U(\Gamma) \;\cong\; \mathsf{After}^{U_2}(\mathsf{After}^{U_1}(\Gamma)) \;\cong\; \mathsf{After}^{U_1}(\mathsf{After}^{U_2}(\Gamma)).$$

The semantic correctness of After is expressed by the following property.

Theorem 1 (After produces weakest precondition). *For any update U and constraint theory Γ, $\mathsf{After}^U(\Gamma)$ is a weakest precondition of Γ with respect to U.*

Proof. We need to show that $D(\mathsf{After}^U(\Gamma)) \cong (D \cup U)(\Gamma)$ for any database state D. Step 2 of definition 8 obviously preserves semantics so we can ignore it. Composition over updates means that we need only consider singleton updates; we start considering a positive update of the form $U = \{p(\vec{a})\}$.

For any database predicate q assume another predicate q' of the same arity, and when writing Φ' for some formula or set of formulas Φ (assumed not to include such primed predicates), we refer to a formula similar to Φ with all occurrences of database predicate q replaced by q'. Let Π be the following program that defines a way of going back and forth between the two classes of predicates.

$$\{p'(\vec{x}) \leftrightarrow \vec{x} \doteq \vec{a} \vee p(\vec{x})\} \;\cup$$
$$\{q'(\vec{x}) \leftrightarrow q(\vec{x}) \mid \text{for any database predicate } q \text{ different from } p\}$$

The theory $D \cup \Pi$ is a combined representation of the states before and after the update, so that formulas without primes are evaluated as in the state before and primed ones as in the state after. Formally we have the following equivalences, where ϕ is any formula without primed predicates.

$$(D \cup \Pi)(\phi) \cong D(\phi)$$
$$(D \cup \Pi)(\phi') \cong (D' \cup U')(\phi') \cong (D \cup U)(\phi)$$

To see that the last line holds, notice that the first two members are equivalent because they have the same definitions for all primed predicates: in the former p' holds when p holds or when its argument is $\vec{a}$ and in the latter p' is just a renaming of p plus the fact $p'(\vec{a})$; all other primed predicates are evidently the same. The last two members are equivalent as they differ only by a consistent renaming of symbols. The two expressions (on the left-hand sides below) that we need to prove equivalent can be represented in the combined theory as follows:

$$D(\mathsf{After}^U(\Gamma)) \cong (D \cup \Pi)(\mathsf{After}^U(\Gamma))$$
$$(D \cup U)(\Gamma) \cong (D \cup \Pi)(\Gamma')$$

However, the two right-hand sides are equivalent as $\mathsf{After}^U(\Gamma)$ can be constructed from Γ' by replacement of expressions that are equivalent in $D \cup \Pi$, i.e., replacing $p'(\vec{t})$ by $(\vec{t} \doteq \vec{a} \vee p(\vec{t}))$ and $q'(\vec{t})$ by $q(\vec{t})$ for any predicate q different from p.

For a negative update of the form $U = \{\neg p(\vec{a})\}$ the proof is symmetric, with the definition of p' in Π being $\{p'(\vec{x}) \leftrightarrow \vec{x} \neq \vec{a} \wedge p(\vec{x})\}$. $\square$

We get immediately composition properties of the Before operator and a dual version of theorem 1 stating that Before^U produces strongest postconditions with respect to update U.

Example 4. Consider a database containing information about marriages, where the binary predicate m indicates that a husband (first argument) is married to a wife (second argument). We expect for this database updates of the form: $U = \{m(\mathbf{a}, \mathbf{b})\}$. The following integrity constraint is given:

$$\phi = \leftarrow m(x, y) \wedge m(x, z) \wedge y \neq z$$

meaning that no husband can be married to two different wives. The first step of definition 8 in the calculation of $\mathsf{After}^U(\{\phi\})$ generates the following:

$$\{\leftarrow (m(x, y) \vee (x \doteq \mathbf{a} \wedge y \doteq \mathbf{b})) \wedge (m(x, z) \vee (x \doteq \mathbf{a} \wedge z \doteq \mathbf{b})) \wedge y \neq z\}.$$

The second step translates it to clausal form:

$$\mathsf{After}^U(\{\phi\}) = \{\ \leftarrow m(x, y) \wedge m(x, z) \wedge y \neq z,$$
$$\leftarrow m(x, y) \wedge x \doteq \mathbf{a} \wedge z \doteq \mathbf{b} \wedge y \neq z,$$
$$\leftarrow x \doteq \mathbf{a} \wedge y \doteq \mathbf{b} \wedge m(x, z) \wedge y \neq z,$$
$$\leftarrow x \doteq \mathbf{a} \wedge y \doteq \mathbf{b} \wedge x \doteq \mathbf{a} \wedge z \doteq \mathbf{b} \wedge y \neq z\ \}. \qquad \Box$$

Example 5. We shall now consider an example of referential integrity, where a relation f (father) is only meaningful if its first argument (the father) is recorded in a relation p (person) with a specific constant value concerning the gender (m for "male"):

$$\phi = \leftarrow f(x, y) \wedge \neg p(x, m).$$

For transactions of the form $U = \{f(\mathbf{a}, \mathbf{b}), p(\mathbf{a}, m)\}$ we have:

$$\mathsf{After}^U(\{\phi\}) = \{\ \leftarrow x \doteq \mathbf{a} \wedge y \doteq \mathbf{b} \wedge \neg(x \doteq \mathbf{a}) \wedge \neg p(x, m),$$
$$\leftarrow x \doteq \mathbf{a} \wedge y \doteq \mathbf{b} \wedge \neg(m \doteq m) \wedge \neg p(x, m),$$
$$\leftarrow f(x, y) \wedge \neg(x \doteq \mathbf{a}) \wedge \neg p(x, m),$$
$$\leftarrow f(x, y) \wedge \neg(m \doteq m) \wedge \neg p(x, m)\}. \qquad \Box$$

Notice that when a predicate that appears in a positive literal is updated positively by a single addition, $\mathsf{After}^U(\{\phi\})$ contains a copy of ϕ (see example 4), whereas for a predicate that appears in a negative literal, $\mathsf{After}^U(\{\phi\})$ contains a formula that is a specialization of ϕ, even when the update is not singleton (see example 5). The effect is symmetric for deletions.

4.2   Normalization of Formulas

The result of the After transformation is obviously not in any "reduced" or "normalized" form, and we introduce an operator Norm to take care of this.

An ideal Norm procedure should produce a constraint theory as output that is minimal in some ordering that reflects an estimate of the time complexity. This can only be an estimate as the actual execution times depend on the database state (that is not available at the time of the simplification process) and is also highly dependent on the applied database technology that may perform optimizations that are not feasible to include in a general definition. We suggest an ordering based on the simple principle of counting literals, although it may be the case that longer constraints are evaluated more efficiently in particular database states (see also section 5.6). We define $\Gamma \prec \Gamma'$ iff Γ has fewer literals than Γ'.

This may appear a bit coarse as it gives the same measure for, say, $\leftarrow 1 \doteq 2$, $\leftarrow p(a)$, and $\leftarrow p(x)$. However, it should be kept in mind that the Norm procedure (as well as the entire simplification process) should return a minimal constraint theory *among those that satisfy the corresponding semantic condition.*

We give a proposal below for a procedure that implements the Norm operation but we do not have a proof that it produces a minimal constraint theory[1]. We are not alone with this problem, as no other work on simplification that we are aware of provides results of this form; in fact, we are not aware of any other work that considers this criterion at all.

In the following definition we also refer to the notion of *expansion* [10]: the expansion of a clause consists in replacing every constant in a database predicate (or variable already appearing elsewhere in database predicates) by a new variable and adding the equality between the new variable and the replaced item. For example, $\leftarrow p(x, a, x)$ can be expanded to $\leftarrow p(x, y, z) \land y \doteq a \land z \doteq x$.

Definition 9 (Normalization). *For a constraint theory Γ, let $\mathsf{Norm}(\Gamma)$ be the result of iterating the following steps on Γ as long as possible, where x is a variable, t is a term, and A, B are (possibly empty) conjunctions of literals.*

> **Variable elimination:** *If a clause $\phi \in \Gamma$ contains an equation $x \doteq t$, remove it and replace all occurrences of x in ϕ by t.*
> **Redundant constraints:** *Remove any denial that is subsumed by another denial in the current set.*
> **Redundancy within constraints:** *In any denial that can be written $\leftarrow A \land B$ so that A logically implies B, remove B (can be done by a straightforward procedure searching for specific patterns such as trivially satisfied (in)equalities).*
> **Contradiction removal:** *Remove any denial $\leftarrow B$ where B is unsatisfiable (can be done by a straightforward procedure searching for specific patterns).*
> **Folding by resolution (FbR):** *If there are two denials that, after expansion, have the form $\leftarrow A \land L$ and $(\leftarrow A \land \neg L \land B)\sigma$ [2], where L is a literal and σ a substitution, the second denial is replaced by $(\leftarrow A \land B)\sigma$.*

---

[1] It is clearly possible to enumerate in finite time all constraint theories preceding the original one in the selected ordering, as the set of symbols is finite. However, the problem of determining whether a constraint theory satisfies a given semantic condition (in this case, being a conditional weakest precondition) is likely to be undecidable. See subsection 4.4 for further discussion.

[2] According to notational convention, the actual negation may appear in either of the two clauses mentioned in FbR.

Notice that if the empty clause is produced during the process, then $\mathsf{Norm}(\Gamma) = false$, as it subsumes every other denial.

The FbR step takes care of a sort of dependency "across" different integrity constraints that is a bit more subtle than the identification of redundant constraints. These cases are not handled in the other approaches to simplification that we have studied, and we can expect that other specific optimizations of the same sort may be recognized in the effort to prove a minimality property. However, there are cases where an unfortunate order of the steps in the nondeterministic Norm procedure makes it fail to remove certain redundant literals, but a refined version not presented here appears to avoid this problem.

Proposition 3 (Semantic correctness of Norm). *The Norm procedure terminates on any input, and for any constraint theory Γ, $\Gamma \cong \mathsf{Norm}(\Gamma)$.*

Proof. Termination follows from the fact that each step in the procedure reduces the constraint theory with respect to the $\prec$ ordering which is obviously well-founded, apart from FbR that may generate an expansion which is anyhow removed by variable elimination. Lemma 1 below shows that FbR preserves the logical meaning. For all the other steps in Norm this property is evident. □

Lemma 1 (Validity of FbR). *Let Γ be a constraint theory and Γ' be another constraint theory obtained by applying FbR on Γ once. Then $\Gamma \cong \Gamma'$.*

Proof. We need only consider the logical equivalence between the two constraints mentioned in definition 9 before and after the replacement in the FbR step (the expansion step clearly preserves equivalence); assume the notation in that definition so that ϕ below represents the before-constraints and ψ the after-constraints, σ a substitution.

$$\phi = \{\leftarrow A \land L, (\leftarrow A \land \neg L \land B)\sigma\}.$$

The first denial is equivalent to $A \rightarrow \neg L$, from which we conclude that $A \land \neg L$ and A are equivalent. Therefore $\phi \cong \{\leftarrow A \land L, (\leftarrow A \land B)\sigma\} = \psi$. □

As a step towards a correct simplification procedure, we notice that the next proposition follows immediately from the previous results.

Proposition 4. *For any constraint theory Γ and update U, $\mathsf{Norm}(\mathsf{After}^U(\Gamma))$ is a weakest precondition of Γ with respect to U.*

4.3   Subsumption Checks

An essential step in the achievement of simpler integrity constraints is to employ the fact that they hold in the current database state, and remove those parts of the condition about the possible updated state that are implied by this. For this purpose, we define a transformation RSub that is used to remove those derived integrity constraints produced by other transformations, that are anyhow subsumed by the original ones.

Definition 10 (Remove subsumed). *Given two constraint theories Γ and Γ', $\mathsf{RSub}^\Gamma(\Gamma')$ refers to a copy of Γ' in which*

- *first, any denial subsumed by a denial in Γ is removed and*
- *then, any remaining denial expandable to the form $(\leftarrow A \wedge \neg L \wedge B)\sigma$, for which a denial expandable to the form $\leftarrow A \wedge L$ is in Γ, is replaced by $(\leftarrow A \wedge B)\sigma$.*

We have immediately the following.

Proposition 5. *Let Γ' be a weakest precondition of Γ with respect to an update pattern U. Then $\mathsf{RSub}^\Gamma(\Gamma')$ is a conditional weakest precondition of Γ with respect to U.*

4.4   Putting together a Simplification Procedure

The transformation operators described in the previous sections comprise tools that can be used to define a procedure for simplification of integrity constraints, where the updates always take place from a consistent state.

Definition 11. *For a constraint theory Γ and an update U, we define*

$$\mathsf{Simp}^U(\Gamma) = \mathsf{RSub}^\Gamma(\mathsf{Norm}(\mathsf{After}^U(\Gamma))).$$

From the previous results we get immediately the following.

Proposition 6. *Let Γ be a constraint theory and U an update. Then $\mathsf{Simp}^U(\Gamma)$ is a conditional weakest precondition of Γ with respect to U.*

Example 6. Consider again the update and the constraint theory from example 4, where we showed the transformation $\mathsf{After}^U(\{\phi\})$. In order to obtain $\mathsf{Simp}^U(\{\phi\})$, we first calculate $\mathsf{Norm}(\mathsf{After}^U(\{\phi\}))$ as follows. The "variable elimination" step of definition 9 applied to $\mathsf{After}^U(\{\phi\})$ generates the following set.

$$\{ \leftarrow m(x,y) \wedge m(x,z) \wedge y \neq z,$$
$$\leftarrow m(\mathbf{a},y) \wedge y \neq \mathbf{b},$$
$$\leftarrow m(\mathbf{a},z) \wedge \mathbf{b} \neq z,$$
$$\leftarrow \mathbf{a} \doteq \mathbf{a} \wedge \mathbf{b} \neq \mathbf{b} \qquad \}.$$

Then, "contradiction removal" eliminates the fourth constraint and, finally, the "redundant constraints" step removes the third constraint, as it is subsumed by the second one[3]. The output of the normalization procedure is therefore the following.

$$\mathsf{Norm}(\mathsf{After}^U(\{\phi\})) = \{ \leftarrow m(x,y) \wedge m(x,z) \wedge y \neq z,$$
$$\leftarrow m(\mathbf{a},y) \wedge y \neq \mathbf{b} \qquad \}.$$

The first constraint is obviously subsumed by ϕ and thus removed by RSub in the simplification procedure.

$$\mathsf{Simp}^U(\{\phi\}) = \{\leftarrow m(\mathbf{a},y) \wedge y \neq \mathbf{b}\}. \qquad \Box$$

---

[3] Alternatively, the second constraint could be removed instead of the third one, as they subsume one another.

Example 7. Reconsider now the update and the constraint theory from example 5. We have here:

$$\mathsf{Simp}^U(\{\phi\}) = \emptyset. \qquad \qquad \square$$

A detailed trace for the evaluation of these simplified formulas will show that RSub removes ϕ from the resulting set of formulas when a predicate with only positive occurrences is updated, and a nontrivial specialization of ϕ when a predicate with a negative occurrence is updated.

The following example shows different combinations of singleton and compound updates for predicates occurring in positive and negative literals.

Example 8. The following transformations hold for the integrity constraint $\phi = \ \leftarrow p(x) \wedge q(x) \wedge \neg r(x)$ and parameters $\mathbf{a}$ and $\mathbf{b}$.

$$\begin{aligned}
\mathsf{Simp}^{\{p(\mathbf{a})\}}(\{\phi\}) &= \{\leftarrow q(\mathbf{a}) \wedge \neg r(\mathbf{a})\} \\
\mathsf{Simp}^{\{q(\mathbf{b})\}}(\{\phi\}) &= \{\leftarrow p(\mathbf{b}) \wedge \neg r(\mathbf{b})\} \\
\mathsf{Simp}^{\{r(\mathbf{a})\}}(\{\phi\}) &= \emptyset \\
\mathsf{Simp}^{\{p(\mathbf{a}),r(\mathbf{b})\}}(\{\phi\}) &= \{\leftarrow q(\mathbf{a}) \wedge \neg r(\mathbf{a}) \wedge \mathbf{a} \neq \mathbf{b}\} \\
\mathsf{Simp}^{\{p(\mathbf{a}),r(\mathbf{a})\}}(\{\phi\}) &= \emptyset \\
\mathsf{Simp}^{\{p(\mathbf{a}),q(\mathbf{b})\}}(\{\phi\}) &= \{\ \leftarrow q(\mathbf{a}) \wedge \neg r(\mathbf{a}), \\
&\qquad \leftarrow p(\mathbf{b}) \wedge \neg r(\mathbf{b}), \\
&\qquad \leftarrow \mathbf{a} = \mathbf{b} \wedge \neg r(\mathbf{a})\ \} \qquad \square
\end{aligned}$$

As shown in examples 6, 7 and 8, the simplified integrity constraints are minimal in the $\prec$ ordering and instantiated as much as possible.

In case the original constraint theory contains redundant constraints (i.e., entailed by other constraints in the set), it is possible to construct examples where the result produced by our procedure would also contain redundancies. Cyclic patterns and recursive definitions can, for instance, be encoded in the integrity constraints, thus rendering the detection of redundancy computationally harder. We have not investigated this phenomenon in depth, but it seems to be undecidable in general whether a given constraint is redundant, as it would amount to the query containment problem in DATALOG, which is known to be undecidable. This means that we can only hope to prove the optimality of our procedure under certain restrictions to the original constraint theory, e.g., that no recursion is encoded.

The following proposition demonstrates the idea that integrity constrains can be "pre-compiled" at design time and then used against specific updates.

Proposition 7. *Let $U(\vec{\mathbf{a}})$ be a generic update request with sequence $\vec{\mathbf{a}}$ of parameters, $\vec{c}$ any matching sequence of ground constants, and Γ a constraint theory. Then*

$$\mathsf{Simp}^{U(\vec{c})}(\Gamma) \quad \equiv \quad \left(\mathsf{Simp}^{U(\vec{\mathbf{a}})}(\Gamma)\right)_{\vec{\mathbf{a}}/\vec{c}}$$

The left-hand side can be thought of as a simplification made at update time, whereas the right-hand side uses a pre-compiled version produced at design time in which the parameters are replaced by the actual ground constants when the update arrives. Note that the former may be simpler (according to $\prec$) than the latter. Apart from [14, 11], most works on simplification have not made such a distinction so that the procedures apply to specific updates only and, thus, need to be employed over and over when the database is running.

5   Other Applications and Examples

We briefly mention here several applications of our transformation operators that go beyond the scope of simplification.

5.1   Generating Consistent Updates by Abductive Reasoning

It may be the case that a proposed update, which in itself will create inconsistency in a given database state, can be extended to an update that preserves consistency. In a database application program, this situation may be handled by entering a dialogue in order to get more information.

Consider as an example the referential integrity constraint of example 5, $\leftarrow f(x, y) \wedge \neg p(x, m)$, and how an application program should handle an update request described by the update pattern $f(\mathbf{a}, \mathbf{b})$; the simplified version of the integrity constraint becomes $\leftarrow \neg p(\mathbf{a}, m)$.

At runtime, with a specific database state and instance of the parameters, the evaluation of this simplified integrity constraint may signal an inconsistency. In that case, the failing constraint gives a proposal for how the consistency may be repaired, namely by an update described by the pattern $p(\mathbf{a}, m)$. This principle is closely related to abduction in logic programming, where literals that otherwise would fail are assumed in order to get a query to succeed.

This extended update should not be suggested to the user in case it conflicts with other integrity constraints. Thus simplified integrity constraints for $\{f(\mathbf{a}, \mathbf{b}), p(\mathbf{a}, m)\}$ need to be checked.

The interesting point is that the different simplifications can be constructed beforehand and added once and for all and embedded as code in the user interface program. In general, this may be structured in a decision tree with each edge labelled by an extension to the update pattern plus a simplified integrity constraints. The tree splits into different branches when there are more than one remaining literal in a failing constraint, i.e., several different ways to achieve consistency may be possible. Either the database designer has made a choice or the user is asked which way to go.

In the example, the insertion of $p(\mathbf{a}, m)$ may conflict with another integrity constraint saying that a person can only have one gender; in this case the dialogue with the user enters a new level.

5.2   Preventing Duplicates

We re-examine here the scenario considered in examples 4 and 6 and include a check to avoid duplicates, i.e., an attempt to add a tuple which is already in the database is rejected. By a simple manipulation of the transformation operators, we can define a new simplification operator that includes this.

Definition 12. *For a constraint theory Γ and an update U, we define*

$$\mathsf{Simp}_{nd}^U(\Gamma) = \mathsf{RSub}^\Gamma(\mathsf{Norm}(\leftarrow U \cup \mathsf{After}^U(\Gamma)))$$

where $\leftarrow U$ is a shorthand for $\{\leftarrow u_1, \ldots, \leftarrow u_n\}$, the elements of U being the variable-free literals $u_1, \ldots, u_n$.

The "nd" subscript stands for "no duplicates", which is characterized here by the fact that any redundancies between the update and the weakest precondition expressed by After should be eliminated by Norm. It is easy to check that with U and ϕ from example 4 we have

$$\mathsf{Simp}_{nd}^U(\{\phi\}) = \{\leftarrow m(\mathbf{a}, y)\} \quad \prec \quad \{\leftarrow m(\mathbf{a}, y) \wedge y \neq \mathbf{b}\} = \mathsf{Simp}^U(\{\phi\}).$$

In the calculation of $\mathsf{Simp}_{nd}^U(\{\phi\})$, FbR applies to the denials $\leftarrow m(\mathbf{a}, \mathbf{b})$ and $\leftarrow m(\mathbf{a}, y) \wedge y \neq \mathbf{b}$ (expanded, respectively, to $\leftarrow m(x, y) \wedge x \doteq \mathbf{a} \wedge y \doteq \mathbf{b}$ and $\leftarrow m(x, y) \wedge x \doteq \mathbf{a} \wedge y \neq \mathbf{b}$), generating $\leftarrow m(x, y) \wedge x \doteq \mathbf{a}$. This example showed how a new assumption could be embedded in the simplification procedure to generate a constraint theory which is clearly minimal in terms of the ordering $\prec$.

5.3   Maintaining Integrity Constraints in Data Mining Applications

Data mining techniques exist that are used to unveil integrity constraints inherent in a database. These integrity constraints may then be used for various purposes, such as semantic query optimization and integrity checking. Suppose that an update comes up that violates the induced integrity. The data miner might either give up the constraint that has been violated, in that it does not model the underlying database anymore, or extend the integrity constraint to use the offending update as a counter-example. For example, let the following be a mined integrity constraint:

$$\phi = \leftarrow p(x) \wedge q(x)$$

and assume that update $U = \{p(a)\}$ violates it. Instead of rejecting ϕ, a perhaps clever approach is to regard U as an exceptional behavior of ϕ and produce a modified version, for example:

$$\phi^U = \leftarrow p(x) \wedge x \neq a \wedge q(x)$$

The transformation from ϕ to ϕ^U is exactly what the Before transformation is doing, as in general $D(\phi) = (D \cup U)(\mathsf{Before}^U(\phi))$ for any database state D.

Some heuristics or application domain information can also be applied here to determine an upper limit to the number of exceptions allowed, above which the system eventually decides to reject ϕ.

Another system might go into a dialogue with the user by questioning whether the mined ϕ is a property of the domain and should be trusted; if yes, the system may continue as described in section 5.1.

5.4   Checking the Integrity after the Update

Although we generally have argued against it, there may be specific applications where database updates should be executed immediately and consistency checked directly on the updated database. Our Before operator can be used in such a case in order to convert our precondition style simplifications into a form that tests the updated state:

Proposition 8. *Let a database D be consistent with a constraint theory Γ. Then the database state $D \cup U$ is consistent with Γ iff $D \cup U$ is consistent with the following:*

$$\mathsf{Norm}(\mathsf{Before}^U(\mathsf{Simp}^U(\Gamma))).$$

Example 9. Consider integrity constraint $\phi =\leftarrow p(x) \wedge q(x) \wedge \neg r(x)$ and update $U = \{p(\mathbf{a}), q(\mathbf{b})\}$. We have:

$$\mathsf{Simp}^U(\{\phi\}) = \{ \leftarrow \mathbf{a} \doteq \mathbf{b} \wedge \neg r(\mathbf{a}),$$
$$\leftarrow p(\mathbf{b}) \wedge \neg r(\mathbf{b}),$$
$$\leftarrow q(\mathbf{a}) \wedge \neg r(\mathbf{a}) \quad \}.$$

Assuming that U was applied to a consistent database state, the updated state is consistent iff the following holds in it:

$$\{ \leftarrow \mathbf{a} \doteq \mathbf{b} \wedge \neg r(\mathbf{a}),$$
$$\leftarrow p(\mathbf{b}) \wedge \neg r(\mathbf{b}),$$
$$\leftarrow q(\mathbf{a}) \wedge \neg r(\mathbf{a}) \quad \}. \qquad \square$$

As it can be seen in this example, the test produced in this way for the updated state is identical to the original, simplified one for the state prior to the update. Whether this indicates a general property is not known at the time of writing.

5.5   Applications for Data Integration

Data integration is the problem of combining two or more existing source databases into a single global one by means of a so-called mediator schema. The global database may be inconsistent even if each of the sources satisfies its particular constraints. In [6] we have adapted the simplification method described in the present paper to a number of different data integration scenarios, where the consistency of the sources is employed, perhaps together with given *a priori* knowledge on their combination.

Example 10 ([6]). Consider two databases containing information about marriages, each of which is known to satisfy the following integrity constraint (no husband has more than a wife):

$$\phi = \leftarrow m(x, y) \wedge m(x, z) \wedge y \neq z.$$

A simplified constraint for checking consistency of the combined database (formed by the union of the tuples) produced by the method is the following, where the subscripts refer to the different local databases.

$$\phi_{1,2} = \leftarrow m_1(x,y) \wedge m_2(x,z) \wedge y \neq z$$

The simplification procedure can also be applied to validate, at the global level, an update reported from one of the local databases, based on the knowledge that the global database was consistent before the update and that the update was checked by the source. If, for example, the update $\{m_1(frederik, mary)\}$ is reported, the simplified check for global consistency is the following:

$$\phi'_{1,2} = \leftarrow m_2(frederik, z) \wedge mary \neq z.$$

If, in addition, it is known that the sets of husbands in the two sources are always disjoint, as expressed by the constraint $\leftarrow m_1(x,y) \wedge m_2(x,z)$, both $\phi'_{1,2}$ and $\phi_{1,2}$ could be further simplified by our method to *true*.   □

5.6   Semantic Query Optimization

We indicate here a potentiality for using the simplification procedure for semantic query optimization by a sketchy example.

Consider again the integrity constraint $\leftarrow f(x,y) \wedge \neg p(x,m)$ and assume that a given database is consistent with it. The query $\leftarrow f(x,y)$ is given to the system. Treat the variables in the query as parameters, thus writing it as $f(\mathbf{a}, \mathbf{b})$, and simplify the integrity constraint with respect to it. This gives for sure that $\leftarrow \neg p(\mathbf{a}, m)$ holds for any $\mathbf{a}$ with $f(\mathbf{a}, \mathbf{b})$ in the database.

This means that we can safely extend the query to the following: $\leftarrow p(x,m) \wedge f(x,y)$. It may be the case that the new literal refers to a very small relation so that the remaining query runs faster (although this is not likely to be the case in the present example, however).

6   Conclusion

We applied program transformation techniques to the generation of simplified integrity constraints. A procedure was constructed that makes use of these transformations and produces the simplification searched for according to a criterion of "minimality" that is relevant for a large class of cases. This minimality and the versatility of the transformation operators are the original contribution of this paper. This, together with the ability of producing a necessary and sufficient condition for checking the integrity before a database transaction, constitutes the main advantage of our method with respect to earlier approaches. Examples are discussed that show how this procedure can be applied and it is also pointed out that the program transformations prove useful in several other contexts.

Although the details were not spelled out, the simplified integrity constraints are assumed to be executable as SQL queries. In this context, an empty answer indicates that the database is consistent, otherwise the tuples returned provide hints for extending the update in order to restore consistency, c.f. section 5.1.

Future directions include the extension of the transaction language to cover the expressive power of today's querying languages, which can be handled by extending the **After** operator with suitable replacement patterns. Extension of the simplification method to databases with recursive views is under consideration.

As we have indicated, there seem to be undecidability results that make it impossible to achieve a general and optimal simplification procedure, so the modest goal we can hope for is to provide a procedure that is proven to produce optimal results under given restrictions to the constraint theory, and acceptable results in all other cases.

Acknowledgements

The authors are grateful to the reviewers for many suggestions and improvements, including a simpler proof of lemma 1. This research is supported in part by the IT-University of Copenhagen.

References

1. Abdennadher, S., Christiansen, H. (2000). An Experimental CLP Platform for Integrity Constraints and Abduction. Proceedings of FQAS2000, Flexible Query Answering Systems, pp. 141–152, Eds. Larsen, H.L., Kacprzyk, J., Zadrozny, S., Andreasen, T., Christiansen, H., *Advances in Soft Computing series*, Physica-Verlag (Springer).
2. Christiansen, H. (1998). Automated reasoning with a constraint-based metainterpreter, *Journal of Logic Programming*, Vol 37(1–3) Oct–Dec, pp. 213–253.
3. Christiansen, H. (1999). Integrity constraints and constraint logic programming (Invited talk). *INAP'99; Proceedings of the 12th International Conference on Application of Prolog*, Science University of Tokyo, Japan. pp. 5–12.
4. Chakravarthy, U., Grant, J., Minker, J. (1990). Logic-based approach to semantic query optimization. *ACM Transactions on Database Systems (TODS)* 15(2), pp. 162–207, ACM Press.
5. Christiansen, H., Martinenghi, D. (2000). Symbolic constraints for meta-logic programming, *Journal of Applied Artificial Intelligence,* vol. 14, pp. 345–367.
6. Christiansen, H., Martinenghi, D. (2004). Simplification of integrity constraints for data integration. Proc. Third International Symposium on Foundations of Information and Knowledge Systems (FoIKS), February 17–20, 2004, Vienna, Austria. *Lecture Notes in Computer Science*, Eds. D. Seipel, J.-M. Turull-Torres, vol. 2942, pp. 31–48.
7. Decker, H. (2002). Translating Advanced Integrity Checking Technology to SQL. *Database Integrity: Challenges and Solutions*, Eds. J. Doorn, L.C.Rivero, Idea Group, pp. 203–249.
8. Decker, H., Celma, M. (1994). A slick procedure for integrity checking in deductive databases. *Logic Programming, Proceedings of the Eleventh International Conference on Logic Programming, June 13-18, 1994*, MIT Press, pp. 456–469.
9. Dijkstra, E.W. (1976). *A Discipline of Programming*. Prentice-Hall.

10. Godfrey, P., Grant, J., Gryz, J., Minker, J. (1998). Integrity Constraints: Semantics and Applications. *Logics for Databases and Information System*, Eds. Chomicki, J. Saake, G., Kluwer, pp. 265–306.

11. Grant, J., Minker, J. (1990). Integrity Constraints in Knowledge Based Systems. In *Knowledge Engineering Vol II, Applications.* H. Adeli, Ed., McGraw-Hill, pp. 1–25.

12. Grant, J., Minker, J. (1992). The Impact of Logic Programming on Databases. *Communications of the ACM* 35(3), pp. 66–81.

13. Hoare, C.A.R. (1969). An axiomatic basis for computer programming. *Communications of the ACM* 12, no. 10. pp. 576–580.

14. Henschen, L., McCune, W., Naqvi, S. (1984). Compiling Constraint-Checking Programs from First-Order Formulas. *Advances in Database Theory*, volume 2. Eds. Gallaire, H., Nicolas, J.-M., Minker, J., Plenum Press, New York, pp. 145–169.

15. Leuschel, M., De Schreye, D. (1998). Creating Specialised Integrity Checks Through Partial Evaluation of Meta-Interpreters. *Journal of Logic Programming* 36(2), pp. 149–193.

16. Lee, S. Y., Ling, T. W. (1996). Further Improvements on Integrity Constraint Checking for Stratifiable Deductive Databases. Proc. of 22th International Conference on Very Large Data Bases (VLDB'96), September 3-6, 1996, Mumbai (Bombay), eds. Vijayaraman, T. M. et al., India. Morgan Kaufmann, pp. 495–505.

17. Lloyd, J., Sonenberg, L., Topor, R. (1987). Integrity Constraint Checking in Stratified Databases. *Journal of Logic Programming* 4(4), pp. 331–343.

18. Lloyd, J., Topor, R. (1985). A Basis for Deductive Database Systems. *Journal of Logic Programming* 2(2), pp. 93–109.

19. Martinenghi, D. (2003). A Simplification Procedure for Integrity Constraints. *World Wide Web*, http://www.dat.ruc.dk/~dm/spic/index.html.

20. Nicolas, J.-M. (1982). Logic for Improving Integrity Checking in Relational Data Bases., *Acta Informatica* 18, pp. 227–253.

21. Nilsson, U., Małuzyński, J. (1995). *Logic, Programming and Prolog (2nd ed.)*, John Wiley & Sons Ltd.

22. Qian, X. (1988). An Effective Method for Integrity Constraint Simplification. *Proc. of the Fourth International Conference on Data Engineering*, IEEE Computer Society, pp. 338–345.

23. Sadri, F., Kowalski, R. (1988). A Theorem-Proving Approach to Database Integrity. *Foundations of Deductive Databases and Logic Programming*, Ed. Minker, J., Kaufmann, Los Altos, CA, pp. 313–362.

Integration and Optimization
of Rule-Based Constraint Solvers

Slim Abdennadher[1] and Thom Frühwirth[2]

[1] Faculty of Information Engineering and Technology,
German University Cairo, Egypt
Slim.Abdennadher@guc.edu.eg
[2] Computer Science Faculty, University of Ulm, Germany
Thom.Fruehwirth@informatik.uni-ulm.de

Abstract. One lesson learned from practical constraint solving applications is that constraints are often heterogeneous. Solving such constraints requires a collaboration of constraint solvers. In this paper, we introduce a methodology for the tight integration of CHR constraint programs into one such program. CHR is a high-level rule-based language for writing constraint solvers and reasoning systems. A constraint solver is well-behaved if it is terminating and confluent. When merging constraint solvers, this property may be lost. Based on previous results on CHR program analysis and transformation we show how to utilize completion to regain well-behavedness. We identify a class of solvers whose union is always confluent and we show that for preserving termination such a class is hard to find. The merged and completed constraint solvers may contain redundant rules. Utilizing the notion of operational equivalence, which is decidable for well-behaved CHR programs, we present a method to detect redundant rules in a CHR program.

1 Introduction

Many real applications of constraint-based reasoning involve heterogeneous constraints. Solving such constraints requires a collaboration of two or more constraint solvers. In this paper, we are concerned with solvers written in CHR language.

CHR (Constraint Handling Rules) [9, 11] is a concurrent committed-choice constraint logic programming language consisting of guarded rules that manipulate conjunctions of constraints. In CHR, we distinguish two kinds of rules: simplification rules replace constraints by simpler constraints. Propagation rules add new constraints which may cause further simplification.

Usually, CHR solvers are *well-behaved*, i.e. terminating and confluent. Confluence means that it does not matter for the result which of the applicable rules are applied in a computation. Once termination has been established [10], there is a decidable, sufficient and necessary test for confluence [1]. Confluence also implies *consistency* of the logical reading of the solver program [1]. We have developed a tool for confluence testing. All solvers of recent CHR releases are terminating

M. Bruynooghe (Ed.): LOPSTR 2004, LNCS 3018, pp. 198–213, 2004.

and only two solvers that rely on variable orderings to achieve termination for variable elimination are not confluent.

Given two well-behaved CHR constraint solvers, then their so-called tight integration is simply the union of their rules. There is no restriction on the signature of the solvers. In particular, solvers may fully or partially define the same constraints. Any computation that was possible in one of the solvers will also be possible in the union of the solvers, since additional rules cannot inhibit the application of old rules (as can be seen from the operational semantics of CHR).

However, the union of the solvers could lose termination and/or confluence, and thus their well-behavedness.

Example 1. Consider a solver program with the single simplification rule {a ⇔ b} that replaces the CHR constraint a by the constraint b and a solver program with the single rule {b ⇔ a} that replaces the CHR constraint b by the constraint a. The union of the two programs, {a ⇔ b, b ⇔ a}, is obviously non-terminating.

Consider a program P_1 with the single rule {a ⇔ b} and a program P_2 with the single rule {a ⇔ c}. Their union {a ⇔ b, a ⇔ c} is terminating, but obviously non-confluent, since a computation for a may result in either b or c depending on the (committed) choice of the rule.

While establishing termination for CHR programs without propagation rules is in practice often rather simple [10], termination is in general undecidable for CHR programs. On the other hand, *completion* can make non-confluent programs confluent [2] by adding new rules. Thus there is a chance to automatically produce from two well-behaved constraint solvers a solver that behaves well, too.

Example 2. Consider the union of P_1 and P_2 of Example 1, which is {a ⇔ b, a ⇔ c}. To make the union confluent, the rule b ⇔ c can be added.

In the paper, we also consider the special case of so-called *non-overlapping* solvers that define different constraints. Non-overlapping solvers may have common (shared) CHR constraints and function symbols and have common built-in constraints. We prove that they are well-behaved if their union is terminating. While confluence is modular (preserved) for well-behaved, non-overlapping solvers, we will argue that it is very hard to find a syntactic class of solver programs that admits modularity for termination.

In practice, non-overlapping solvers are integrated using so-called *bridge rules* between the different constraints they define. These bridge rules often destroy well-behavedness and we show by example how completion fares with such solvers.

The resulting constraint solver may contain *redundant rules*. Since propagation in a rule-based constraint solver corresponds to a fixpoint computation with its rules, it is preferable to have a minimal number of rules to accelerate the fixpoint computation. Based on the operational equivalence notion [3], we present a method to detect and remove redundant rules in a CHR constraint solver.

Related Work. There is a renewed interest in languages and models for constraint solver cooperation. An overview of the issues in cooperative constraint solving can be found in [14]. Recent work in this area includes BALI [16], a scheme for integrating heterogeneous solvers by encapsulation: a cooperation language based on strategies is compiled into solver specific communication code. Similarly, the framework of [8] relies on strategies to specify when component solvers are to be applied. The framework of [15] requires specific interfaces from the constraint solvers and a meta constraint solver to coordinate the cooperating solvers. Examples and implementations of this framework concentrate on numerical constraints.

When CHR is used as an implementation language for constraint solvers, desirable properties like confluence and operational equivalence can be decided once termination has been established. There is no need for specific interfaces, because the constraint solvers communicate freely via shared variables using their common built-in constraints. In well-behaved CHR solvers, it does not matter which of the applicable rules are applied. In particular, in well-behaved merged solvers, it does not matter from which solvers the rules are coming. Thus any type of cooperation strategies [14], be it hard-coded, be it based on priorities or explicit operators, is possible. Moreover, the strategies can be very fine-grained, at the level of the application of a single rule from the solver program, i.e. single computation step.

The work of [18, 7] focuses on building a constraint solver for the union of theories with given decision procedures. These theories are usually casted as equational theories. In [7], the theories are assumed to be disjoint. In [18], combination of theories sharing constructors have been investigated. In CHR, equalities referring to distinct theories are assumed to be represented by different constraint symbols. CHR programs represent first-order theories, that can be unioned without any requirements. Operationally, however, we want to make sure that the resulting solver is still well-behaved. The constraint solvers we are interested in are not necessarily decision procedures, but trade efficiency for completeness.

In the term rewriting literature, there is a considerable body of work on modularity of termination and also work on modularity of confluence [17, 13, 6]. Although CHR borrows notions and techniques from term rewriting systems (TRS), it is not clear how these results would apply to CHR, since CHR are rather different to classical TRS:

- CHR propagation rules cannot be directly expressed as terminating TRS.
- CHR manipulate constraints, which usually contain free variables, while terms that are rewritten in TRS are usually ground (variable-free).
- Rule application in CHR relies on AC-matching of conjunctions of atomic CHR constraints (relations), and not on matching of terms at arbitrary positions as in TRS.
- Built-in constraints do not appear in TRS. CHR guards use built-in constraints only and differ from conditions in extended TRS that refer to comparison of normal forms of TRS reductions.

- Multiple occurences of variables are allowed on both sides of CHR rules. Variables are allowed to occur only in one side of the rule, in particular variables can be introduced on the right hand side of a rule.

To the best of our knowledge, there does not exist a TRS with all these properties for which modularity results have been obtained. Clearly this does not preclude non-trivial future work to relate aspects of modularity in CHR with aspects of modularity results in TRS.

Outline of Paper. In Section 2, we define the CHR language and summarize previous results on confluence, completion, and operational equivalence. In the next section of the paper, we show how to merge CHR constraint solvers utilizing completion. We then investigate when termination and confluence are preserved under union of solver programs. We consider the special case of so-called non-overlapping solvers that define different constraints and introduce the notion of so-called bridge rules to integrate such solvers. In Section 6, we show how to remove redundant rules from a solver utilizing operational equivalence. A preliminary version of this paper was presented at JFPLC'02 [4].

2   Preliminaries

In this section we give an overview of syntax and semantics for constraint handling rules (CHR) as well as previous results on confluence, completion, and operational equivalence. Detailed presentations can be found in [12, 1, 5, 2, 3].

2.1   Syntax of CHR

We use two disjoint sets of predicate symbols for two different kinds of constraints: *built-in constraint symbols* and *CHR constraint symbols (user-defined symbols)*. We call an atomic formula with a constraint symbol a *constraint*. Built-in constraints are handled by predefined constraint black-box solvers. We assume that these solvers are well-behaved. Built-in constraints include $=$, *true*, and *false*. The semantics of the built-in constraints is defined by a consistent first-order *constraint theory CT*. In particular, CT defines $=$ as the syntactic equality over finite terms.

CHR constraints are defined by a CHR program.

Definition 1. A *CHR program* is a finite set of rules. There are two kinds of rules: A *simplification rule* is of the form *Name* @ $H \Leftrightarrow C \mid B$. A *propagation rule* is of the form *Name* @ $H \Rightarrow C \mid B$, where *Name* is an optional, unique identifier of a rule, the *head H* is a non-empty conjunction of CHR constraints, the *guard C* is a conjunction of built-in constraints, and the *body B* is a goal. A *goal* is a conjunction of built-in and CHR constraints. For convenience, a trivial guard "*true*" can be omitted together with "⊺".

A CHR symbol is *defined* in a CHR program if it occurs in the head of a rule in the program.

Example 3. We define a CHR constraint for a partial order relation $\leq$:

r1 @ X$\leq$X $\Leftrightarrow$ *true*.
r2 @ X$\leq$Y $\wedge$ Y$\leq$X $\Leftrightarrow$ X=Y.
r3 @ X$\leq$Y $\wedge$ Y$\leq$Z $\Rightarrow$ X$\leq$Z.
r4 @ X$\leq$Y $\wedge$ X$\leq$Y $\Leftrightarrow$ X$\leq$Y.

The CHR program implements reflexivity (r1), antisymmetry (r2), transitivity (r3) and redundancy (r4) in a straightforward way. The reflexivity rule r1 states that X$\leq$X is logically true. The antisymmetry rule r2 means X$\leq$Y $\wedge$ Y$\leq$X is logically equivalent to X=Y. The transitivity rule r3 states that the conjunction of X$\leq$Y and Y$\leq$Z implies X$\leq$Z. The redundancy rule r4 states that X$\leq$Y $\wedge$ X$\leq$Y is logically equivalent to X$\leq$Y.

2.2   Operational Semantics of CHR

The operational semantics of CHR is given by a transition system. A state is simply a goal, i.e. a conjunction of built-in and CHR constraints. Let P be a CHR program. We define the transition relation $\mapsto_P$ by introducing two computation steps (transitions), one for each kind of CHR rule (cf. Figure 1). In the figure, all meta-variables stand for conjunctions of constraints. The notation G_{bi} denotes the built-in constraints of G. Since the two transitions are structurally very

Simplify

If $(H \Leftrightarrow C \mid B)$ is a fresh variant of a rule with variables $\bar{x}$
and $CT \models \forall \, (G_{bi} \rightarrow \exists \bar{x}(H=H' \wedge C))$
then $(H' \wedge G) \mapsto_P^{\text{Simplify}} (G \wedge B \wedge C \wedge H=H')$

Propagate

If $(H \Rightarrow C \mid B)$ is a fresh variant of a rule with variables $\bar{x}$
and $CT \models \forall \, (G_{bi} \rightarrow \exists \bar{x}(H=H' \wedge C))$
then $(H' \wedge G) \mapsto_P^{\text{Propagate}} (H' \wedge G \wedge B \wedge C \wedge H=H')$

Fig. 1. Computation Steps of Constraint Handling Rules

similar, we first describe their common behavior and only at the end point out their differences.

A fresh variant of a rule is *applicable to a state* $H' \wedge G$ if H' matches its head H and if its guard C is implied by the built-in constraints appearing in G. A *fresh variant* of a rule is obtained by renaming its variables to fresh variables, listed in the sequence $\bar{x}$. *Matching* (one-sided unification) succeeds if H' is an instance of H, i.e. it is only allowed to instantiate (bind) variables of H but not variables of H'. Matching is logically expressed by equating H' and H but existentially quantifying all variables from the rule, $\bar{x}$. This equation $H'=H$ is shorthand for pairwise equating the arguments of the constraints in H' and H, provided their constraint symbols are equal. Note that conjuncts can be permuted.

If an applicable rule is applied, the equation $H=H'$, its guard C and its body B are added to the resulting state. A rule application cannot be undone (CHR is a committed-choice language without backtracking). When a simplification rule is applied in the transition **Simplify**, the matching CHR constraints H' are removed from the state. The **Propagate** transition is like the **Simplify** transition, except that it keeps the constraints H' in the resulting state. Trivial non-termination caused by applying the same propagation rule again and again is avoided by applying it at most once to the same constraints [1].

A *computation* of a goal G in a program P is a sequence $S_0, S_1, \ldots$ of states with $S_i \mapsto_P S_{i+1}$ beginning with the initial state S_0 for G and ending in a final state or diverging. A *final state* is one where either no computation step is possible anymore or where the built-in constraints are inconsistent. $\mapsto_P^*$ denotes the reflexive and transitive closure of $\mapsto_P$. When it is clear from the context, we will drop the reference to the program P.

Example 4. Recall the solver program for $\leq$ of Example 3. Operationally the rule r1 removes occurrences of constraints that match X≤X. The antisymmetry rule r2 means that if we find X≤Y as well as Y≤X in the current store, we can replace them by the logically equivalent X=Y. The transitivity rule r3 propagates constraints. We add the logical consequence X≤Z as a redundant constraint. The redundancy rule r4 absorbs multiple occurrences of the same constraint.

A computation of the goal A≤B ∧ C≤A ∧ B≤C proceeds as follows:

$$
\begin{array}{ll}
\text{A≤B} \wedge \text{C≤A} \wedge \text{B≤C} & \mapsto \text{Propagate} \\
\text{A≤B} \wedge \text{C≤A} \wedge \underline{\text{B≤C}} \wedge \text{C≤B} & \mapsto \text{Simplify} \\
\text{A≤B} \wedge \underline{\text{B≤A}} \wedge \text{B=C} & \mapsto \text{Simplify} \\
\text{A=B} \wedge \text{B=C}
\end{array}
$$

2.3   Confluence

The confluence property of a program guarantees that any computation for a goal results in the same final state no matter which of the applicable rules are applied.

Definition 2. A CHR program is *confluent* if for all states S, S_1, S_2: If $S \mapsto^* S_1$ and $S \mapsto^* S_2$ then the pair of states (S_1, S_2) is joinable.

A pair of states (S_1, S_2) is *joinable* if there exist states T_1 and T_2 such that $S_1 \mapsto^* T_1$ and $S_2 \mapsto^* T_2$ where T_1 and T_2 are identical up to renaming of variables and logical equivalence of built-in constraints.

To analyze confluence of a given CHR program we cannot check joinability starting from any given ancestor state S, because in general there are infinitely many such states. However for terminating programs, one can restrict the joinability test to a finite number of "minimal" states, the so-called critical states as explained below.

A CHR program is called *terminating*, if there are no infinite computations. For many existing CHR programs simple well-founded orderings are sufficient to prove termination [10]. In general, such orderings are not sufficient because of non-trivial interactions between simplification and propagation rules. In this paper we assume that the constraint solvers are terminating.

Definition 3. Let R_1 be a simplification rule and R_2 be a (not necessarily different) rule, whose variables have been renamed apart. Let $H_i \wedge A_i$ be the head and C_i be the guard of rule R_i ($i = 1, 2$). Then a *critical ancestor state of R_1 and R_2* is

$$(H_1 \wedge A_1 \wedge H_2 \wedge (A_1 = A_2) \wedge C_1 \wedge C_2),$$

provided A_1 and A_2 are non-empty conjunctions and $CT \models \exists((A_1 = A_2) \wedge C_1 \wedge C_2)$.

Let S be a critical ancestor state of R_1 and R_2. If $S \mapsto S_1$ using rule R_1 and $S \mapsto S_2$ using rule R_2 then the tuple (S_1, S_2) is a *critical pair* of R_1 and R_2.

The following theorem from [1, 5] gives a decidable, sufficient and necessary condition for confluence of a terminating CHR program:

Theorem 1. *A terminating CHR program is confluent iff all its critical pairs are joinable.*

Example 5. Recall the program for $\leq$ of Example 3. Consider a critical ancestor state of r2 and r3 where $A_1 = A_2 = \text{X} \leq \text{Y}$. This critical state is $\text{X} \leq \text{Y} \wedge \text{Y} \leq \text{X} \wedge \text{Y} \leq \text{Z}$ and gives raise to the following critical pair

$$(S_1, S_2) = (\text{X} = \text{Y} \wedge \text{X} \leq \text{Z}, \quad \text{X} \leq \text{Y} \wedge \text{Y} \leq \text{X} \wedge \text{Y} \leq \text{Z} \wedge \text{X} \leq \text{Z})$$

which is joinable: S_1 is a final state, i.e. no further computation step is possible. A computation beginning with S_2 results in S_1:

$$\underline{\text{X} \leq \text{Y}} \wedge \underline{\text{Y} \leq \text{X}} \wedge \text{Y} \leq \text{Z} \wedge \text{X} \leq \text{Z} \quad \mapsto^{\text{Simplify}}$$
$$\underline{\text{X} \leq \text{Z}} \wedge \underline{\text{X} \leq \text{Z}} \wedge \text{X} = \text{Y} \quad \mapsto^{\text{Simplify}}$$
$$\text{X} \leq \text{Z} \wedge \text{X} = \text{Y}$$

2.4   Completion

Completion is the process of adding rules to a non-confluent program until it becomes confluent. Rules are built from a non-joinable critical pair to allow a transition from one of the states into the other while maintaining termination. In contrast to other completion methods, in CHR we need in general more than one rule to make a critical pair joinable: a simplification rule and a propagation rule [2]. When these rules are added, new critical pairs may be produced, but also old non-joinable critical pairs may be removed, because the new rules make them joinable. Completion tries to continue introducing rules this way until the program becomes confluent. The essential part of a completion algorithm is the introduction of rules from critical pairs.

Definition 4. Let $\gg$ be a termination order and let $(C_{ud1} \wedge C_{bi1}, C_{ud2} \wedge C_{bi2})$ be a critical pair, where the states are ordered such that C_{ud1} is a non-empty conjunction and $C_{ud1} \gg C_{ud2}$. Then the *orientation* of the critical pair results in the rules:

$$C_{ud1} \Leftrightarrow C_{bi1} \mid C_{ud2} \wedge C_{bi2}$$
$$C_{ud2} \Rightarrow C_{bi2} \mid C_{bi1}$$

The second rule is needed if C_{ud2} is a non-empty conjunction and $CT \not\models C_{bi2} \rightarrow C_{bi1}$.

Examples of completion will be shown in the next section of the paper. In these examples, unless otherwise noticed, a simple termination order will suffice, where $C_1 \gg C_2$ if $C_1 = (C_2 \wedge C)$, i.e. the conjunction C_1 contains all conjuncts of C_2 and more (C is non-empty).

In [2] it was shown that if the completion procedure stops successfully, then the resulting program is well-behaved. But completion cannot always be successful: completion is aborted if a critical pair cannot be transformed into rules. Completion may not terminate, because new rules produce new critical pairs.

2.5   Operational Equivalence

The following definition clarifies when two programs are operationally equivalent: if for each goal, all final states in one program are the same as the final states in the other program.

Definition 5. Let P_1 and P_2 be programs. A state S is P_1, P_2-*joinable*, iff there are two computations $S \mapsto^*_{P_1} S_1$ and $S \mapsto^*_{P_2} S_2$, where S_1 and S_2 are final states, and S_1 and S_2 are identical up to renaming of variables and logical equivalence of built-in constraints.

Definition 6. Let P_1 and P_2 be programs. P_1 and P_2 are *operationally equivalent* if all states are P_1, P_2-joinable.

In [3], we gave a decidable, sufficient and necessary syntactic condition for operational equivalence of well-behaved CHR programs: when testing operational equivalence, similar to our confluence test, we can restrict ourselves to a finite number of *critical states* that consist of the head and the guard of a rule. These critical states are run in both programs, and their outcome must be the same.

Definition 7. Let P_1 and P_2 be programs. Then a *critical state of P_1 and P_2* is defined as follows:

$$H \wedge C \text{ where } (H \odot C \mid B) \in P_1 \cup P_2 \text{ and } \odot \in \{ \Leftrightarrow, \Rightarrow \}$$

Theorem 2. Two well-behaved programs P_1 and P_2 are operationally equivalent iff all critical states of P_1 and P_2 are P_1, P_2-joinable.

Examples for operational equivalence can be found in the subsequent sections.

3   Tight Integration of CHR Constraint Solvers with Completion

In the introduction, Example 1 illustrated that the union of two well-behaved (i.e. terminating and confluent) programs is not necessarily well-behaved. Once termination of the union has been established, we can use our confluence test to check if the union of well-behaved programs is confluent again. We call such programs "compatible".

Definition 8. Let P_1 and P_2 be two well-behaved CHR programs and let the union of the two programs, $P_1 \cup P_2$, be terminating. P_1 and P_2 are *compatible* if $P_1 \cup P_2$ is confluent.

The critical pairs of $P_1 \cup P_2$ are the critical pairs of P_1 unioned with the critical pairs of P_2 unioned with critical pairs coming from one rule from P_1 and one rule from P_2. Since P_1 and P_2 are already confluent, for compatibility it suffices to check only those critical pairs coming from rules in different programs (cf. proof of upcoming Theorem 3). In other words, the confluence test can be made incremental in the addition of rules.

If the compatibility test succeeds, we can just take the union of the rules in the two programs. This holds even for constraints that are fully or partially defined in more than one of the programs which are merged.

Example 6. The well-behaved program P_1 contains the following CHR rules defining max, where max(X,Y,Z) means that Z is the maximum of X and Y:

max(X,Y,Z) $\Leftrightarrow$ X<Y | Z=Y.
max(X,Y,Z) $\Leftrightarrow$ X$\geq$Y | Z=X.

whereas well-behaved P_2 defines max by

max(X,Y,Z) $\Leftrightarrow$ X$\leq$Y | Z=Y.
max(X,Y,Z) $\Leftrightarrow$ X>Y | Z=X.

Note that $<$, $\leq$, and $\geq$ are built-in constraints in this example.

In order to perform the union of the two programs, we check whether the definitions of max are compatible. There are three critical ancestor states coming from one rule in P_1 and one rule in P_2:

max(X,Y,Z) $\wedge$ X<Y $\wedge$ X$\leq$Y
max(X,Y,Z) $\wedge$ X$\geq$Y $\wedge$ X$\leq$Y
max(X,Y,Z) $\wedge$ X$\geq$Y $\wedge$ X>Y

Since the critical pairs of these critical ancestor states are joinable, the two definitions of max are compatible. Hence we can just take the union of the rules and define max by all four rules.

Note that the constraint max is *"operationally stronger"* in $P_1 \cup P_2$ than in each program alone, in the sense that more computation steps are possible: in $P_1 \cup P_2$ (and P_1) we have the computation

max(X,Y,Z) $\wedge$ X$\geq$Y $\mapsto_{P_1 \cup P_2}$ Z=X $\wedge$ X$\geq$Y while in P_2 the goal cannot reduce at all, it is a final state. But like P_2, P_1 is not as strong as $P_1 \cup P_2$: the goal $\max(\text{X},\text{Y},\text{Z}) \wedge \text{X} \leq \text{Y}$ is a final state in P_1, while it has a non-trivial computation in $P_1 \cup P_2$ and P_2.

Example 7. Here we consider a variation on a solver for $\max$ that does not use any built-in constraints (except for implicit syntactical equality). We define $\max$ with the inequalities as CHR constraints in two steps.

Given the constraint solver for $\leq$ (example 3), we add the following simplification rule describing the interaction of $\max$ and $\leq$:

max1 @ max(X,Y,Z) $\wedge$ X$\leq$Y $\Leftrightarrow$ Z=Y $\wedge$ X$\leq$Y.

The resulting solver is non-confluent. The critical ancestor state $\max(\text{X},\text{X},\text{Z}) \wedge \text{X} \leq \text{X}$ of the rule max1 and of the reflexivity rule r1 of $\leq$ produces the non-joinable critical pair $(\text{X=Z} \wedge \text{X} \leq \text{X}, \max(\text{X},\text{X},\text{Z}))$. We use *completion* to make the solver confluent. For the above-mentioned critical pair it adds the rule:

max2 @ max(X,X,Z) $\Leftrightarrow$ Z=X.

Now, we consider a solver for $<$ which is well-behaved

X<X $\Leftrightarrow$ *false*.
X<Y $\wedge$ X<Y $\Leftrightarrow$ X<Y.
X<Y $\wedge$ Y<Z $\Rightarrow$ X<Z.

and we add the rule describing the interaction of $\max$ and $<$:

max3 @ max(X,Y,Z) $\wedge$ Y<X $\Leftrightarrow$ Z=X $\wedge$ Y<X.

The resulting solver remains well-behaved.

Finally, we union the solvers for $\leq$ and for $<$ that have been extended by the three rules for $\max$, i.e. max1, max2, and max3. The union of these solvers is not confluent. The completion method adds the following rule to make a non-joinable critical pair stemming from the rules max1 and max3 joinable:

X$\leq$Y $\wedge$ Y<X $\Leftrightarrow$ *false*.

The rules derived by completion revealed interesting properties of $\max$, i.e. rules max2 and max3, and the interaction of $\leq$ and $<$. The completed program is well-behaved.

4   Modularity of Termination and Confluence

We have seen that well-behavedness is not modular, i.e. it is not preserved under union of programs. We may ask ourselves if there are syntactic criteria for classes of programs that admit modularity of well-behavedness. In this section we will show that while for confluence, the answer is positive and simple (presupposing termination), the situation seems very difficult for termination.

When the two solvers do not have any *defined* CHR constraints in common (i.e. a CHR symbol occurring in the head of the rules in a solver does not occur in the head of the rules in the other solver), we call them *non-overlapping*. Note that non-overlapping solvers may have common (shared) CHR constraints and function symbols and have common built-in constraints (by definition, at least syntactical equality). We can show that the union of two non-overlapping well-behaved solvers is always well-behaved if the union is terminating.

Theorem 3. Let P_1 and P_2 be two well-behaved CHR programs and let the union of the two programs, $P_1 \cup P_2$, be terminating. If P_1 and P_2 are non-overlapping then $P_1 \cup P_2$ is confluent.

Proof. To show that $P_1 \cup P_2$ is confluent, we only have to show that all critical pairs of $P_1 \cup P_2$ are joinable, since $P_1 \cup P_2$ is terminating. The set of critical pairs of $P_1 \cup P_2$ consists of all critical pairs stemming from two rules appearing in P_1 (case 1. below), all critical pairs stemming from two rules appearing in P_2 (case 2) and all critical pairs stemming from one rule appearing in P_1 and one rule appearing in P_2 (case 3).

1. P_1 is well-behaved, thus all critical pairs stemming from two rules appearing in P_1 are joinable. Therefore, these critical pairs are also joinable in $P_1 \cup P_2$.
2. Analogous to case 1.
3. Critical pairs from rules of different programs can only exist, if the head of the rules have at least one constraint in common. Since P_1 and P_2 are non-overlapping, there exists no critical pair stemming from one rule in P_1 and one rule in P_2. □

For modularity of termination, the situation seems very difficult: even if two terminating programs do not have common CHR constraint symbols, their union may be non-terminating.

Example 8. Consider the following two programs:

```
P1: c(f(X))  ⇔  X=g(Y) ∧ c(Y).
P2: d(g(Y))  ⇔  Y=f(Z) ∧ d(Z).
```

Any goal (of finite size) terminates in each of the two programs, but the goal c(f(X)) ∧ d(X) does not terminate in the union of the programs (due to common function symbols).

c(f(X)) ∧ d(X)	↦Simplify
X=g(Y) ∧ c(Y) ∧ d(g(Y))	↦Simplify
X=g(f(W)) ∧ Y=f(W) ∧ c(f(W)) ∧ d(W)	↦Simplify ...

Actually, even if there are no common symbols in the program text, we may run into trouble.

Example 9. The previous example can be rewritten such that instead of common function symbols one uses built-in constraints to the same effect:

```
P1: c(FX)  ⇔  f1(FX,X) | g1(X,Y) ∧ c(Y).
P2: d(GY)  ⇔  g2(GY,Y) | f2(Y,Z) ∧ d(Z).
```

where $f1(X,Y)$ and $f2(X,Y)$ are both defined as $X = f(Y)$ in the constraint theory for the built-in constraints and analogously for $g1(X,Y)$ and $g2(X,Y)$. There are no common symbols in the CHR program itself, but only in the constraint theory. Any goal terminates in each of the two programs, but the goal `c(FX)` $\wedge$ `f1(FX,X)` $\wedge$ `d(X)` does not terminate in the union of the programs.

Summarizing, as soon as there are common symbols, no matter if they are CHR constraints, built-in constraints or function symbols (even when only shared in the built-in constraint theories), termination is in danger. But any non-trivial integration of constraint solvers will at least share some function symbols, otherwise there could not be shared variables in goals, and without shared variables there is no non-trivial communication between the solvers.

5   Cooperation Using Bridge Rules and Completion

In practice, one will often add to the union of non-overlapping solvers a few so-called *bridge rules*. These are rules that may translate constraints from one solver to constraints of the other solver to improve the overall solving power, i.e. more propagation is possible. In general, they relate constraints from different solvers to enable non-trivial cooperation. In other words, they define *communication* between the solvers by sharing data (constraints).

When adding bridge rules, care has to be taken to maintain termination. On the other hand, bridge rules can be used to re-introduce termination: we may make a union of solvers terminating by renaming symbols apart and using bridge rules to control the interaction between the solvers. In any case, terminating bridge rules will typically cause non-confluence and thus will be the starting point for completion.

Example 10. We want to build a Boolean constraint solver from a well-behaved program P_1 defining conjunction and a well-behaved program P_2 defining implication. In P_1, the constraint `and(X,Y,Z)` stands for X $\wedge$ Y $\leftrightarrow$ Z and in P_2, `imp(X,Y)` stands for X $\rightarrow$ Y.

```
P1:  and(X,X,Z)  ⇔  X=Z.
      and(X,Y,1)  ⇔  X=1 ∧ Y=1.
      and(X,1,Z)  ⇔  X=Z.
      and(X,0,Z)  ⇔  Z=0.
      and(1,Y,Z)  ⇔  Y=Z.
      and(0,Y,Z)  ⇔  Z=0.
      and(X,Y,Z) ∧ and(X,Y,Z1)  ⇔  and(X,Y,Z) ∧ Z=Z1.

P2:  imp(0,X)  ⇔  true.
      imp(X,0)  ⇔  X=0.
      imp(1,X)  ⇔  X=1.
      imp(X,1)  ⇔  true.
      imp(X,Y) ∧ imp(Y,X)  ⇔  X=Y.
```

We add the following bridge rule:

and(X,Y,X) ⇔ imp(X,Y).

The program containing P_1 and P_2 together with the bridge rule is not confluent: the critical pair (*true*, imp(X,X)) stemming from the critical ancestor state and(X,X,X) of the first rule of and and the bridge rule is not joinable. Completion generates the following rules from the non-joinable critical pairs:

imp(X,X) ⇔ *true*.
imp(X,Y) ∧ imp(X,Y) ⇔ imp(X,Y).
imp(X,Y) ∧ and(X,Y,Z) ⇔ imp(X,Y) ∧ X=Z.

Again, the automatically derived rules reveal interesting properties of the constraints.

6   Removal of Redundant Rules with Operational Equivalence

Since propagation in a rule-based constraint solver corresponds to a fixpoint computation with its rules, it is preferable to have a minimal number of rules to accelerate the fixpoint computation and thus to improve the efficiency of the constraint solver. A smart fixpoint engine may detect redundant rules at run-time, but it is obviously cheaper to remove them at compile time or before.

We can use a variation of the operational equivalence test [3] between programs to remove redundant rules from the (completed) union of constraint solvers.

Definition 9. A rule R is *redundant* in a CHR program P iff for all states S: If $S \mapsto_P^* S_1$ then $S \mapsto_{P \setminus \{R\}}^* S_2$, where S_1 and S_2 are final states and S_1 and S_2 are identical up to renaming of variables and logical equivalence of built-in constraints.

Example 11. In example 6, the union of the two programs defining max

r1 @ max(X,Y,Z) ⇔ X<Y | Z=Y.
r2 @ max(X,Y,Z) ⇔ X≥Y | Z=X.
r3 @ max(X,Y,Z) ⇔ X≤Y | Z=Y.
r4 @ max(X,Y,Z) ⇔ X>Y | Z=X.

was operationally stronger than each program alone. However, the union contains redundant rules. For example, rule r3 can always make a transition when rule r1 does, with the same result, but not vice versa. Hence rule r1 is redundant, and analogously for rule r4.

Redundant rules can be discovered using operational equivalence: We remove one rule from the program and compare it with the original program. If the two programs are operationally equivalent, then the rule was obviously redundant and we can remove it. We continue until we have tried to remove all rules. The final program found this way is not necessarily unique, since the result may depend on the order in which rules are tried and removed.

However, Theorem 2 may not be applicable for our redundancy check: If we remove a rule from a well-behaved program, it may become non-confluent. In order to come up with a decidable rule redundancy test, we first have to test confluence of the program without the candidate rule for redundancy. If the program is not confluent, it cannot be operationally equivalent to the initial program, and hence the candidate rule cannot be redundant. If the program is confluent, we can and must check for operational equivalence.

Theorem 4. Let P be a well-behaved program. A rule R is redundant with respect to P iff $P\backslash\{R\}$ is well-behaved and all critical states of P and $P\backslash\{R\}$ are $P, P\backslash\{R\}$-joinable.

Proof. $\Rightarrow$ First, we prove the claim that $P\backslash\{R\}$ is well-behaved by contradiction. Assumption: $P\backslash\{R\}$ is not well-behaved. We can distinguish two cases:
1. $P\backslash\{R\}$ is non-terminating, thus P is also non-terminating, which is a contradiction to the fact that P is well-behaved.
2. $P\backslash\{R\}$ is non-confluent, thus there exists a state S such that $S \mapsto^*_{P\backslash\{R\}}$ S_1 and then $S \mapsto^*_{P\backslash\{R\}} S_2$, where S_1 and S_2 are final states, and S_1 and S_2 are not identical up to renaming of variables and logical equivalence of built-in constraints. R is redundant with respect to P, therefore there exists a state S_3 such that $S \mapsto^*_P S_3$, where S_3 is a final state, and S_3 and S_1 as well as S_3 and S_2 are identical up to renaming of variables and logical equivalence of built-in constraints. This is a contradiction to the claim that S_1 and S_2 are not identical up to renaming of variables and logical equivalence of built-in constraints.

Now we prove that all critical states of P and $P\backslash\{R\}$ are $P, P\backslash\{R\}$-joinable. R is redundant with respect to P, thus for all states S the following holds: $S \mapsto^*_P S_1$ then $S \mapsto^*_{P\backslash\{R\}} S_2$, where S_1 and S_2 are final states and S_1 and S_2 are identical up to renaming of variables and logical equivalence of built-in constraints. Therefore, all states are $P, P\backslash\{R\}$-joinable. $\qquad\square$

It is easy to see that we can specialize our operational equivalence test for redundancy removal: We only have to check if the computation step due to the candidate rule that is tested for redundancy can be performed by the remainder of the program, but we do not have to consider any other rule prefixes.

Example 12. The critical states of the program P in Example 11 are

```
cs1: max(X,Y,Z) ∧ X<Y
cs2: max(X,Y,Z) ∧ X≥Y
cs3: max(X,Y,Z) ∧ X≤Y
cs4: max(X,Y,Z) ∧ X>Y
```

Note that any subset of the program in Example 11 is still well-behaved. A program $P\backslash\{R\}$ ($R \in \{\texttt{r1}, \texttt{r2}, \texttt{r3}, \texttt{r4}\}$) obviously cannot contribute any new critical states. So if we try to remove rule r1 we only have to check the critical state from rule r1, that is cs1, by running it in both programs:

$$\texttt{max(X,Y,Z)} \wedge \texttt{X<Y} \mapsto_P \texttt{X<Y} \wedge \texttt{Z=Y} \qquad \text{by rule } \texttt{r1}$$
$$\texttt{max(X,Y,Z)} \wedge \texttt{X<Y} \mapsto_{P \backslash \{\texttt{r1}\}} \texttt{X<Y} \wedge \texttt{Z=Y} \qquad \text{by rule } \texttt{r3}$$

Since rule r3 enables the same transition, rule r1 must be redundant. In an analogous way, redundancy of rule r4 can be shown. Rule r2, however, is not redundant:

$$\texttt{max(X,Y,Z)} \wedge \texttt{X} \geq \texttt{Y} \mapsto_P \texttt{X} \geq \texttt{Y} \wedge \texttt{Z=X} \qquad \text{by rule } \texttt{r2}$$
$$\texttt{max(X,Y,Z)} \wedge \texttt{X} \geq \texttt{Y} \not\mapsto_{P \backslash \{\texttt{r2}\}}$$

In program $P \backslash \{\texttt{r2}\}$, the critical state is a final state. Hence (the only) redundancy free program consists of the rules r2 and r3.

7   Conclusions

In this paper, we have shown that terminating and confluent, i.e. well-behaved CHR constraint solvers can be merged provided termination is preserved: their tight integration is the union of the rules, even if some constraints are fully or partially defined and/or used in several solvers or program parts. In case that the resulting solver becomes non-confluent, we use our completion method to improve its behavior.

Non-overlapping solvers do not define common constraints but may freely share them otherwise. We have shown that their union is always well-behaved if it is terminating. We argued that a similar modularity result for termination is likely to be very hard to obtain. Future work will investigate how to maintain termination of the union, i.e. modularity results, trying to build on work in term rewriting systems such as [17, 13, 6].

We have discussed bridge rules as a communication means to integrate solvers with disjoint constraints utilizing completion. Finally, we have introduced a method to remove redundant rules from a CHR solver using our operational equivalence test and our confluence test to improve the efficiency of the CHR solver. An implementation of the approach on the basis of our confluence testing tool is certainly desirable to gain more practical experience.

For future work, we are also interested in general notions of confluence and completion, since we have found that on larger examples, their current requirements are unnecessarily strict. A more efficient method for detecting and removing redundant rules should be found.

Another open question is how the results that we obtained for CHR can be transferred to rewrite systems and other rule-based languages. Our work could serve as a starting point for developing a methodology for integration that is supported by semi-automatic tools.

Last but not least we would like to thank the anonymous referees for often detailed and crucial comments that helped to improve and clarify our paper.

References

1. S. Abdennadher. Operational semantics and confluence of constraint propagation rules. In *Third International Conference on Principles and Practice of Constraint Programming, CP97*, LNCS 1330. Springer-Verlag, 1997.
2. S. Abdennadher and T. Frühwirth. On completion of constraint handling rules. In *4th International Conference on Principles and Practice of Constraint Programming, CP98*, LNCS 1520. Springer-Verlag, 1998.
3. S. Abdennadher and T. Frühwirth. Operational equivalence of constraint handling rules. In *Fifth International Conference on Principles and Practice of Constraint Programming, CP99*, LNCS. Springer-Verlag, 1999.
4. S. Abdennadher and T. Frühwirth. Using program analysis for integration and optimization of rule-based constraint solvers. In *Onziemes Journees Francophones de Programmation Logique et Programmation par Contraintes (JFPLC'2002)*, 2002.
5. S. Abdennadher, T. Frühwirth, and H. Meuss. Confluence and semantics of constraint simplification rules. *Constraints Journal*, 4(2), May 1999.
6. T. Arts, J. Giesl, and E. Ohlebusch. Modular termination proofs for rewriting using dependency pairs. *Journal of Symbolic Computation*, 34(1):21–58, 2002.
7. F. Baader and K. U. Schulz. Combining constraint solving. In *Constraints in Computational Logics*, volume 2002 of *Lecture Notes in Computer Science*, pages 104–158. Springer, 2001.
8. C. Castro and E. Monfroy. Basic operators for solving constraints via collaboration of solvers. In *Proceedings of AISC 2000*, LNAI 1930. Springer-Verlag, 2000.
9. T. Frühwirth. Theory and practice of constraint handling rules. *Journal of Logic Programming*, 37(1-3):95–138, 1998.
10. T. Frühwirth. Proving termination of constraint solver programs. In E. M. K.R. Apt, A.C. Kakas and F. Rossi, editors, *New Trends in Constraints*, LNAI 1865. Springer-Verlag, 2000.
11. T. Frühwirth. Constraint handling rules web pages, www.informatik.uni-ulm.de/pm/mitarbeiter/fruehwirth/chr-intro.html, 2004.
12. T. Frühwirth and S. Abdennadher. *Essentials of Constraint Programming*. Springer, 2003.
13. B. Gramlich. On termination and confluence properties of disjoint and constructor-sharing conditional rewrite systems. *Theoretical Computer Science*, 165(1):97–131, 1996.
14. L. Granvilliers, E. Monfroy, and F. Benhamou. Cooperative solvers in constraint programming: A short introduction. In *Workshop on Cooperative Solvers in Constraint Programming (CoSolv) at CP 2001*, 2001.
15. P. Hofstedt. Better communication for tighter cooperation. In *First Intl. Conference on Computational Logic (CL 2000)*, LNAI 1861. Springer-Verlag, 2000.
16. E. Monfroy. The constraint solver collaboration language of BALI. In *Frontiers of Combining Systems 2*, Vol. 7 of Studies in Logic and Computation. Research Studies Press/Wiley, 2000.
17. E. Ohlebusch. Modular properties of composable term rewriting systems. *Journal of Symbolic Computation*, 20(1), 1995.
18. C. Tinelli and C. Ringeissen. Unions of non-disjoint theories and combinations of satisfiability procedures. *Theoretical Computer Science*, 290(1):291–353, Jan. 2003.

Introducing ESRA, a Relational Language for Modelling Combinatorial Problems*

Pierre Flener, Justin Pearson, and Magnus Ågren**

Department of Information Technology
Uppsala University, Box 337, S – 751 05 Uppsala, Sweden
{pierref,justin,agren}@it.uu.se

Abstract. Current-generation constraint programming languages are considered by many, especially in industry, to be too low-level, difficult, and large. We argue that solver-independent, high-level relational constraint modelling leads to a simpler and smaller language, to more concise, intuitive, and analysable models, as well as to more efficient and effective model formulation, maintenance, reformulation, and verification. All this can be achieved without sacrificing the possibility of efficient solving, so that even time-pressed or less competent modellers can be well assisted. Towards this, we propose the ESRA relational constraint modelling language, showcase its elegance on some well-known problems, and outline a compilation philosophy for such languages.

1   Introduction

Current-generation constraint programming languages are considered by many, especially in industry, to be too low-level, difficult, and large. Consequently, their solvers are not in as widespread use as they ought to be, and constraint programming is still fairly unknown in many application domains, such as molecular biology. In order to unleash the proven powers of constraint technology and make it available to a wider range of problem modellers, a solver-independent, higher-level, simpler, and smaller modelling notation is needed.

In our opinion, even recent commercial languages such as OPL [31] do not go far enough in that direction. Many common modelling patterns have not been captured in special constructs. They have to be painstakingly spelled out each time, at a high risk for errors, often using low-level devices such as reification.

In recent years, modelling languages based on some logic with sets and relations have gained popularity in formal methods, witness the B [1] and Z [29] specification languages, the ALLOY [16] object modelling language, and the *Object Constraint Language* (OCL) [35] of the *Unified Modelling Language* (UML) [27]. In semantic data modelling this had been long advocated; most notably via entity-relationship-attribute (ERA) diagrams.

---

* A previous version of this paper appears pages 63–77 in the informally published proceedings of the *Second International Workshop Modelling and Reformulating CSPs*, available at http : //www − users.cs.york.ac.uk/~frisch/Reformulation/03/

** The authors' names are ordered according to the Swedish alphabet.

M. Bruynooghe (Ed.): LOPSTR 2004, LNCS 3018, pp. 214–232, 2004.

Sets and set expressions started appearing as modelling devices in some constraint languages. Set variables are often implemented by the set interval representation [13]. In the absence of such an explicit set concept, modellers usually painstakingly represent a set variable by its characteristic function, namely as a sequence of $0/1$ integer variables, as long as the size of the domain of the set.

Relations have not received much attention yet in constraint programming languages, except total functions, via arrays. Indeed, a total function f can be represented in many ways [15], say as a 1-dimensional array of variables over the range of f, indexed by its domain, or as a 2-dimensional array of Boolean variables, indexed by the domain and range of f, or as a 1-dimensional array of set variables over the domain of f, indexed by its range, or even with some redundancy. Other than retrieving the (unique) image under a total function of a domain element, there has been no support for relational expressions.

Matrix modelling [8, 10, 31] has been advocated as one way of capturing common modelling patterns. Alternatively, it has been argued [11, 15] that functions, and hence relations, should be supported by an abstract datatype (ADT). It is then *the compiler* that must (help the modeller) choose a suitable representation, say in a contemporary constraint programming language, for each instance of the ADT, using empirically or theoretically gained modelling insights.

We here demonstrate, as originally conjectured in [9], that a suitable first-order relational calculus is a good basis for a high-level, ADT-based, and solver-independent constraint modelling language. It gives rise to very natural and easy-to-maintain models of combinatorial problems. Even in the (temporary) absence of a corresponding high-level search language, this generality does not necessarily come at a loss in solving efficiency, as abstract relational models are devoid of representation details so that the results of analysis can be exploited.

Our aims here are only to justify and present our new language, called ESRA, to illustrate its elegance and the flexibility of its models by some examples, and to argue that it can be compiled into efficient models in lower-level (constraint programming) languages. The syntax, denotational semantics, and type system of the proposed language are discussed in full detail in an online appendix [12] and a second prototype of the advocated compiler is under development.

The rest of this paper is organised as follows. In Section 2, we present our relational language for modelling combinatorial problems and deploy it on three real-life problems before discussing its compilation. This allows us to list, in Section 3, the benefits of relational modelling. Finally, in Section 4, we conclude as well as discuss related and future work.

2   Relational Constraint Modelling with ESRA

In Section 2.1, we justify the design decisions behind our new ESRA constraint modelling language, targeted at constraint programmers. Then, in Section 2.2, we introduce its concepts, syntax, type system, and semantics. Next, in Section 2.3, we deploy ESRA on three real-life problems. Finally, in Section 2.4, we discuss the design of our prototype compilers for ESRA.

2.1 Design Decisions

The key design decisions for our new relational constraint modelling language —
called ESRA for *Executable Symbolism for Relational Algebra* — were as follows.

We want to capture common modelling idioms in a new abstract datatype
for relations, so as to design a high-level and simple language. The constructs of
the language are orthogonal, so as to keep the language small. Computational
completeness is not aimed at, as long as the language is useful for elegantly
modelling a large number of combinatorial problems.

We focus on *finite*, discrete domains. Relations are built from such domains
and sets are viewed as unary relations. Theoretical difficulties are sidestepped
by supporting only bounded quantification, but not negation nor sets of sets.

The language has an ASCII syntax, mimicking mathematical and logical
notation as closely as possible, as well as a LATEX-based syntax, especially used
for pretty-printing models in that notation.

2.2 Concepts, Syntax, Type System, and Semantics of ESRA

For reasons of space, we only give an informal semantics. The interested reader
is invited to consult [12] for a complete description of the language. Essentially,
the semantics of the language is a conservative extension of existential second-
order logic. Existential quantification of relations is used to assert that relations
are to be found that satisfy sets of first-order constraints. This is in contrast
with extensions of logic programming [6, 25] where second-order relations can
be specified recursively using Horn clauses, which needs a much more careful
treatment of the fixed-point semantics.

Code excerpts are here provided out of the semantic context of any particular
problem statement, just to illustrate the syntax, but a suggested reading in plain
English is always provided. In Section 2.3, we will actually start from plain
English problem statements and show how they can be modelled in ESRA. Code
excerpts are always given in the pretty-printed form, but we indicate the ASCII
notation for every symbol where it necessarily differs.

An ESRA model starts with a sequence of declarations of named *domains*
(or types) as well as named *constants* and *decision variables* that are tied to
domains. Then comes the *objective*, which is to find values for the decision variables within their domains so that some *constraints* are satisfied and possibly
some *cost expression* takes an optimal value.

The Type System. A *primitive domain* is a finite, extensionally given set of
new names or integers, comma-separated and enclosed as usual in curly braces.
An integer domain can also be given intensionally as a finite integer interval,
by separating its lower and upper bounds with '...' (denoted in ASCII by '..'),
without using curly braces. When these bounds coincide, the corresponding singleton domain $n \ldots n$ or $\{n\}$ can be abbreviated to n. Context always determines
whether an integer n designates itself or the singleton domain $\{n\}$. A domain
can also be given intensionally using set comprehension notation.

The only *predefined* primitive domains are the sets $\mathbb{N}$ (denoted in ASCII by 'nat') and $\mathbb{Z}$ (denoted in ASCII by 'int'), which are '0...sup' and 'inf...sup' respectively, where the predefined constant identifiers 'inf' and 'sup' stand for the smallest negative and largest positive representable integers respectively. *User-defined* primitive domains are declared after the 'dom' keyword and initialised at compile-time, using the '=' symbol, or at run-time, via a datafile, otherwise interactively.

Example 1. The statement

$$\text{dom } Varieties, Blocks$$

declares two domains called *Varieties* and *Blocks* that are to be initialised at run-time. As in OPL [31], this neatly separates the problem model from its instance data, so that the actual constraint satisfaction problem is obtained at run-time.

Similarly, the statement

$$\text{dom } Players = 1\ldots g*s, \ \ Weeks = 1\ldots w, \ \ Groups = 1\ldots g$$

where g, s, w are integer-constant identifiers (assumed previously declared, in a way shown below), declares integer domains called *Players*, *Weeks*, and *Groups* that are initialised at compile-time.

Finally, the declaration

$$\text{dom } Even = \{i \mid i : 0\ldots 100 \mid i \% 2 = 0\}$$

initialises the domain *Even* of all even natural numbers up to 100.

The usual binary infix $\times$ constructor (denoted in ASCII by '#') allows the construction of Cartesian products.

The only *constructed domains* are relational domains. In order to simultaneously capture frequently occurring multiplicity constraints on relations, we offer a parameterised binary infix $\times$ domain constructor. The relational domain $A \ ^{M_1}\times^{M_2} B$, where A and B are (possibly Cartesian products of) primitive domains, designates a set of binary relations in $A \times B$. The optional M_1 and M_2, called *multiplicities*, must be integer sets and have the following semantics: for every element a of A, the number of elements of B related to a must be in M_1, while for every element b of B, the number of elements of A related to b must be in M_2 [1]. An omitted multiplicity stands for $\mathbb{N}$.

Example 2. The constructed domain

$$Varieties \ ^r\times^k Blocks$$

designates the set of all relations in *Varieties* $\times$ *Blocks* where every variety occurs in exactly r blocks and every block contains exactly k varieties. These are two occurrences where an integer abbreviates the singleton domain containing it.

---

[1] Note that our syntax is the opposite of the UML one, say, where the multiplicities are written in the other order, with the *same* semantics. That convention can however *not* be usefully upgraded to Cartesian products of arity higher than 2.

In the absence of such facilities for relations and their multiplicities, a relational domain would have to be modelled using arrays, say. This may be a premature commitment to a concrete data structure, as the modeller may not know yet, especially prior to experimentation, which particular (array-based) representation of a relational decision variable will lead to the most efficient solving. The problem constraints, including the multiplicities, would have to be formulated in the constraints part of the model, based on the chosen representation. If the experiments revealed that another representation should be tried, then the modeller would have to first painstakingly reformulate the declaration of the decision variable as well as all its constraints. Our ADT view of relations overcomes this flaw: it is now *the compiler* that must (help the modeller) choose a suitable representation for each instance of the ADT by using empirically or theoretically gained insights. Also, multiplicities need not become counting constraints, but are succinctly and conveniently captured in the declaration.

We view sets as unary relations: $A\ M$, where A is a domain and M an integer set, constructs the domain of all subsets of A whose cardinality is in M. The multiplicity M is mandatory here; otherwise there would be ambiguity whether a value of the domain A is an element or an arbitrarily sized subset of A.

For total and partial functions, the left-hand multiplicity M_1 is $1\ldots 1$ and $0\ldots 1$ respectively. In order to dispense with these left-hand multiplicities for total and partial functions, we offer the usual $\longrightarrow$ and $\nrightarrow$ (denoted in ASCII by '->' and '+>') domain constructors respectively, as shorthands. They may still have right-hand multiplicities though.

For injections, surjections, and bijections, the right-hand multiplicity M_2 is $0\ldots 1$, $1\ldots\text{sup}$, and $1\ldots 1$ respectively. Rather than elevating these particular cases of functions to first-class concepts with an invented specific syntax in ESRA, we prefer keeping our language lean and close to mathematical notation.

Example 3. The constructed domain

$$(Players \times Weeks) \longrightarrow^{s*w} Groups$$

designates the set of all total functions from *Players* × *Weeks* into *Groups* such that every group is related to exactly sw (player,week) pairs.

We provide no support (yet) for bags and sequences, as relations provide enough challenges for the time being. Note that a *bag* can be modelled as a total function from its domain into $\mathbb{N}$, giving the repetition count of each element. Similarly, a *sequence* of length n can be modelled as a total function from $1\ldots n$ into its domain, telling which element is at each position. This does *not* mean that the representation of bags and sequences is fixed (to the one of total functions), because, as we shall see in Section 2.4, the various relations (and thus total functions) of a model need not have the same representation.

Modelling the Instance Data and Decision Variables. All identifier declarations are strongly typed and denote variables that are implicitly universally quantified over the entire model, with the constants expected to be ground before search begins while the decision variables can still be unbound at that moment.

Like the user-defined primitive domains, constants help describe the instance data of a problem. A constant identifier is declared after the 'cst' keyword and is tied to its domain by ':', meaning set membership. Constants are initialised at compile-time, using the '=' symbol, or at run-time, via a datafile, otherwise interactively. Again, run-time initialisation provides a neat separation of problem models and problem instances.

Example 4. The statement

$$\text{cst } r, k, \lambda : \mathbb{N}$$

declares three natural number constants that are to be initialised at run-time.

As already seen in Examples 2 and 3, the availability of total functions makes arrays unnecessary. The statement

$$\text{cst } CrewSize : Guests \longrightarrow \mathbb{N}, \; SpareCap : Hosts \longrightarrow \mathbb{N}$$

declares two natural-number functions, to be provided at run-time.

A decision-variable identifier is declared after the 'var' keyword and is tied to its domain by ':'.

Example 5. The statement

$$\text{var } BIBD : Varieties \; {}^r\times{}^k \; Blocks$$

declares a relation called *BIBD* of the domain of Example 2.

Modelling the Cost Expression and the Constraints. *Expressions* and first-order logic *formulas* are constructed in the usual way.

For *numeric expressions*, the arguments are either integers or identifiers of the domain $\mathbb{N}$ or $\mathbb{Z}$, including the predefined constants 'inf' and 'sup'. Usual unary ($-$, 'abs' for absolute value, and 'card' for the cardinality of a set expression), binary infix ($+$, $-$, $*$, $/$ for integer quotient, and $\%$ for integer remainder), and aggregate ($\sum$, denoted in ASCII by 'sum') arithmetic operators are available. A sum is indexed by local variables ranging over finite sets, which may be filtered on-the-fly by a condition given after the '|' symbol (read 'such that').

Sets obey the same rules as domains. So, for *set expressions*, the arguments are either set identifiers or (intensionally or extensionally) given sets, including the predefined sets $\mathbb{N}$ and $\mathbb{Z}$. Only the (unparameterised) binary infix domain constructor $\times$ and its specialisations $\longrightarrow$ and $\nrightarrow$ are available as operators.

Finally *function expressions* are built by applying a function identifier to an argument tuple. We have found no use yet for any other operators on functions (but see the discussion of future work in Section 4).

Example 6. The numeric expression

$$\sum_{g:Guests \;|\; Schedule(g,p)=h} CrewSize(g)$$

denotes the sum of the crew sizes of all the guest boats that are scheduled to visit host h at period p, assuming this expression is within the scope of the local variables h and p. The nested function expression $CrewSize(g)$ stands for the size of the crew of guest g, which is a natural number according to Example 4.

Atoms are built from numeric expressions with the usual comparison predicates, such as the binary infix $=$, $\neq$, and $\leq$ (denoted in ASCII by '=', '!=', and '=<' respectively). Atoms also include the predefined 'true' and 'false', as well as references to the elements of a relation. We have found no use yet for any other predicates. Note that '$\in$' is unnecessary as $x \in S$ is equivalent to $S(x)$.

Example 7. The atom $BIBD(v_1, i)$ stands for the truth value of variety v_1 being related to block i in the $BIBD$ relation of Example 5.

Formulas are built from atoms. The usual binary infix connectives ($\wedge$, $\vee$, $\Rightarrow$, $\Leftarrow$, and $\Leftrightarrow$, denoted in ASCII by '/\', '\/', '=>', '<=', and '<=>' respectively) and quantifiers ($\forall$ and $\exists$, denoted in ASCII by `forall` and `exists` respectively) are available. A quantified formula is indexed by local variables ranging over finite sets, which may be filtered on-the-fly by a condition given after the '|' symbol (read 'such that'). As we provide a rich (enough) set of predicates, we are only interested in models that can be formulated positively, and thus dispense with the negation connective. The usual typing and precedence rules for operators and connectives apply. All binary operators associate to the left.

Example 8. The formula

$$\forall(p : Periods,\ h : Hosts) \left(\sum_{g:Guests\ |\ Schedule(g,p)=h} CrewSize(g) \right) \leq SpareCap(h)$$

constrains the spare capacity of any host boat h not to be exceeded at any period p by the sum of the crew sizes of all the guest boats that are scheduled to visit host h at period p.

A generalisation of the $\exists$ quantifier turns out to be very useful. We define

$$\text{count}(Multiplicity)(x : Set\ |\ Condition)$$

to hold if and only if the cardinality of the set comprehension $\{x : Set | Condition\}$ is in the integer set *Multiplicity*. So

$$\exists(x : Set\ |\ Condition)$$

is actually syntactic sugar for

$$\text{count}(1 \ldots \sup)(x : Set\ |\ Condition)$$

Example 9. The formula

$$\forall(v_1 < v_2 : Varieties)\ \text{count}(\lambda)(j : Blocks\ |\ BIBD(v_1, j) \wedge BIBD(v_2, j))$$

says that each ordered pair of varieties v_1 and v_2 occurs together in exactly λ blocks, via the *BIBD* relation. Regarding the excerpt '$v_1 < v_2 : Varieties$', note that multiple local variables can be quantified at the same time, and that a filtering condition on them may then be pushed across the '|' symbol.

Example 10. Assuming that the function *Schedule* is of the domain of Example 3 and thus returns a group, the formula

$$\forall(p_1 < p_2 : Players)\ \text{count}(0 \ldots 1)(v : Weeks \mid Schedule(p_1, v) = Schedule(p_2, v))$$

says that there is at most one week where any ordered pair of players p_1 and p_2 is scheduled to play in the same group.

A *cost expression* is a numeric expression that has to be optimised. The *constraints* on the decision variables of a model are a conjunction of formulas, using $\wedge$ as the connective. The *objective* of a model is either to solve its constraints:

solve Constraints

or to minimise the value of its cost expression subject to its constraints:

minimise CostExpression such that Constraints

or similarly for maximising. A *model* consists of a sequence of domain, constant, and decision-variable declarations followed by an objective, without separators.

Example 11. Putting together code fragments from Examples 1, 4, 5, and 9, we obtain the model of Figure 2 two pages ahead, discussed in Section 2.3.

The grammar of ESRA is described in Figure 1. For brevity and ease of reading, we have omitted most syntactic-sugar options as well as the rules for identifiers, names, and numbers. The notation $\langle nt \rangle^{s^*}$ stands for a sequence of zero or more occurrences of the non-terminal $\langle nt \rangle$, separated by symbol s. Similarly, $\langle nt \rangle^{s^+}$ stands for one or more occurrences of $\langle nt \rangle$, separated by s. The typing rules ensure that the equality predicates $=$ and $\neq$ are only applied to expressions of the same type, that the other comparison predicates, such as $\leq$, are only applied to numeric expressions, and so on.

2.3   Examples

We now showcase the elegance and flexibility of our language on three real-life problems, namely Balanced Incomplete Block Designs, the Social Golfers problem, and the Progressive Party problem.

Balanced Incomplete Block Designs. Let V be any set of v elements, called *varieties*. A *balanced incomplete block design* (BIBD) is a bag of b subsets of V, called *blocks*, each of size k (constraint C_1), such that each pair of distinct

⟨*Model*⟩ ::= ⟨*Decl*⟩$^+$ ⟨*Objective*⟩

⟨*Decl*⟩ ::= ⟨*DomDecl*⟩ | ⟨*CstDecl*⟩ | ⟨*VarDecl*⟩

⟨*DomDecl*⟩ ::= dom ⟨*Id*⟩ [= ⟨*Set*⟩]

⟨*CstDecl*⟩ ::= cst ⟨*Id*⟩ [= ⟨*Tuple*⟩ | ⟨*Set*⟩] : ⟨*SetExpr*⟩

⟨*VarDecl*⟩ ::= var ⟨*Id*⟩ : ⟨*SetExpr*⟩

⟨*Objective*⟩ ::= solve ⟨*Formula*⟩
         | (minimise | maximise) ⟨*NumExpr*⟩ such that ⟨*Formula*⟩

⟨*Expr*⟩ ::= ⟨*Id*⟩ | ⟨*Name*⟩ | ⟨*Tuple*⟩ | ⟨*NumExpr*⟩ | ⟨*SetExpr*⟩ | ⟨*FuncAppl*⟩ | (⟨*Expr*⟩)

⟨*NumExpr*⟩ ::= ⟨*Id*⟩ | ⟨*Int*⟩ | ⟨*Nat*⟩ | inf | sup | ⟨*FuncAppl*⟩
        | ⟨*NumExpr*⟩ (+ | - | * | / | %) ⟨*NumExpr*⟩
        | (- | abs) ⟨*NumExpr*⟩
        | card ⟨*SetExpr*⟩
        | sum (⟨*QuantExpr*⟩) (⟨*NumExpr*⟩)

⟨*SetExpr*⟩ ::= ⟨*Set*⟩ | ⟨*SetExpr*⟩ [⟨*Set*⟩]
        | ⟨*SetExpr*⟩ ([[⟨*Set*⟩]#[⟨*Set*⟩]] | #) ⟨*SetExpr*⟩
        | ⟨*SetExpr*⟩ ([->[⟨*Set*⟩]] | -> | [+>[⟨*Set*⟩]] | +>) ⟨*SetExpr*⟩

⟨*Set*⟩ ::= ⟨*Id*⟩ | int | nat
        | { ⟨*Tuple*⟩,* } | { ⟨*ComprExpr*⟩ }
        | ⟨*NumExpr*⟩..⟨*NumExpr*⟩ | ⟨*NumExpr*⟩

⟨*ComprExpr*⟩ ::= ⟨*Expr*⟩ | (⟨*IdTuple*⟩$^{\&+}$ in ⟨*SetExpr*⟩)$^{/\backslash+}$ [| ⟨*Formula*⟩]

⟨*FuncAppl*⟩ ::= ⟨*Id*⟩ ⟨*Tuple*⟩

⟨*Tuple*⟩ ::= (⟨*Expr*⟩,$^+$) | ⟨*Expr*⟩

⟨*Formula*⟩ ::= true | false | ⟨*RelAppl*⟩
        | ⟨*Formula*⟩ (/\ | \/ | => | <= | <=>) ⟨*Formula*⟩
        | ⟨*NumExpr*⟩ (< | =< | = | >= | > | !=) ⟨*NumExpr*⟩
        | forall (⟨*QuantExpr*⟩) (⟨*Formula*⟩)
        | count (⟨*Set*⟩) (⟨*QuantExpr*⟩)

⟨*RelAppl*⟩ ::= ⟨*Id*⟩ ⟨*Tuple*⟩

⟨*QuantExpr*⟩ ::= ((⟨*RelQvars*⟩ | ⟨*IdTuple*⟩$^{\&+}$) in ⟨*SetExpr*⟩),$^+$ [| ⟨*Formula*⟩]

⟨*RelQvars*⟩ ::= ⟨*Expr*⟩ (< | =< | = | >= | > | !=) ⟨*Expr*⟩

⟨*IdTuple*⟩ ::= ⟨*Id*⟩ | (⟨*Id*⟩,$^+$)

Fig. 1. The grammar of ESRA

varieties occurs together in exactly λ blocks (C_2), with $2 \leq k < v$. An implied constraint is that each variety occurs in the same number of blocks (C_3), namely $r = \lambda(v - 1)/(k - 1)$. A BIBD is parameterised by a 5-tuple $\langle v, b, r, k, \lambda \rangle$ of

dom *Varieties*, *Blocks*
cst $r, k, \lambda : \mathbb{N}$
var *BIBD* : *Varieties* $^r \times^k$ *Blocks*
solve
    $\forall(v_1 < v_2 : Varieties) \; \text{count}(\lambda)(j : Blocks \mid BIBD(v_1, j) \wedge BIBD(v_2, j))$

Fig. 2. A pretty-printed ESRA model for BIBDs

```
dom Varieties, Blocks
cst r, k, lambda : nat
var BIBD : Varieties [r#k] Blocks
solve
    forall (v1 < v2 : Varieties)
       count (lambda) (j : Blocks | BIBD(v1,j) /\ BIBD(v2,j))
```

Fig. 3. An ESRA model for BIBDs

parameters. Originally intended for the design of statistical experiments, BIBDs also have applications in cryptography and other domains. See Problem 28 at http://www.csplib.org for more information.

    The instance data can be declared as the two domains *Varieties* and *Blocks*, of implicit sizes v and b respectively, as well as the three natural-number constants r, k, and λ, as in Examples 1 and 4. A unique relational decision variable, *BIBD*, can then be declared as in Example 5, thereby immediately taking care of the constraints C_1 and C_3. The remaining constraint C_2 can be modelled as in Example 9. Figure 2 shows the resulting pretty-printed ESRA model, while Figure 3 shows it in ASCII notation.

    For comparison, an OPL [31] model is shown in Figure 4, where '= ...' means that the value is to be found in a corresponding datafile. The decision variable BIBD is a 2-dimensional array of integers 0 or 1, indexed by the varieties and blocks, such that BIBD[i,j] = 1 iff variety i is contained in block j. Furthermore, the constraints C_1 and C_3, which we could capture by multiplicities in the ESRA model, need here to be stated in more length. Finally, the constraint C_2 is stated using a higher-order constraint[2]: for each ordered pair of varieties v1 and v2, the number of times they appear in the same block, that is the number of blocks j where BIBD(v1,j) = 1 = BIBD(v2,j) holds, must equal lambda.

    In an OPL model, one needs to decide what concrete datatypes to use for representing the abstract decision variables of the original problem statement. In this case, we chose a 2-dimensional 0/1 array BIBD, indexed by Varieties and Blocks. We could just as well have chosen a different representation, say (if OPL had set variables) a 1-dimensional array BIBD, indexed by Blocks, of subsets of Varieties. Such a choice affects the formulation of every constraint and the cost expression, but is premature as even expert intuition is weak in predicting which representation choice leads to the best solving efficiency. Consequently, the modeller has to frequently reformulate the constraints and the cost expression

---

[2] A higher-order constraint refers to the truth value of another constraint. In OPL, the latter is nested in parentheses, truth is represented by 1, and falsity by 0.

```
enum Varieties = ..., Blocks = ...;
int r = ...; int k = ...; int lambda = ...;
range Boolean 0..1;
var Boolean BIBD[Varieties,Blocks];
solve {
    forall(j in Blocks) sum(i in Varieties) BIBD[i,j] = k;
    forall(i in Varieties) sum(j in Blocks) BIBD[i,j] = r;
    forall(ordered v1,v2 in Varieties)
      sum(j in Blocks) (BIBD[v1,j] = 1 = BIBD[v2,j]) = lambda;
    ... symmetry-breaking code ...
};
```

Fig. 4. An OPL model for BIBDs

while experimenting with different representations. No such choices have to be made in an ESRA model, making ESRA a more convenient modelling language.

As a consequence to such representation choices, one often introduces an astronomical amount of symmetries into an OPL model that are not present in the original problem statement [10]. For example, given a solution, any two rows or columns in the array BIBD can be swapped, giving a different, but symmetrically equivalent, solution. Such symmetries need to be addressed in order to achieve efficient solving. Hence, symmetry-breaking code [10, 32] would have to be inserted, as indicated in Figure 4. Since such choices are postponed to the compilation phase in ESRA (see Section 2.4), any symmetries consciously introduced can be handled (automatically) in that process.

The Social Golfers Problem. In a golf club, there are n players, each of whom plays golf once a week (constraint C_1) and always in g groups of size s (C_2), hence $n = gs$. The objective is to determine whether there is a schedule of w weeks of play for these golfers, such that there is at most one week where any two distinct players are scheduled to play in the same group (C_3). An implied constraint is that every group occurs exactly sw times across the schedule (C_4). See Problem 10 at http://www.csplib.org for more information.

The instance data can be declared as the three natural-number constants g, s, and w, via 'cst $g, s, w : \mathbb{N}$', as well as the three domains *Players*, *Weeks*, and *Blocks*, as in Example 1. A unique decision variable, *Schedule*, can then be declared using the functional domain in Example 3, thereby immediately taking care of the constraints C_1 (because of the totality of the function) and C_4. The constraint C_3 can be modelled as in Example 10. The constraint C_2 can be stated using the count quantifier, as seen in the pretty-printed ESRA model of Figure 5.

Note the different style of modelling sets of unnamed objects, via the separation of models from the instance data, compared to Figure 2. There we introduce two sets without initialising them at the model level, while here we introduce three uninitialised constants that are then used to arbitrarily initialise three domains of desired cardinalities. Both models can be reformulated in the other style. The benefit of such sets of unnamed objects is that their elements are indistinguishable, so that lower-level representations of relational decision variables whose domains involve such sets are known to introduce symmetries.

cst $g, s, w : \mathbb{N}$
dom $Players = 1 \ldots g * s$, $Weeks = 1 \ldots w$, $Groups = 1 \ldots g$
var $Schedule : (Players \times Weeks) \xrightarrow{s*w} Groups$
solve

$\forall(p_1 < p_2 : Players)$ count$(0 \ldots 1)(v : Weeks \mid Schedule(p_1, v) = Schedule(p_2, v))$
$\land \; \forall(h : Groups, v : Weeks)$ count$(s)(p : Players \mid Schedule(p, v) = h)$

Fig. 5. A pretty-printed ESRA model for the Social Golfers problem

dom $Guests, Hosts, Periods$
cst $SpareCap : Hosts \longrightarrow \mathbb{N}$, $CrewSize : Guests \longrightarrow \mathbb{N}$
var $Schedule : (Guests \times Periods) \longrightarrow Hosts$
solve

$$\forall(p : Periods, \; h : Hosts) \left(\sum_{g:Guests \;\mid\; Schedule(g,p)=h} CrewSize(g) \right) \leq SpareCap(h)$$
$\land \; \forall(g : Guests, h : Hosts)$ count$(0 \ldots 1)(p : Periods \mid Schedule(g, p) = h)$
$\land \; \forall(g_1 < g_2 : Guests)$ count$(0 \ldots 1)(p : Periods \mid Schedule(g_1, p) = Schedule(g_2, p))$

Fig. 6. A pretty-printed ESRA model for the Progressive Party problem

The Progressive Party Problem. The problem is to timetable a party at a yacht club. Certain boats are designated as hosts, while the crews of the remaining boats are designated as guests. The crew of a host boat remains on board throughout the party to act as hosts, while the crew of a guest boat together visits host boats over a number of periods. The spare capacity of any host boat is not to be exceeded at any period by the sum of the crew sizes of all the guest boats that are scheduled to visit it then (constraint C_1). Any guest crew can visit any host boat in at most one period (C_2). Any two distinct guest crews can visit the same host boat in at most one period (C_3). See Problem 13 at http://www.csplib.org for more information.

The instance data can be declared as the three domains $Guests$, $Hosts$, and $Periods$, via 'dom $Guests, Hosts, Periods$', as well as the two functional constants $SpareCap$ and $CrewSize$, as in Example 4. A unique functional decision variable, $Schedule$, can then be declared via 'var $Schedule : (Guests \times Periods) \longrightarrow Hosts$'. The constraint C_1 can now be modelled as in Example 8. The constraints C_2 and C_3 can be stated using the count quantifier, as seen in the pretty-printed ESRA model of Figure 6.

2.4 Compiling Relational Models

A compiler for ESRA is currently under development. It is being written in OCAML (http://www.ocaml.org) and compiles ESRA models into SICStus Prolog [5] finite-domain constraint programs. Our choice of target language is motivated by its excellent collection of global constraints and by our collaboration with its developers on designing new global constraints.

We already have an ESRA-to-OPL compiler [36, 15], written in Java, for a restriction of ESRA to functions, now called Functional-ESRA. That project gave us much of the expertise needed for developing the current compiler.

The solver-independent ESRA language is so high-level that it is very small compared to such target languages, especially in the number of necessary primitive constraints. The full panoply of features of such target languages can, and must, be deployed during compilation. In particular, the implementation of decision-variable indices into matrices is well-understood.

In order to bootstrap our new compiler quickly, we decided to represent initially *every* relational decision variable by a matrix of 0/1 variables, indexed by its participating sets. This first version of the new compiler is thus deterministic.

The plan is then to add alternatives to this unique representation rule, depending on the multiplicities and other constraints on the relation, achieving a *non-deterministic compiler*, such as our existing Functional-ESRA-to-OPL compiler [36, 15]. The modeller is then invited to experiment with her (real-life) instance data and the resulting compiled programs, so as to determine which one is the 'best'. If the compiler is provided with those instance data, then it can be extended to automate such experiments and generate rankings.

Eventually, more intelligence will be built into the compiler via *heuristics* (such as those of [15]) for the compiler to rank the resulting compiled programs by decreasing likelihood of efficiency, without any recourse to experiments. Indeed, depending on the multiplicities and other constraints on a relation, certain representations thereof can be shown to be better than others, under certain assumptions on the targeted solver, and this either theoretically (see for instance [33] for bijections and [15] for injections) or empirically (see for instance [28] for bijections). We envisage a hybrid interactive/heuristic compiler.

Our ultimate aim is of course to design an actual *solver for relational constraints*, without going through compilation.

3   Benefits of Relational Modelling

In our experience, and as demonstrated in Section 2.3, a relational constraint modelling language leads to more *concise and intuitive models*, as well as to more *efficient and effective model formulation and verification*. Due to ESRA being *smaller* than conventional constraint programming languages, we believe it is easier to learn and master, making it a good candidate for a teaching medium. All this could entail a better dissemination of constraint technology.

Relational languages seem a good trade-off between generality and specificity, enabling *efficient solving* despite more generality. Relations are a *single*, powerful concept for elegantly modelling many aspects of combinatorial problems. Also, there are *not too many* different, and even *standard*, ways of representing relations and relational expressions. Known and future modelling insights, such as those in [15, 28, 33], can be built into the compilers, so that even time-pressed or less competent modellers can benefit from them. Modelling is unencumbered by early if not uninformed commitments to representation choices. Low-level modelling devices such as reification and higher-order constraints can be encapsulated as implementation devices. The number of decision variables being reduced, there is even hope that directly solving the constraints at the high relational level can be faster than solving their compiled lower-level counterparts. All this illustrates that more generality need not mean poorer performance.

Relational models are more amenable to *maintenance* when the combinatorial problem changes, because most of the tedium is taken care of by the compiler. Model maintenance at the relational level reduces to adapting to the new problem, with all representation (and solving) issues left to the compiler. Very little work is involved here when a multiplicity change entails a preferable representation change for a relation. Maintenance can even be necessary when the statistical distribution of the problem instances that are to be solved changes [22]. If information on the new distribution is given to the envisaged compiler, a simple recompilation will take care of the maintenance.

Relational models are at a more suitable level for possibly automated model *reformulation*, such as via the inference and selection of suitable *implied constraints*, with again the compiler assisting in the more mundane aspects. In the BIBD and Social Golfers examples, we have observed that multiplicities provide a nice framework for discovering and stating some implied constraints. Indeed, the language makes the modeller think about making these multiplicities explicit, even if they were not in the original problem formulation.

Relational models are more amenable to *constraint analysis*. Detected properties as well as properties consciously introduced during compilation into lower-level programs, such as symmetry or bijectiveness, can then be taken into account during compilation [10], especially using tractability results [32].

There would be further benefits to an abstract modelling language if it were adopted as a *standard front-end language* for solvers. Models and instance data would then be *solver-independent* and could be shared between solvers, whatever their technology. Indeed, the targeted solvers need not even use constraint technology, but could just as well use answer-set programming, linear programming, local search, or propositional satisfiability technology, or any hybrid thereof. This would facilitate fair and homogeneous comparisons, say via new standard benchmarks, as well as foster competition in fine-tuning the compilers.

4   Conclusion

We have argued that solver-independent, abstract constraint modelling leads to a simpler and smaller language; to more concise, intuitive, and analysable models; as well as to more efficient and effective model formulation, maintenance, reformulation, and verification. All this can be achieved without sacrificing the possibility of efficient solving, so that even time-pressed or less competent modellers can be well assisted. Towards this, we have proposed the ESRA relational modelling language, showcased its elegance on some well-known problems, and outlined a compilation philosophy for such languages. To conclude, let us look at related work (Section 4.1) and future work (Section 4.2).

4.1   Related Work

We have here generalised and re-engineered our own work [11, 36, 15] on a pre-decessor of ESRA, now called Functional-ESRA, that only supports functional decision variables, by pursuing the aim of relational modelling outlined in [9]. Elsewhere, such ideas have recently inspired a related project [3], incorporating partition decision variables. Constraints for bag decision variables [2, 7, 34] and sequence decision variables [2, 26] have also been proposed.

This research owes a lot to previous work on relational modelling in formal methods and on ERA-style semantic data modelling, especially to the ALLOY object modelling language [16], which itself gained much from the Z specification notation [29] (and learned from UML/OCL how not to do it). Contrary to ERA modelling, we do not distinguish between attributes and relations.

In constraint programming, the commercial OPL [31] stands out as a medium-level modelling language and actually gave the impetus to design ESRA: see the BIBD example in Section 2.3 and consult [9] for a further comparison of elegant ESRA models with more awkward (published) OPL counterparts that do not provide all the benefits of Section 3. Other higher-level constraint modelling languages than ESRA have been proposed, such as ALICE [18], $CLP(Fun(D))$ [14], CLPS [2], CONJUNTO [13], EACL [30], $\{log\}$ [7], NCL [37], and the language of [24]. Our ESRA shares with them the quest for a practical declarative modelling language based on a strongly-typed fuller first-order logic than Horn clauses, with sequence, set, bag, functional, or even relational decision variables, while often dispensing with recursion, negation, and unbounded quantification. However, ESRA goes way beyond them, by advocating an ADT view (of relations), so that representations need not be fixed in advance, by providing an elegant notation for multiplicity constraints, and by promising intelligent compilation.

In the field of knowledge representation, answer-set programming (ASP) has recently been advocated [21] as a practical constraint solving paradigm, especially for dynamic domains such as planning. A set of (disjunctive) function-free clauses, where classical negation and negation as failure are allowed, is interpreted as a constraint, stating when an atom is in a solution, called an answer set or a stable model. This non-monotonic approach differs from constraint (logic) programming, where statements are used to add atomic constraints on decision variables to a constraint store, whereupon propagation and search are used to construct solutions. Implementation methods for computing the answer sets of ground programs have advanced significantly over recent years, possibly using propositional satisfiability (SAT) solvers. Also, effective grounding procedures have been devised for some classes of such programs with (schematic) variables. Sample ASP systems are DLV [19] and SMODELS [23]. Closely related are *ConstraintLingo* [8] and NP-SPEC [4]. The languages of these systems include useful features, such as cardinality and weight constraints, aggregate functions, and soft constraints. They have strictly more expressive power than propositional logic and traditional constraint (logic) programming/modelling languages, including ESRA. Again, our objective only is a language that is useful for elegantly modelling a large number of combinatorial problems. The cardinality constraint

dom *Cities*
cst *Distance* : (*Cities* × *Cities*) $\longrightarrow \mathbb{N}$
var *Next* : *Cities* $\longrightarrow^1$ *Cities*
minimise $\sum_{c:Cities}$ *Distance*(*c*, *Next*(*c*))
such that $\forall(c_1 \& c_2 : Cities)$ *Next*$^*(c_1) = c_2$

Fig. 7. A pretty-printed ESRA model for the Travelling Salesperson problem

of SMODELS is a restriction of the ESRA 'count' quantifier to interval multiplicities, as opposed to set multiplicities. Speed comparisons with SAT solvers were encouraging, but no comparison has been done yet with constraint solvers.

4.2 Future Work

Most of our future work has already been listed in Sections 2.4 and 3 about the compiler design and long-term benefits of relational modelling, such as the generation of implied constraints and the breaking of symmetries.

We have argued that our ESRA language is very small. This is mostly because we have not yet identified the need for any other operators or predicates. An exception to this is the need for *transitive closure relation constructors*. We aim at modelling the well-known Travelling Salesperson (TSP) problem as in Figure 7, where the transitive closure of the bijection *Next* on *Cities* is denoted by *Next**. This general mechanism avoids the introduction of an *ad hoc* 'circuit' constraint as in ALICE [18].

As we do not aim at a complete constraint modelling language, we can be very conservative in what missing features shall be added to ESRA when they are identified. Also, for manpower reasons, we do not yet propose other ADTs, say for bags or sequences, although this was originally part of our original vision (see Section 3.3 of [11]).

Our request for explicit model-level distinction between constants and decision variables may be eventually lifted, as the default is run-time initialisation: we could treat as constants any universally quantified variable that was actually initialised and treat all the others as decision variables. This requires a convincing example, though, as well as just-in-time compilation.

In [20], a type system is derived for binary relations that can be used as an input to specialised filtering algorithms. This kind of analysis can be integrated into the *relational solver* we have in mind.

Also, a *graphical language* could be developed for the data modelling, including the multiplicity constraints on relations, so that only the cost expression and the constraints would need to be textually expressed.

Finally, a *search language*, such as SALSA [17] or the one of OPL [31], but at the level of relational modelling, should be adjoined to the constraint modelling language proposed here, so that more expert modellers can express their own search heuristics.

Acknowledgements

This work is partially supported by grant 221-99-369 of VR, the Swedish Research Council, and by institutional grant IG2001-67 of STINT, the Swedish Foundation for International Cooperation in Research and Higher Education. We thank Nicolas Beldiceanu, Mats Carlsson, Esra Erdem, Brahim Hnich, Daniel Jackson, Zeynep Kızıltan, François Laburthe, Gerrit Renker, Christian Schulte, Mark Wallace, and Simon Wrang for stimulating discussions, as well as the constructive reviewers of previous versions of this paper.

References

1. J.-R. Abrial. *The B-Book: Assigning Programs to Meanings.* Cambridge University Press, 1996.
2. F. Ambert, B. Legeard, and E. Legros. Programmation en logique avec contraintes sur ensembles et multi-ensembles héréditairement finis. *Techniques et Sciences Informatiques*, 15(3):297–328, 1996.
3. A. Bakewell, A. M. Frisch, and I. Miguel. Towards automatic modelling of constraint satisfaction problems: A system based on compositional refinement. In *Proceedings of the 2nd International Workshop on Modelling and Reformulating CSPs*, pages 3–17, 2003. Available at http://www-users.cs.york.ac.uk/~frisch/Reformulation/03/.
4. M. Cadoli, L. Palopoli, A. Schaerf, and D. Vasile. NPSPEC: An executable specification language for solving all problems in NP. In G. Gupta, editor, *Proceedings of PADL'99*, volume 1551 of *LNCS*, pages 16–30. Springer-Verlag, 1999.
5. M. Carlsson, G. Ottosson, and B. Carlson. An open-ended finite domain constraint solver. In H. Glaser, P. Hartel, and H. Kuchen, editors, *Proceedings of PLILP'97*, number 1292 in LNCS, pages 191–206. Springer-Verlag, 1997.
6. M. Denecker, N. Pelov, and M. Bruynooghe. Ultimate well-founded and stable semantics for logic programs with aggregates. In *Proceedings of ICLP'01*, volume 2237 of *LNCS*, pages 212–226. Springer-Verlag, 2001.
7. A. Dovier, C. Piazza, E. Pontelli, and G. Rossi. Sets and constraint logic programming. *ACM Transactions on Programming Languages and Systems*, 22(5):861–931, 2000.
8. R. Finkel, V. Marek, and M. Truszczyński. Tabular constraint-satisfaction problems and answer-set programming. In *Proceedings of the AAAI Spring Symposium on Answer-Set Programming*, 2001. Available at http://www.cs.nmsu.edu/~tson/ASP2001/.
9. P. Flener. Towards relational modelling of combinatorial optimisation problems. In C. Bessière, editor, *Proceedings of the IJCAI'01 Workshop on Modelling and Solving Problems with Constraints*, pages 31–38, 2001. Available at http://www.lirmm.fr/~bessiere/ws_ijcai01/.
10. P. Flener, A. M. Frisch, B. Hnich, Z. Kızıltan, I. Miguel, and T. Walsh. Matrix modelling: Exploiting common patterns in constraint programming. In *Proc. of the 1st Int'l Workshop on Reformulating CSPs*, pages 27–41, 2002. Available at http://www-users.cs.york.ac.uk/~frisch/Reformulation/02/.
11. P. Flener, B. Hnich, and Z. Kızıltan. Compiling high-level type constructors in constraint programming. In I. Ramakrishnan, editor, *Proceedings of PADL'01*, volume 1990 of *LNCS*, pages 229–244. Springer-Verlag, 2001.

12. P. Flener, J. Pearson, and M. Ågren. The Syntax, Semantics, and Type System of esra. Technical report, ASTRA group, April 2003. Available at `http://www.it.uu.se/research/group/astra/`.

13. C. Gervet. Interval propagation to reason about sets: Definition and implementation of a practical language. *Constraints*, 1(3):191–244, 1997.

14. T. J. Hickey. Functional constraints in CLP languages. In F. Benhamou and A. Colmerauer, editors, *Constraint Logic Programming: Selected Research*, pages 355–381. The MIT Press, 1993.

15. B. Hnich. *Function Variables for Constraint Programming*. PhD thesis, Department of Information Science, Uppsala University, Sweden, 2003. Available at `http://publications.uu.se/theses/`.

16. D. Jackson, I. Shlyakhter, and M. Sridharan. A micromodularity mechanism. *Software Engineering Notes*, 26(5):62–73, 2001. Proceedings of FSE/ESEC'01.

17. F. Laburthe and Y. Caseau. SALSA: A language for search algorithms. *Constraints*, 7:255–288, 2002.

18. J.-L. Laurière. A language and a program for stating and solving combinatorial problems. *Artificial Intelligence*, 10(1):29–127, 1978.

19. N. Leone, G. Pfeifer, W. Faber, T. Eiter, G. Gottlob, S. Perri, and F. Scarcello. The DLV system for knowledge representation and reasoning. In *ACM Transactions on Computational Logic*, forthcoming. Available at `http://arxiv.org/ps/cs.AI/0211004`.

20. D. Lesaint. Inferring constraint types in constraint programming. In P. Van Hentenryck, editor, *Proceedings of CP'02*, volume 2470 of *LNCS*, pages 492–507. Springer-Verlag, 2002.

21. V. Lifschitz. Answer set programming and plan generation. *Artificial Intelligence*, 138:39–54, 2002.

22. S. Minton. Automatically configuring constraint satisfaction programs: A case study. *Constraints*, 1(1–2):7–43, 1996.

23. I. Niemelä. Logic programs with stable model semantics as a constraint programming paradigm. *Annals of Mathematics and AI*, 25(3–4):241–273, 1999.

24. N. Pelov and M. Bruynooghe. Extending constraint logic programming with open functions. In *Proceedings of PPDP'00*, pages 235–244. ACM Press, 2000.

25. N. Pelov, M. Denecker, and M. Bruynooghe. Partial stable models for logic programs with aggregates. In *Proceedings of LPNMR'04*, volume 2923 of *LNCS*, pages 207–219. Springer-Verlag, 2004.

26. G. Pesant. A regular language membership constraint for sequences of variables. In *Proceedings of the 2nd International Workshop on Modelling and Reformulating CSPs*, pages 110–119, 2003. Available at `http://www-users.cs.york.ac.uk/~frisch/Reformulation/03/`.

27. J. Rumbaugh, I. Jacobson, and G. Booch. *The Unified Modeling Language Reference Manual*. Addison-Wesley, 1999.

28. B. M. Smith. Modelling a permutation problem. Technical Report 18, School of Computing, University of Leeds, UK, 2000. Also in *Proceedings of the ECAI'00 Workshop on Modelling and Solving Problems with Constraints*.

29. J. M. Spivey. *The Z Notation: A Reference Manual*. Prentice Hall, second edition, 1992.

30. E. Tsang, P. Mills, R. Williams, J. Ford, and J. Borrett. A computer-aided constraint programming system. In J. Little, editor, *Proceedings of PACLP'99*, pages 81–93. The Practical Application Company, 1999.

31. P. Van Hentenryck. *The OPL Optimization Programming Language*. The MIT Press, 1999.

32. P. Van Hentenryck, P. Flener, J. Pearson, and M. Ågren. Tractable symmetry breaking for CSPs with interchangeable values. In *Proceedings of IJCAI'03*, pages 277–282. Morgan Kaufmann, 2003.

33. T. Walsh. Permutation problems and channelling constraints. In R. Nieuwenhuis and A. Voronkov, editors, *Proc. of LPAR'01*, number 2250 in LNCS, pages 377–391. Springer-Verlag, 2001.

34. T. Walsh. Consistency and propagation with multiset constraints: A formal viewpoint. In F. Rossi, editor, *Proceedings of CP'03*, number 2833 in LNCS, pages 724–738. Springer-Verlag, 2003.

35. J. Warmer and A. Kleppe. *The Object Constraint Language: Precise Modeling with UML*. Addison-Wesley, 1999.

36. S. Wrang. Implementation of the ESRA Constraint Modelling Language. Master's thesis, Master's Thesis in Computing Science 223, Department of Information Technology, Uppsala University, Sweden, 2002. Available at `ftp://ftp.csd.uu.se/pub/papers/masters-theses/`.

37. J. Zhou. Introduction to the constraint language NCL. *Journal of Logic Programming*, 45(1–3):71–103, 2000.

Author Index

Lecture Notes in Computer Science

For information about Vols. 1–2987

please contact your bookseller or Springer-Verlag